Dedicated to
Our parents,
family members,
peers
and dear students

About the Authors

Harmeet Kaur is currently working as Senior Computer Teacher, Department of Computer Science at Heritage Xperiential Learning School, Gurugram. She has over 21 years of experience in the field of education; teaching Computer Science, Informatics Practices and Multimedia and Web Technologies to grades XI and XII along with a background of mentoring, IT curriculum development for STEM integration, and staff training and development. She has led various inhouse projects such as Learning Management System to propagate collaborative personalized e-learning. She is well adept in Google Apps for Education and uses it as a primary platform for her classroom teaching. She integrates multiple teaching styles to build digital literacy skills in millennial learners while strongly promoting safe and ethical use of technology. She believes in driving the experiential and project-based pedagogy by imparting mobile computing skills to high school students. She has conducted various workshops in and around Delhi-NCR to train teachers with latest pedagogies of classroom management, incorporating Tech to teach STEM education and "learning by doing" hands-on workshops. She has authored training material for in-house teacher training and been constructive in ICT curriculum development.

Sangita Chadha has been working as Head of Computer Department in Ambience Public School, Safdarjung Enclave, New Delhi from last 12 years. She has over twenty years of experience in the field of education; teaching Computer Science, Informatics Practices and Multimedia & Web Technology to grades XI and XII; and has been multifold responsibilities at her school (Result In-charge, ERP, Website, Almanac, Magazine). She is a passionate learner and committed educator consistently working to make learning enjoyable for the learners.Her foremost classroom pedagogy is centered around project-based learning. She has conducted ICT and Net safety workshops for all stakeholders. She has been part of the curriculum development team for classes IX and X Information and Communication Technology, NCERT. She has co-authored class IX and X ICT for NCERT. She also co-authored Class XII Informatics Practices and Computer Science, NCERT. She has conducted Teacher Training workshops for SCERT Teachers.

New Edition

Artificial Intelligence

TEXTBOOK

(As per CBSE Syllabus Code 417)

Authors
Harmeet Kaur
Sangita Chadha

FIRST EDITION 2020
REPRINT 2024

ISBN: 978-93-89845-09-9

LIMITS OF LIABILITY AND DISCLAIMER OF WARRANTY

CBSE is no way connected with this book. This book is written solely for the benefit and guidance for CBSE examination.

Distributors:

BPB PUBLICATIONS
20, Ansari Road, Darya Ganj
New Delhi-110002
Ph: 23254990/23254991

DECCAN AGENCIES
4-3-329, Bank Street,
Hyderabad-500195
Ph: 24756967/24756400

MICRO MEDIA
Shop No. 5, Mahendra Chambers,
150 DN Rd. Next to Capital Cinema,
V.T. (C.S.T.) Station, MUMBAI-400 001
Ph: 22078296/22078297

BPB BOOK CENTRE
376 Old Lajpat Rai Market,
Delhi-110006
Ph: 23861747

Published by Manish Jain for BPB Publications, 20 Ansari Road, Darya Ganj, New Delhi-110002 and Printed at Akash Press, New Delhi

www.bpbonline.com

About the Reviewer

Rekha Verma is a 1st class MCA degree holder and has a teaching experience of 19 years, with a strong command of Python, C++, Java and current software. She had received recommendation letters from HRD Minister-Smriti Irani for board results.

Acknowledgements

We would like to acknowledge the contributions of all the educators, data scientists, scientists, professionals from various fields for their valuable suggestions in developing the content for this book.

We would like to express our gratitude to everyone at BPB Publications for giving us this opportunity to write the book. We are thankful to all the resource persons at BPB Publications for editing, technical reviewing and language editing the book. We would like to thank our technical reviewer, Mrs. Rekha Verma for her thoughtful insights while refining the manuscript of this book.

We are thankful to each other and our families for being supportive in numerous ways and for giving their unconditional love and support at all times.

Lastly, but not the least, we would like to thank God for bearing us with courage and humility to be able to write this book for our students.

— Harmeet Kaur

— Sangita Chadha

Preface

Artificial Intelligence is a growing and important field in Computer Science. AI has become very popular in today's times. The goals of scientists in recent times has been to create technology to allow computers to be able to take human-like smart decisions and behave in intelligent manner. AI has become a prevalent jargon dueto increasing dependency on big data; algorithms working on the bulk of data collection and improving capabilities in computing and storage. It is impacting the life of everyone in the field of education, entertainment, transport, and many more.

Artificial Intelligence is an important aspect of policy decision makers in many countries. In India, the lawmakers have been focusing on including AI in multiple fields to propagate economic growth. The impact of AI is visible in multiple arenas affecting the young and old in a similar manner. The understanding of Artificial Intelligence is very crucial in the deployment of various solutions proliferating sustainable development goals in today's times.

The primary objective in the development of this book is to create a pedagogical approach that emphasizes on the basic concepts of Artificial Intelligence. This book contains many examples to make the student learn, understand about various domains of Artificial Intelligence easily using various activities. Each activity is connected with real life scenario to make the learner connected with the world and become a global citizen. Learners understand the simulations in real time. They are even able to develop some of the simulations without knowing the programming language and hence, efficiently employ the potentials of AI in a viable manner.

The book is based on the CBSE curriculum (Code 417) for class 9 designed for the purpose of teaching Artificial Intelligence to the students. This book is divided into 4 Parts and it provides a detailed description of the basic concepts of Artificial Intelligence.

PART A

Chapter 1 introduces the communication process along with its importance and characteristics. Various elements in communication cycles, along with communication methods, along with factors that affect perspective communication. It also gives the knowledge of basic writing skills such as phrase, sentence, and speech, Articles that helps you in writing the paragraph.

Chapter 2 discusses the self-management and its importance, self-management Skill, what is self-confidence, factors influencing is and building it along with SWOT Analysis.

Chapter 3 defines Information and Communication Technology, tools, and the role of ICT along with its usage in workplace. It also defines computer systems and basic things related to it, Internal and external memory, various peripheral devices, and various Operating System.

Chapter 4 define business, entrepreneur skills, types of business, and its enterprises in our community, define entrepreneur and its various phases. It also covers various factors that affect the growth of entrepreneurship.

Chapter 5 is also a key chapter that contains the categorization of environment, define ecosystem and its primary components, the relationship between Man and environment, define ecological imbalance, and conservation of natural resources.

PART B

Chapter 1 excites the learners to explore and get motivated about Artificial Intelligence applications in their daily lives. The chapter reviews the content knowledge learnt by the students in class 8.

Chapter 2 begins with an explanation about the AI Project Cycle. AI Project Cycle defines each step that needs to be taken in order to get the desired output which includes Problem Scoping, Data Acquisition, Data Exploration, Data Modelling and Evaluation of the Project.

Chapter 3 defines the concept about Problem Scoping. Problem Scoping focuses on identifying, analyzing and choosing the problem that the learner wishes to solve using his AI knowledge. The learner clearly defines goals in Problem Scoping. In this chapter, they will understand how to use the 4Ws - Project Canvas technique with the help of which they can identify the key elements of the problem. By the end of the chapter, they will be able to transform Project Canvas into Problem Statement template for better understanding.

Chapter 4 focuses on acquiring data for the project; hence the process of learning about Data acquisition While reading this chapter, learners will be able to acquire skills to interpret, identify and categorize data. They will be able to differentiate between training data and testing data. They can demonstrate the importance of relevant and authentic data as training data and also how and from where these data should be acquired for their project.

Chapter 5 talks about various methods for the learner to be able to interpret and classify data visualization into different categories. Data exploration helps in classifying, comparing and analyzing the data which has been gathered from various relevant sources. To understand and interpret data; data exploration and visualization aids the same using various methods such as charts, graphs, mind maps, sketches, etc. This technique is very clearly explained in this chapter which helps the learner to construct and evaluate patterns and trends effectively.

Chapter 6 focuses on various techniques which are used to make the machine intelligent i.e. AI model. The learner will be able to interpret and classify AI models using rule based and learning based approach. They will be able to identify and relate the applications based upon different techniques. The learner will also be able to identify, create, examine, evaluate and construct the decision tree algorithm for rule-based learning which focuses on set of rules rather than data.

Chapter 7 focuses on how Neural Network works and its relationship with human nervous system. The learner will be introduced to common regression, classification and clustering models. Neural Network is a series of algorithms that interpret a set of data without programmer's intervention and performs a particular task. They will be learning some of the features of Neural Network. They will be able to identify, classify and interpret the use of different types of layers in Neural Network.

Chapter 8 teaches the basics of how a learner can acquire basic programming skills through gamified platforms. The learner explores CodeCombat portal, a game-based computer science program where they type real code and see their characters react in real time.

Chapter 9 paves the techniques for the learner to formulate introductory Python programming skills in a very user-friendly format by going through lessons on Python Basics. The flow of the module empowers the learner to understand and enumerate examples exhibiting the step by step solution of a problem statement

Chapter 10 introduces the learner to recognize the use of data structure list, to store pieces of information. The module explains multiple List operations helping the learning acquire knowledge about basic programming skills.

PART C

It consists of viva questions based on Python and its programming.

PART D

It consists of Programming based questions based on Python.

SYLLABUS

OBJECTIVE

The objective of this module/curriculum - which combines both Inspire and Acquire modules is to develop a readiness for understanding and appreciating Artificial Intelligence and its application in our lives. This module/ curriculum focuses on:

1. Helping learners understand the world of Artificial Intelligence and its applications through games, activities and multi-sensorial learning to become AI-Ready.
2. Introducing the learners to three domains of AI in an age appropriate manner.
3. Allowing the learners to construct meaning of AI through interactive participation and engaging hands-on activities.
4. Introducing the learners to AI Project Cycle.
5. Introducing the learners to programming skills - Basic Python coding language.

LEARNING OUTCOMES

Learners will be able to

1. Identify and appreciate Artificial Intelligence and describe its applications in daily life.
2. Relate, apply and reflect on the Human-Machine Interactions to identify and interact with the three domains of AI: Data, Computer Vision and Natural Language Processing and undergo assessment for analysing their progress towards acquired AI-Readiness skills.
3. Imagine, examine and reflect on the skills required for futuristic job opportunities.
4. Unleash their imagination towards smart homes and build an interactive story around it.
5. Understand the impact of Artificial Intelligence on Sustainable Development Goals to develop responsible citizenship.
6. Research and develop awareness of skills required for jobs of the future.
7. Gain awareness about AI bias and AI access and describe the potential ethical considerations of AI.
8. Develop effective communication and collaborative work skills.
9. Get familiar and motivated towards Artificial Intelligence and Identify the AI Project Cycle framework.
10. Learn problem scoping and ways to set goals for an AI project and understand the iterative nature of problem Scoping in the AI Project Cycle.
11. Brainstorm on the ethical issues involved around the problem selected.

12. Foresee the kind of data required and the kind of analysis to be done, identify data requirements and find reliable sources to obtain relevant data.
13. Use various types of graphs to visualise acquired data.
14. Understand, create and implement the concept of Decision Trees.
15. Understand and visualise computer's ability to identify alphabets and handwritings.
16. Understand and appreciate the concept of Neural Network through gamification and learn basic programming skills through gamified platforms.
17. Acquire introductory Python programming skills in a very user-friendly format.

SCHEME OF UNITS (SESSION 2020-2021)

Total Marks: 100 (Theory-50 + Practical-50)

This course is a planned sequence of instructions consisting of units meant for developing employability and vocational competencies of students of Class IX opting for skill subject along with other education subjects. The unit-wise distribution of hours and marks for class IX is as follows:

ARTIFICIAL INTELLIGENCE (417) Class IX (Session 2020-21)			
	UNITS	**NO. OF HOURS for Theory and Practical 200**	**MAX. MARKS for Theory and Practical 100**
Part A	**Employability Skills**		
	Unit 1 : Communication Skills-I	10	10
	Unit 2 : Self-Management Skills-I	10	
	Unit 3 : ICT Skills-I	10	
	Unit 4 : Entrepreneurial Skills-I	15	
	Unit 5 : Green Skills-I	05	
	Total	**50**	**10**
Part B	**Subject Specific Skills**		**Marks**
	Unit 1: Introduction to Artificial Intelligence (AI)		40
	Unit 2: AI Project Cycle		
	Unit 3: Neural Network		
	Unit 4: Introduction to Python* (* To be assessed in Practicals only)		
	Total		**40**
Part C	**Practical Work – PYTHON** **Unit 4: Introduction to Python**		
	Practical Examination		35
	Viva Voce		
	Total		**35**
Part D	**Project Work/Field Visit**		
	Practical File/ Student Portfolio		15
	Viva Voce		
	Total		15
	GRAND TOTAL	**200**	**100**

DETAILED CURRICULUM/TOPICS FOR CLASS IX:

Part-A: EMPLOYABILITY SKILLS

S. No.	Units	Duration in Hours
1.	Unit 1: Communication Skills-I	10
2.	Unit 2: Self-management Skills-I	10
3.	Unit 3: Basic Information and Communication Technology Skills-I	10
4.	Unit 4: Entrepreneurial Skills-I	15
5.	Unit 5: Green Skills-I	05
	TOTAL	**50**

NOTE: For Detailed Curriculum/ Topics to be covered under Part A: Employability Skills can be downloaded from CBSE website.

Part-B – SUBJECT SPECIFIC SKILLS

- Unit 1: Introduction to Artificial Intelligence (AI)
- Unit 2: AI Project Cycle
- Unit 3: Neural Network
- Unit 4: Introduction To Python (to be assessed through Practicals)

UNIT 1: INTRODUCTION TO AI

SUB-UNIT	LEARNING OUTCOMES	SESSION / ACTIVITY / PRACTICAL
Excite	To identify and appreciate Artificial Intelligence and describe its applications in daily life.	**Session:** Introduction to AI and setting up the context of the curriculum.
		Ice Breaker Activity: Dream Smart Home idea • Learners to design a rough layout of floor plan of their dream smart home.
	To relate, apply and reflect on the Human-Machine Interactions. To identify and interact with the three domains of AI: Data, Computer Vision and Natural Language Processing.	**Recommended Activity:** The AI Game • Learners to participate in three games based on different AI domains. – Game 1: Rock, Paper and Scissors (based on data). – Game 2: Mystery Animal (based on Natural Language Processing - NLP). – Game 3: Emoji Scavenger Hunt (based on Computer Vision - CV).
	To undergo an assessment for analysing progress towards acquired AI-Readiness skills.	**Recommended Activity:** • AI Quiz (Paper Pen/Online Quiz)

SUB-UNIT	LEARNING OUTCOMES	SESSION / ACTIVITY / PRACTICAL
	To imagine, examine and reflect on the skills required for futuristic job opportunities.	**Recommended Activity:** To write a letter Writing a Letter to one's future self • Learners to write a letter to self-keeping the future in context. They will describe what they have learnt so far or what they would like to learn someday.
Relate	Learners to relate to application of Artificial Intelligence in their daily lives.	**Video Session:** To watch a video • Introducing the concept of Smart Cities, Smart Schools and Smart Homes
	To unleash their imagination towards smart homes and build an interactive story around it. To relate, apply and reflect on the Human-Machine Interactions.	**Recommended Activity:** Write an Interactive Story • Learners to draw a floor plan of a Home/ School/City and write an interactive story around it using Story Speaker extension in Google docs.
Purpose	To understand the impact of Artificial Intelligence on Sustainable Development Goals to develop responsible citizenship.	**Session:** • Introduction to UN Sustainable Development Goals.
		Recommended Activity: Go Goals Board Game • Learners to answer questions on Sustainable Development Goals.
Possibilities	To research and develop awareness of skills required for jobs of the future. To imagine, examine and reflect on the skills required for the futuristic opportunities. To develop effective communication and collaborative work skills.	**Session:** Theme-based research and Case Studies • Learners will listen to various case-studies of inspiring start-ups, companies or communities where AI has been involved in real-life. • Learners will be allotted a theme around which they need to search for present AI trends and have to visualise the future of AI in and around their respective theme.
		Recommended Activity: Job Ad Creating activity • Learners to create a job advertisement for a firm describing the nature of job available and the skill-set required for it 10 years down the line. They need to figure out how AI is going to transform the nature of jobs and create the Ad accordingly.
AI Ethics	To understand and reflect on the ethical issues around AI.	**Video Session:** Discussing about AI Ethics **Recommended Activity:** Ethics Awareness • Students play the role of major stakeholders and they have to decide what is ethical and what is not for a given scenario.

SUB-UNIT	LEARNING OUTCOMES	SESSION / ACTIVITY / PRACTICAL
	To gain awareness around AI bias and AI access.	**Session:** AI Bias and AI Access • Discussing about the possible bias in data collection. • Discussing about the implications of AI technology.
	To let the students analyse the advantages and disadvantages of Artificial Intelligence.	**Recommended Activity:** Balloon Debate • Students divide in teams of 3 and 2 teams are given same theme. One team goes in affirmation to AI for their section while the other one goes against it. • They have to come up with their points as to why AI is beneficial/ harmful for the society.

UNIT 2: AI PROJECT CYCLE

SUB-UNIT	LEARNING OUTCOMES	SESSION / ACTIVITY / PRACTICAL
Problem Scoping	**Identify the AI Project Cycle framework.**	**Session:** Introduction to AI Project Cycle • Problem Scoping • Data Acquisition • Data Exploration • Modelling • Evaluation
	Learn Problem Scoping and ways to set goals for an AI Project.	**Activity:** Brainstorm around the theme provided and set a goal for the AI Project. • Discuss various topics within the given theme and select one. • List down/ Draw a mindmap of problems related to the selected topic and choose one problem to be the goal for the project.
	Identify stakeholders involved in the problem scoped. Brainstorm on the ethical issues involved around the problem selected.	**Activity:** To set actions around the goal. • List down the stakeholders involved in the problem. • Search on the current actions taken to solve this problem. • Think around the ethics involved in the goal of your project.
	Understand the iterative nature of problem scoping for in the AI project cycle. Foresee the kind of data required and the kind of analysis to be done.	**Activity:** Data and Analysis • What are the data features needed? • Where can you get the data? • How frequent do you have to collect the data? • What happens if you don't have enough data? • What kind of analysis needs to be done? • How will it be validated? • How does the analysis inform the action?
	Share what the students have discussed so far.	**Presentation:** Presenting the goal, actions and data.

SUB-UNIT	LEARNING OUTCOMES	SESSION / ACTIVITY / PRACTICAL
Data Acquisition	Identify data requirements and find reliable sources to obtain relevant data.	**Activity:** Introduction to data and its types. • Students work around the scenarios given to them and think of ways to acquire data.
Data Exploration	To understand the purpose of Data Visualisation	**Session:** Data Visualisation • Need of visualising data. • Ways to visualise data using various types of graphical tools.
	Use various types of graphs to visualise acquired data.	**Recommended Activity:** Let's use Graphical Tools • To decide what kind of data is required for a given scenario and acquire the same. • To select an appropriate graphical format to represent the data acquired. • Presenting the graph sketched.
Modelling	Understand, create and implement the concept of Decision Trees.	**Session:** Decision Tree • To introduce basic structure of Decision Trees to students.
		Recommended Activity: Decision Tree • To design a Decision Tree based on the data given.
	Understand and visualise computer's ability to identify alphabets and handwritings.	**Recommended Activity:** Pixel It • To create an "AI Model" to classify handwritten letters. • Students develop a model to classify handwritten letters by diving the alphabets into pixels. • Pixels are then joined together to analyse a pattern amongst same alphabets and to differentiate the different ones.

UNIT 3: NEURAL NETWORK

LEARNING OUTCOMES	SESSION / ACTIVITY / PRACTICAL
Understand and appreciate the concept of Neural Network through gamification.	**Session:** Introduction to Neural Network • Relation between the Neural Network and nervous system in human body. • Describing the function of Neural Network.
	Recommended Activity: Creating a Human Neural Network • Students split in four teams each representing input layer (X students), hidden layer 1 (Y students), hidden layer 2 (Z students) and output layer (1 student) respectively. • Input layer gets data which is passed on to hidden layers after some processing. The output layer finally gets all information and gives meaningful information as output.

UNIT 4: INTRODUCTION TO PYTHON

NOTE: Python should be assessed through Practicals only and should not be assessed with the Theory Exam.

LEARNING OUTCOMES	SESSION / ACTIVITY / PRACTICAL
Learn basic programming skills through gamified platforms.	**Recommended Activity:** • Introduction to programming using Online Gaming portals like Code Combat.
Acquire introductory Python programming skills in a very user-friendly format.	**Session:** • Introduction to Python language. • Introducing Python programming and its applications.
	Practical: Python Basics • Students go through lessons on Python Basics (Variables, Arithmetic Operators, Expressions, Data Types - integer, float, strings, using print() and input() functions). • Students will try some simple problem solving exercises on Python Compiler.
	Practical: Python Lists • Students go through lessons on Python Lists (Simple operations using list). • Students will try some basic problem solving exercises using Lists on Python Compiler.

Contents

Part A	
1. Communication Skills	1
2. Self-Management Skills	18
3. Information and Communication Technology Skills-I	28
4. Entrepreneurial Skills	57
5. Green Skills	70
Part B	
1. Review of Concepts	87
2. Introduction to AI Project Cycle	106
3. Problem Scoping	119
4. Data Acquisition	133
5. Data Exploration	152
6. Data Modelling	177
7. Understanding the Neural Network Framework	197
8. Understanding the Programming Basics	223
9. Python Programming Language	241
10. Python List	278
Part C	289
Viva Questions and Answers	289
Part D	
Practical Exercises	297
Appendixes 1-5	323
Co-Curricular Activities	341
Sample Question Papers - 1 & 2	342
Chapterwise Solutions	353

Part–A

OTHER TITLES OF INTEREST

for Class 9th...

Sample Papers – Computer Applications for Class IX (165)
ISBN: 9789389845129

Sample Papers – Information Technology for Class IX (402)
ISBN: 9789390684335

Information Technology – Textbook for Class IX (402)
ISBN: 9789391392437

for Class 10th...

Computer Applications – Textbook for Class X (165)
ISBN: 9789391030773

Sample Papers – Computer Applications for Class X (165)
ISBN: 9789389845020

Information Technology – Textbook for Class X (402)
ISBN: 9789391392710

Artificial Intelligence *Made Simple* Textbook for **Class 10** (417)
ISBN: 9789390684014

for Class 12th...

Computer Science with **Python**: Question Bank for (Term-1) Class XII (083)
ISBN: 9789390684847

Computer Science with **Python**: Question Bank for Class XII (083)
ISBN: 9789389845051

Sample Papers – Computer Science for Class XII (083)
ISBN: 9789390684243

for Class 11th...

Computer Science with **Python Language** Made Simple Class XI (083)
ISBN: 9789388176224

1 Communication Skills

Structure Bot

In this chapter, we will discuss the following topics:

- Communication process
- Importance and characteristics of communication
- Methods of communication

Objective Bot

At the end of this chapter, you should be able to:

- Understand the concept of communication process
- Discuss the characteristics of communication
- Demonstrate/discuss/elaborate the importance of communication
- Explain the methods of communication

Communication is the process of sharing information between two or more people. It involves the ability to listen, understand and give the right message to another person.

For communication to take place, there must be a sender and receiver; in which the sender sends the message and in response, gets feedback from the receiver. (Figure 1.1)

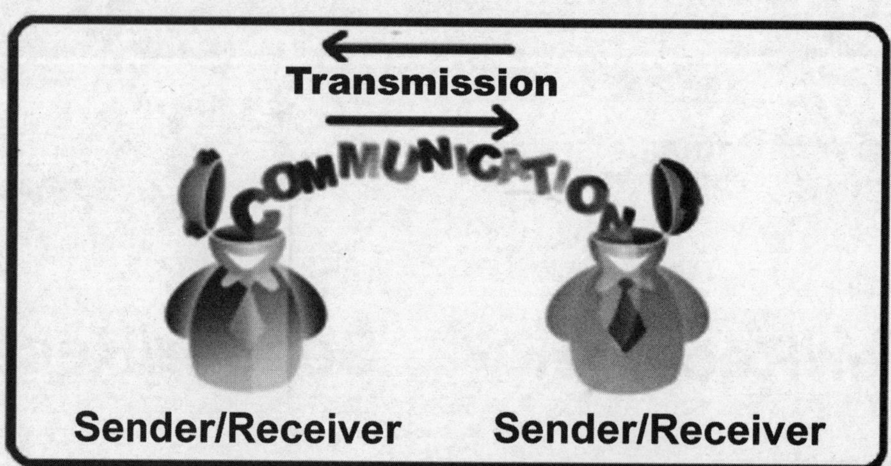

Figure 1.1: *Communication process*

Effective Communication

When the messages are successfully delivered to the receiver and is understood by receiver, then the communication is said to be an effective communication.

Characteristics of Communication

The characteristics of communication are:

- **Continuous process:** The nature, situation and contents of the communication keep changing.
- **Social activity:** Communication is a process of sharing messages.
- **Mutual understanding:** For communication and to understand it, there must an understanding among the sender and receiver.
- **Two-way process:** Communication involves both sender-receiver and they must respond to each other to have an effective communication.
- **Lead to reaction or response:** To have a successful communication, there is a need for quick and right response from the sender; once the sender understands the message.

KNOWLEDGE BOT

A message should be clear. It should convey the right meaning to others.

Importance of Communication Skills

Communications not only include verbal communication, but it includes everything's like posture, visual aspects, body language which appeals to the listener. The importance of communication skills is the ability to listen, speak, and write with clarity.

MEMORY BOT

Reading, writing and listening carefully are the three most important communication skills for everyone.

Elements of a Communication Cycle

The sender or source translates the message or information by encoding and then an encoded message is transmitted via communication channel to receiver. Then, at the receiver side, it is decoded, and feedback is given to the sender.

Various elements of the communication cycle are: (Figure 1.2)

- **Message:** Information to be conveyed.
- **Sender:** Source who sends information or message.
- **Encoding:** Converting data or information into the coded language which is not understood by any other person.
- **Receiver:** Person who will receive the sent information or message by sender and understand it by decoding.
- **Communication channel:** An appropriate channel or medium (electronic mail, telephone call) through which the sender send a message.
- **Decoding:** Receiver decode an encoded information to understand the sent message or information.
- **Feedback:** Response given to sender by receiver.

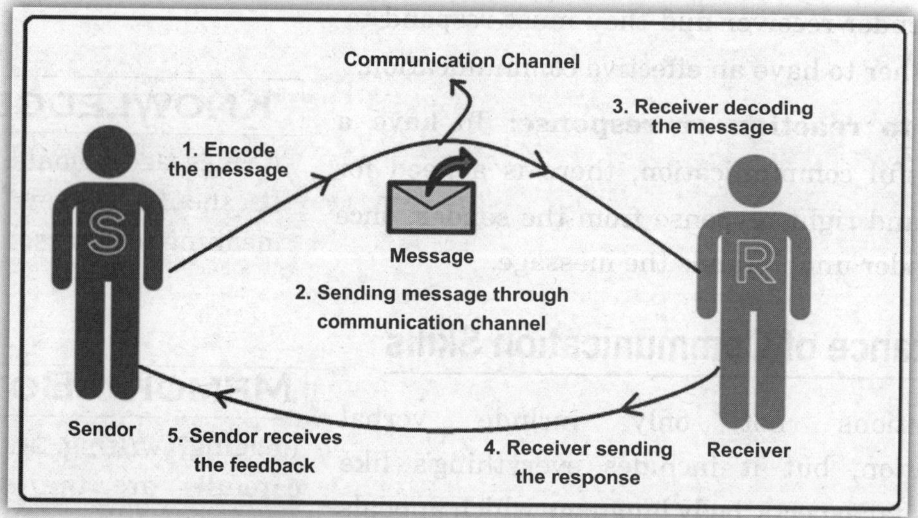

Figure 1.2: *Communication cycle*

Methods of Communication

There are three methods of communication:

- Verbal communication
- Non-verbal communication
- Visual communication

Verbal Communication

- In verbal communication, message is delivered by using words.
- It is the most powerful and accurate tool for expressing and sharing ideas.
- Verbal communication can be done orally or by writing. (Figure 1.3)

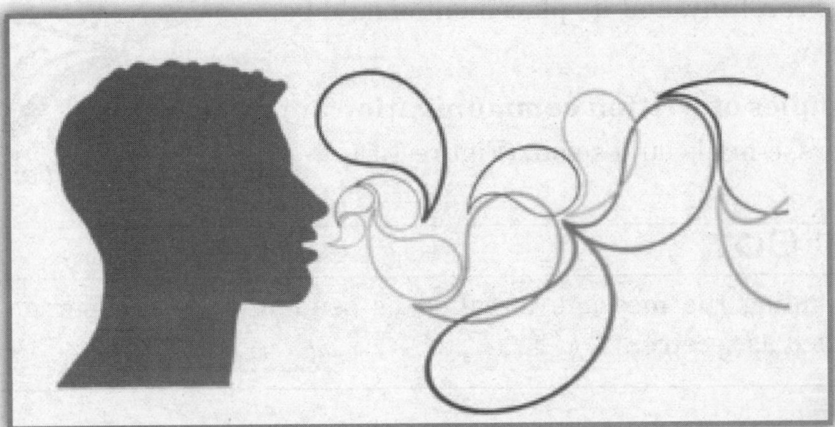

Figure1.3: *VerbalCommunication*

TIP BOT

Communication skills are vital to healthy and efficient workplace.

Types of Verbal Communication

- **Oral communication:**
  - In this the ideas and information is expressed through spoken words.
  - It is the natural form of communication as in this immediate clarification and feedback is involved.
  - Both sender and receiver must be present in this type of communication as one will listen and respond accordingly.
  - The message should be concise and short. (Figure 1.4)

Figure 1.4: *Oral Communication*

- **Written communication:**
  - In this written messages are used to convey a message.
  - It is a most formal way of communication as while writing you should have to choose words carefully, and its placement should be inorder.
  - **Examples of written communication** are Letters, e-mails, and so on. (Figure 1.5)

Figure 1.5: *Written Communication*

MEMORY BOT

The person sending the message is called as sender while the person receiving the message is called as receiver.

Non-Verbal Communication

- In non-verbal communication, information is exchanged by using all other things except word.
- It includes **gestures** (pointing fingers, waving, body and hand movement), **facial expressions** (most noticeable aspect), **body language** (eye movements, postures, hand gestures), **eye gaze** (movement of eyes like staring, looking and blinking), **voice** (person other than the speaker read its voice and listen to words).

Figure 1.6: *Non-verbal Communication*

FACT BOT

Non-verbal communication was introduced by Psychiatrist Jurgen Ruesch and Weldon Kees in 1956.

Definition Bot

Non-verbal communication is the process of sending and receiving messages without words, either spoken or written.

Visual Communication

- Any method which relies on pictures, illusions, and graphics for sharing messages is **visual communication.**
- **Examples of visual communication:** PowerPoint presentation, Charts, Graphs, Maps, White and blackboards and Paper handouts.
- Visual communication involves visual images using textures, colors, shapes which communicate messages along with emotions, experiences, concepts, textures and lifestyles. (Figure 1.7)

Figure 1.7: *Visual Communication*

KNOWLEDGE BOT

Visual technique can be used with oral communication.

Perspective in Communication

Perspective is the point of view of an individual through which one understands every communication and the event happening around us. Every people interpret and convey the messages through the filters of their motives, beliefs, knowledge, and understanding.

Factors affecting perspective in communication

The important factors affecting the perspective in communication are:

- **Visual perspective:** It is a tendency by which people will only focus on the parts of a scenario which is most disposed to notice.

  Consider an example: In figure 1.8, some will see a face, on the other hand, some will see an old women

Figure 1.8: *Visual perspective*

walking towards back, and tree. Firstly what you will see depends on your visual perception.

- **Language perspective:** In the interpretation of words, perception plays an important role in the communication process. In this the sender and receiver must be able to understand each other language. (Figure 1.9)

Figure 1.9: *Language perspective*

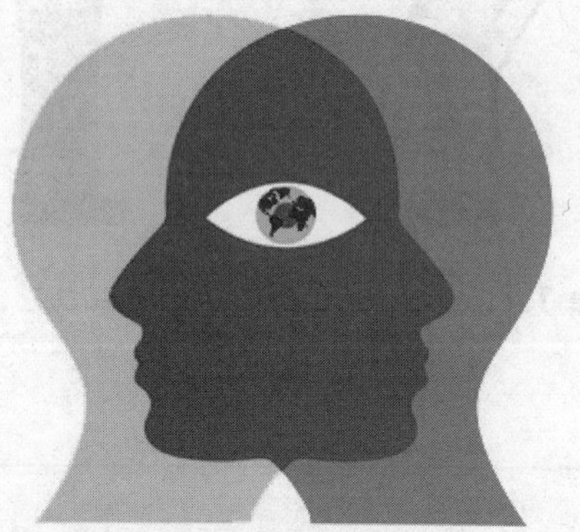

Figure 1.10: *Past experience perspective*

- **Past experience:** Sometimes, when you face a situation to which you have gone through earlier, you predict what going to happen next as you will have face the same situation in the past. That past experience will shape your attitude towards the situation, place or people. (Figure 1.10)

- **Prejudices:** Prejudices is a prejudgment which is not based on any experience, logic, or any fact. If either sender or receiver have prejudices in their mind, then it can result in communication failure. (Figure 1.11)

Figure 1.11: *Prejudices*

Figure 1.12: *Feelings*

- **Feelings:** In communication, the most important role is played by our mind. As people will react to same situation in many ways when they are sad and happy; but how someone's feeling at a particular time will only depend on the way they reach on a particular situation and the way they interact with people around them. (Figure 1.12)

Basic Writing Skills

To express ourselves, sentences (group of words which communicate the right message) must be written correctly as not to change its meaning. Writing correct sentence includes the correct choices of words and the organization of words in the right sequence of a sentence.

Seven Elements of Communication

Seven elements of communication are used to improve the professional communication skills.

These 7C's are:

a. Clear (message should be clear)

b. Correct (No spelling and grammatical errors)

c. Complete (Message should include all the required information)

d. Concrete (Message must be supported with figures and facts)

e. Concise (Message should be short and to the point)

f. Consideration (Message must covers the points as suggested by receiver)

g. Courteous (Message should consider the viewpoints and feelings of the receiver)

KNOWLEDGE BOT

Written communication is more formal and less flexible than oral communication.

Writing Skills

To have an effective written communication, both sender and receiver must be able to share their message without any confusion. As if there is any lap of communication on the sender or receiver side it will lead to miss-communication. An important aspect of writing skill involves the use of correct grammar, selection of right words and easy sentence structure.

Phrase

Phrase are the group of words which do not make any sense. It only gives us hint about the message sender want to communicate. It doesn't have an object and a subject

Example: I am going, behind the chair.

Example shown above, are not sentences as they are not making complete sense and so, are known as phrases.

For example:

- **Phrase:** I am sitting.
- **Sentence:** I am sitting on the chair.

To make phrase a sentence, simple add finite verbs or objects in the phrase then it becomes a sentence.

Type of Phrases

There are five types of phrases:

a. **Noun phrase:** It act like a noun in a sentence. **Example:** The red car is for sale. Here, the red car is a noun phrase.

b. **Verb phrase:** It is a group of helping and main verbs within a sentence. **Example:** She was walking quickly towards the car. Here, was walking is a verb.

c. **Adjective phrase:** It is built around an adjective and consist of articles and adjectives. **Example:** The woman sitting in car is my aunty. Here, in the car is an adjective.

d. **Adverbial phrase:** It is built around adverb by adding words before or after it. **Example:** After winning an award, Deepak screams in joy. Here, in joy is an adverbial phrase.

e. **Prepositional phrase:** It always begins with a preposition followed by a noun. **Example:** The vegetable store at the corner sells ready to eat food also. Here, at the corner is a prepositional phrase.

Sentence

Sentence is a group of words that make complete sense. It must consist of predicate and subject.

Examples: I am sitting on the chair.

Types of Sentences

- **Asserted or declarative sentence:** Sentence which reports events, describe things and state facts.

  Example: This is my favorite song.

- **Interrogative sentence:** Sentences which makes enquiries and asks for information. At the end question mark is used and it starts with words like Why, What, When and How.

  Example: What are you doing?

- **Imperative sentence:** Sentences which express an order, advice, request, suggestion, direction, etc. It ends with a full stop.

  Example: Don't go outside, it's raining.

- **Exclamatory sentence:** Sentence which express wonder, surprise, happiness, sorrow, sympathy or gratitude. It can form by either selecting how, what like words or oh, ah, hurrah, alas, oops like interjections.

  Example: Wao! Well done!

Parts of Sentence

Subject (word or group of words that convey the name of things or persons about whom you are speaking) and predicate (part of a sentence which contains verbs and state something about the subject) are the two parts of every complete sentence.

Example: Deepak is a good boy: Here, Deepak is subject and is a good boy is a predicate.

Parts of Speech

According to the functions in a sentence, it is classified into eight types:

a. **Noun:** Word (except a pronoun) that identifies a person, place or thing, or names.

b. **Adjective:** It describes noun or pronoun. It specifies quality, size and number.

c. **Verb:** It shows state or action.

d. **Conjunction:** Words that link other words, phrases, or clauses together.

e. **Preposition:** It refers to the word which specifies a location and shows the relation of a noun, noun phrase, a sentence with another word.

f. **Article:** Word used before noun.

g. **Interjection:** It coveys strong emotion, and is usually put an exclamatory sign in the end.

h. **Adverb:** Word used to modify a verb, an adjective, or another adverb.

Articles and its use

An article is a word used before a noun (person, object, place or idea. There are two types of Article:

a. **Definite article:** The (I like the pen you gave me).

b. **Indefinite article:** A, An (A beautiful flower, An orange).

'A' is used before the words starting with constants, and 'an' is used before words starting with vowels (A, E, I, O, U).

Paragraph Writing

Paragraph is a number of related sentences which focus on an idea. It forms a part of a larger piece of writing, such as a composition.

Before writing the paragraph writer should be clear about the topic and the contents.

Essential sections of the paragraph are:

- **Paragraph topic:** Paragraph subject or topic.
- **Introduction:** Start the paragraph with the introduction about a paragraph and is known as topic sentence.
- **Explanation:** Give information about topic sentence in 7-8 sentences.
- **Conclusion:** It summarizes the whole sentences written about the topic.
- **Proofread:** In this writer should check the paragraph for grammatical mistakes and sentence making.

TECH BOT

- **Communication:** It is the way the process of exchanging information, data, and ideas among various people throughout the world.
- **Visual Perspective:** It is the ability to see to see and interpret the visual information that surrounds us.
- **Effective communication:** When the sent message are successfully delivered to the receiver and understand by them, then communication is said to be effective communication.

Recap Bot

- Communication is the process of sharing information between two or more people.
- For communication to take place, there must be a sender and receiver; in which the sender sends the message and in response, gets feedback from the receiver.
- There are three methods of communication:
  - Verbal communication
  - Non-verbal communication
  - Visual communication
- Perspective is the point of view of an individual through which one understands every communication and the event happening around us.
- To express yourselves, sentences (group of words which communicate the right message) must be written correctly as not to change its meaning.
- To have an effective written communication, both sender and receiver must be able to share their message without any confusion.
- Phrase are the group of words which do not make any sense. It only gives us hint about the message sender want to communicate.
- Sentence is a group of words that make complete sense. It must consist of predicate and subject.
- Subject (word or group of words that convey the name of things or persons about whom you are speaking) and predicate (part of a sentence which contains verbs and state something about the subject) are the two parts of every complete sentence.
- An article is a word used before a noun (person, object, place or idea).
- Paragraph is a number of related sentences which focus on an idea. It forms a part of a larger piece of writing, such as a composition.

A. Multiple choice questions.

1. The communication word is derived from the Latin word communis that means:
   a. To share
   b. Impart
   c. Both a. and b.
   d. None of these
2. What is the purpose of the receiver in communication?
   a. Understand the message and respond to it
   b. Send message
   c. Take response
   d. None of these
3. In verbal communication message is delivered using:
   a. Spoken or written message
   b. Message that uses words of any language
   c. Both a. and b.
   d. None of these
4. Which of the following is not an example of written communication?
   a. E-mails
   b. Reports
   c. Body language
   d. Letters
5. Which of the following is not a factor affecting perspective in communication?
   a. Feelings
   b. Prejudice
   c. Attitude
   d. Love
6. Perspective is an individual's:
   a. Point of view
   b. Activity
   c. Body language
   d. None of these
7. Which of the following is not the 7C's or elements of communication?
   a. Clear
   b. Complete
   c. Concentrate
   d. Concise
8. _______ article is used before words starting with vowels.
   a. A
   b. An
   c. The
   d. Definite article
9. Which of the following is not a type of phrase?
   a. Noun
   b. Adjective
   c. Adverbial
   d. Pronoun
10. Which of the following is not a type of speech?
   a. Noun
   b. Pronoun
   c. Adverb
   d. Adjective

B. Fill in the blanks.

1. _______________ must consist of predicate and subject.
2. In verbal communication, message is delivered by using _______________.
3. Any method which relies on pictures, illusions, and graphics for sharing messages is _______________.
4. Communication is a process of sharing _______________.
5. Visual technique can be used with _______________ communication.

C. Answer the following questions.

1. What are the various characteristics of communication?
2. Define effective communication.
3. What do you understand by barriers to effective communication?
4. Define non-verbal communication. List the main elements of non-verbal communication.
5. What is visual communication? Give its any two advantages and disadvantages.
6. Enlist the factors affecting the perspective of communication.
7. How prejudices can affect the perception of communication.
8. Differentiate between phrase and sentence with example.

D. Project Work

1. **Blindfold Game:** Blindfold Game builds trust, listening and instructional skills.

   What you'll need:
   - Four or more people blindfold
   - Private room or recreational area
   - Various "obstacles" such as boxes, chairs or books

   How to play: Construct an obstacle course with your various items. Divide your players into teams of two. Tie a blindfold on one member and have them stand at the "start" of the obstacle course. The second member must then guide the blindfolded member through the course by calling out directions.

2. **Listen and Draw:** This game is easy to play but not so easy to "win." It requires participants' full attention and active listening. Gather your group of participants together and hand out a piece of paper and a pen or pencil to each player. Tell them you will give them verbal instructions on drawing an object, one step at a time.

   For example, you might give them instructions like:
   - Draw a square, measuring 5 inches on each side.
   - Draw a circle within the square, such that it fits exactly in the middle of the square.
   - Intersect 2 lines through the circle, dividing the circle into 4 equal parts.

Worksheet

A. State whether the statements are True or False.

1. Prejudices is the process of sharing information between two or more people.
2. Paragraph is a number of related sentences which focus on an idea.
3. Examples of written communication are football and chess.
4. There are four methods of communication.
5. Sentence is a group of words that make complete sense.
6. Example of visual communication is PowerPoint presentation.

B. Fill in the blanks.

1. ______________ involves both sender- receiver and they must respond to each other to have an effective communication.
2. An appropriate channel or medium (electronic mail, telephone call) through which the sender send a ______________________.
3. ________________communication is more formal and less flexible.
4. ______________are the group of words which do not make any sense.
5. A ________________ should be clear.
6. Subject and predicate are two parts of every complete ____________________.

C. Answer the following questions.

1. What is the phrase? Name a different kind of phrases?
2. Describe four types of sentences with an example of each.
3. Write a short note on effective paragraph writing.
4. What do you mean by article and its usage?

Exam Tips

1. Relate everything with your day to day life to keep things in mind for long time.
2. More workout on practical work.
3. Focus on part of speech by checking more examples.
4. Check the examples of various types of communication for better understanding the differences.

QUIZ CARD

Multiple choice questions.

1. Sender sends a message and in response gets ________ from receiver.
   a. Nothing ☐ b. Result ☐
   c. Feedback ☐ d. All of these ☐
2. ____________ is the process of converting coded information into original form.
   a. Communication ☐ b. Encoding ☐
   c. Feedback ☐ d. Decoding ☐
3. One way communication is __________ due to absence of receiver response.
   a. Difficult ☐ b. Steady and slow ☐
   c. Fast ☐ d. Effective ☐
4. Dress code is an example of __________ communication.
   a. Verbal ☐ b. Non-verbal ☐
   c. Written ☐ d. Spoken ☐
5. Pronouns always begin with ___________ letters.
   a. Small ☐ b. Capital ☐
   c. Numerical ☐ d. Any ☐
6. The message may be misinterpreted because of ___________.
   a. Barriers ☐ b. Distortions ☐
   c. Distractions ☐ d. Noise ☐
7. Which of the following is the negative attitude, especially when it is related to hatred for some people?
   a. Feelings ☐ b. Attitude ☐
   c. Prejudices ☐ d. Language ☐
8. Communication is a non-stop ___________.
   a. Paper ☐ b. Process ☐
   c. Programme ☐ d. Plan ☐
9. Who is the person who notices and decodes and attaches some meaning to a message?
   a. Receiver ☐ b. Driver ☐
   c. Sender ☐ d. Cleaner ☐
10. The response to a sender's message is called________.
    a. Channel ☐ b. Decoded message ☐
    c. Feedback ☐ d. None of these ☐

2 Self-Management Skills

Structure Bot

In this chapter, we will discuss the following topics:

- Self-management, self-management skills and its Importance of self-management
- Self-confidence, Factors influencing and building self-confidence
- SWOT analysis

Objective Bot

At the end of this chapter, you should be able to:

- Understand the concept of self-management
- Discuss the self-management skills
- Demonstrate/discuss/elaborate the importance of self-management
- Determine the factors influence and building self-confidence
- Explain SWOT analysis

Introduction

Self-management refers to the self-regulation or self-control; to one's thoughts, emotions, and behaviour effectively in various situations. It is about organizing your time, regulating actions, to achieve pre-determined goals. (Figure 2.1)

Figure 2.1: *Self- Management*

Self- management skills include:

- Self-awareness
- Self-control
- Self-confidence
- Problem solving
- Self-motivation
- Positive thinking
- Managing our emotions
- Anger
- Learning new ideas and team work

What is Self-management?

Self-management makes you organized, disciplined, helps in achieving goals, completing all work on time and effectively. It enhances your self-confidence, develops problem solving skills, and more.

Self-management can be achieved by learning:

- Time management
- Settings goals and priorities
- Accepting people from different cultures
- Managing your emotions, mood, anger, team working ability, etc. (Figure 2.2)

Figure 2.2: *Achieving self-management*

Self-management skills

Key skills of self-management are:

a. **Initiative:** Ability to work without getting instructions of what to do. In this, people need to believe on their own capabilities.

Initiative means doing the right thing without being told what to do.

To grow your Initiative skills:

- Look for various ways to simplify tasks.
- Keep yourself organized and stay on top of activities.
- Keep you plans and ambitions clear.

b. **Organization:** It involves planning time, energy and resources in work and life. When you are organized, you will save your energy and time and complete your tasks effectively and get the more productive results.

Organization involves:

- Defining and identification of specific tasks.
- Breaking your goals into smaller and fruitful tasks using SMART strategy.
- Managing time slots to activities as per their importance.

Organization includes:

- Planning
- Fix time slots
- Prioritize and schedule
- Spend right time on right activity

Knowledge Bot

In SMART strategy, S stands for Specific, M stands for Measurable, A stands for Achievable, R stands for Realistic and T stands for Time bound.

c. **Accountability:** In this, the person will be responsible and have to answer for his/her actions. If you say to yourself that you are accountable then it means you take ownership of responsibilities that come to your way.

Characteristics of accountability are:

- **Avoid procrastination:** It means avoiding the important tasks which need to be completed and doing an easy task.
- Problem solving attitude to achieve goals on time.
- Manage your emotions and work towards the best and constructive solutions. (Figure 2.3)

Figure 2.3 : *Self--management skills*

Importance of Self-management

Self-management is important in every field of life as it teaches you to be productively and efficiently achieve your goals.

> **KNOWLEDGE BOT**
>
> Self-management gives you confidence that you can control every situation.

Self-management helps you to:

- **Organized:** Skills of organizing and allocating their time and resources while planning a task.
- **Disciplined:** Organized schedule and commitments to follow.
- **Attain goals:** To attain goals on time organized all the tasks and allocated the right amount of time.
- **Enhance Self-confidence:** Set goals and achieve them to get self-confidence and achieve more challenging tasks. (Figure 2.4)

Figure 2.4 : *Importance of Self-management*

Self-confidence

Self-confidence is the sense of trusting one's own abilities. If you have self-confidence then you will start believing in your own capabilities; and willing to take risks and ready to accept any challenges. (Figure 2.5)

Figure 2.5 : *Self confidence*

Definition Bot

Self-confidence is a feeling of trust in one's own judgement.

Various factors influencing self-confidence are:

- **Social factors:** Society (school, friends, family and neighbourhood)all plays an important role in building and shaping your self-confidence.
- **Cultural factors:** It includes culture behaviour and development in different cultures through specific inputs from their environment.
- **Physical factors:** Your behaviour, body language and way of speaking reflect the level of confidence.

Building self-confidence

Building self-confidence is the process which takes efforts and commitment and it requires having a positive attitude about yourself.

Factors and techniques which help in having self-confidence are:

- **Self-efficiency:** It is the belief in your own ability in dealing with various challenges and events.
- **Positive thinking:** Focusing on the positives even in the time of adversity.
- **Self-esteem:** General feeling about your own self. People with low self-esteem are more affected by others' opinions about them and people with high self-esteem have positive feelings about themselves.

Figure 2.6 : *Building Self-confidence*

- **Self-monitoring:** Extent to which you base your behavior on cues from other people and situations.
- **SWOT:** The SWOT means, S- Strength, W- Weakness, O-Opportunity, and T- Threat and it is a useful technique for understanding opportunities and challenges. SWOT analysis helps in recognizing the one's abilities and talents along with choosing opportunities utilizing their core strengths. (Figure 2.6)

TIP BOT

Use the SMART strategy to outline a suitable goal for yourself.

MEMORY BOT

Skills are very important because it makes you more organised and it becomes easier to work.

TECH BOT

- **Self-management:** It is the process by which you manage yourself and do the daily task or coordinate among them successfully.
- **Accounting:** It means holding yourself answerable for the completion of the task.

Recap Bot

- Self-management is the self-regulation or self-control; to one's thoughts, emotions, and behavior effectively in various situations.
- Self-management makes you organized, disciplined, helps in achieving goals, completing all work on time and effectively. It enhances your self-confidence, develops problem solving skills, and more.
- Self-management is important in every field of life as it teaches you to be productively and efficiently achieve your goals.
- Self-confidence is the sense of trusting one's own abilities. If you have self-confidence then you will start believing in your own capabilities; and willing to take risks and ready to accept any challenges.
- Building self-confidence is the process which takes efforts and commitment and it requires having a positive attitude about yourself.

A. Multiple choice questions.

1. Self-management skills do not involve:
   a. Initiative
   b. Organization
   c. Management
   d. Accountability
2. Which of the following shows the ability to participate as a team member?
   a. Interpersonal skills
   b. Communication skills
   c. Entrepreneur skills
   d. None of these
3. Which of the following is not a factor influencing self-confidence?
   a. Social factors
   b. Personal factors
   c. Cultural factors
   d. Physical factors
4. People with self-confidence have a __________ outlook.
   a. Negative
   b. Arrogant
   c. Outward
   d. Positive
5. In SWOT, O stands for __________.
   a. Operation
   b. Organization
   c. Opportunity
   d. Openly
6. People with low self-esteem are more affected by:
   a. Personal matters
   b. Others thinking about them
   c. Work load
   d. None of these
7. R in SMART strategy stands for________.
   a. Real
   b. Rate
   c. Realistic
   d. Required
8. ________ is the ability to work without always getting instructions from others.
   a. Self-confidence
   b. Organization
   c. Initiative
   d. Accountability
9. Which of the following refers to a belief about your own ability to deal with events and challenges?
   a. Self-esteem
   b. Self-confidence
   c. Self-monitoring
   d. Self-efficacy
10. In SWOT, T stands for __________.
    a. Threat
    b. Time
    c. Timestamp
    d. Timer

B. Fill in the blanks.

1. ______________includes culture behaviour and development in different cultures through specific inputs from their environment.
2. Social, cultural and __________factors influences the self-confidence.
3. Self-management skills comprises of ______key skills.
4. ____________is the ability to work without always getting instructions for what needs to be done.
5. ____________________ enhances your self-confidence, develops problem solving skills, and more.

C. Answers the following questions.

1. Name the three factors influencing self-confidence.
2. Explain SWOT technique for improving self-confidence.
3. Give any five factors for building self-confidence.
4. What do you mean by self-esteem?
5. Give two characteristics of accountability.
6. Name the three factors influencing self-confidence.

D. Project work

1. Practise the team building exercise yourself first to check that it works, check timings, materials, and to ensure you have all the answers. Anticipation and planning are vital.
2. Observe the head girl of your school and write points on how she helps others, solves problems of every student, and handles different situations.

Worksheet

A. State whether the following statements are True or False.

1. Self-confidence is a sense of trusting one's own abilities and self.
2. Self-management is a general feeling about your own self.
3. Organization involves defining and identification of specific tasks.
4. To attain goals on time organized all the tasks and allocated the right amount of time.
5. Self-management can be achieved by learning thread management.
6. Accounting means holding yourself answerable for the completion of the task.

B. Fill in the blanks.

1. ______________ helps in recognizing the one's abilities and talents along with choosing opportunities utilizing their core strengths.
2. ______________ all plays an important role in building and shaping your self-confidence.
3. __________________means avoiding the important tasks which need to be completed and doing an easy task.
4. Self- management skills include ________________________.
5. ______________________is the process by which you manage yourself and do the daily task or coordinate among them successfully.

C. Answer the following questions.

1. Name the three factors influencing self-confidence.
2. Explain SWOT technique for improving self-confidence.
3. Give any five factors for building self-confidence.
4. What do you mean by self-esteem?

Exam tips

1. Apply the self-management skills in your life to better understand its benefits.
2. Observe the various factors that influence the self-confidence in one individual then divide into different categories such as Social, Cultural and Physical factors.
3. For checking the practical feasibility of SWOT technique, identify your core strengths, weaknesses, opportunities and threat.
4. More check the examples of accountability and responsibility to understand the differences.

QUIZ CARD

Multiple choice questions.

1. Which of the following shows the ability to participate as a team member?
   a. Interpersonal skills ☐ b. Communication skills ☐
   c. Entrepreneur skills ☐ d. None of these ☐
2. ________ is your ability to participate as a team member.
   a. Rational Abilities ☐ b. Personal qualities ☐
   c. Interpersonal skill ☐ d. Communication skill ☐
3. People with low self-esteem are more affected by:
   a. Personal matters ☐ b. Others thinking about them ☐
   c. Work load ☐ d. None of these ☐
4. Which of the following refers to a belief about your own ability to deal with events and challenges?
   a. Self-esteem ☐ b. Self-confidence ☐
   c. Self-monitoring ☐ d. Self-efficacy ☐
5. Which of the following is not a self-management skill?
   a. Rational ability ☐ b. Personal quality ☐
   c. Both a. and b. ☐ d. None of these ☐
6. Which one is not considered a self-management skill?
   a. Problem solver ☐ b. Stress-resistance ☐
   c. A bargain hunter ☐ d. Communication ☐
7. What does it mean to be stress-resistant?
   a. You never have stress in life ☐
   b. You know how to handle stress efficiently ☐
   c. You have too much stress in your life ☐
   d. You enjoy stress ☐
8. Which of the following is not a self-management skill?
   a. Problem solving ☐ b. Bargaining ☐
   c. Understanding self ☐ d. Confidence building ☐
9. Grooming is a term associated with:
   a. Time management ☐ b. Problem solving ☐
   c. Neat and clean appearance ☐ d. Self-management ☐
10. What steps should one take to build confidence?
   a. Set goals in life ☐
   b. Appreciate oneself for all the achievements ☐
   c. Always think positively ☐ d. Talk to people who are confident ☐

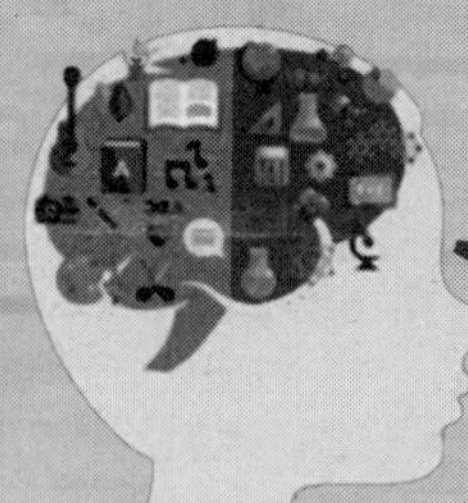

3 Information and Communication Technology Skills-I

Structure Bot

In this chapter, we will discuss the following topics:

- Information and communication technology, its tools and role
- Computer system and its basic components
- Computer memory
- Various peripheral devices
- Software and its types

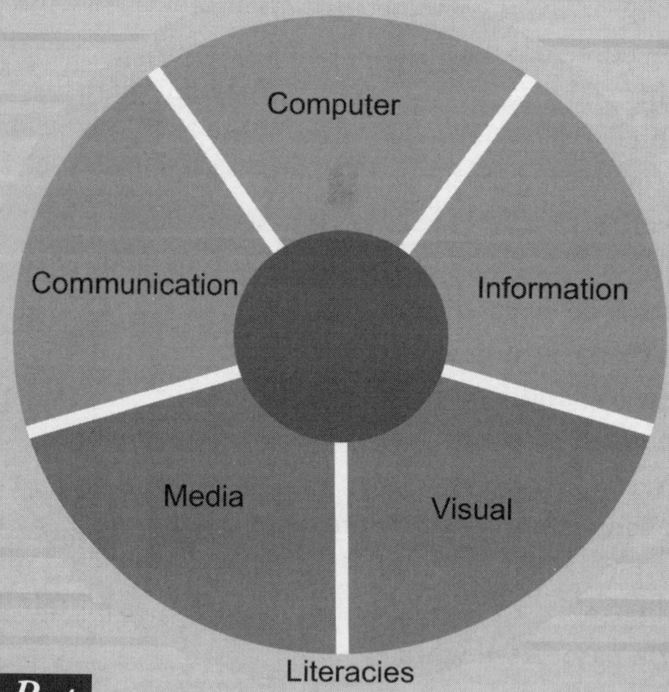

Objective Bot

At the end of the chapter, you should be able to:

- Define the operating system
- Understand the Internet and its uses of the Internet
- Know the e-mail application
- Learn about the social media like Twitter, Facebook, YouTube, and WhatsApp

Introduction to Information and Communication Technology (ICT)

Information and Communication Technology (ICT) includes a set of technological resources and tools which are used for communication, creation, storing, managing, and disseminating information. (Figure 3.1)

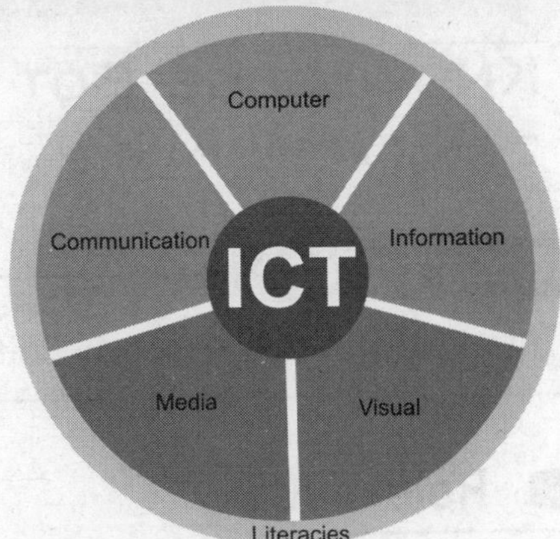

Figure 3.1: *Information and Communication Technology*

Definition Bot

ICT is defined as a diverse set of technologies tools and resources used to communicate, and to create, disseminate, store and manage information.

Tools of ICT

The ICT tools includes television, radio, computers, satellite systems, networks, and mobile phones. The video conferencing, teleconferencing, and social networking, like various applications and services associated with these technologies, come under ICT.

Definition Bot

IT tools are devices or objects used in Information and Communication Technology.

Some of the ICT tools are:

- **Radio:** It is used as a transmission device, music listening device and so on.
- **Mobile:** It is used for making calls and has many applications used for money transfer (Paytm, Goggle Pay), messaging (WhatsApp) and Games.
- **TV:** It is used for watching movies, listening news and many more.
- **E-mail (Electronic mail):** Outlook by Microsoft, Yahoo mail, Hotmail, Rediff mail, and Gmail are major carriers of e-mail messages. (Figure 3.2)

Figure 3.2: *Tools of ICT*

Memory Bot

Radio seeks to build up the listener's attitudes favourable towards the new information useful to them.

Knowledge Bot

TV and Mobile is the simplest and easiest way of communication.

Fact Bot

In 1971, Ray Tomlinson invented and developed electronic mail.

Role of ICT

ICT has given access to information and various services and products, by changing the way of living, working, communicating with each other.

Some of the applications, where ICT are being used are given below:

- **Information access:** Accessing information regarding health, social aspects, education, and so on.

- **E-commerce:** Buying or selling products online through the Internet. It will save time and money as one can get the product at home.

- **Learning and teaching:** Various learning tools (GSuit, YouTube, and Scribed) are now available for students, parents, and teachers.

- **E-banking:** With e-banking, you can make the transaction anytime, anywhere, through the Internet. You can transfer money to any account, can check account details, make online payments.

- **Entertainment:** Watching movies on TV, Live TV, Amazon prime video, Netflix, and many more.

- **Social media and communication:** Social media applications, such as Facebook, Twitter, Snapchat, and WhatsApp helps people to stay connected with their friends and family living far away or near to them.

- **Personal healthcare:** Wearable gadgets (Fitbit, I watch) help in monitoring heart rate and provide information on other physical fitness.

- **Industries:** Industries are using robots and Artificial Intelligence in manufacturing their products.

- **E-governance:** Government apps and websites, with the help of which one can interact directly with the government.

  For digital empowerment, various apps are launched by the government are:
  - Bharat Interface for Money (BHIM)
  - UMANG
  - Swachh Bharat Abhiyaan App

- **Medical services:** In diagnose of diseases, treatment, and monitoring of patients.

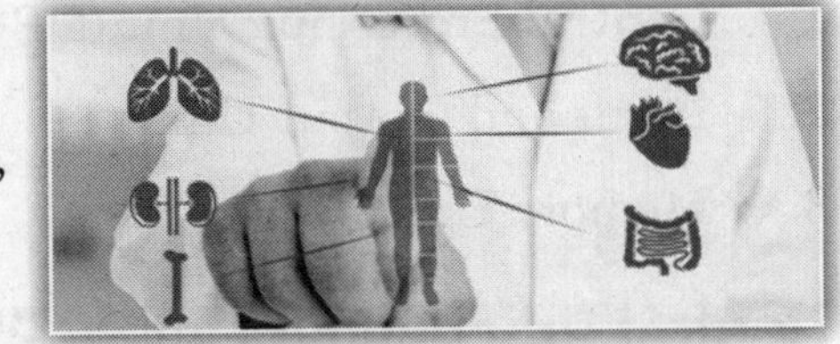

Knowledge Bot

ICT is used in the pharmaceutical sector for cutting research and manufacturing.

Computer System

Figure 3.3: *Computer System*

The word **Computer** is derived from word compute that means to calculate. It is a calculating device that can perform arithmetic operations at an enormous speed and operates upon data.

A computer is an electronic device that can perform a variety of operations according to a given set of instructions called a program. It then displays or prints the result. (Figure 3.3)

Computer is a combination of hardware and software, which instruct to perform operations.

- **Hardware:** The physical components of a computer, it may be electronic, electrical, magnetic, mechanical or optical components. Examples of components are microprocessors, ICs.
- **Software:** It is the set of computer programs, procedures, and associated documentation related to the effective operation of a computer system.

KNOWLEDGE BOT

All the tangible parts of a computer system, no matter how small or big, are part of hardware.

Components of Computer System

The major components of a digital computer are:

1. Central Processing Unit (CPU)
2. Input and Output Unit
3. Memory Unit

Central Processing Unit (CPU)

The CPU is the brain of a computer. Its primary job is to run program and perform the logical, arithmetic, input-output operation of system.

A block diagram of the basic computer organization is shown in Figure 3.4.

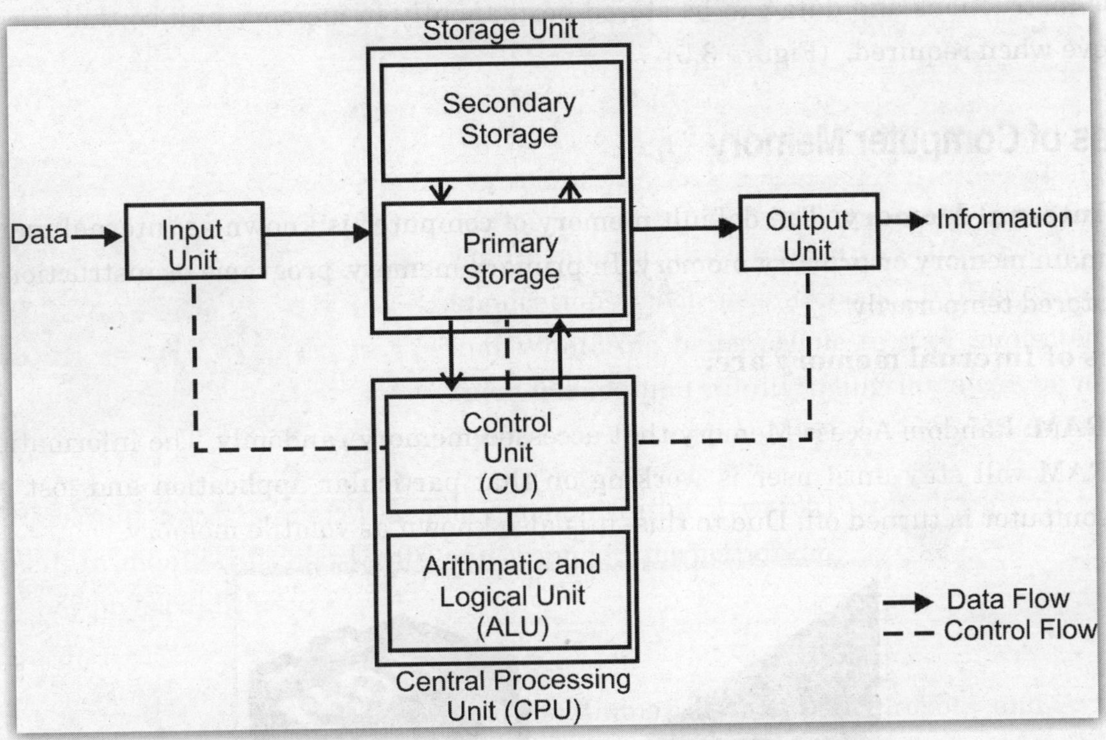

Figure 3.4: *Block diagram of the basic computer organization*

The five units of computer system are:

- **Inputting:** Process of entering data into the computer, by the user using an input device.
- **Storing:** Holding of data and instructions in the computer's main memory, for manipulations.
- **Processing:** Performing operations (both arithmetic and logical) or manipulation of data.
- **Outputting:** Process of showing the information or result to the user either on screen (monitor) or on paper (through printer).
- **Controlling:** Directing all the above processes, in coordination, by the Control Unit (CU).

MEMORY BOT

The speed of the CPU is measured in Megahertz.

Memory unit is a principle storage of computer that stores both instructions and data. These instructions and data can be stored permanently in memory unit so that it can be retrieve when required. (Figure 3.5)

Types of Computer Memory

a. **Internal Memory:** The default memory of computer is known as internal memory, main memory or primary memory. In primary memory, programs or instructions are stored temporarily.

Types of Internal memory are:

- **RAM:** Random Access Memory that accessed memory randomly. The information in RAM will stay until user is working on that particular application and lost when computer is turned off. Due to this, it is also known as volatile memory.

Figure: 3.5: *RAM and ROM*

Types of RAM

- DRAM stands for Dynamic Random Access Memory that stores data temporarily and to retain data it is refreshed periodically.
- SRAM stands for Static RAM are more expensive and faster than DRAM.
- SDRAM stands for Synchronous DRAM that transmit large amount of data on highspeed through synchronous interface.
- DDR stands for Double Data Rate Memory used in Intel Pentium 4 systems and needless power to process with double speed of SDRAM.

- **ROM:** Read Only Memory and also known as non-volatile memory as it stores information permanently. It is mainly used in booting process and when power is turned off an initial program to start computer is saved in ROM.

Types of ROM:

- PROM stands for Programmable Read Only Memory or One-Time Programmable ROM(OTP) because in this only one program can be done at one time by manufacturer while manufacturing it and after that changes can't be done in it.
- EPROM stands for Erasable PROM in which data can be erased multiple times by exposing it to ultraviolet rays and it will erase the entire data present on the chip.
- EEPROM stands for Electronically EPROM that erase and reprogrammed the contents in blocks instead of one byte at a time and in this selective data can be erased.
- Flash memory is a specific type of EEPROM that keep information even without power source.
- Masked ROM contents are programmed at the time of manufacturing by burning the software mask on chip during designing phase.

Knowledge Bot

The primary use of ROM is during the booting process.

- **Cache Memory:** It is a fast speed memory can be inserted as a part of CPU or motherboard that stores repeatedly required instructions to run program. It is faster because it does not require the motherboard system bus for transferring data.

b. **External Memory:** It is also known as secondary or auxiliary memory and used due to expensive, temporary and less storage capacity of internal memory. When required, the data can be transferred to external memory from internal memory.

Types of secondary memory or secondary storage devices

- **Magnetic Disk:** Magnetic disk permits direct access to individual records. This means that the computer system does not have to search the entire file (as in the case of sequential file tape) to find record disk storage. (Figure 3.6)

Figure: 3.6: *Magnetic Disk*

The two types of magnetic disk are:

a. **Hard Disk:** Hard Disk is a non-volatile secondary storage device. It is an electromechanical device and used as the main storage device of the computer.

b. **Floppy Disk:** Floppy disk is another magnetic storage media. It is widely used in personal computers. It is a flat, 3.5-inch disk of polyester film with a magnetic coating. The maximum storage capacity of this disk is 1.44 MB.

- **Optical Disk:** An optical disk is a computer disk that uses optical storage technology to read and write data. Laser beams are used to store data digitally and even to read and write data to and from the disk. (Figure 3.7)

Figure: 3.7: *Optical Disk*

The various types of optical disks are:

a. **Compact Disc (CD):** It is used to store video, images, sound recording etc. it is costs less then hard disk or RAM. CDs are categorized as CD-ROM, CD-R, CD-W, and CD-RW.

b. **Digital Versatile Disc (DVD):** A DVD is capable of storing data such as movies, games and can also be used for installing small applications.

- **Flash memories**

  a. **Blu- Ray Disc:** The name Blu-ray is derived from the blue-violet laser technology and is used to read and write information on these discs. It is the successor to DVD. It is used for HD content and optical data storage and is fast enough for High Definition (HD) quality video recording.

  b. **Memory Stick:** A memory stick is also known as memory card which is used to read and write information in it. A large amount of data can be stored in memory stick. (Figure 3.8)

Figure: 3.8: *Flash Memory*

2. Arithmetic Logic Unit

Fundamental building block of CPU, where the actual execution of instructions takes place. It loads data from input register, performs the operations as directed by control unit, and then stores the result in output register.

ALUs are designed to perform:

- **Arithmetic operations:** Add, subtract, multiply, and divide.
- **Logical operations:** AND, OR, NOT, and XOR.
- **Comparison operations:** Less than, equal to, greater than, less than equal to, and greater than equal to.

- **Bit-shifting operators:** Shifting the word by specific number of bits either to left or right.

3. Control Unit (CU)

It controls the entire working of the computer, by generating timing and control signals. It also controls the transfer of data between memory and input/output devices, operations and entire processing.

Input Unit

Input is the process of entering and collecting the data into the computer.

Definition Bot

An input device is a piece of hardware used to provide data to a computer used for interaction and control.

Some Input devices are:

- **Keyboard:** Programs and data are entered into a computer through a keyboard. It contains alphabets, digits, special characters, function keys and some control keys. When a key is pressed, an electronic signal is produced which is detected by an electronic circuit called keyboard encoder.

KNOWLEDGE BOT

Keyboards are of two sizes 84 keys or 101/102 keys, but now keyboards with 104 keys or 108 keys are also available for Windows and Internet.

- **Mouse:** It performs functions by detecting two- dimensional motion. It is held in one handand moved across a flat surface, generally it consist of two buttons: left and right button.

- **Scanner:** Information in the form of text or image is entered and then transformed into digital file, which allows the computer to read or display the scanned object.

- **Joystick:** A joystick is used to move the cursor continuously in the previously pointing direction on a monitor screen.

MEMORY BOT

Joystick is mainly used in Computer Aided Designing (CAD) and playing computer games.

- **Graphics tablet/ digitizer/ digitizing tablet:** It consists of an electronic writing area and a pressure sensitive pen for getting different strokes of various widths. It is widely used by artist to create hand-made image.

- **Touch Screen:** It's an electronic visual display which detects the touch within a display area. The touch screen sends a signal to the computer which gives the location on the screen which has been touched.

- **Touchpad/Track pad:** It translates motion and position of user's fingertip to relative position on the screen. It is used in Laptops.

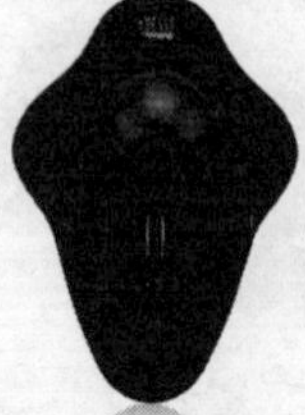

- **Trackball:** It has ball on its top, which can be rolled by finger. It is widely used in CAD workstation.

- **Microphone:** This input device is used to store sound in the computer with **.wav** as extension. It is mainly used in radio broadcasting, video conferencing, sound amplifying systems, speech recognition programs and recording.

- **Light Pen:** It is mainly used to select or modify the data on screen by allowing user to point on displayed objects or draw it on the screen.

Output Unit

The processed data is display by using an output unit.
Some of commonly used devices are:

- **Monitor:** It is a most common output device that is also known as Electronic Visual Display or Visual Display Unit for computer. The output is display on screen.

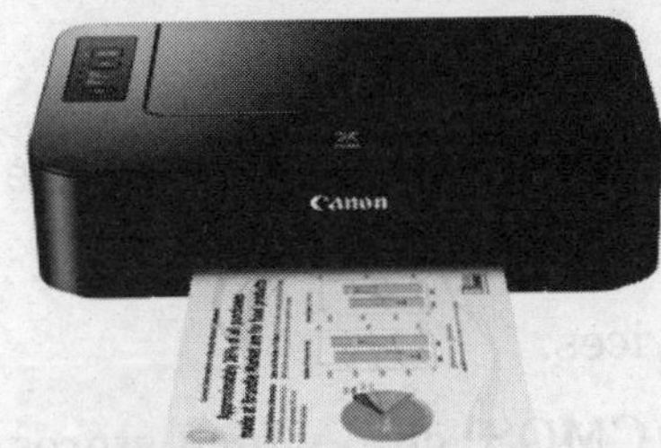

- **Printers:** It produces a hard copy of documents which is stored in an electronic form on physical print media.

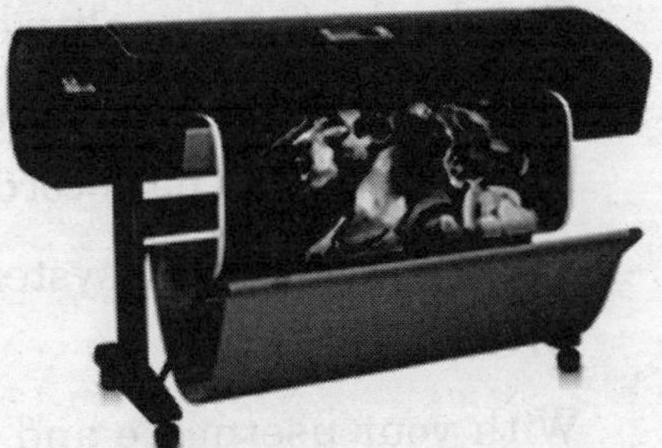

- **Plotters:** These are used to produce precise and good quality graphics and drawings under control of the computer, by using an ink pen or inkjet.

- **Speaker:** It receives sound in form of electric current form sound card and then converts itinto sound format.

TIP BOT

Drives such as a CD-ROM, DVD, floppy diskette drive, and USB flash drive are considered storage devices.

Peripheral Devices

One can connect some external or internal devices to computer systems that is known as peripheral devices.

These are attached to the computer system when there is a need for to perform special functions like video recording, image capturing and connecting to the Internet, and more.

The peripheral devices can be easily attached and removed from the computer system.

Starting Computer

To start a computer:

1. Switch on the main power supply.
2. Switch on the UPS.
3. Switch on the monitor.

Process which happens between when you switch on the UPS to when the Desktop screen appears.

a. Booting process begins which check all the hardware and software installed in the computer and are working properly or not and then load all the needed files.

b. Checks the functionality of all the connected hardware devices.

c. Checking of Complementary Metal-Oxide-Semiconductor (CMOS) chip which stores the settings like password, date, and time of Basic Input-Output System (BIOS).

d. Then, the operating system is loaded on the RAM after completion of all the steps of BIOS.

e. With your username and password, you can log in to the computer system, and the operating system desktop will appear if you have entered the correct credentials.

Shut Down a Computer

To shut down the computer:

1. Click on Start button present on Taskbar.
2. Various options appears.
3. Click on Shut down option
4. This will fade away the desktop, and the computer will gradually shut down.

Software

Software is a set of instructions or programs instructing a computer to do specific tasks.

The two types of software are:

1. System software
2. Application software

1. System Software

It is collections of single or multiple programs which manage or control the overall performance and operation of a computer system.

Types of system software:

a. **Operating system:** It is an interface between hardware and software of a computer that manages the overall functionality of the computer and its resources.

Examples: Windows, Macintosh (Mac), DOS, and Unix.

Components of OS

- **Shell:** It is an interface and outermost layer of OS that handle the interaction with users.
- **Kernel:** It is an interface and core component of OS that handles the interaction between data processing and applications done at the hardware level.

Functioning of OS

- Management of processor, memory, file, devices, security and detection of error.

Types of OS

- **Single User Operating System:** It allows only one user to work on a computer at a time. Example: Windows XP.
- **Multiuser Operating System:** It allows a number of users to work together on a single computer by providing a terminal connected to a single computer. Example: Unix.
- **Single-Tasking Operating System:** It executes a single job / program at a time. Example: MS-DOS.
- **Multitasking Operating System:** It supports the execution of more than one task at a time. Example: Windows 2012.
- **Multiprogramming Operating System:** In this, several programs can be run at the same time via time sharing mechanism. Example: Linux.
- **Real Time Operating System:** It responds to an event within a pre-determined time. Example: Windows CE.
- **Batch Processing Operating System:** Similar types of tasks are grouped under batch and then these tasks are executed without any user interruption. Example: MS-DOS.

- **Multiprocessing Operating System:** It uses more than two CPUs within a single computer system. Example: LINUX and UNIX.

Disk Operating System

Disk Operating System (DOS) is a type of system software that runs from a hard disk drive. This also refers to the specific family of DOS, which is known as a Microsoft Disk Operating System (MS-DOS).

DOS support:

- Multiple networking
- Text editing functions
- Multiple directories
- Enhanced management of memory
- Disk compression and fragmentation

FACT BOT

DOS was most commonly found OS in IBM PCs that were developed by Microsoft in 1981.

Linux

Linux OS is an open and free source that was developed by Linus Torvalds in 1991 at AT & T's Bell Laboratories. The main function of Linux OS is to manage the system resources or hardware and can act as an interface between user and computer system just like other OS. It was designed by considering UNIX compatibility; that's why its functioning is similar to UNIX. From the last 2 decades, it has become very popular due to its various features, as given in the below section.

Edubuntu

It has a Graphical User Interface (GUI) that is known as Unity that allows users to interact with the computer system using graphical icons. It allows accessing your data on the web or your computer in a faster way. Earlier its name was Ubuntu Education Edition as it is built on the Ubuntu base. It is one of the best available free software that is designed for homes and computers.

b. **Language Processor:** Language processor is known as translator that converts the program written in high level language into low level language (machine language).

c. **Device Drivers:** In order to run Input/output devices, there is a need of driver which translates the commands from the operating system into commands that the specific hardware can understand.

Application Software

Application software are also known as applications which are meant for end users. For example, software for preparing school result, library management system, accounting bills and so on.

Application software can be categorized as:

a. **General Purpose Application Software:** The software that help in managing files in database, creating text documents and formatting it, preparing presentations and designing graphics are called general purpose application software.

b. **Customized (Bespoke) Software:** Customized software is also known as tailor-made software or bespoke software as it is developed according to the need or requirement of a client/user. For example, if the owner of a restaurant requires an automatic bill generator, then the software company will develop and customize the software as per owner`s requirement.

c. **Specific Purpose Software:** The software which is used for some specific purpose such as calculator, computer game, imusic, reservation software etc., is known as specific purpose software.

Internet

Internet is an interconnection of multiple networks. The word internet (lowercase i) is different from Internet (uppercase I). While internet means network of networks, Internet is the term used to refer to a specific worldwide network, WWW (World Wide Web).

The Internet carries a vast array of information resources and services, most notably the interlinked hypertext documents of the World Wide Web (WWW) and the infrastructure to support electronic mail.

Uses of internet

With the help of Internet, you can:

- Exchange messages using e-mail (Electronic mail).

- Transfer files as well as software.
- Browse through information on any topic on web.
- Communicate in real time (chat) with others connected to the Internet.
- Search databases of government, individuals and organizations.
- Read news available from leading news groups.
- Send or receive animation and picture files from distant places.
- Set up a site with information about your company's products and services.

Common terms

- **Website:** Website can be defined as a collection of information stored as Web pages which may be on one or more computers. A Web page is an electronic document written in computer language called HTML.
- **Web Page:** A web page is an electronic document written in computer language called HTML (Hypertext Markup Language). It contains text, links or tags that will display graphics, video, audio, and downloaded files and other web pages. Each web page has a unique address, called a URL (Uniform Resource Locator) that identifies its location on the network.

KNOWLEDGE BOT

The basic elements of a web page are Page title, header area, navigation menu, content area and footer.

- **Website Address:** A website address is known as a URL. It is an Internet name that points to a location where a file, directory or website page is hosted. The first page of the website is called the Home page.
- **URL (Uniform Resource Locator):** Uniform Resource Locators, or URLs, are the unique addresses of Internet resources. URLs contain information about the access method to use and also about the resource itself.

FACT BOT

The first web page was created at CERN by Tim Berners-Lee on August 6, 1991.

TIP BOT

You can view all of the code by viewing the source code of the web page.

- **E-mail:** It stands for Electronic mail, is the most popular internet application used to send or receive messages between various users.
- **E-mail account:** It is an electronic mailbox on a network where a user sends e-mails or messages.
- **E-mail address:** The e-mail address of the user is a must to use the services the e-mail services that are a unique name to identify accounts on a network.

Creating a Gmail account

1. Open web browser (Google chrome) by double click on it. Following screen appears:

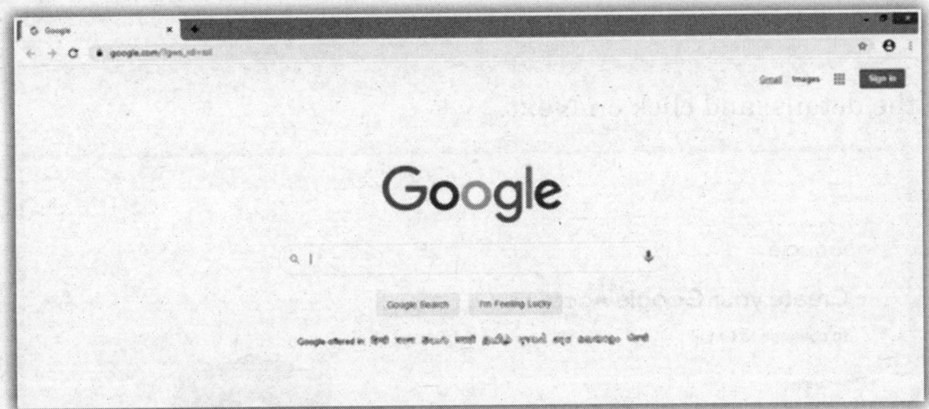

2. Click on Gmail. Following screen appears:

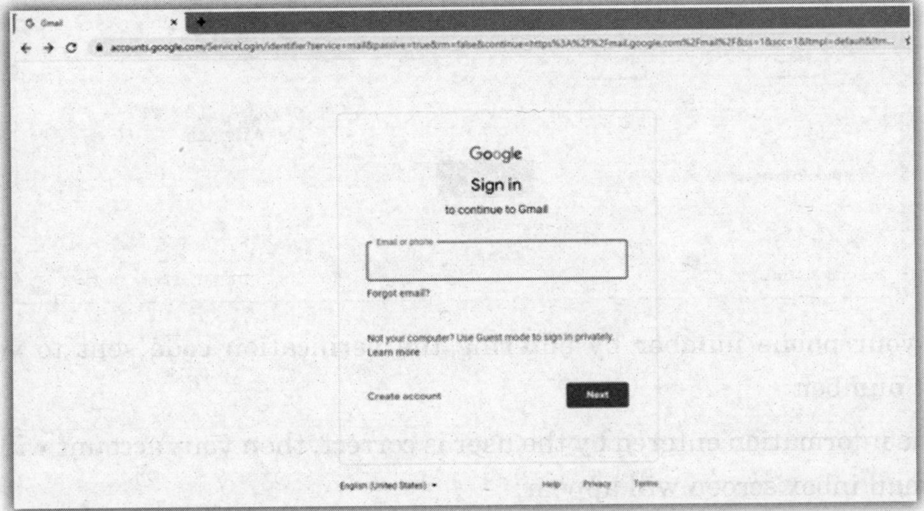

3. Click on **Create** account. A registration form will appear on the screen:

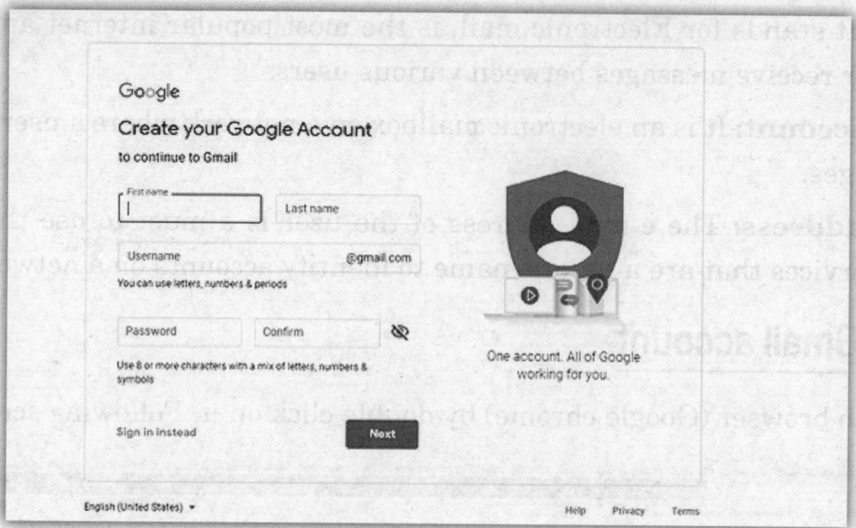

4. Fill all the details, and click on **Next**.

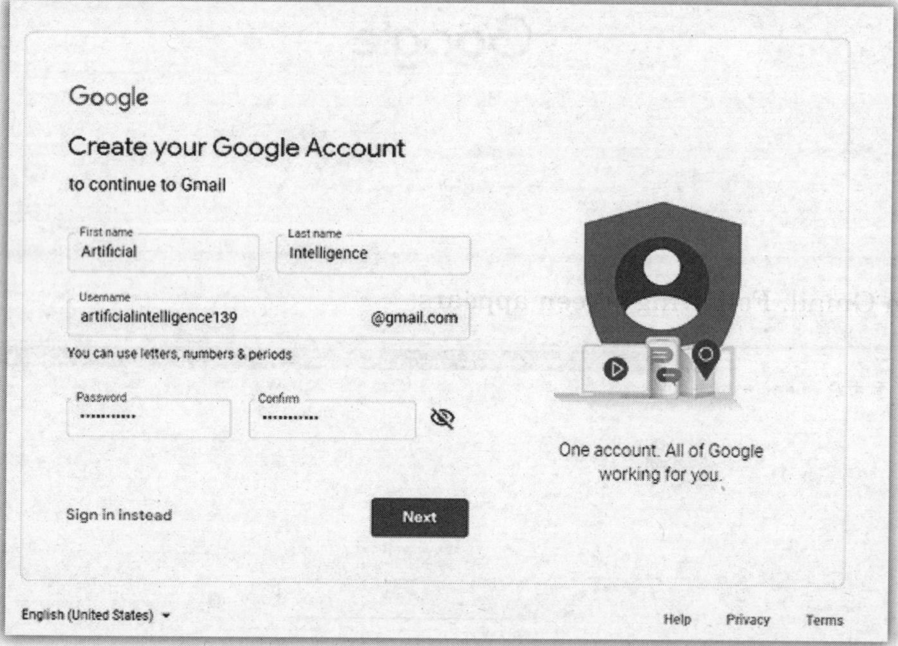

5. Verify your phone number by entering the verification code sent to your entered contact number.
6. If all the information entered by the user is correct, then your account will be created, and Gmail inbox screen will appear:

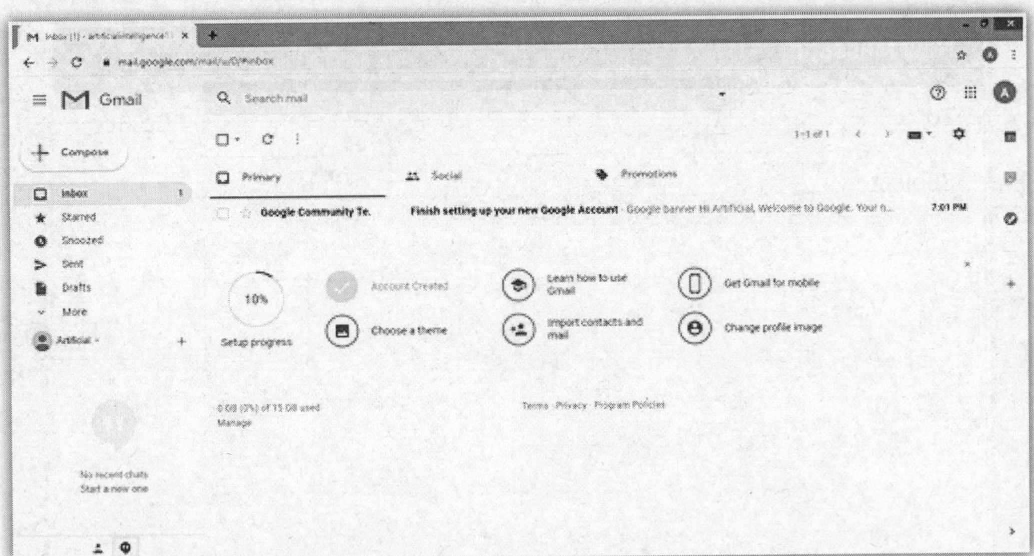

To sign out from Gmail account is:

1. Click on username drop-down arrow.
2. Select your account from the list and click on the **Sign out** button.

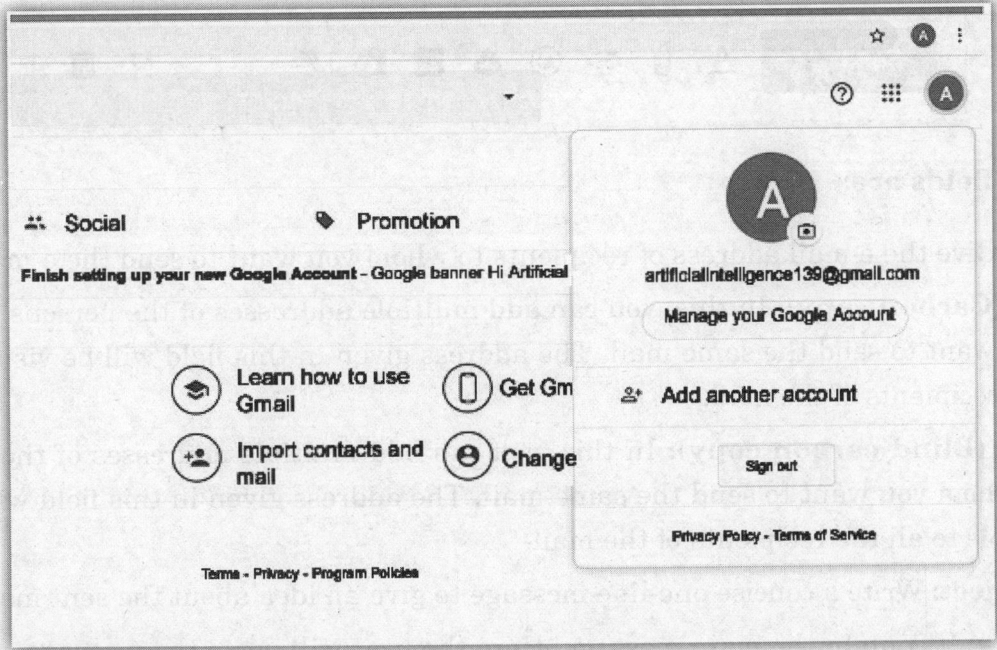

To compose a mail:

Click on **Compose** button given on the upper left corner of Gmail, the following screen appears:

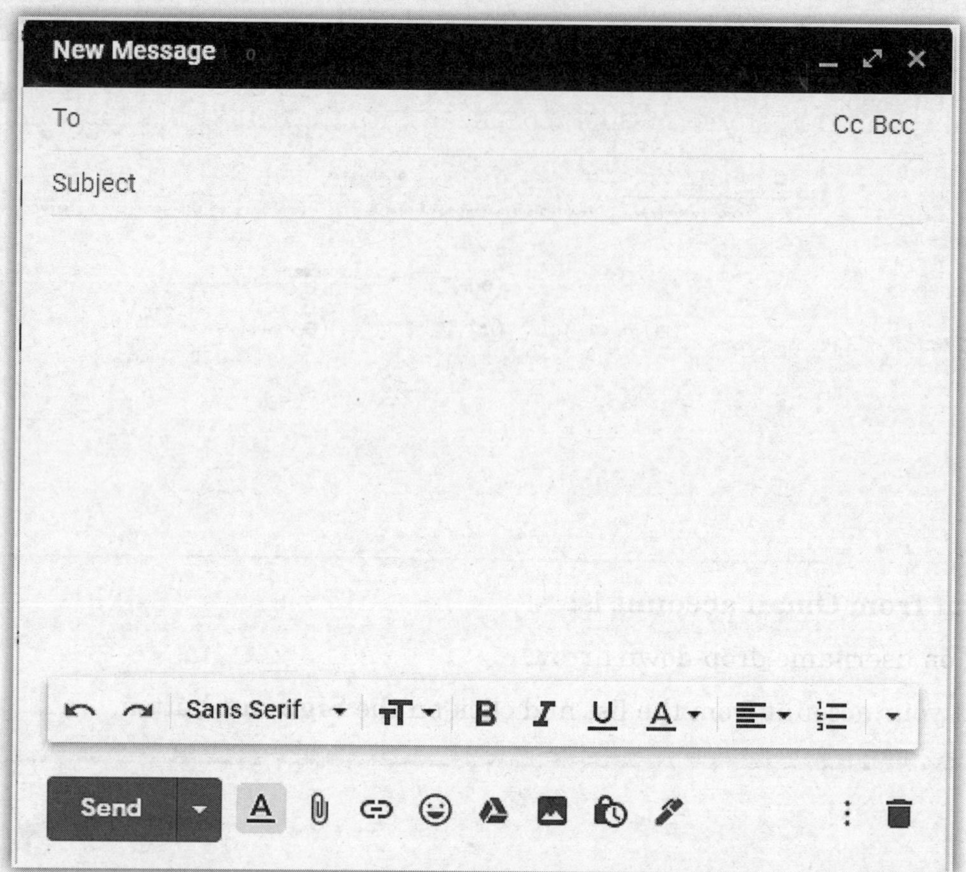

Various fields are:

- **To:** Give the e-mail address of recipients to whom you want to send the e-mail.
- **Cc (Carbon copy):** In this, you can add multiple addresses of the persons to whom you want to send the same mail. The address given in this field will be visible to all the recipients of the mail.
- **Bcc (Blind carbon copy):** In this, you can add multiple addresses of the persons to whom you want to send the same mail. The address given in this field will not be visible to all the recipients of the mail.
- **Subject:** Write a concise one-line message to give an idea about the sent mail.
- **Body:** It contain the main message. Here the user will write the message according to the type of mail, whether formal or informal.
- **Attach file:** In this, you can add various files like audio, document, video,and more.
- **Send:** Once you are done with writing and attaching files, click on the **Send** button given on the lower left side.

Receiving e-mails

All received e-mails are stored in the Inbox along with the details like the sender's name, subject line, time, date, and some content in the mail when you receive an e-mail.

To open a mail:

1. Click on the Inbox button.
2. Take the cursor on particular mail you want to open and double click on it.

Three tabs in the Inbox are:

- **Primary tab:** It consists of e-mails from your friends, family, colleagues, and more.
- **Social tab:** It consists of e-mails from social media like Facebook, Twitter, and more.
- **Promotion tab:** It consists of e-commerce related emails like promotional offers, adds, and more.

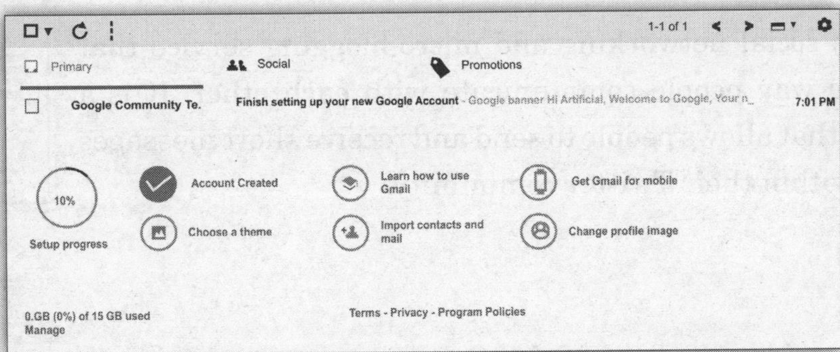

To reply an e-mail:

1. Click on received e-mail from a particular person.
2. You will find Reply, Reply All, and Forward option or only Reply and Forward option right below the opened message.
3. Once you have read the received message, click on Reply arrow, this will appear a new Compose Window below the original mail and type your message.
4. Click on the Send button.

Social Networking

A social networking service is an online service, platform, or site that focuses on building and reflecting of social networks or social relations among people, e.g., who share common interests and/or activities.

Most social network services are Web based and provide means for users to interact over the Interet, such as e-mail and instant messaging, video calling, chat, file sharing, discussion groups, voice chats, e-mails, blogging and so on.

Examples of social networking sites:

Facebook

Facebook is a social networking Website intended to connect friends, family, and business associates. It is the largest networking site. By creating Facebook profile, the user can fill different information about himself and share content such as text, pictures, music, video etc. with others.

Twitter

Twitter is a free social networking and micro-blogging service that has changed the way people communicate with each other. It is a message service that allows people to send and receive short messages (called tweets) within their Twitter community.

YouTube

It is a free online video sharing service that has now acquired by Google. One can search for video, songs, movies, exercise tips, comedy, and tutorial to learn something on it. Any person can upload their video on YouTube by creating user Id and password, and all other person can see it. One can also have access of some videos by subscribe it and give view, rate, share, like, add to favourite and comments on it.

WhatsApp

It is a firmware and cross-platform messaging service that allows sending messages, pictures, and videos. One can also do voice or video call with other person across the world.

Digital India

'Digital India' is a program initiated by Prime Minister Mr. Narendra Modi. The motive behind the Digital India mission is to build participative, transparent, and responsive governance to reach out the citizens.

Aadhaar, Digilocker, Permanent Account Number (PAN), All IndiaCouncil of Technical Education (AICTE), e-District, Passport, Central Board of Secondary Education (CBSE), Indian railway ticket booking, and many more are services provided by Digital India.

FACT BOT

Twitter was created in March 2006 by Jack Dorsey, Noah Glass, Biz Stone, and Evan Williams, launched in July of that year.

TECH BOT

- **Hardware:** The physical components of a computer that you can see and touch.
- **Software:** It is a set of instructions, data or programs used to operate computers and execute specific tasks.
- **Operating System:** It acts as an interface between the user and the computer hardware.
- **WWW:** It is a means of accessing information over the internet.
- **Webpage:** A Web page is a document for the World Wide Web that is identified by a unique uniform resource locator (URL).
- **E-mail:** It is defined as the transmission of messages over communications networks.

Recap Bot

- Information and Communication Technology (ICT) includes a set of technological resources and tools which are used for communication, creation, storing, managing, and disseminating information.
- The ICT tools includes television, radio, computers, satellite systems, networks, and mobile phones.

- ICT has given access to information and various services and products, by changing the way of living, working, communicating with each other.
- Word "Computer" is derived from word compute that means to calculate. It is a calculating device that can perform arithmetic operations at an enormous speed and operates upon data.
- The CPU is the brain of a computer. Its primary job is to run program and perform the logical, arithmetic, and input-output operation of a system.
- Memory unit is a principle storage of computer that stores both instructions and data.
- Arithmetic Logic Unit is the fundamental building block of CPU, where the actual execution of instructions takes place. It loads data from input register, performs the operations as directed by control unit, and then stores the result in output register.
- Control unit controls the entire working of the computer, by generating timing and control signals.
- Input is the process of entering and collecting the data into the computer.
- The processed data is display by using an output unit.
- One can connect some external or internal devices to computer systems that is known as peripheral devices.
- Software is a set of instructions or programs instructing a computer to do specific tasks.
- System software is collections of single or multiple programs which manage or control the overall performance and operation of a computer system.
- Operating system is an interface between hardware and software of a computer that manages the overall functionality of the computer and its resources.
- Language processor is known as translator that converts the program written in high level language into low level language (machine language).
- To run Input/output devices, there is a need of driver which translates the commands from the operating system into commands that the specific hardware can understand.
- Application software are also known as applications which are meant for end users. For example, software for preparing school result, library management system, accounting bills and so on.
- Internet is an interconnection of multiple networks. The word internet (lowercase i) is different from Internet (uppercase I).
- A social networking service is an online service, platform, or site that focuses on building and reflecting of social networks or social relations among people, e.g., who share common interests and/or activities.

A. Multiple choice questions.

1. Which of the following is not a tool of ICT?
   a. Radio b. Mobile
   c. E-mail d. Software
2. Which of the following helps the user to stay connected with their friends and family?
   a. Talk b. WhatsApp
   c. Art d. All of these
3. Which of the following is a volatile memory?
   a. ROM b. Internal
   c. External d. RAM
4. __________ is not an internal peripheral device.
   a. Modem b. Wi-Fi adaptor
   c. NIC d. Memory card reader
5. Password, date, and time settings of BIOS are stored in ___________.
   a. Internal memory b. CMOS chip
   c. External memory d. Booting process
6. Through ________ OS one can perform multiple tasks using a single CPU.
   a. Time-sharing OS b. Batch OS
   c. Multi-user OS d. Single user OS
7. Which of the following component of Internet is the interface between World Wide Web and user?
   a. Internal b. Internet Browser
   c. Web pages d. Web portal
8. ________ and ________ are two parts of e-mail address.
   a. Portal address and e-mail address b. User name and domain name
   c. Portal address and domain name d. E-mail address and user name
9. In Twitter,_________ term is used to handle user account name.
   a. Tweets b. Twitter feed
   c. Twitter handle d. Hashtags
10. _________company is not providing e-mail service.
    a. Google b. Amazon
    c. Yahoo d. Microsoft

B. Fill in the blanks.

1. ____________ is an online news and social networking service on which users post and interact with messages known as tweets.
2. ___________ in Facebook is a list of people whom you are accepted to see your profile and information shared by you.
3. ___________ tab contain e-mails from social media websites.
4. Full form of CC and BCC is ____________ and ____________.
5. ____________ is the brain of computer.
6. CMOS stands for ____________.
7. _________ support multiple networking, text editing functions, multiple directories, enhanced management of memory, disk compression and fragmentation.
8. Linux OS was developed by ________ in 1991 at ATc and T's Bell Lab.

C. Match the columns.

	Column A		Column B
1.	Facebook	i.	ROM
2.	Non-volatile	ii.	RAM
3.	Volatile	iii.	Input device
4.	Monitor	iv.	Output device
5.	Keyboard	v.	Mark Zuckerberg

D. Answers the following questions.

1. Name any five Input and output devices.
2. Differentiate between volatile and non-volatile memory.
3. Define ICT?
4. Give full form of MODEM, CPU, ALU, NIC, and Wi-Fi.
5. Write down the steps to start computer?
6. What do you mean by peripheral? How peripheral helps in doing various task.
7. Briefly explain the role of ICT in detail.
8. What is the full form of e-mail? Write down the steps to compose an e-mail message and send it.

Lab Activity

1. Check the hard disk and RAM size of your computer system. Check all input and output devices connected to your system and analyse its usage in it.
2. Make a presentation on various types of operating system. Open DOS and observe their various features.
3. Organise a presentation in computer lab and give presentation on various parts of computer and everyone should contribute their presence in it.

Worksheet

A. State whether the following statements are True or False.

1. Government apps and websites, with the help of which one can interact directly with the government.
2. Hardware is the set of computer programs, procedures, and associated documentation related to the effective operation of a computer system.
3. Read Only Memory that accessed memory randomly.
4. External Memory is also known as secondary or auxiliary memory.
5. The motive of Digital India program is to build participative, transparent, and responsive government to reach out the citizen.
6. ICT is used in Medical services, Sports, Education, and training, Research, etc.

B. Fill in the blanks.

1. Through ____________ one can buy or sell products online through the Internet after comparing them online and selecting the best one as per your requirements.
2. Transactions can be done anytime, anywhere through the Internet by _________.
3. The taxes collection, licenses, exchange of information with citizens and other government departments can become possible by ______ and __________.
4. BHIM app was launched for digital empowerment, here BHIM stands for __________.
5. ________________ is an online news and social networking service on which users post and interacts with messages known as tweets.
6. ____________________ permits direct access to individual records.
7. ____________________ produces a hard copy of documents which is stored in an electronic form on physical print media.

C. Write down the full form of the following.

1. CPU ______________________________
2. MU ______________________________
3. RAM ______________________________
4. ROM ______________________________
5. DOS ______________________________

C. Answer the following questions.

1. Write down the components of OS.
2. Define Internet and its uses.
3. What is the full form of e-mail? Write down the steps to compose an e-mail message and send it.
4. Describe the radio and mobile as ICT tools.
5. When and who has developed the Linux. Give various features of Linux.

QUIZ CARD

Multiple choice questions.

1. Which of the following is not a learning app?
   - a. Javatpoint ☐
   - b. Khan Academy ☐
   - c. WhatsApp ☐
   - d. Kindle books ☐
2. A web page is written using________________language.
   - a. HTML ☐
   - b. Python ☐
   - c. C++ ☐
   - d. Java ☐
3. ____________ unit carries out the basic calculations and comparison operations on the data.
   - a. CPU ☐
   - b. Control unit ☐
   - c. ALU ☐
   - d. ROM ☐
4. _________ is not an internal peripheral devices.
   - a. Modem ☐
   - b. Wi-fi adaptor ☐
   - c. NIC ☐
   - d. Memory card reader ☐
5. Operating system has two components used to perform and achieve the objectives.
   - a. System Software and Application software ☐
   - b. Software and hardware ☐
   - c. Kernel and Shell ☐
   - d. Software and technologies ☐
6. _________ is not a feature of Linux.
   - a. Potable ☐
   - b. Open-source ☐
   - c. Single programming ☐
   - d. Hierarchical File system ☐
7. Which of the following component of Internet is the interface between World Wide Web and user?
   - a. Internal ☐
   - b. Internet Browser ☐
   - c. Web pages ☐
   - d. Web portal ☐
8. The maximum length of tweet is:
   - a. 120 words ☐
   - b. No limit ☐
   - c. 140 words ☐
   - d. 280 words ☐
9. To avail government services to every citizen is the objective of ____________.
   - a. Satya Nadella ☐
   - b. Digital India ☐
   - c. AICTE ☐
   - d. All of these ☐
10. In Twitter, ________ term is used to handle user account name.
    - a. Tweets ☐
    - b. Twitter feed ☐
    - c. Twitter handle ☐
    - d. Hashtags ☐

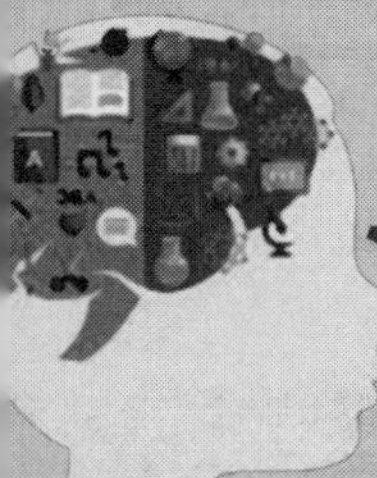

4 Entrepreneurial Skills

Structure Bot

In this chapter, we will discuss the following topics:

- Entrepreneur skills
- Business activities and its types
- Various types of business enterprises in our community
- Entrepreneurship development and various phases of entrepreneurship development
- Factors affecting the growth of entrepreneurship
- Characteristics, Role and reward of entrepreneurship

Objective Bot

After studying this chapter, you should be able to:

- Identify various types of business activities
- Know about various types of business enterprises in our community
- Understand the meaning and various phases of entrepreneurship development
- Know about the characteristics, role and reward of entrepreneurship

Introduction

Figure 4.1: *Entrepreneur*

Business is an economic activity which is related to regular and continuous production and the distribution of services or goods which satisfy the human needs. Businesses can be for non-profit or for profit organizations. There may be a gap among your needs and the availability (can be used as an opportunity by some people who are ready to take a risk) which can be fill by providing necessary services and products. People who fills this gap is known as **Entrepreneurs**. (Figure 4.1)

Entrepreneur Skills

An entrepreneur can be an educator, businessman, artist, restaurateur, inventor or professional. (Figure 4.2)

Some famous entrepreneurs are:

- **Mark Zuckerberg**, a youngest billionaires with his skills and talent in computers. He launched his website Facebook from his dormitory room in 2004.
- **William Bill Gates**, an American business magnate, software developer, investor, and philanthropist. He is the second richest man on the planet.

Figure 4.2: *Entrepreneur Skills*

To be a successful entrepreneur you must have:

- An ambition
- Willingness to learn
- Creativity
- Courage
- Or take risk

What is business?

Business is an activity which is related to trade; for earning profits. It involves sales and purchase of services or goods. (Figure 4.3)

Figure 4.3: *Business*

Definition Bot

A business is defined as an organization or enterprising entity engaged in commercial, industrial, or professional activities.

Types of Business

Business is broadly classified as:

- **Service:** It's a business which provides products with no physical form. It involves the execution of specialized personal services on the basis of training. Example: Lawyers and Chartered accountant.
- **Manufacturing:** It involves the transformation and manufacturing of raw materials, labor, and other production processes to manufacture goods. Example: To make cotton cloth, thread are used as raw materials in cotton and wool/textile companies.

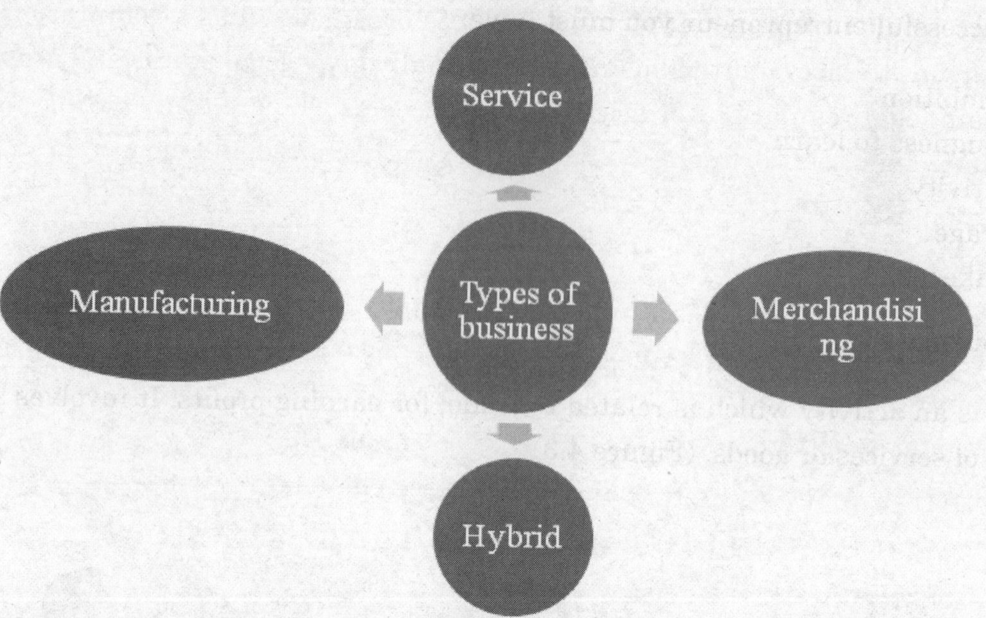

- **Merchandising / trading / buy and sell business:** In this, merchandise business firms buy products at wholesale prices and further sell it at retail prices to other customers or retailers.
- **Hybrid:** It is a company which is classified into more than one type of business or it is a mixed type of business. Example: Restaurant (In this meals are prepared (manufacturing), cold drinks are sold (merchandising) and the food is served (service)).

KNOWLEDGE BOT

Business activities are activities which involve the provision of goods or services with an aim of earning a profit.

Various types of Business Enterprises in our Community

The first step of entrepreneur is to choose the form of business which you wants to start and then organize (owned by single person (sole proprietorship) or by a group of persons).

In case of Joint stock and cooperative society, which comes under co-operative form of business enterprises. In this, the identity of the enterprise is separate from its owners.

In case of non-cooperative, the form of ownership, the identity of owners and enterprise is same and in case of any obligation owner is responsible for it.

- **Joint stock Company:** It forms a business organization as a voluntary association of persons to carry out the business. It normally gives legal status and is subjected to certain legal regulations or association of persons who are contributing money for a common purpose. Example: Reliance Industries Limited and more.
- **Cooperative society:** It is a society whose purpose is to render services to its members and to the public. It works on the principle of mutual self-help and has very less liability on its members. Example: Amul.
- **Sole proprietorship:** In this, the business is owned by a single person who provides the entire capital, bears all the risks and independently manages it. Example: Grocery store, and sweets shop.
- **Partnership:** It's an another form of non-cooperative form of enterprise. In this more than one person carry a lawful business and share its profits.

In this, each member of the group is known as partner and collectively all members are known as partnership firm.

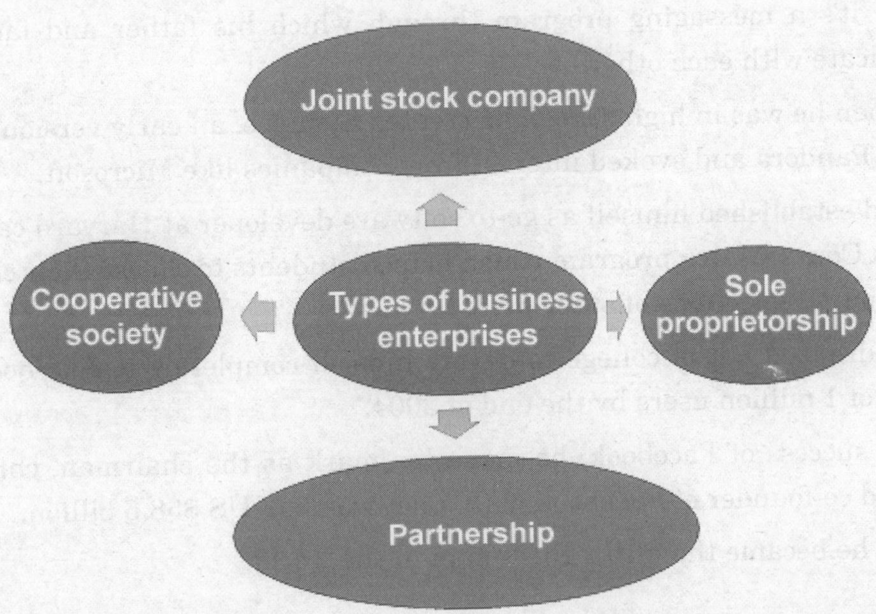

KNOWLEDGE BOT

Wholesale price is the price charged for goods that are sold in bulk or large quantities to a businessman or a trader.

Retail price is the price of goods or products when they are sold to customers for consumption, and not for sale.

What is Entrepreneur and Entrepreneurship?

An entrepreneur is a designer or a creator who designs new businesses and ideas according to its own passion but according to the requirements of market.

Entrepreneurship is the art of starting a new company or business that makes creative products, process, and services.

Story of Mark Zuckerberg

Mark Zuckerberg:

- He has made one of the most famous social networking websites, Facebook.
- He created Facebook at the age of 19 in 2004;
- He is the one of the most powerful entrepreneurs in the world.
- He had interest in computers since he was 12 years old. At that time he had created Zucknet, it's a messaging program through which his father and family used to communicate with each other.
- Then, when he was in high school, he created Synapse, an early version of the music software Pandora and evoked interest from companies like Microsoft.
- Mark had established himself as go-to software developer at Harvard campus where he built a CourseMatch program which helped students to choose their classes on the basis of course selections of other users.
- Then he dropped out of college to devote himself completely to Facebook as he got response of 1 million users by the end of 2004.
- With the success of Facebook, he made his mark as the chairman, chief executive officer and co-founder of Facebook with a net worth of US $58.6 billion.
- And then he became the fifth richest man in the world.

Entrepreneurship Development

Entrepreneurship is the process of improving the skills and knowledge of entrepreneurs through various training and classroom programs.

MEMORY BOT

The whole point of Entrepreneurship development is to increase the number of entrepreneurs.

Phases of Entrepreneurship Development

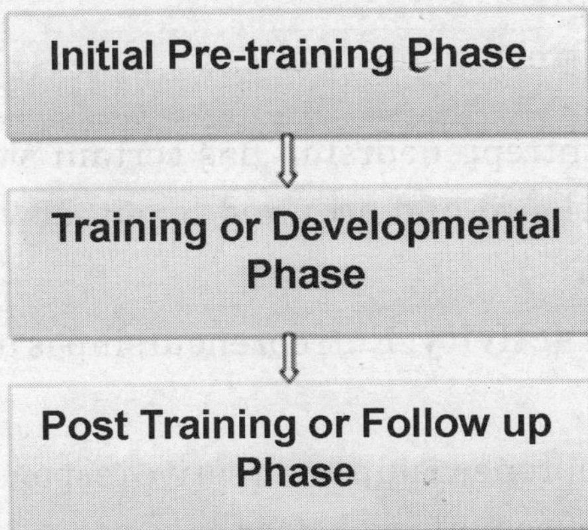

- **Pre-training or initial phase:** This phase includes all the activities and preparation required to launch the training program.
- **Training or development phase:** In this stage, trainers have to judge how far trainees have moved in their entrepreneurial pursuits.
- **Post-training or follow-up phase:** This last phase involves the assessment to judge how far the objectives of the program have been achieved.

Factors Affecting the Growth of Entrepreneurship

The growth of Entrepreneurship gets affected by:

- **Economic factors:** It includes the absence of opportunities and unavailability of jobs people choose entrepreneurship.
- **Social factors:** Entrepreneurial behavior of people also gets affected by social factors or environment in which people grow.
- **Psychological factors:** Many Entrepreneurial theorists have developed theories of entrepreneurship that are based on psychological factors. These factors are need of achievement, withdrawal of status, respect, and motives.

TIP BOT

A business plan is a good place to start – defining your skills and weaknesses, what you offer, how it's unique and how you plan on growing your offering.

Characteristics of Entrepreneurship

Common characteristics of entrepreneurs are:

- **Systematic activity:** Entrepreneurship has certain skills and other requirements that can be learnt, developed and acquired by either vocational training or formal educational.
- **Purposeful and lawful activity:** Entrepreneurship is a goal oriented activity whose object is lawful business.
- **Creative activity:** Entrepreneurship is a creative response to changes in environment. It involves introduction of something better or new.
- **Organizing of production:** Production implying creation of place, form, time, requires combined utilization of diverse factors of land, capital, technology, and labor.
- **Risk bearing activity:** Risk is inseparable and inherent from entrepreneurship.
- **Initiative taking:** Entrepreneurship should take initiative to take up new and challenging tasks.

Role of Entrepreneurship

- **In economic development:** The entrepreneur or entrepreneurship initiate and sustain the process of economic development by Capital information and Generation of employment.
- **In social development:** Business started by an entrepreneur is usually a very small business in the beginning. There is expansion of business if that small business becomes successful and grows. As it grows there is need for more work to be done, so it creates more jobs. Good quality jobs lead to more people earning money and having a good life.
- **In psychological development:** It includes development of confidence, increase motivationand instils a drive for achievement.

KNOWLEDGE BOT

Entrepreneur plays a vital role in economic development. Entrepreneurs serve as the catalysts in the process of industrialization and economic growth.

- You become the boss
- You have freedom to do anything
- You become creative
- You build an enterprise
- You make your own schedule

TECH BOT

- **Business:** It is defined as an economic activity involving the production and sale of goods and services to earn profits by satisfying human needs.
- **Entrepreneurship:** It is the act of setting up a business and taking on financial risks in the hope of making a profit.
- **Entrepreneurship development:** It is the inculcation, development, and polishing of entrepreneurship skills in a person to enable him to establish and successfully run an enterprise.

Recap Bot

- Business is an economic activity which is related to regular and continuous production and the distribution of services or goods which satisfy the human needs.
- An entrepreneur can be an educator, businessman, artist, restaurateur, inventor or professional.
- Business is an activity which is related to trade; for earning profits. It involves sales and purchase of services or goods.
- An entrepreneur is a designer or a creator who designs new businesses and ideas according to its own passion but according to the requirements of market.
- Entrepreneurship is the art of starting a new company or business that makes creative products, process, and services.

A. Multiple choice questions.

1. Which of the following skills are required to be a successful entrepreneur?
   a. Ambition
   b. Creativity
   c. Team management
   d. All of these
2. __________ is not a business activity.
   a. Service
   b. Manufacturing
   c. Creativity
   d. Merchandising
3. Entrepreneur is derived from French verb 'enterprendre' which means:
   a. To communicate
   b. To understand
   c. To take
   d. All of these
4. Which of the following factors is affects the growth of entrepreneurship?
   a. Economic factors
   b. Social factors
   c. Psychological factors
   d. All of these
5. Services given by lawyers or doctors comes under which business activities:
   a. Service
   b. Manufacturing
   c. Merchandising
   d. Hybrid
6. Grocery store, stationary store, vegetable shop, and more are examples of __________ form of business enterprises.
   a. Joint stock company
   b. Cooperative society
   c. Sole Proprietorship
   d. Partnership firm
7. An entrepreneur ______________.
   a. Sets the interest rates of banks
   b. Manages financial investments
   c. Takes risks to earn profits
   d. Enforces government regulations
8. Which of the following is the non-cooperate type of business enterprise?
   a. Joint stock company
   b. Cooperative society
   c. Sole Proprietorship
   d. None of these
9. Which of the following skills are required to be a successful entrepreneur?
   a. Ambition
   b. Creativity

c. Team management

d. All of these

10. _______ is a process of improving skills and knowledge of entrepreneurs through various training and classroom programs.

a. Enterprise

b. School

c. Entrepreneurship development

d. College

B. Fill in the blanks.

1. _____________ is a business organization that which provide goods and services, create jobs, contributes to national income, exports, imports or it is a business venture.
2. __________phase of entrepreneurship development includes all the activities and preparation required to launch a training program.
3. ___________ is the funds for investment to start a new business venture.
4. One of the psychological factors that helps entrepreneurship is that it increases__________.
5. _____________ is a person who takes risk to produce goods and services in search of profit.

C. Answers the following questions.

1. Name the three factors influencing self-confidence.
1. Who is entrepreneur? Give a few important skills to become a successful entrepreneur.
2. Name four types of business activities. Explain any two of it.
3. Give types of business enterprises in our community.
4. Give any five characteristics of entrepreneurship.
5. Give various rewards of entrepreneurship.

D. Project work

1. The teacher brings in a cake to celebrate the end of a successful session. Participants cannot eat it until they have cut it. They cannot make more than three cuts and they must divide the cake into eight pieces.
2. Tell students they are going to create a new product and then try to convince the class it's a great idea.

Worksheet

A. State whether the following statements are True or False.

1. Restaurant is agood example of hybrid business activity.
2. Joint Stock Company is a type of non-cooperative form of business enterprise.
3. Entrepreneur is a self-employed person who is willing to take risk and start.
4. An entrepreneur can be an educator, businessman, artist, restaurateur, inventor or professional.
5. Wholesale price is the price charged for goods that are sold in bulk or large quantities to a businessman or a trader.
6. Entrepreneurship is the art of starting a new company or business that makes creative products, process, and services.

B. Fill in the blanks.

1. All business activities are classified into ____________ broad categories.
2. ____________________ is a company that is classified into more than one type of businessor it is a mixed type of business.
3. Lawyers and chartered accountant are the examples of service.
4. Entrepreneurship is a ________________ activity.
5. The whole point of entrepreneurship development is to increase the number of ______________.

C. Answer the following questions.

1. Name any four types of business activities.
2. Give any two examples of manufacturing business activity.
3. Define integrity.
4. Name the phases of entrepreneurship development.
5. Give various characteristics of entrepreneurship.

Exam tips

1. Read the Stories of great entrepreneurs to know more about entrepreneurs and important skills required to be a successful entrepreneurs.
2. Make a list of various shops, factories in your city then divide it into different category of business activities.
3. Make a presentation on various forms of business enterprises and alternate student will cover the different type in detail that helps in easy learning of all types.
4. Do the same task individually then in group after that note down the advantages of being working in partnership.

QUIZ CARD

Multiple choice questions.

1. Entrepreneurs attributes includes:
   a. Preservence ☐ b. Hard working ☐
   c. Determination ☐ d. All of above ☐
2. Entrepreneurs skills includes:
   a. Creative problem solving ☐ b. Persuading ☐
   c. Negotiation ☐ d. All of above ☐
3. The term "entrepreneurs" was applied to business initially by the French economist in the 18th century:
   a. Cantillon ☐ b. Jan Tinbergen ☐
   c. J.S.Mill ☐ d. None of above ☐
4. Which business function do experts agree, you should focus on first when preparing to start a business?
   a. Financing ☐ b. Marketing vision ☐
   c. Operation ☐ d. None of above ☐
5. Which of the following is not something that can be invested?
   a. Energy ☐ b. Experties ☐
   c. Money ☐ d. Time ☐
6. What is the need of entrepreneurship?
   a. For new innovation ☐ b. To fill gap in growth ☐
   c. For healthy competition ☐ d. All of above ☐
7. Which one of the following is the process of entrepreneur developing new products that over time make current products obsolete?
   a. New business model ☐ b. Anatomization ☐
   c. Creative Destruction ☐ d. None of above ☐
8. The level at which an individual is viewed by society is called:
   a. Financial status ☐ b. Qualification ☐
   c. Social Status ☐ d. Achievement ☐
9. In real life, entrepreneurs are those that:
   a. Robbers that exploit their workers ☐
   b. Generate business success ☐
   c. Generate business success through hard and long hours of work ☐
   d. Robbers that exploit their workers and generate business success ☐
10. The definition of entrepreneurship holds the promise of:
   a. Financial difficulties and hardship ☐
   b. Limited expansion ☐
   c. Growth, unlimited expansion and long-term financial gain ☐
   d. Growth, expansion and long term financial gain ☐

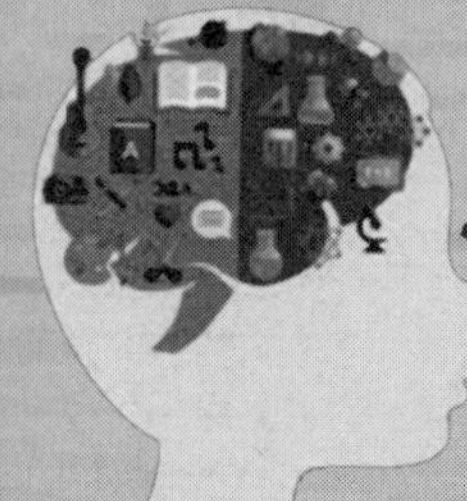

5 Green Skills

Structure Bot

In this chapter, we will discuss the following topics:

- Environment and its categorization
- Ecosystem and its three primary components
- Relationship between man and environment
- Effects of human activities on environment
- Ecological imbalance
- Green skills and green economy
- Importance of green economy

Objective Bot

After studying this chapter, you should be able to:

- Learn about the environment and its categories
- Explain ecosystem and its primary components
- Discuss the relationship between man and environment
- Identify the effects of human activities on environment
- Discuss conservation of natural resources
- Know about the green economy and its importance

Introduction

Figure 5.1: *Environment*

Environment is made up of everything around us and our lives depend on the flora and fauna around us. Same as that, your school environment is made of socio-culture and physical environment (includes school building and the library, and playground).

The word environment has been derived from French word environ which means to surround or encircle. Environment refers to the sum total of conditions that surround us at a given point in time and space. Environment comprised of non-living or abiotic aspects (water, air, and land) and living or biotic organisms (plants, animals, and time). (Figure 5.1)

Definition Bot

Environment is defined as the circumstances and physical conditions that surround and affect an organism or a group of organism.

Categorization of Environment

Environment is categorized into two types:

- **Natural environment:** It includes living and non-living things like air, animals, water, land and plants.

The natural environment is subdivided into biotic components (living components of anecosystem. It include animals, plants, bacteria, and fungus) and abiotic components (Physical or chemical factors that act on living organisms at any part of their life. It includes Light, soil, air, water, and minerals). (Figure 5.2)

Figure 5.2: *Natural environment*

Knowledge Bot

The biotic factors depend on the abiotic factors to fulfil their requirements to grow and survive.

- **Human-made environment:** Human beings interact with the environment and modify it according to their needs. The needs grew with time and various new ways were learned by humans to change and use the environment. It includes bridges, markets, and houses. (Figure 5.3)

Figure 5.3: *Man made environment*

Ecosystem

Ecosystem can be defined as a functional unit of nature in which living organisms interact with each other and also with surrounding physical environment. Ecosystem can be as small as pond or as large as sea or forest. (Figure 5.4)

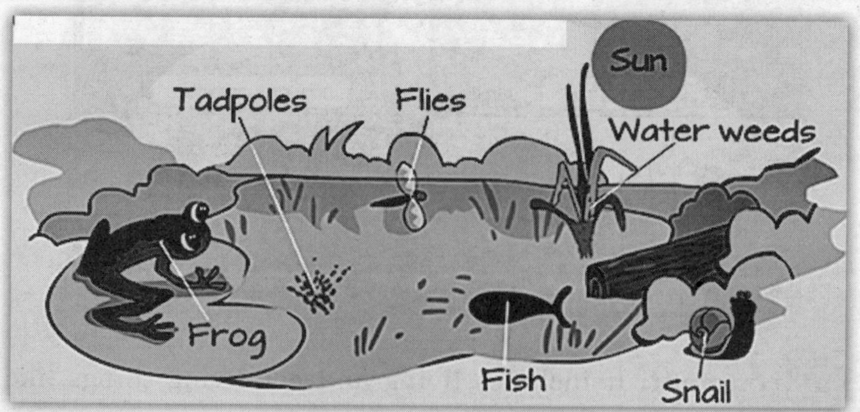

Figure 5.4: *Ecosystem*

Categories of ecosystem:

- Aquatic (river, estuary, wetland, lake, and pond)
- Terrestrial (grasslands, deserts and forests)

An ecosystem is a community of living and non-living components that depend on each other.

Primary components of all ecosystems are:

a. **Autotrophs:** Autotrophs are producers of energy and majority of autotrophs in an ecosystem are made by plants as they convert energy from sun or other sources into food.

b. **Heterotrophs/consumers:** Heterotrophs are the consumers of energy and these organisms directly or indirectly depend upon the autotrophs of their food.

c. **Non-living matter:** It is leaf litter, soil, sediments and other organic matter found on ground or at the bottom of an aquatic system. (Figure 5.5)

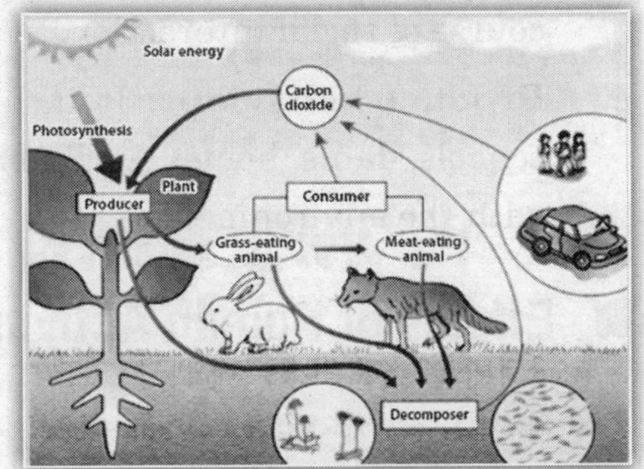

Figure 5.5: *Primary components of all ecosystems*

Relationship between Man and Environment

During different stages of the evolution of humans and their society there is variation in relation. In this relationship, a human being's life gets influenced by environment. The changing environment is adapted by humans but sometimes according to their requirements there is modification in natural environment. (Figure 5.6)

Figure 5.6: *Primary components of all ecosystems*

The survival of early humans depended on natural environment as their clothing, shelter and food all came from their natural habitat. Due to these reasons they lived in harmony with nature and devised various ways of preserving their natural environment.

MEMORY BOT

Nature was worshipped in different forms as a way to honour the natural environment.

Major components of human-environment interaction, such as:

a. **Physical environment:** It includes temperature, flora, terrain, climate, fauna, rainfall, and more.

b. **Social-culture environment:** It includes all aspects of cultural environment such as customs, socialization, process and norms.

c. **Environmental orientation:** It refers to the beliefs that people hold about their environment.

d. **Environmental behaviour:** It refers to the use of environment by people in the course of social interactions.

e. **Product behaviour:** It includes the outcomes of people's actions such as cities, schools, dams, homes, and more. This means these are outcomes or products dealing with the environment.

Effects of Human Activities on Environment

The environment gets affected by various activities done by human beings like:

- Driving scooter, car or motor cycle
- Use of pesticides

Environmental Degradation

Environmental degradation has now become a global problem. Over the past few decades, millions of people have died due to natural disasters. The effect of human activities like air pollution is long term and irreversible that eventually affects the lives of generations. (Figure 5.7)

Causes of environmental degradation:

- Earthquakes
- Forest fires
- Volcanic eruption
- Floods

Figure 5.7: *Environmental degradation*

Ecological imbalance

Figure 5.8: *Ecological imbalance*

Ecological imbalance takes place when a human or naturally caused disturbance disrupts the natural balance of an ecosystem. (Figure 5.8)

The ecosystem gets imbalanced by:

- Volcanic eruptions
- Floods
- Natural fires
- Logging a forest
- Overhunting of a species

Some other factors of ecosystem are:

- **Greenhouse Gas emission:** In greenhouse effect, the short wavelength of visible light from the sun pass through a transparent medium, that is, CO, SO_2, CO_2, and get absorbed. But the longer wavelengths of the infrared radiation from the heated objects are unable to pass through that medium and are trapped causing more heat and a higher resultant temperature.

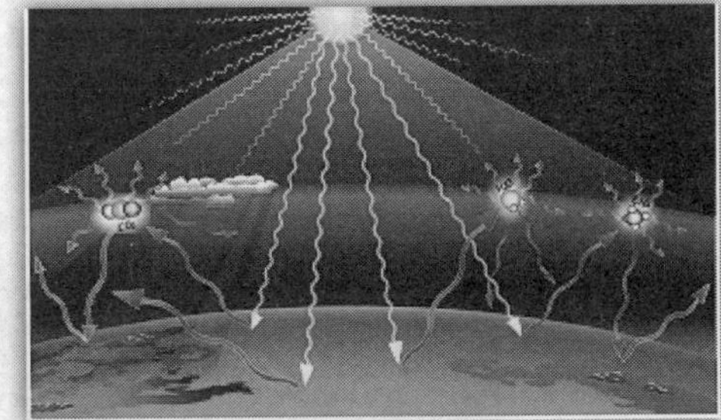

TIP BOT

The best place to start saving and reducing Greenhouse Gases is by choosing the right lighting options for your living space or office.

- **Habitat distinction:** Clearing forests to obtain timber and space for urban or agricultural zones, results in deforestation.

- **Radioactive wastes:** Nuclear reactors generate nuclear wastes and are real threat to life on Earth. Exposures to radioactive elements have severe health effects on human being that can result in irreparable DNA damage that lead to tumours, cancers and other life threatening conditions.

- **Nuclear weapons:** Nuclear bombs are possessed by several countries so an extreme global and climate environmental change can take place if a major nuclear conflict happens. This will result in significant health implications and may destroy life on earth.

- **Overexploitation of natural resources:** It means overuse of natural resources to such extent that it almost reaches a stage off conversation.

- Environmental pollution: Any disturbance in air, water and land is reflected in the deviation from natural balance in living beings. This undesirable change in the composition of air, water and land and the disturbed inter-relation (ecology) is called environmental pollution.

- **Biotechnological misuse:** Another threat to environment and mankind is production of disease producing bacteria, fungi, viruses for biological welfare.

Conservation of Natural Resources

Conservation is the proper management of a natural resource to prevent its exploitation, destruction, or degradation.

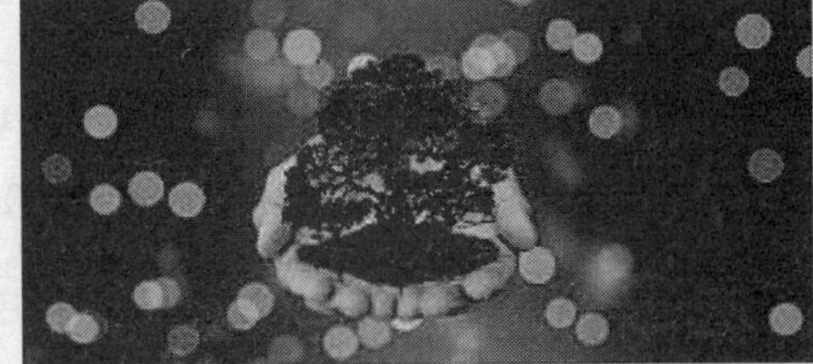

Figure 9: *Conservation of natural resources*

Conservation is the sum total of activities, which can derive benefits from natural resources but at the same time prevent excessive use, which may lead to destruction or degradation. It means using them more efficiently and less wastefully. (Figure 5.9)

The consumption of resources is getting increased by urbanization and industrialization and due to increase in population. There will be no resources left for future if you human beings keep exploiting nature.

Steps taken to conserve natural resources are:

- **Soil conservation:** It means checking soil erosion and improving the fertility of soil by control on grazing, reforestation, terracing and so on.
- **Water conservation:** For survival of plants, mankind and animals there is a need to conserve and manage water.

- **Food conservation:** Food is also preserved through various methods to prevent the spoilage due to harmful bacteria and other micro-organisms.
- **Forest conservation:** Forest conservation means the retention of existing forests or the creation of new forests at the levels prescribed by the State or local authority.

Tips to Conserve Natural Resources

The 3Rs (Reduce, Reuse, and Recycle) can be applied in daily life to conserve natural resources. The 3Rs are:

- **Reduce:** Do not use what is not required.
- **Reuse:** Reuse the materials for other purposes.
- **Recycle:** Recycling is reusing some components of waste that may have some economic value.

Environment Protection and Conservation

Conservation of environment means proper use and management of natural resources that can be water, air, land, wildlife, natural vegetation, earth deposits, and more.

Some of the essential steps for environment conservation are:

- Turned off electrical appliances when not in use or when no one is present in the room.
- Don't dump things in rivers, lakes and seas, and not even on land.
- Instead of using incandescent bulbs make use of CFL and LED bulbs.
- Use solar heaters, solar cookers like appliances that utilize renewable energy sources.
- Buy electrical appliances (air conditioners and refrigerators) according to their energy star ratings. Less power consumption by these appliances result in reduction of global warming.
- Practice rainwater harvesting at home by encouraging the use of drip irrigation.
- Use biofuels and biogas at home.

TIP BOT

It is not the responsibility of government and big companies only to take steps to conserve the environment.

Green Skills

Green skills are skills used for promoting green economy which are needed in areas like renewable energy, climate resilient cities, solid waste management, sewer water treatment and green construction. The green skills agreement defines skills for sustainability. (Figure 5.10)

Figure 10: *Green skills*

Green skills are:

- Technical skills and values
- Knowledge and attitudes needed in the workspace for supporting and development of sustainable economic
- Social and environment outcomes in industry
- Business and community

Knowledge Bot

Areas in which green skills has contributed to sustainable development are:

- Solar, wind, and power renewable energy
- Management of waste and water
- Energy conservation
- Rain water harvesting
- Reducing pollution

Green Economy

Green economy results in improved human well-being and social equity while reducing ecological scarcities and environmental risks. This system helps in economic growth along with taking care of environment. The economy is a system of institutions and organizations that either facilitate or play a role in the production and distribution of goods and services among the members of society. (Figure 5.11)

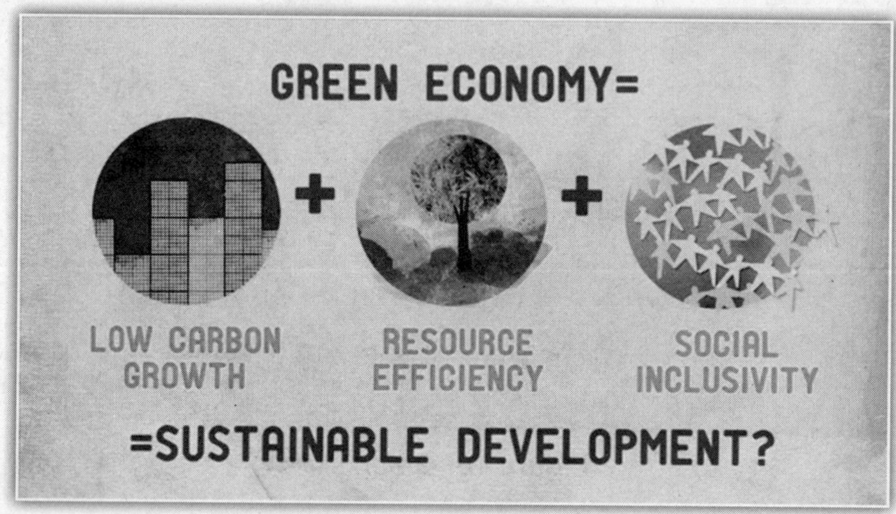

Figure 11: *Green economy*

Definition Bot

A green economy is defined as low carbon, resource efficient and socially inclusive.

The concept of green economy has become a global agenda and some of the important global events over the last few decades focusing on green economy are:

- 1972 Stockholm conference
- 1987 Brundtland Report
- 1992 Earth Summit and Agenda 21
- 2012 Rio+20Conference

For attainment of green economy, United Nations Environment Programme (UNEP) are:

- **Low carbon growth:** The concentration of CO_2, Nitrogen oxide, methane like Greenhouse Gases in the environment is getting increased by burning fossil fuels.

- **Resource efficiency:** By overusing and exploiting the natural resources, they are getting depleted. These resources can be conserved by green economy.
- **Social inclusion:** It essentially means sharing the responsibility and benefits of economic growth across all sections of society. There is need for investments from both private and public sectors that result in growth of income and employment through green jobs.

KNOWLEDGE BOT

The skill India mission of the government of India, Ministry of Environment, Forest and Climate Change, has started the Green Skill Development Programme.

MEMORY BOT

Climate change and pollution are posing an alarming and fast approaching threats to us and for our future generations.

Importance of Green Economy

- Green economy leads to economic growth in renewable energy and bio-fuels areas.
- Green economy contributes in prevention of melting glaciers and resulting rise of sea levels.
- Green economy fights against global warming, loss of diversity and desertification.
- Green economy helps in improving the quality of air, water, and soil.
- Green economy prevents climate changes such as variation in temperature, rainfall, and
- Reduction in disease and deaths of living beings.

TECH BOT

- **Ecosystem:** It is any community of living and non-living things that function together.
- **Green Skill:** They are the knowledge, abilities, values and attitudes needed to live in, develop and support a society which reduces the negative impact of human activity on the environment.
- **Green economy:** It is an economy that results in improved human well-being and social equity while significantly reducing environmental risks and ecological scarcities.

Recap Bot

- Ecosystem can be defined as a functional unit of nature in which living organisms interact with each other and also with surrounding physical environment.
- During different stages of the evolution of humans and their society there is variation in relation. In this relationship, a human being's life gets influenced by environment.
- Environmental degradation has now become a global problem. Over the past few decades, millions of people have died due to natural disasters.
- Ecological imbalance takes place when a human or naturally caused disturbance disrupts the natural balance of an ecosystem.
- Conservation is the proper management of a natural resource to prevent its exploitation, destruction, or degradation.
- The 3Rs (Reduce, Reuse, and Recycle) can be applied in daily life to conserve natural resources.
- Conservation of environment means proper use and management of natural resources that can be water, air, land, wildlife, natural vegetation, earth deposits, and more.
- Green skills are skills used for promoting green economy which are needed in areas like renewable energy, climate resilient cities, solid waste management, sewer water treatment and green construction. The green skills agreement defines skills for sustainability.
- Green economy results in improved human well-being and social equity while reducing ecological scarcities and environmental risks. This system helps in economic growth along with taking care of environment.

A. Multiple choice questions.

1. The word environment has been derived from the French word environ which means:
   a. To protect
   b. To surround
   c. To circle
   d. None of these
2. Which of the following primary components of the ecosystem that are producers of energy?
   a. Autotrophs
   b. Heterotrophs
   c. Non-living matter
   d. All of these
3. The Greenhouse Gases, otherwise called radioactively active gases includes:
   a. Carbon dioxide
   b. CH_4
   c. N_2O
   d. All of these
4. Algal boom results in:
   a. Global Warming
   b. Salination
   c. Eutrophication
   d. Biomagnification
5. A high Biological oxygen demand indicates that:
   a. Water is pure
   b. Absence of microbial action
   c. Low level of microbial pollution
   d. High level of microbial pollution
6. The effects of radioactive pollutants depends upon:
   a. Rate of difficult
   b. Energy releasing capacity
   c. Rate of deposition of the contaminant
   d. All of these
7. The range of normal human hearing is in the range of:
   a. 10 Hz to 80 Hz
   b. 50 Hz to 80 Hz
   c. 50 Hz to 15000 Hz
   d. 15000 Hz and above
8. Soap and detergent are the source of organic pollutants like:
   a. Glycerol
   b. Polyphosphates
   c. Sulphonated hydrocarbons
   d. All of these
9. The main atmospheric layer near the surface of earth is:
   a. Troposphere
   b. Mesophere
   c. Ionosphere
   d. Stratosphere

10. The unfavourable alteration of environment due to human activities is termed as:

a. Ecological disturbance　　b. Catastrophe

c. Ecological degradation　　d. Pollution

11. The pollution which does not persistent harm to life supporting system is:

a. Noise pollution　　b. Radiation pollution

c. Organo-chlorine pollution　　d. All of these

B. Fill in the blanks.

1. Examples of abiotic components are ____________.
2. All living organisms are included in __________ components of ecosystem.
3. __________ are the consumers of energy and these organisms directly or indirectly depend on the autotrophs of their food.
4. ____________ is a deep layer in earth's atmosphere that contains ozone which is naturally occurring molecule containing three oxygen atoms.
5. The full form of 3Rs that can be appliedin daily life to conserve natural resources are __________.

C. Match the following.

Column A	Column B
1. Environ	i. Sun
2. Natural environment	ii. Recycle, Reuse and Reduce
3. Paper bag	iii. Surrounding
4. 3 R's	iv. Recycle

D. Answers the following questions.

1. What do you mean by the word environment?
2. What do you mean by conservation of environment?
3. Define the term ecosystem. Name its three primary components.
4. Why is conservation of environment important?
5. List any three human activities that affect the environment.
6. How our environment gets affected by Greenhouse Gases?
7. What do you mean by term the sustainable development?

D. Project work

1. Deforestation or cutting of trees is getting increased that putting negative effects on environment, aware people of your surrounding and plant more trees in your school and living area.
2. Implement the 3Rs concept to conserve the natural resources and observe the changes after every 1 month.

Worksheet

A. State whether the following statements are True or False.

1. Conservation of environment means proper use and management of natural resources.
2. The green economy agreement defines skills for sustainability.
3. Environmental behaviour refers to the beliefs that people hold about their environment.
4. Ecosystem can be as small as pond or as large as sea or forest.
5. The natural environment is subdivided into three components.
6. In greenhouse effect, the short wavelength of visible light from the sun pass through a transparent medium, that is, CO, SO_2, CO_2, and get absorbed.

B. Fill in the blanks.

1. _________ building preserves precious natural resources and improves the quality of life.
2. Green economy is essential for _________ sustainability and future prosperity.
3. Green economy emphasizes on becoming more ___________ efficient.
4. Transition towards a ______________ can help us in countering the ecological problems.
5. Green economy will not lead to _______________.

C. Write down the full form of the following.

1. GHG ____
2. 3 R'S ____
3. CNG ____
4. UNEP ____

D. Answer the following questions.

1. Define the term ecological imbalance.
2. Define Greenhouse Gases?
3. What do you understand by overexploitation of natural resources?
4. Define habitat distinction.
5. Give some essential steps for environment conservation.

QUIZ CARD

Multiple choice questions.

1. Which of the following primary components of the ecosystem that are producers of energy?
   a. Autotrophs ☐ b. Heterotrophs ☐
   c. Non-living matter ☐ d. All of these ☐
2. All living organisms are included in __________ components of ecosystem.
   a. Abiotic ☐ b. Biotic ☐
   c. Environment ☐ d. Forest ☐
3. ____________ is a deep layer in earth's atmosphere that contains ozone which is naturally occurring molecule containing three oxygen atoms.
   a. Earth crust ☐ b. Lithosphere ☐
   c. Troposphere ☐ d. Ozone layer ☐
4. Which of the following is not a Greenhouse Gas?
   a. Carbon dioxide ☐ b. Nitrogen ☐
   c. Methane ☐ d. Nitrogen oxide ☐
5. Green skills are the ability to __________.
   a. Protect trees ☐ b. Plant trees ☐
   c. Conserve the environment ☐ d. Identify tree ☐
6. Green economy will not lead to ____________.
   a. More employment ☐ b. Energy efficiency ☐
   c. Economic growth ☐ d. More pollution ☐
7. Green economy is essential for ________ sustainability and future prosperity.
   a. Human ☐ b. Animal ☐
   c. Life ☐ d. Resource ☐
8. Green economy emphasizes on becoming more __________ efficient.
   a. Green ☐ b. Resource ☐
   c. Environmental ☐ d. Life ☐
9. Soil erosion can be prevented by:
   a. Deforestation ☐ b. Afforestation ☐
   c. Overgrazing ☐ d. Removal of vegetation ☐
10. Which of the following is an inorganic natural resource?
    a. Water ☐ b. Fossil fuels ☐
    c. Plants ☐ d. Animals ☐

Part – B

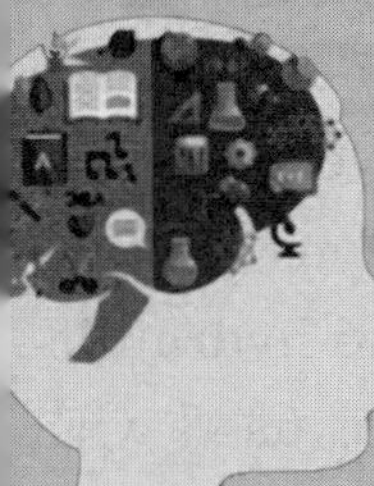

1 Review of Concepts

Structure Bot

In this chapter, we will discuss the following topics:

- What is the meaning of the term Artificial Intelligence?
- Applications of Artificial Intelligence in your daily lives
- Three domains of Artificial Intelligence – Data for AI, NLP, and Computer Vision
- Create and play an interactive story using Google Story Speaker
- Identify themes and social areas affected by local and global issues listed under UN's agenda 2030 of 17 SDGs

Objective Bot

After studying this chapter, you should be able to:

- Understand the concept of Artificial Intelligence
- Demonstrate/discuss/elaborate the use of AI applications in Smart Home/ Smart City daily lives and can make a Smart Home/ Smart City
- Determine, interact, and explain the use of AI domains in various applications
- Interact and create an interactive story using Story Speaker add-on around an ultramodern home
- Learn to relate with Artificial Intelligence domains, namely, data for Artificial Intelligence, Natural Language Processing, and Computer Vision
- Understand, summarize and relate the societal issues where AI can determine and solve the issues, locally and globally
- Identify and gain awareness on the skill sets needed for jobs in the field of AI

Artificial Intelligence is quite relevant in Modern Times. Everyone surely remembers the classic movie of the immortal Charlie Chaplin, Modern Times. The film portrayed different scenarios of Industrial Revolution with machines but who can forget the famous scene of feeding lunch to Little Tramp (character played by Charlie Chaplin) with the hydraulic-based robots. In 1936, it was just a thought that machines could harm if not used with conscience. Now, you are at the 4th generation of industrial revolution which is solely based on digitalization implemented through Artificial Intelligence and Machine Learning.

Figure 1.1: *Artificial Intelligence*

AI techniques have become an essential part of the technology industry and help to solve many challenging problems. As you are getting more and more dependent on machines, Artificial Intelligence is becoming a reality in your daily lives. Internet of Things (IoT) has evolved due to the convergence of multiple technologies, real-time analytics and Machine Learning. IoT technology is most synonymous with products pertaining to the concept of the Smart Home, which can be controlled through smartphones and smart speakers.

Definition Bot

Artificial Intelligence refers to the simulation of human intelligent behaviour in computers.

Alternatively, there are a number of serious concerns about dangers in the growth of IoT, such as the areas of privacy and security. Many sectors such as healthcare, transport, manufacturing industries, cyber security, telecommunication, data science, e-commerce, weather risk management and education are getting benefited from the applications of AI.

AI is the new technology that has arrived to alter your lives. Tremendous amount of research is being conducted in AI. Concerns around areas like transparency, bias, and accountability are still under discussion. In a global context, the biggest challenge would be to remove bias in AI data sets in terms of providing equal representation to the plethora of social, economic, gender, regional and religious classes. Most of the AI products prevalent in the market must be customized to remove any bias. Additionally, data privacy and

KNOWLEDGE BOT

The purpose of Artificial Intelligence is to create robots that can interact with humans without controls.

transparency laws need to be augmented to give consumers more control over data taken by the service providers and more information regarding its usage. AI systems need to have well-defined ethical requirements.

AI holds the key to solve most of the current social and economic problems of the human race from eradicating poverty to building society and uplifting women to ensure food for all. AI is a decision tool. With an increase in the computing power and data storage capacity, you now are in a position to hunt for a needle in a trillion data stack using AI, thus making better-targeted decisions to solve any problem efficiently and in minimum time. Amazon Alexa, Apple Siri, and Google Assistant are all getting better at understanding and answering one's questions while cooking, driving, or running. Amazon, Flipkart, Netflix, Spotify and so on, recommend items based on the user's browsing history and behavioral characteristics. Social media sites like YouTube, Instagram, Facebook, and so on, present the users with targeted ads after perusing through the users' online profile and learning their actions.

Apps like Google Maps calculate traffic and instruct in order to find the quickest route to user's destination. AI plays an important role in technologies like self-driving car, metro, flight to diagnosing life-threatening diseases, conducting stock trades in nanoseconds, making recommendations for the best long-term investment, and developing prosthetic limbs for human-machine interaction.

FACT BOT

Artificial Intelligence was first invented by John McCarthy in 1956.

UNESCO's Sustainable Development Goals support and take initiatives to tackle some of the world's greatest problems like hunger management, pollution control, and several socio-economic challenges. In agriculture, new AI advancements are showing improvements in gaining yield of various crops. Crop and soil monitoring uses new algorithms and data collected on the field to manage and track the health of crops, thus making it easier and more sustainable for the farmers. Bio-medical systems such as medical image processing, heart-sound analysis, and EEG signal analysis are one of the fundamental driving forces for the AI revolution to take place. AI is a major tool leading towards a better and efficient e-commerce industry. Weather prediction is a thinking tool being addressed by AI systems. Face recognition and speech recognition are some directions of AI which are used to identify criminals.

You have already studied in Class VIII about the Artificial Intelligence and three pillars of Artificial Intelligence. You played various games to understand the various pillars of AI. By now, you know which pillar of AI is used when and where Artificial Intelligence

MEMORY BOT

SDG fall under the three domain pillars such as Economic, Social and Environment.

makes the machine work intelligently so as to help us in performing the various tasks easily and accurately. You also studied some of the examples of Artificial Intelligence in the previous class. Let us attempt some of the activities in this chapter to test your knowledge and understanding of the topics done in the previous class.

Activity 1.1

Write the three pillars of Artificial Intelligence.

____

____

____

Activity 1.2

Write the definition of Artificial Intelligence.

____

____

____

Activity 1.3

Write how Artificial Intelligence is used in the following apps/features areas.

App /Features/Areas	Function/ use
Chatbot	
Smart Car	
Google Maps	
Amazon Entertainment	

Activity 1.4

You played three games in the previous class. Write the domain of AI and any three learning outcomes for the game specified.

Game	Domain	Learning Outcome
Rock, Paper, Scissor		
Mystery Animal		
Emoji Scavenger Hunt		

A Smart Home is a home that can be managed remotely to control the items/ appliances/ gadgets/systems such as TV, AC, fridge, and so on, with your device. All these devices can be operated once they are connected through the internet. A Smart Home is actually a home with automation and is also known as Home Automation. The dream of home automation wouldn't be possible without the use of smartphones and internet connectivity.

The Internet of Things (IoT) is used for building Smart Homes and Smart Cities with automation and safety as priority for many of us. The Internet of Things (IoT) refers to all the objects/devices that have sensors, network connectivity, software, and so on, to connect to the network using the internet, thus making them responsive. Examples of IoT are security systems, electronic appliances, speakers, cars, and many more.

A Smart City is an urban city which uses Internet of Things to collect data and information to improve the quality of government services easily and effectively.

Story Speaker is an add-on Google tool used to utilize Google's voice recognition capabilities that allows you to create talking, interactive stories without using and learning any coding language. You can write a story in Google Docs, push a button, and play it instantly on your Google Home or any other device with the Google Assistant.

Story Speaker provides the templates, that is, a framework to write an interactive story. It has two templates—the basic and advanced template. The basic template only has two options for every choice, and you can simply go and change what is provided there as what you want to say. The advanced template provides the GOTO command and allows you to add randoms to the make story look different each time you play it and add saves so that the information taken from the user can be integrated into the story.

1. Write the prerequisites for Story Speaker.

   - ______________________________
   - ______________________________
   - ______________________________

2. Design the interactive story using Story Speaker using the advanced feature of Story Speaker. You can use the same story template to be modified done in the previous class.

   ____
   ____
   ____
   ____
   ____
   ____
   ____

Activity 1.6

Write the steps to create an interactive story using Story Speaker.

____

____

____

____

____

____

____

____

You have moved from one age to another and now to a digital age from the past so many years. To understand the digital age and become a responsible citizen of the world, you have to be an industrious, caring, conscientious and a contributing member of the society. Displaying empathy and compassion to one and all while being helpful and considerate towards one's society and environment reflects towards the good qualities of a citizen. It is very important to be part of the change which affects the world in which you live.

You have studied about the 17 SDG laid by UN which are to be achieved by 2030. Many countries have committed to taking action to meet these goals which will aid in creating positive change globally.

FACT BOT

SDG come on effect from January 1, 2016.

Activity 1.7

Write any four reasons to understand and learn about SDG.

1. ____
2. ____
3. ____
4. ____

Activity 1.8

Write the name/goal/aim for the image shown in the table.

SDG - Image	Name/ Goal/ Aim
1 NO POVERTY	
7 AFFORDABLE AND CLEAN ENERGY	
11 SUSTAINABLE CITIES AND COMMUNITIES	
13 CLIMATE ACTION	
15 LIFE ON LAND	

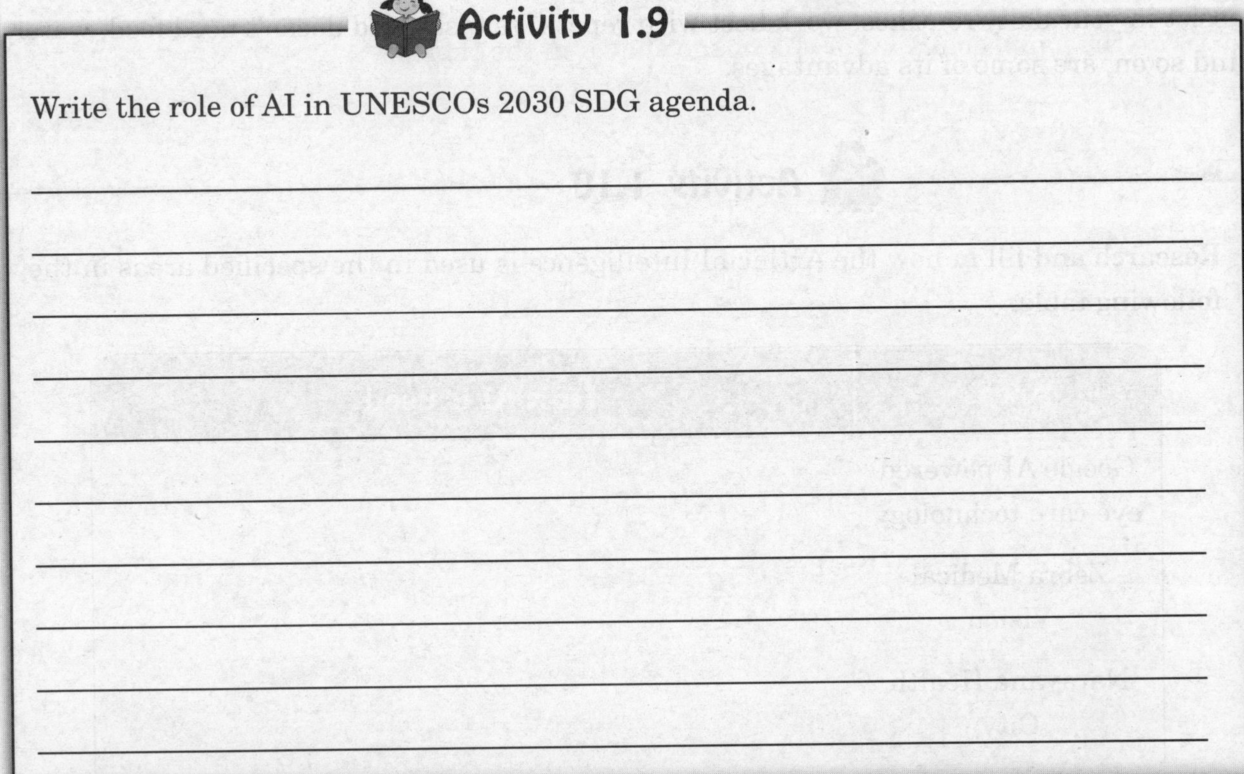

TIP BOT

Artificial Intelligence covers a broad range of domains and applications and is expected to impact every field in the future.

The impact of Artificial Intelligence on Sustainable Development Goals is to develop responsible global citizens. Ethics can be defined as the study of values; generating moral values for good and bad, right and wrong.

Bias is a phenomenon that occurs when an algorithm produces results that are discriminatory due to the built-in biases created by the programmer.

AI Access can be defined as the mission where world's information can be organized and made available to all.

AI inclusion suggests making researches, tools, systems and scientific developments available to solve problems. The main idea of AI inclusion is to provide an ease of access to AI technology which can help to solve certain common challenges together. AI can be used in any of the applications such as healthcare, transport, education, security, entertainment and services. AI machine can work tirelessly, take decisions quickly, gives accurate results, assist in your daily routines, work best with repetitive tasks and doesn't need food, water, and so on, are some of its advantages.

Activity 1.10

Research and fill in how the Artificial Intelligence is used in the specified areas in the following table.

Areas	How AI is used?
Google AI powered eye-care technology	
Zebra Medical Vision	
Narayana Health City	
Qure.ai	
Sigtuple	
CureSkin	

Activity 1.11

List any five soft skills and technical skills each.

Activity 1.12

Write a short note on AI ethics.

TECH BOT

- **Artificial Intelligence:** It is the creation of intelligent machines that work and react like humans.
- **Smart Home:** It is a home that can be controlled remotely by smartphone or computer.
- **Smart City:** It is a city that uses information and communication technologies (ICT) to increase operational efficiency, share information with the public and improve both the quality of government services and citizen welfare.
- **SDG:** It is a blueprint to achieve a better and the more sustainable future for all.

Recap Bot

- Artificial Intelligence is quite relevant in Modern Times.
- A Smart Home is actually a home with automation and is also known as Home Automation.
- IoT is used for building smart homes and smart cities with automation and safety as priority for many of us.
- A Smart City is an urban city which uses IoT to collect data and information to improve the quality of government services easily and effectively.
- AI inclusion suggest making researches, tools, systems and scientific development available to solve problems.

BRAIN BOT

A. Multiple choice questions.

1. Which technique have become an essential part of the technology industry and help to solve many challenging problems?

   a. MI b. IoT

   c. AI d. None of these

2. ________________is quite relevant in Modern Times.

   a. Artificial Intelligence b. IoT

   c. Both a. and b. d. None of these

3. Who can be controlled through smartphones and smart speakers?

   a. Smart Home Device b. Smart Home

   c. IoT d. Both b. and c.

4. Which of the following is an application of AI?

   a. Data Science b. Transport

   c. Manufacturing industries d. None of these

5. ____________ app calculate traffic and instruct in order to find the quickest route to user's destination.

a. Google Maps
b. Google Music
c. Both a. and b.
d. None of these

6. AI plays an important role in ____________ technologies.

a. Self-driving car
b. Metro
c. Both a. and b.
d. None of these

7. ________________ is a thinking tool being addressed by Al systems.

a. E-commerce industry
b. Weather prediction
c. Metro
d. None of these

8. Which are used in AI to identify criminals?

a. Face recognition
b. Speech recognition
c. Both a. and b.
d. None of these

B. Fill in the blanks.

1. Al is a major tool leading towards a better and efficient ____________ industry.
2. Electronic appliances is an example of ________________.
3. ________________ can write a story in Google Docs.
4. The ____________ template provides the GOTO command.
5. SDG laid by UN which are to be achieved by ____________.

C. Match the following.

Column A	Column B
1. SDG	i. AI Inclusion
2. TV, AC, fridge	ii. E-commerce
3. Healthcare	iii. 17 goals
4. Benefitted from the application of AI	iv. Pillars of AI
5. Economic	v. Smart Home gadgets

D. Answer the following questions.

1. What is the purpose of Smart City?
2. Define AI.
3. Explain the use of AI inclusion.
4. Write down the following:

a. Bias b. Ethics c. AI Access

Create your own sound maker

1. Go to the link: https://experiments.withgoogle.com/sound-maker

   The following page appears.

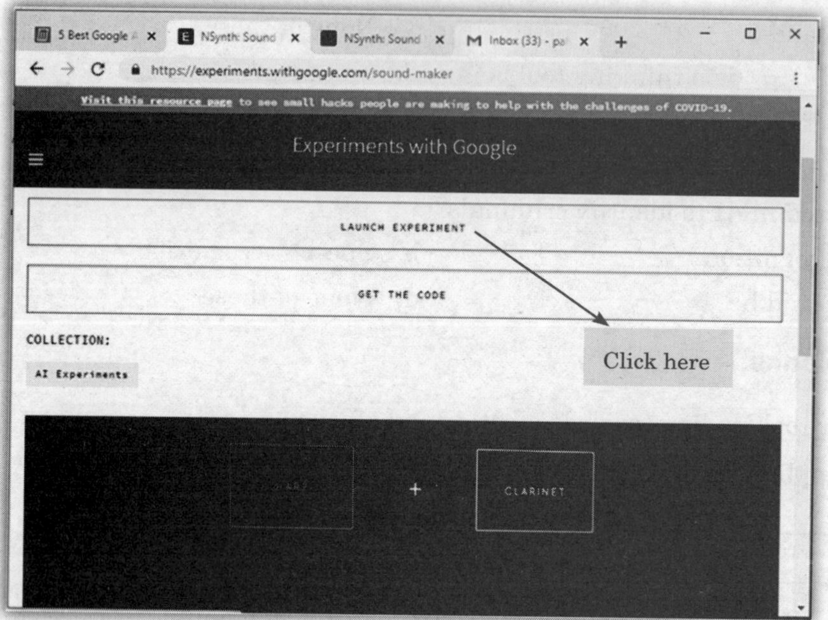

2. Click on the Launch Experiment button. The following screen appears.

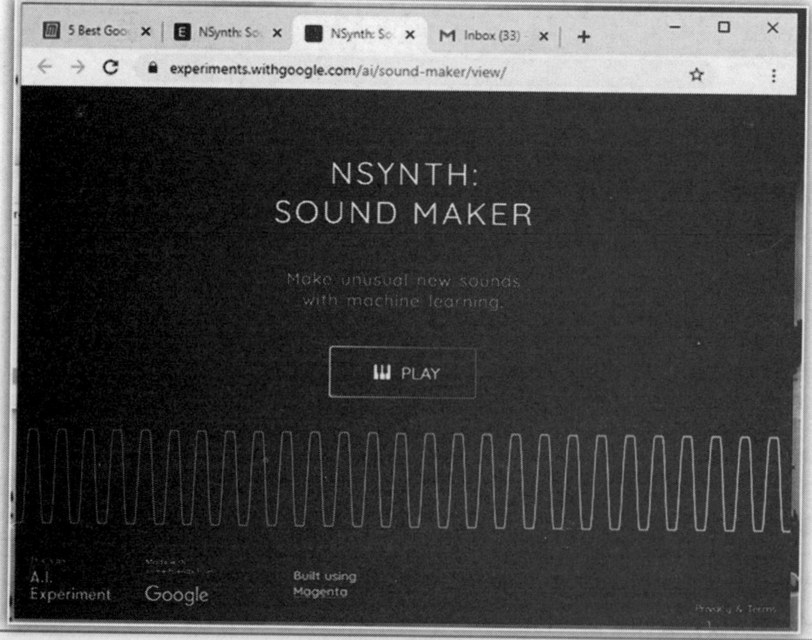

3. Click on Play button. The following screen appears.

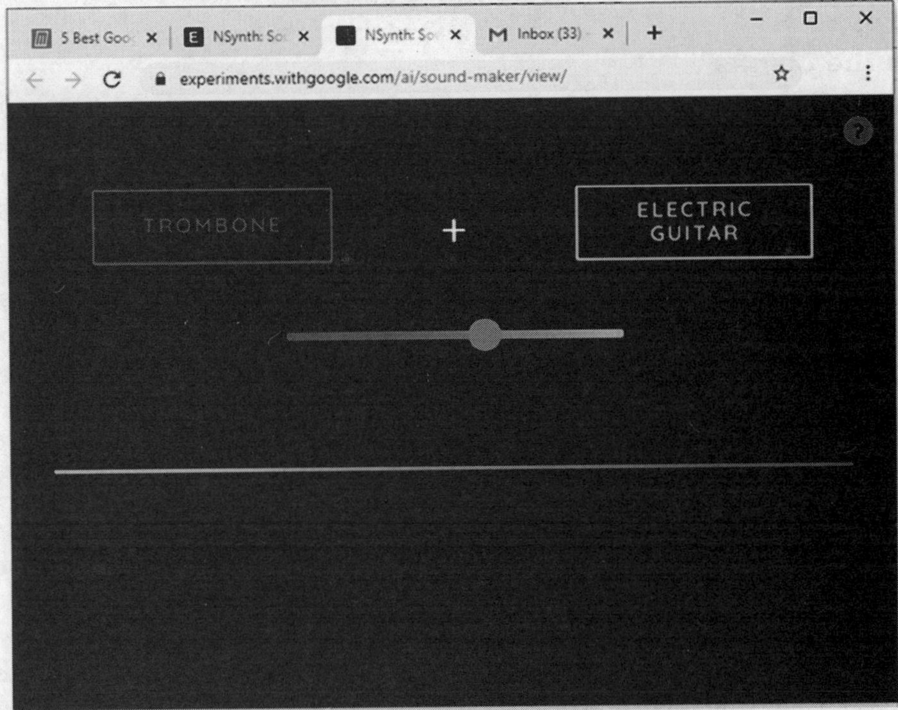

4. Select either TROMBONE or ELECTRIC GUITAR. The desired sound will be produced like in the given screenshot.

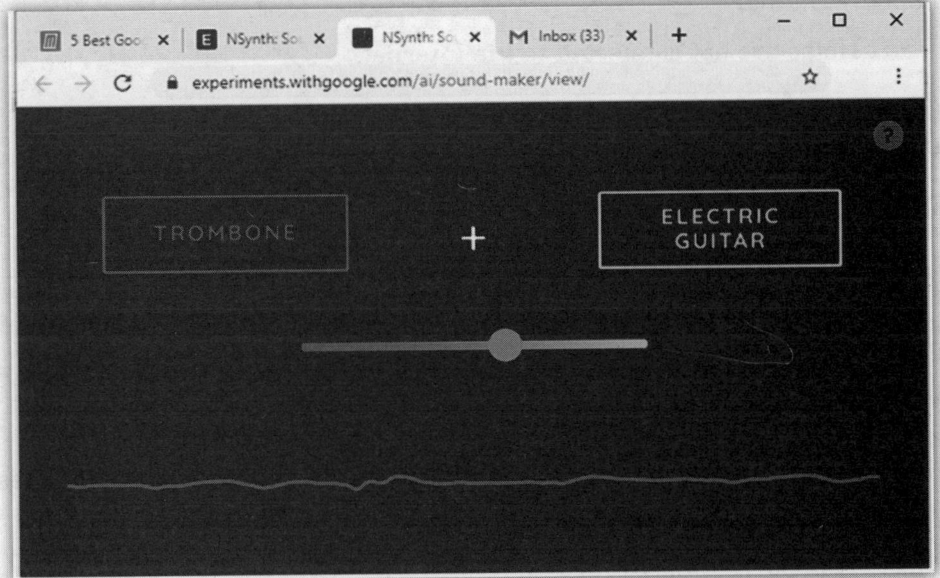

Worksheet

A. Fill in the blanks.

1. AI ______________________suggests making researches, tools, systems and scientific developments available to solve problems.
2. AI __________________can be defined as the mission where world's information can be organised and made available to all.
3. ______________can be defined as the study of values; generating moral values for good and bad, right and wrong.
4. A __________is a home that can be managed remotely to control the items/appliances/gadgets/systems such as TV, AC and so on, with your devices.
5. The impact of __________________on Sustainable Development Gaols is to develop responsible global citizens.
6. Story Speaker has _____________template.

B. State whether the following statements are True or False.

1. AI makes the machine work intelligently so as to help us in performing the various tasks easily and accurately.
2. Security systems is an example of Internet of Things.
3. Face recognition and speech recognition are some directions of AI which are used to identify criminals.
4. Smart Home are not connected to the internet.

C. Write down the full form of the following.

1. AI ____
2. ML ____
3. IoT ____
4. SDGs ____
5. NLP ____

D. Answer the following questions.

1. Write down the two applications of Artificial Intelligence in your daily lives.
2. Explain Smart Home and Smart City.
3. What is the purpose of AI?
4. What do you mean by Internet of Things?

QUIZ CARD

Multiple choice questions.

1. How many pillars of AI are available?
   - a. Two ☐ b. Three ☐
   - c. Four ☐ d. Five ☐
2. ______________________ can be controlled through smartphones and smart speakers.
   - a. Smart Home ☐ b. Smart City ☐
   - c. Bias ☐ d. Ethics ☐
3. Which refers to all objects that have sensors, network connectivity, software, and so on, to connect to the network?
   - a. IoT ☐ b. AI ☐
   - c. ML ☐ d. DL ☐
4. Another name of Smart Home is:
   - a. Home Automation ☐ b. Home Communication ☐
   - c. Home appliances ☐ d. Smart Appliances ☐
5. ______________________ is a phenomenon that occurs when an algorithm produces results that are discriminatory due to the built-in biases created by the programmer.
   - a. Smart City ☐ b. Smart Home ☐
   - c. Bias ☐ d. Ethics ☐
6. Who coined the term "Artificial Intelligence" in 1955?
   - a. John McCarthy ☐ b. Charles Babbage ☐
   - c. Tim Berners Lee ☐ d. None of these ☐
7. ________________ is the first goal of SDG.
   - a. No Poverty ☐ b. Zero Hunger ☐
   - c. Quality Education ☐ d. Gender Equality ☐
8. Another name of SDG is:
   - a. Global Goals ☐ b. Hunger Goals ☐
   - c. Local goals ☐ d. Both b. and c. ☐
9. SDG are 17 goals with _______________ targets.
   - a. 168 ☐ b. 169 ☐
   - c. 170 ☐ d. 171 ☐
10. There are ________________ types of AI.
    - a. 2 ☐ b. 3 ☐
    - c. 4 ☐ d. 5 ☐

2 Introduction to AI Project Cycle

Structure Bot

In this chapter, we will discuss the following topics:

- Describe the stages of an AI Project Cycle of a project
- Identify and describe the various stages of AI Project Cycle that is, Problem Scoping, Data Acquisition, Data Exploration, Modelling and Evaluation
- Reflect and paraphrase to set the goals for any specific topic/problem

Objective Bot

After studying this chapter, you should be able to:

- Describe the various stages of an AI Project Cycle
- Get started with any of AI Project
- Understand the concept of water scarcity and need for water conservation
- Demonstrate various tools to solve the problem of water conservation
- Divide a problem into different stages to understand how AI can solve the problem

In the previous chapters, you have learnt the various stages of identifying a crucial social problem and importance of steps required towards working an affordable and approachable solution for all members of the community. The solutions to global goals such as the UNESCOs SDG Agenda 2030 requires effective planning with guaranteed results at local levels. The key to successful results comes hand in hand with effective project planning.

Artificial Intelligence plays a vital role in planning of a project with ulterior social goals. The planning of such a project requires ascertaining and analysing important factors with all of the major stakeholders. Once the scope of the project has been defined, it becomes very clear to set the goals and objectives to determine the deliverables. A track of all the milestones as per the project schedule is maintained. Further, a periodic assessment check of the intermediate results helps us in reaching your said goals successfully.

Activity 2.1

Let us try to phrase a basic definition for various components of an AI Project Cycle as per your readings and understanding so far.

Problem Scoping	Problem Scoping is________________________ ____________________________________ ____________________________________
Data Acquisition	Data Acquisition is_______________________ ____________________________________ ____________________________________
Data Exploration	Data Exploration is______________________ ____________________________________ ____________________________________
Modelling	Modelling is____________________________ ____________________________________ ____________________________________
Evaluation	Evaluation is __________________________ ____________________________________ ____________________________________

Definition Bot

AI Project cycle is a framework which is used to design an AI project taking all the crucial factors into consideration.

Let us begin to understand, identify and describe different components of an AI Project Cycle with the help of a social problem. **Example:** Water Conservation.

Preface

Water is a valuable resource and an essential part of your lives. Our earth has three-fourth of its surface area covered with water. About 97% of water is found in oceans and seas, remaining 3% from rivers, lakes, ponds, streams, etc. All plants, animals and human beings need water to survive. Human beings needs water for day-to-day activities like bathing, cleaning, drinking, washing, irrigation, generating electricity, etc. Hence, you can establish that water is important for all of us for our day-to-day activities but at the same time you know that the world has started facing water crisis. Overuse of usable water has led to the problem of water scarcity.

Practice Time

Fill in the blanks.

1. __________ needs water for day-to-day activities.
2. ________________ is a valuable resource and an essential part of our lives.

Background Information

You will have to research about your facts and understandings to form the basis of information required for setting your goals and objectives.

Let us watch the following video links and collate your observations in the graphic organizer.

- Uses of water: https://youtu.be/Q6l6RHfLluA
- Water cycle: https://youtu.be/z5G4NCwWUxY
- Need to conserve water: https://youtu.be/CFSmuGPv8eU

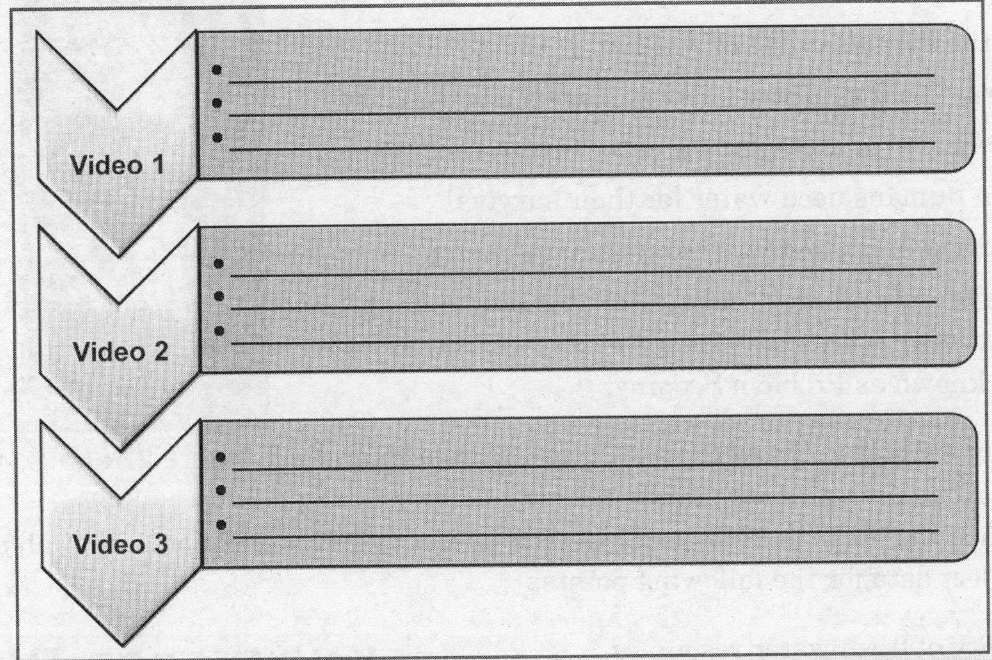

Brief Description

Water Conservation is a global issue where every little bit helps. A lot of people across the world are doing their little bits which adds up to a whole lot. Lifestyle changes will modify the course of our water and its quality while making a huge difference to the environment. Since each of us depends on water for life, it is our collective responsibility to learn about water conservation and how you can help keep your water pure and safe for generations to come and enjoy these benefits.

It is important to remember on an everyday basis that water equals life. There is only a finite limit of fresh water resources available. Protecting our natural eco-systems from further damage is equally critical, especially for the survival of some endangered species.

Saving water also means using less energy which reduces your carbon footprint and helps your lives become more energy independent.

You have read about the various uses of water and how it is important for us to conserve it smartly. Let us list down all the factors which you need to consider while framing the AI Project Cycle on water conservation.

Figure 2.1: *Save Water*

The goal/ aim of water conservation project cycle is to:

- Discuss the various usage of water.
- To devise methods as to how water wastage can be controlled.
- To ensure the availability of water for future generations.
- Ascertain humans need water for their survival.
- Conservation helps to preserve our environment.

While you have defined the goal/aim of the problem which you want to achieve with the help of the project, the process component is known as Problem Scoping.

The next important step in the AI Project Cycle is to understand and collect various data points for your set goal. Now, as you have established the importance of water in your lives and how it is important for all of us, let us now collect data for the following points:

- Availability of fresh water resources.
- Availability of water resources which can be directly used by us.
- Distribution of water resources.
- Various usage of water in your day-to-day lives.
- Areas affected by water scarcity.

KNOWLEDGE BOT

In Problem Scoping, steps with the help of which you can scope the problem and finalize the goal/aim of the problem in your project.

Once you start collecting data, you actually collect data in various forms like photographs, videos or text from different places like website, newspaper, journals, and so on. You have to check the authenticity of the collected data. The data collected needs to be accurate and reliable to work efficiently. This process component is called Data Acquisition.

After Data Acquisition, you will find that you have different types of information from different sources. Now you need to put all the data in a simplified format to interpret it. The data can be organised in one of the following manner:

- Create a table and put the information gathered in a proper columns.
- Create a table by interpreting the data regarding various sources of fresh water.
- Create a table by interpreting the data regarding various usages of water.
- Create a table for interpreting the data regarding the water scarcity.

Data can be interpreted to understand some useful information about the data. You should be able to interpret the data on the basis of the following too:

- Pre and Post Industrialization
- Pre and Post Urbanization
- State-wise Analysis

Data needs to be uniformly arranged for a better understanding. Visualizing the acquired data in user-friendly format helps us to quickly get a sense of the trends, relationships and patterns contained within the data and communicate the same to others effectively. This basis helps us comprehend and define strategies for later use. This AI component is known as Data Exploration.

After exploring the data, you need to develop different exhibition workable models in order to ensure water conservation and management. These projects can be undertaken with adequate funding from various resources along with NGOs and government aid.

You can take certain examples into consideration as following:

- Afforestation or planting of more trees to replenish water table
- Rain water harvesting
- Efficient watering systems
- Multi-purpose river Project
- Building dams
- Irrigation hours and frequency should be reduced
- Economical use of water for various home purposes
- Treatment of industrial and domestic waste water in sewage plants before its disposal

To implement on the ideas, let us evaluate each and every model by checking the advantages and disadvantages of the models. Choose the best model which gives the most efficient and reliable result. This AI Component stage is known as Modelling.

FACT BOT

In 1963, IBM produced computers which specialized in Data Acquisition.

The Water Conservation system is now done. The last stage is the most important. This is the point where you shall evaluate the efficiency of the model selected on the basis of the results expected versus the results obtained. This stage is important to identify and work on the data points where AI-enabled technologies can be incorporated to increase the efficiency of the project. The component of AI project cycle is known as Evaluation.

Figure 2.2: *Save Water*

Activity 2.3

It is time to reflect on our thoughts once again. Explain the concept of AI Project cycle with the help of a suitable example as described in the chapter. You can pick up any of the following topics.

- Security and Surveillance
- Saving the Birds
- Food Preservation

Goal/Aim of the Project
Brief Description
AI Project Cycle

TIP BOT

- Planning is the key for the successful results for any project.
- Carefully select the data sets for your proposed AI solution.

TECH BOT

- **Problem Scoping:** It refers to understanding a problem and finding out various factors which affect the problem.
- **Data Acquisition:** It is the process of collection of data accurately and it must be reliable to work.
- **Data Exploration:** Process of gathering data which needs to be arranged uniformly for the better understanding is called Data Exploration.
- **Modelling:** It means to present the results of the modern researches in the artificial intelligence.
- **Evaluation:** It is the method of understanding the reliability of an AI model, evaluation is based on the outputs which is received by feeding the test dataset into the model and then comparing the output with the actual answers.

Recap Bot

- The components of AI Project Cycle is Problem Scoping, Data Acquisition, Data Exploration, Modelling and Evaluation.
- Artificial Intelligence plays a vital role in planning of a project with ulterior social goals.
- Overuse of usable water has led to the problem of water scarcity.
- Carbon footprint is the amount of carbon which is released in the atmosphere by various activities like burning of fuels for energy, deforestation, and so on.
- Saving water also means using less energy which reduces your carbon footprint.
- Water conservation is a global issue where each one of us is helping in our own ways.
- The Problem Scoping is the first component of the Project Cycle which is used to define the goal/aim of the project.
- Data Acquisition is used to collect the data in the form of text, video, images, and so on, regarding the project and it should be accurate and reliable.
- Data can be collected from various sources like newspaper, journals, internet, and so on.
- Data Exploration is the process in which data gathered needs to be uniformly arranged for a better understanding.
- Modelling is the process in which different models based on the previous components can be created and checked for the advantages and disadvantages of each model.
- Evaluation is the important component which is used to identify and work on the data points where AI-enables technologies can be incorporated to increase the efficiency of the project.

A. Multiple choice questions.

1. The process of collecting the rainwater for use is called:
   a. Rainwater
   b. Rainwater harvesting
   c. Rain pumping
   d. Water conservation
2. Which one of the following is the last component of the AI Project Cycle?
   a. Data Exploration
   b. Modeling
   c. Evaluation
   d. Project Scoping
3. The process of preventing the overuse of water to balance our natural ecosystem is known as:
   a. Water scarcity
   b. Water conservation
   c. Rainwater harvesting
   d. None of the above
4. Scarcity means:
   a. Shortage
   b. Lack
   c. Inadequacy
   d. All of the above
5. The AI Project stage which is used to set the goal for the problem is:
   a. Data Exploration
   b. Evaluation
   c. Problem Scoping
   d. Data Validation
6. Water Conservation means:
   a. Saving water
   b. Protecting water
   c. Water management
   d. All of the above

B. Fill in the blanks.

1. __________ helps us to preserve your environment.
2. __________ stage of project cycle is used to collect data.
3. Problem Scoping, ________, ________ and ________ are the first four components of Project Cycle.
4. Saving water also means using ______ energy which reduces your __________ footprint.
5. About __________ of water is found in oceans and seas.
6. Our earth has ______________ of its surface area covered with water.
7. The data needs to be ___________ and ___________ to work efficiently.
8. Arranging data in a uniform manner so as to sense it for data interpretation is known as ________________.

C. Match the following.

	Column A		Column B
1.	Water	i.	Water
2.	Three-fourth	ii.	Global issue
3.	Shortage	iii.	Collect Data
4.	Saving	iv.	Data arranged in organised manner
5.	Water conservation	v.	Valuable resource
6.	Aim / Goal	vi.	Scarcity
7.	Data Acquisition	vii.	Conservation
8.	Data Exploration	viii.	Problem Scoping

D. Answer the following questions.

1. Write the various uses of water in your life. Also, write what all can you do to conserve water?
2. Define Data Acquisition. Also, write the various sources for Data Acquisition.
3. Unscramble the following letters to form a word.

   a. A C E I O O N N S R V T

   b. A A C F I II L R T
4. Define the following:

   a. AI Project Cycle

   b. Water Scarcity

   c. Water Conservation
5. Write any two ways to conserve water.

Lab Activity

Giorgio Cam: This is an AI experiment that takes a picture and tells what the object is in the picture, while putting it into music lyrics.

1. Go to the link: https://experiments.withgoogle.com/ai/giorgio-cam/view/

   The following page appears.

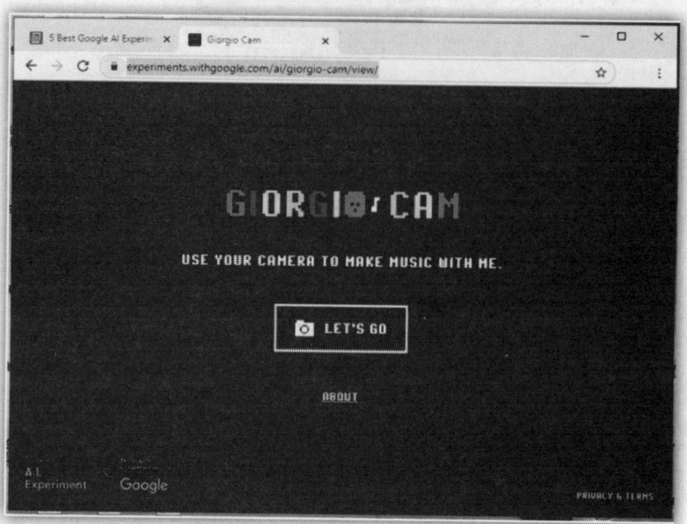

2. Click on the  button.

3. Take an image then Giorgio Cam creates rhymes and adds rhythm to the music. Then it identifies the object, while using the photo to create entertainment with music.

Worksheet

A. Fill in the blanks.

1. ______________________is a valuable resource and an essential part of our lives.
2. _____________water also means using less energy which reduces your carbon footprint.
3. The data collected needs to be accurate and ________________to work efficiently.
4. ________________is the first component of the Project Cycle.
5. _______________is a global issue where each one of you is helping in your own way.
6. __________________is the last component of the Project Cycle.
7. ____________can be collected from various sources like newspaper, journals, internet, and so on.
8. _______________component helps us comprehend and define strategies for later use.

B. State whether the following statements are True or False.

1. AI is the key to successful results for any project.
2. Your earth has three-fourth of its surface area covered with water.
3. Modelling is the process in which data gathered needs to be uniformly arranged for a better understanding.
4. Usage of water is one of the goal of water conservation Project Cycle.
5. Overuse of usable water has led to the problem of water scarcity.
6. Planning plays a vital role in planning of a project with ulterior social goals.
7. Evaluation is used to define the goal/aim of the project.

C. Reorder the AI Project Cycle components in the following fashion.

1. Evaluation
2. Modelling
3. Data Exploration
4. Problem Scoping
5. Data Acquisition

D. Answer the following questions.

1. Explain Problem Scoping.
2. How data can be organised in Data Acquisition?
3. Write down the components of AI Project Cycle.
4. What do you mean by Data Exploration?

QUIZ CARD

Multiple choice questions.

1. Which is the fourth component of AI project cycle?
   a. Modelling ☐ b. Problem Scoping ☐
   c. Data Acquisition ☐ d. Data Exploration ☐
2. How many components of AI Project Cycle are available?
   a. Four ☐ b. Five ☐
   c. Six ☐ d. Seven ☐
3. Which AI project cycle is used to collect the data in the form of text, video, images and so on?
   a. Modelling ☐ b. Problem Scoping ☐
   c. Data Acquisition ☐ d. Data Exploration ☐
4. ______________________is the amount of carbon which is released in the atmosphere by various activities.
   a. Carbon ☐ b. Carbon Dioxide ☐
   c. Carbon foot d. Carbon footprint ☐
5. Which AI project cycle is to understand and collect various data points for your set goals?
   a. Modelling ☐ b. Problem Scoping ☐
   c. Data Acquisition ☐ d. Data Exploration ☐
6. ________________needs to be uniformly arranged for a better understanding.
   a. Datasets ☐ b. Data ☐
   c. Database ☐ d. Both a. and b. ☐
7. Which component is used to identify and work on the data points?
   a. Evaluation ☐ b. Problem Scoping ☐
   c. Data Acquisition ☐ d. Data Exploration ☐
8. ______________is the process in which different models based on the previous components can be created for the advantages and disadvantages of each model.
   a. Modelling ☐ b. Problem Scoping ☐
   c. Data Acquisition ☐ d. Data Exploration ☐
9. Building dams is an example of:
   a. Evaluation ☐ b. Problem Scoping ☐
   c. Data Acquisition ☐ d. Data Exploration ☐
10. About ______________of water is found in oceans and seas.
    a. 96% ☐ b. 97% ☐
    c. 98% ☐ d. 99% ☐

3 Problem Scoping

Structure Bot

In this chapter, we will discuss the following topics:

- Choose a theme from three dimensions (environment, social and economic) of SDG
- Identify, analyse and choose the problem that the learner wish to solve using AI knowledge
- Exploring the 4Ws Problem Canvas
- Deliberating the Problem Statement Template
- Reflect and paraphrase to set the goals for any specific topic/problem

Objective Bot

After studying this chapter, you should be able to:

- Scope a problem to further take action for solutions i.e. to set a goal for a problem
- Identity various elements to the problem so as to set actions which can work around the problem
- Compare and contrast various data features needed and how this data is to be collected and used for data analysis
- Recapitulate and reflect about the goal, action and data

So far, you have learnt how to identify the goals for a social problem by identifying the data points collected based on different sources. This process helps in preparing the best possible model with workable solution. The successful deliverables of the model help us ascertain that the goals set at the beginning of the AI Project Cycle play the most important role. In this chapter, you will learn in depth about Problem Scoping as it is the first stage of AI Project Cycle. You all know that each one of us is surrounded by one or many problems. The problem can be person specific, religion specific, country specific or world problem. A problem influences many individuals and many people strive to find solutions. Figuring out the problem requires us a need to work towards finding an effective solution for it. To find any solution to a problem, you need to find out the root causes of the problem. Hence, let us first understand how the goals of the problem should be finalised.

Figure 3.1: *Defining a problem*

To understand the concept better, you shall take a problem which you later want to be solved using AI integration. The process starts with choosing a theme from one of the three domain pillars of UNSECOs Agenda 2030. A theme is a broader term which has many other things in it, related to the theme.

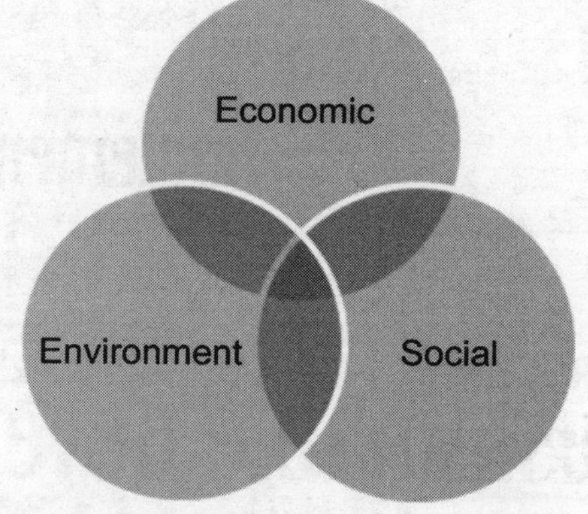

Figure 3.2: *Three domain pillars*

Definition Bot

Problem Scoping refers to understanding a problem and finding out various factors which affect the problem.

Activity 3.1

Let us take the theme of environment for this chapter to understand how to set the goal for the project by undergoing various activities.

You know that environment is a very big topic. So, you need to break it further to know about various goals of SDG which comes under this domain. The various topics under environment are as given in the following.

For example: In Sustainable Development Goals, you have 17 goals that fall under any of the three domain pillars. These themes are Economic, Social and Environment.

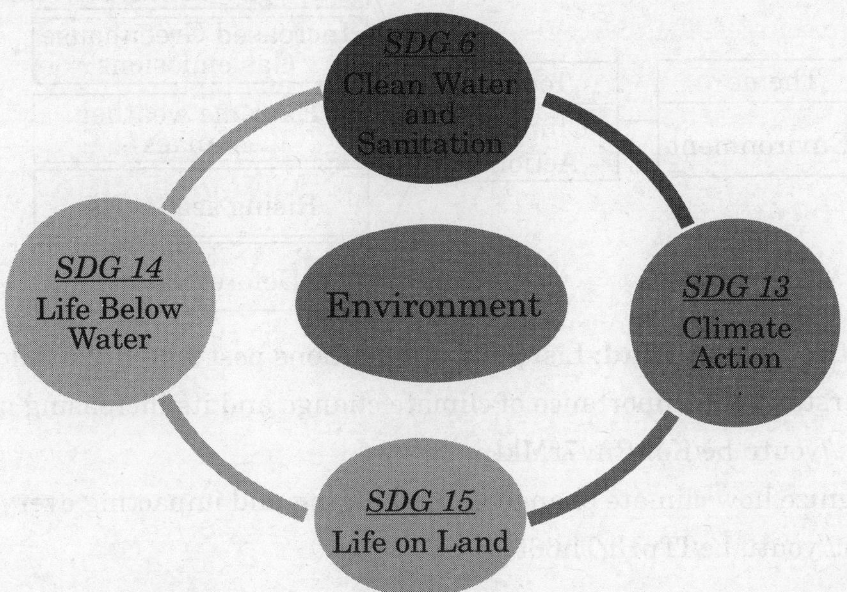

Activity 3.2

Let us take any one topic from the above stated SDG goals to further understand the various concerns regarding the topic and research regarding the topic to list out various problems associated with it.

Topic Undertaken for This Activity: Climate Action (SDG 13)

The change in climate is increasing and its impact is seen and observed by each one of us which is further impacting everyone's life in more than one way. By doing this activity, you will not only able to only scope the problem but also learn about each other by sharing your personal experiences and feelings regarding the climate change.

Observe the filled up the boxes in the given figure to understand the hierarchy of the problem and to explore how the bigger problems can be solved by following various steps to identify, analyse and find solutions.

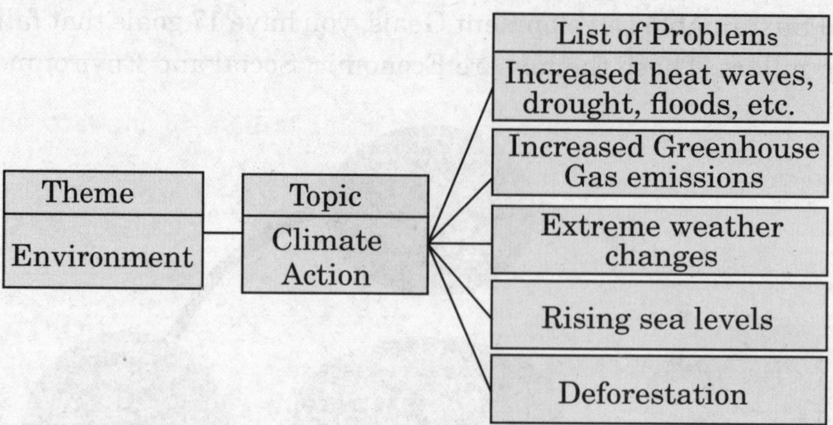

Researching the background: List your observations post watch the following videos.

Video 1: Understand the importance of climate change and its increasing impacts.
https://youtu.be/KJbRnv7rMkk

Video 2: Recognize how climate change is threatening and impacting every one's life.
https://youtu.be/ITpHgTh66tY

Observations:

- ______________________________
- ______________________________
- ______________________________
- ______________________________

You have listed so many problems that comes under climate action. Let us take any one problem from the list mentioned above as your goal of the project. It finally emerges as the target for AI Project to be solved using AI enabled technologies.

The goal taken for the next activity is Greenhouse Gas(GHG) emissions.

Activity 3.3

List the goal statement here. The goal can be stated as how you can help in reducing the Greenhouse Gas emission and improve the situation for everyone.

Write the goal of Greenhouse Gases (GHG) emission theme below:	
•	Describe Greenhouse Gas emission.
•	Understand and identify the causes of GHG emissions.
•	Once you know the problem and the causes have been listed, you can work on how to protect yourselves from those problems.

Activity 3.4

To understand and demonstrate more about the impact of climate change due to Greenhouse Gases, let us prepare a step by step scoping to this problem using 4Ws Problem Canvas framework.

This canvas will help us identify four different parameters for Problem Scoping.

The four parameters of 4Ws Problem Canvas are:

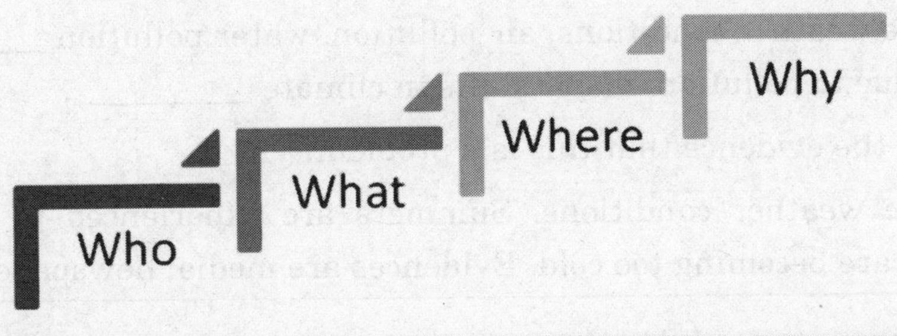

- Who: This is the first block of the 4W Problem Canvas. It helps us in comprehending and categorizing who all are getting effected directly or indirectly with the problem. This step includes cataloguing the information regarding what all you know about the problem. The details about the stakeholders who are directly and indirectly affected by the problem are an important basis of the 4W Canvas.

Let us fill in the following questions to get the answer for WHO block of the 4W Problem Canvas.

WHO
• Who has the problem (that is, who is the stakeholder)? Concerns every one of us _________. People, animals, sea life, places __________. • Does the said stakeholder consider it a problem? Yes, each one of us has observed/ faced this problem in one or the other way __________. Pollution, diseases due to increasing pollution _________.

FACT BOT

In September 2015, Canada and all other 192 United Nations Member States adopted the 2030 Agenda for Sustainable Development at the UN General Assembly.

- What: This is the second block of the 4W Problem Canvas. It helps in understanding and identifying the nature of the problem and how do you get to know about this as a problem.The details should be supported by relevant and valid evidences about the existence of the said problem.

Fill in the following questions to get the answer for WHAT block of the 4W Problem Canvas.

WHAT?
• What is the problem? Extreme weather conditions, air pollution, water pollution __________. Health issues due to pollution, major shifts in climate __________. • What is the evidence that this is a problem? Extreme weather conditions. Summers are experienced to be too hot and winters are becoming too cold. Evidences are media, newspaper, and so on.

- **Where:** This is the third block of the 4W Problem Canvas. Using the previous two blocks, you came to know about what the problem is and whom it is affecting. Now in this block, let us concentrate on where this problem comes from. The context, situation and location where the problem is most prominent, plays an important role here.

Fill in the following questions to get the answer for WHERE block of the 4W Problem Canvas.

WHERE
• Where does this problem arise (location/ situation)? Carbon dioxide emissions from burning, pollution due to increasing vehicles on road, gases emissions from the factories, deforestation, Landfill__________. • Have you observed/experienced this statement as a problem? Yes, each one of us has experienced directly or indirectly this statement as a problem __________. As these Greenhouse Gases are effecting your health by causing respiratory diseases from smog and air pollution ______________.

- Why: By now, you have the answers to what is the problem, who has the problem and from where the problem is arising. Let us get the answer for why you need to solve this and how the solution will improve the situation for an individual and the society as a whole.

Fill in the following questions to get the answer for WHY block of the 4W Problem Canvas.

WHY
• Why is the problem worth solving? Health is the major concern. If this problem is addressed properly then so many problems which are dependent on this will also improve __________. The problem is worth solving for people, animals, sea life and places __________.
• How the solution will improve the situation? Clean air will improve the life of people, animals, plant life, sea life, and so on. Reduction in the death rate by diseases caused due to pollution __________.

KNOWLEDGE BOT

In Who 4Ws Problem Canvas, you can get the information about what all you know about the problem.

Activity 3.5

Problem Statement Template is used to put the problem stated using 4Ws Problem Canvas in paragraph form. It has clear description to tell who has the problem, what the problem is, from where it comes and why you need to address it. Let us summarise all the key points into this template.

Our	[stakeholders] People, sea life and animals are facing lot of problem.	Who
Has/have a problem that	[issue, problem, need] Greenhouse Gas emissions, which is increasing the carbon dioxide in the atmosphere and thus pollution, shift in climate, extreme weather conditions.	What
When/ while	[context, situation] Due to which people are facing lot of respiratory diseases, facing floods, droughts, and so on.	Where
An ideal solution would	[benefit of solution] Control of Carbon dioxide will improve the health conditions, sea life and animal life too. Balance in ecosystem.	Why

TIP BOT

Problem statement is used to put the 4Ws Problem Canvas in the paragraph form for better understanding.

Identify a theme which can be classified as a social problem. Fill up the 4W Problem Canvas which shall establish 'Problem Scoping' and establish the goals for the project by undergoing various activities.

GOALS	• ______ • ______	
OUR	[stakeholders] • ______ • ______ • ______	WHO
HAS/HAVE A PROBLEM THAT	[issue, problem, need] • ______ • ______ • ______	WHAT
WHEN/ WHILE	[context, situation] • ______ • ______ • ______	WHERE
AN IDEAL SOLUTION WOULD	[benefit of solution] • ______ • ______ • ______	WHY

TECH BOT

- **Project Scoping:** Steps with the help of which you can scope the problem and finalize the goal/aim of the problem in your project.
- **4Ws Problem Canvas:** It consists of 4 components that is, Who, What, Where and Why.
- **Problem Statement:** A problem statement is a clear description of the issue(s), it includes a vision, issue statement, and method used to solve the problem.
- **Theme:** It is a broader term, which has various components which are further attached to it.

Recap Bot

- Project Scoping is the first component of AI Project Cycle.
- To solve any problem, you need to first break down it into further components to understand it properly using 4Ws Problem Canvas.
- Who block is the first component that focuses on the people who are actually facing the problem.
- What block focuses on the problem that is, what exactly is the problem.
- Where block tells from where the problem is coming.
- Why block is used to understand what are the benefits for solving such a problem.
- Greenhouse Gases (GHG) cause the greenhouse effect. The Greenhouse gases are carbon dioxide, methane, water vapour and ozone.
- GHG emission is the release of the gases mainly carbon dioxide in the earth atmosphere that causes greenhouse effect.
- Greenhouse effect is the problem state which is caused due to increased quantities of gases such as carbon dioxide in the air.
- Carbon dioxide is the primary Greenhouse Gas emission that is effecting the global climate change.
- The increased rate of carbon dioxide in the atmosphere is due to man-made activities such as burning of fossil fuels for heat, electricity and transportation.

A. Multiple choice questions.

1. Which one of the following is not a component of AI Project Cycle?
   a. Data Acquisition
   b. Data Analyst
   c. Problem Scoping
   d. Data Exploration
2. Which one of the following is the first component of the AI Project Cycle?
   a. Data Exploration
   b. Modeling
   c. Evaluation
   d. Project Scoping
3. Which one of the following is not the component of 4Ws Problem Canvas?
   a. Who
   b. How
   c. What
   d. Where
4. The full form of GHG :
   a. Greenhouse Gas
   b. Grasshouse Gas
   c. Greenhouse Gas
   d. Genesis Housing Gas
5. Which of the following SDG comes under the Environment domain?
   a. Clean Water and Sanitation
   b. Life Below Water
   c. Climate Action
   d. All of the above
6. Which of the following is the Greenhouse Gas?
   a. Hydrogen
   b. Nitrogen
   c. Methane
   d. Life on Land

B. Fill in the blanks.

1. __________ defines the various steps with the help of which you can scope the problem and finalise the goal of the project.
2. The first block in 4Ws Problem Canvas is __________.
3. Who, _________, ________ and ________ are the 4 components of 4Ws Problem Canvas.
4. Greenhouse Gases cause the greenhouse __________.
5. __________ block focuses on the people who face the problem.
6. ______________ is used to put the 4Ws Problem Canvas in the paragraph form.
7. The Greenhouse Gases are _________________, methane, ________ and water vapour.

C. Match the following.

	Column A		Column B
1.	Problem Scoping	i.	Burning of fossil fuels
2.	4Ws Problem Canvas	ii.	Broader term
3.	GHG	iii.	Who, What, Where, Why
4.	Increased CO_2 due to	iv.	Is the last block of 4Ws Problem Canvas
5.	Greenhouse Gas	v.	Cutting trees
6.	Theme	vi.	Greenhouse Gas
7.	Deforestation	vii.	Carbon dioxide
8.	Why	viii.	Defines the goal of the project

D. Answer the following questions.

1. What are the two main Greenhouse Gases?
2. Unscramble the following letters to form a word.
   a. IONCPGS b. AACNSV
3. Define the following:
   a. Problem Scoping b. Greenhouse Gas c. Greenhouse effect
4. Write the causes of increased carbon dioxide in the atmosphere.
5. Write down the name of 4Ws Problem Canvas.

Lab Activity

Create a bird sounds: This experiment organize thousands of recordings of different bird sounds using only audio analysis technology putting the most similar sounds together.

1. Go to the link: https://experiments.withgoogle.com/bird-sounds
   The following page appears.

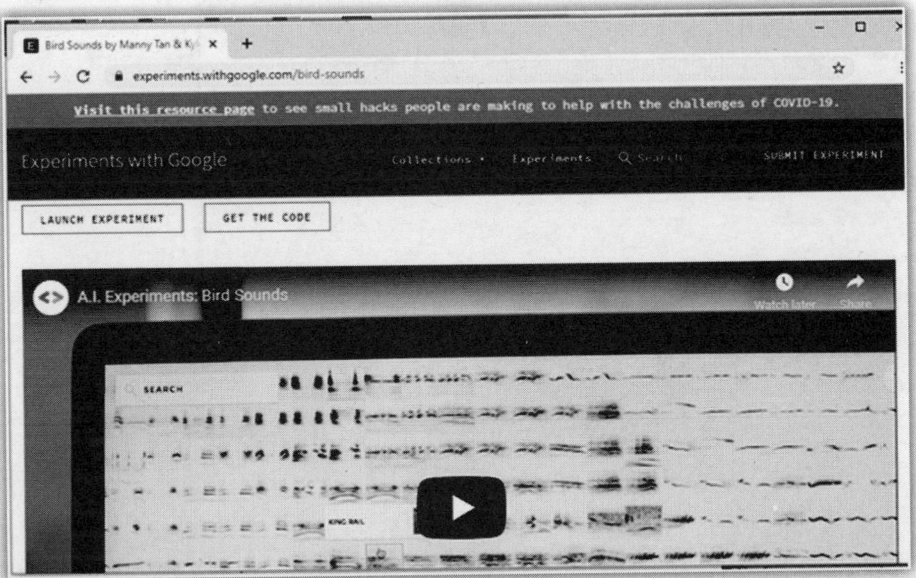

1. Click on the Launch Experiment button.

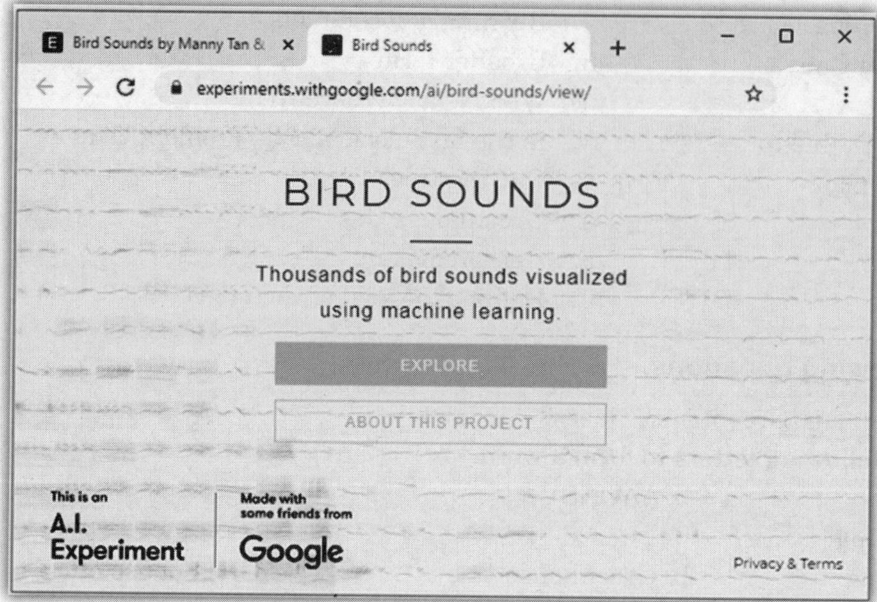

2. Click on Explore button.
3. Click on any part of the screen the desired sound will be produced.

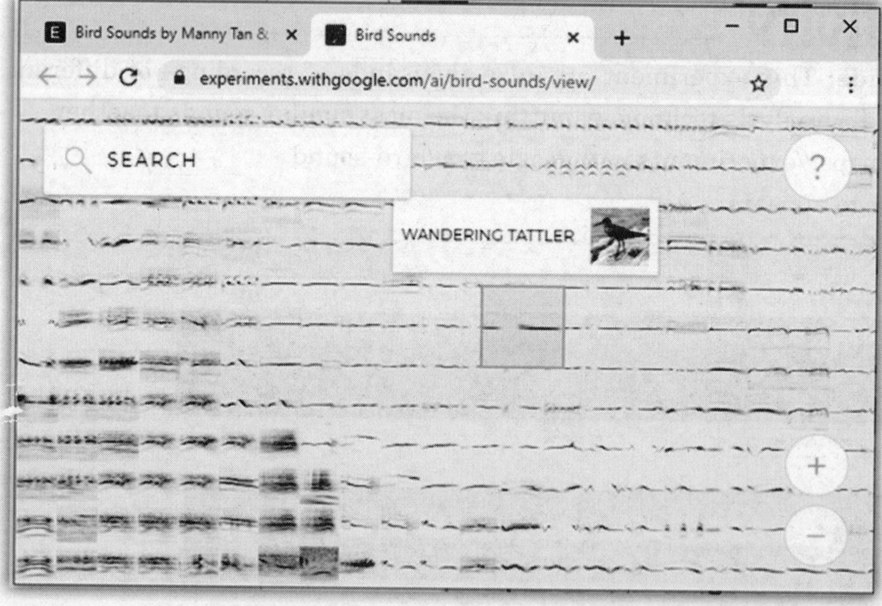

Worksheet

A. Fill in the blanks.

1. The problem can be person specific, _______________specific, country specific or world specific.
2. A ____________is a border term which has many other things in it.
3. ______________is the full form of GHG.
4. ________________is the second block of the 4W Problem Canvas.
5. ______________step includes cataloguing the information regarding what all you know about the problem.
6. ________________canvas help us to identify the four different parameters of Problem Scoping.
7. ________________helps in understanding and identifying the nature of the problem.

B. State whether the following statements are True or False.

1. In what block, context and location regarding problem plays an important role.
2. What block helps in identifying how do you get to know about this problem.
3. The 4 parameters of 4Ws are Why, what, where and Whom.
4. Where block is used to understand what are the benefits for solving such a problem.
5. Problem Statement is used to put 4Ws Problem Canvas in the paragraph form for better understanding.
6. Project Scoping is the second component of AI Project Cycle.
7. Methane is the primary GHG emission that is effecting the global climate change.
8. Where blocks tells from where the problem is coming.

C. Write down the full form of the following.

1. GHG ________________________________
2. CO_2 ________________________________
3. SDG ________________________________

D. Answer the following questions.

1. Explain Why block in detail.
2. What do you mean by Greenhouse Gases?
3. What is Problem Statement?
4. Write down the goals of GHG emission theme.
5. Write down the names of 4Ws Problem Canvas.

QUIZ CARD

Multiple choice questions.

1. Which one of the following is not a 4Ws Problem Canvas?

   a. Whom ☐ b. Who ☐

   c. What ☐ d. Where ☐

2. Which template is used to put the problem stated using 4Ws Problem Canvas in paragraph form?

   a. Problem Scoping ☐ b. Problem Statement ☐

   c. Problem Understand ☐ d. None of these ☐

3. Which block helps us in comprehending and categorizing who all are getting effected directly or indirectly with the problem?

   a. Who b. What ☐

   c. Where d. None of these ☐

4. ________________________is the problem state which is caused due to increased quantities of gases.

   a. Greenhouse Gases ☐ b. Greenhouse effect ☐

   c. Co_2 ☐ d. None of these ☐

5. Which block focuses on the problem that is, what exactly is the problem?

   a. Who ☐ b. What ☐

   c. Where ☐ d. None of these ☐

6. A ________________influences many individuals and many people strive to find solutions.

   a. Theme ☐ b. Figuring ☐

   c. Problem ☐ d. Both a. and b. ☐

7. Themes are economic, social and __________________.

   a. Religion ☐ b. Quality ☐

   c. Environment ☐ d. None of these ☐

8. ______________is the third block of 4Ws Problem canvas.

   a. Why ☐ b. What ☐

   c. Whom ☐ D. Where ☐

9. Understand and identify the causes of GHG emissions is a goal of:

   a. GHG Emission ☐ b. Why ☐

   c. Both a. and b. ☐ d. None of these ☐

10. To solve any problem. You need to first break down it into further components to understand it problem using:

    a. 4Ws Problem Canvas ☐ b. Problem Statement ☐

    c. Problem Understand ☐ d. None of these ☐

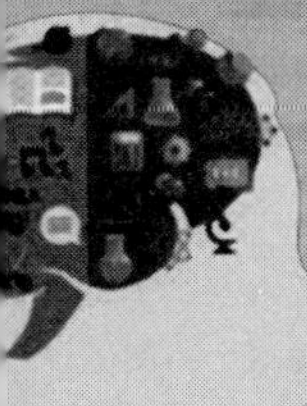

4 Data Acquisition

Structure Bot

In this chapter, we will discuss the following topics:

- Create the 4W Problem Canvas to acquire all aspects data for a theme
- Introduction to data and research about these data points as per the AI Project theme taken
- Elaborate data features and the need to acquire data from reliable, authentic, and relevant resources to interpret, identify, and categorize it
- Illustrate thinking in systems using System Maps designed with the online tool–LOOPY

Objective Bot

At the end of this chapter, you should be able to:

- Identify and relate the data points for the problem scoped
- Identity various elements of a process/system to set actions which can work around the problem
- Compare and contrast various data features needed and see how one data feature is connected with the other
- Validate data collection methods and check the authenticity and reliability of the data collected
- Demonstrate the connectivity between the data features using a System Map

Definition Bot

Data Acquisition is the process of collection of data accurately and it must be reliable to work.

Activity 4.1

Let us evaluate and take an example by Problem Scoping for a topic theme.

Topic Theme: How driving crowds out walking and biking?

The 4Ws Problem Canvas can be summed up as follows:

- Who:
  - Who has the problem (stakeholders)?
    - Community (People and environment)
  - Can you prove this as a problem?
    - Yes, we face this problem in our daily life.
- What:
  - What is the problem statement?
  - How driving crowds out walking and biking?
  - What is the evidence that this is a problem?
    - Congestion on the roads and in the market place as well.
    - People don't walk and face health and obesity issues.
    - Air Quality Index is bad due to rise in emission of harmful gasses.
- Where:
  - Where does this problem arise (location/situation)?
    - Roads are full of cars, scooters, bikes as mode of transportation is based on petrol/diesel.
    - Congestion on the roads/congestion in the market place too.
    - No space to walk/no space to walk in the market place too.
    - Air pollution due to lot of emissions from transportation.
  - Have you observed/experienced this statement as a problem?
    - Yes, air pollution is the biggest issue due to imbalance of CO_2 in the environment due to emissions as well as deforestation.
- Why:
  - Why is the problem worth solving?
    - Public health benefits.
    - Energy and environmental health benefits.
  - How the solution will improve the situation?
    - People will start walking and biking.
    - Reducing the congestion on the roads.
    - Less vehicles on road means less emissions in the environment.

In the previous chapter, you learned how to review all aspects of a social problem to the base of a problem and how it can be used to draft the goal for a theme project. Once the goal of the project is set, the 4Ws Problem Canvas is used to pen down all the elements that are directly or indirectly affecting the problem of the project.

Activity 4.2

Summarize the 4Ws Problem Canvas in a Problem Statement template.

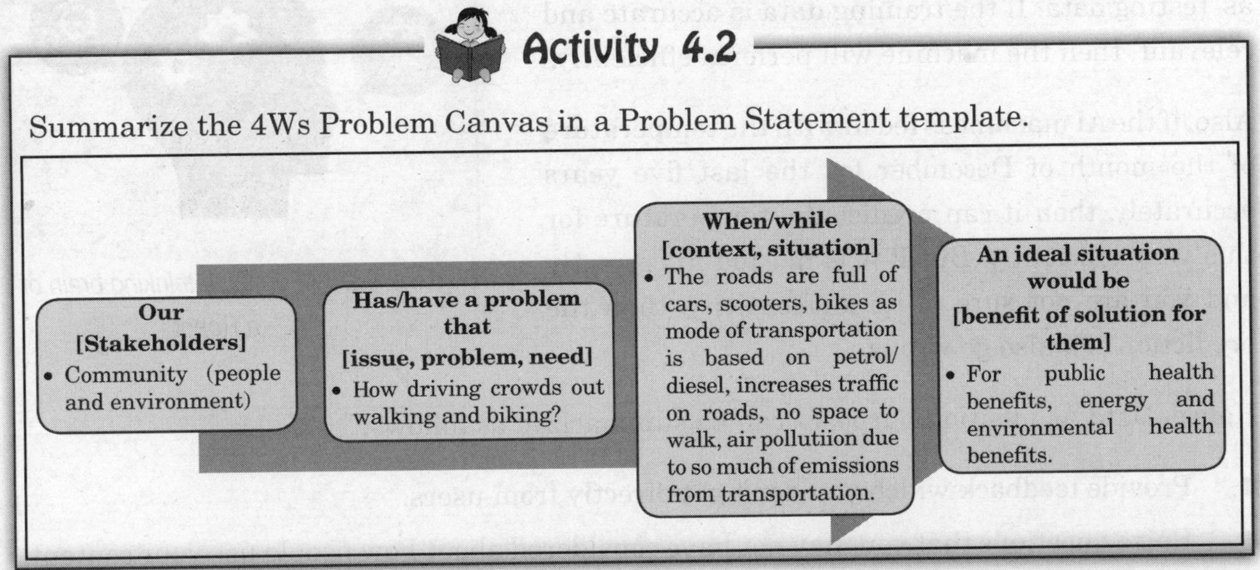

Data Acquisition is the second element in the AI Project Cycle which is used to collect data for the problem scoped and this data has to be reliable, authentic, and efficient. Before you begin with the data acquisition methods, let us talk about data.

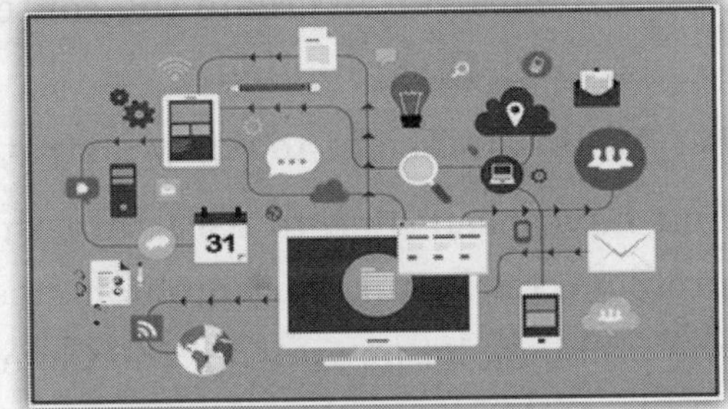
Figure 4.1: *Data Acquisition*

Data is the raw fact which when combined together to form information needs to be processed further for any kind of analysis. The Artificial Intelligence machine always works only if it has been fed in with some sample data to be processed to predict outputs further.

FACT BOT

In 1981, IBM introduced the IBM Personal Computer and Scientific Solutions introduced the first PC data acquisition products.

For example, if you want the artificially intelligent system to give access of the machine based on finger prints, then the machine has to be fed with the finger prints of the authorized person from all possible ways so that it can give access to only that person whose finger print matches with the system. The machine has to be trained with all the data (that is, fingerprints) for all those who will be given permission for accession. This data is known as Training data and while accessing using one's finger prints out of the set which is already fed in is known as Testing data. If the training data is accurate and relevant, then the machine will perform efficiently.

Figure 4.2: *AI-enabled thinking brain of a Robot*

Also, if the AI machine is fed in with the temperature of the month of December for the last five years accurately, then it can predict the temperature for this year efficiently. But if it is not fed in correctly and you are not sure of its authenticity, then the prediction can also go wrong.

Hence, Data Acquisition purposes can be summarized as follows:

- Provide feedback which you don't get directly from users.
- Raise questions that you may not have considered about how people use your content.
- Enables you to create the content wanted by your audience in contrast to what you thought they wanted.
- Gain an insight to apply a strategic approach for future planning.

You have been able to ascertain that data plays a very important role in solving any problem. Each and every problem has some of the factors associated with it. Once you have the problem, let us take out the factors that create the problem statement. To do this, yo u need to take out the factors, that is, data features of the problem scoped.

TIP BOT

Training data's output is available to model whereas testing data is the unseen data for which predictions have to be made.

Activity 4.3

Let us look back at Activity 4.2 and list down the data features required regarding the problem scoped. Data features required regarding your goal. How driving crowds out walking and biking?

Data Features

- Walking
- Biking
- Driving
- Safe streets
- Emissions

Once you list down the data features regarding the problem scoped, you have to collect data regarding these data features and also need to check that the sources from where you are collecting data are authentic and reliable for the machine to work efficiently. As you know by now that the data plays very important role in the AI Project Cycle. Therefore, the data acquired should be authentic and reliable to get the efficient results.

The data can be collected from various sources, for example:

- Newspapers
- Web Scraping
- Cameras
- Surveys
- Observations
- Application Program Interfaces (API)
- Questionnaires

Figure 4.3: *Scraping Data*

Most of the time, you use internet to collect the data for your project. You find various websites to collect the information regarding a particular topic. One website gives some information regarding the topic and the other gives some other information. Now, the question arises which information is correct, which is the authentic website to refer to for the data collection. Also, you have to understand the rules for copying data. You just cannot copy someone's data without any permission.

Using someone's data without permission is a cybercrime. So, there are websites from where you can take data, and these websites are authentic, reliable, and open-sourced which are hosted by government for public interest. These government portal websites are created in the public interest to help them to get general information regarding various common topics like health and wellness, money and taxes, electricity, water and local services, and so on.

Some of the open-sourced Indian government portals are:

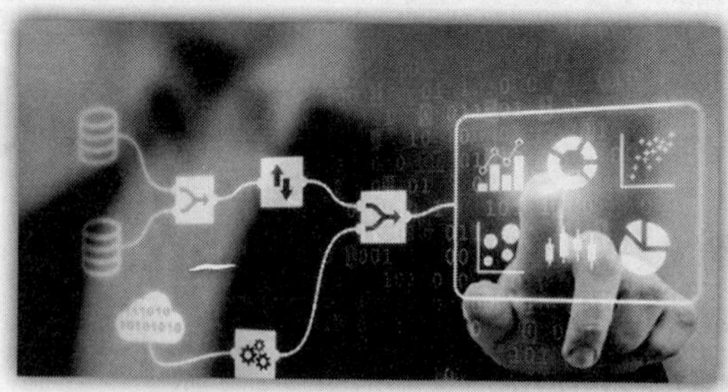

Figure 4.4: *Web Scraping*

- india.gov.in: Official website with access to information and services being provided by the Indian Government.
- data.gov.in: It is a platform for supporting open data initiative of Government of India.
- nic.in: National Informatics Centre.
- incometaxindia.gov.in: Income Tax Department – Tax law, rules, and notifications.
- indianrail.gov.in: The official website with information on trains, fares and availability.

MEMORY BOT

Artificial Intelligence can be allowed to replace a whole system, making all decisions end-to-end, or it can be used to enhance a specific process.

Open source website are the website from where you can get the information.

Activity 4.4

List down the ways of acquiring data for the project theme.

Project Goal: How driving crowds out walking and biking?

- https://www.epa.gov/transportation-air-pollution-and-climate-change/what-you-can-do-reduce-pollution-vehicles-and-engines - An official website of the US Government.
- Articles published on Twitter/Wikipedia/others
- Paper surveys
- Questionnaires
- User surveys (Survey Monkey,Type Form)
- Newsletters
- Blogs
- Facebook posts
- YouTube videos
- Publishing platforms (Hootsuite, sprinklr, and so on)
- Ad platforms
- Board displays

System Maps

The core of understanding the complexities of any system requires basic understanding of all elements that build up that system along with the nature of relationship among the elements of the system. All elements are interconnected. The concept of loops exists in the system which defines the causes and effects equation in the element relationships. The system outcome can easily change based on the changes you do in the system. You can either change the elements or change their relationships. The change in one factor affects the consequences of the other.

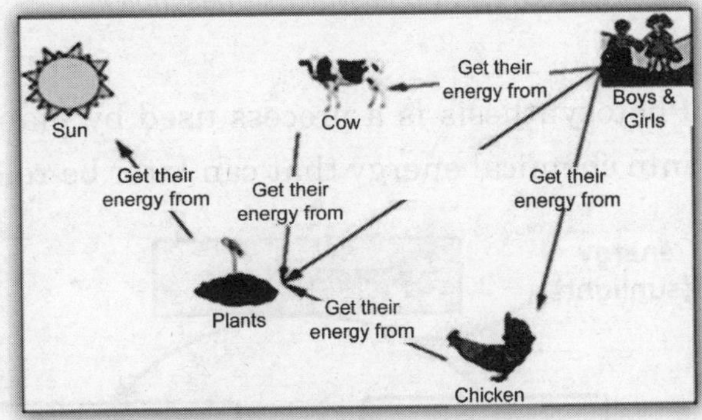

Figure 4.5: *System Map*

A loop in the system defines a chain of events which signifies the cause and effects amongst system elements. Two or more elements are connected with each other by directional arrows which signify the relationship between them. The longer arrow is referred as time delay; demonstrating the nature of relationship between them. The + and – signs with the arrows signify the relationship between them. A change in the system can be predicted with the change of elements or making a change in the relationship pattern to observe a different outcome.

Let us take the example of energy and photosynthesis to understand the concept of a working system with elements and relationships. All livings beings extract their energy from one form of food item or other. The energy changes its form in the food chain to maintain the ecological balance of the environment. Energy is a quantitative property which changes its form but is neither created nor destroyed. It is the power derived from the utilization of physical or chemical resources to provide light, heat or to work with machines. All elements in the energy cycle influence the energy output. Removing or changing any element relationship will imbalance the system.

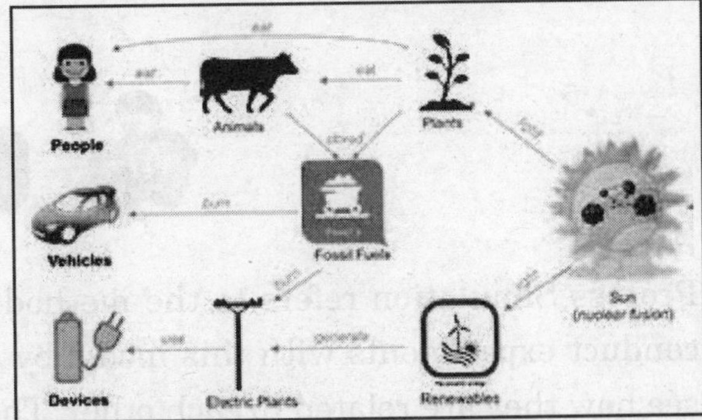

Figure 4.6: *Energy forms*

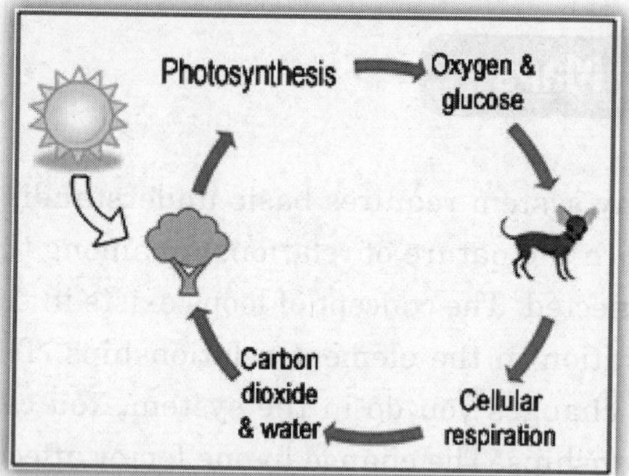

Figure 4.7: *Photosynthesis description*

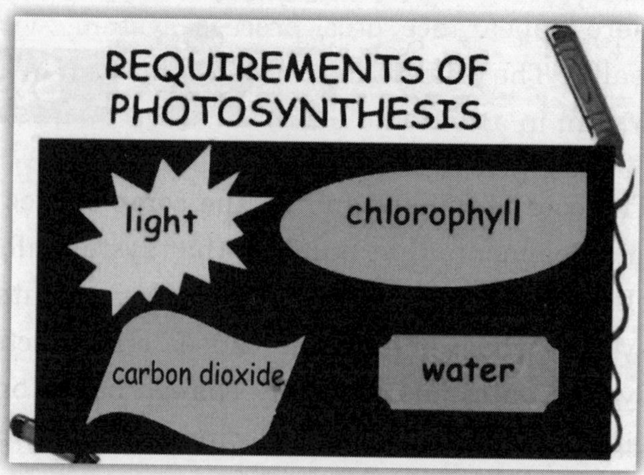

Figure 4.8: *Photosynthesis requirements*

Photosynthesis is a process used by plants and other organisms to convert light energy into chemical energy that can later be released to fuel the organisms' activities.

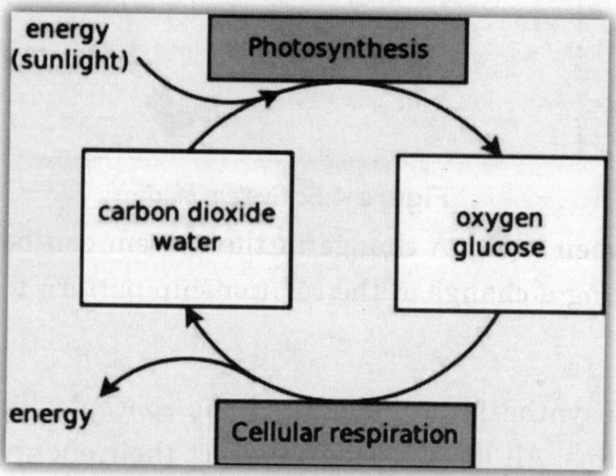

Figure 4.9: *Photosynthesis*

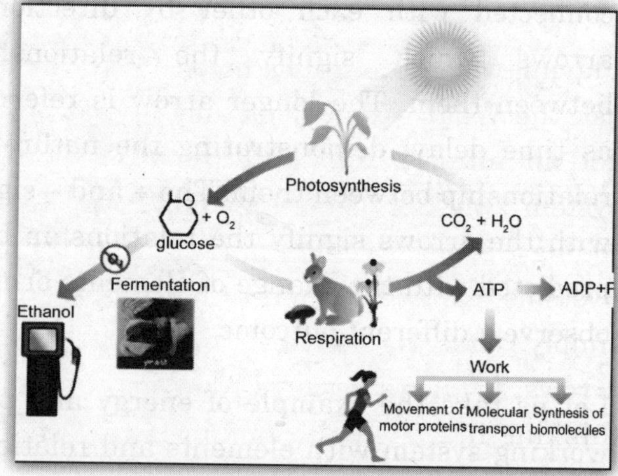

Figure 4.10: *Photosynthesis system map*

Process Simulation refers to the method of designing a model of a real system. You can conduct experiments with this model by changing the values of individual elements and see how they are related to each other. The purpose of such a change over is to understand the behavior of various operations of the system. In short, simulation lets us assume the mere appearance of a process system, without the reality. The conceptualization of the system shows the system in action and lets us observe the results based on multiple inputs. Some of the advantages can be seen in the adjoining diagram.

PROBLEM SOLVING

QUESTION ANSWERING

TIME OPTIMIZING

MONEY SAVING

Figure 4.11: *Advantages of simulation*

Online Process Simulation Portal

https://ncase.me/loopy/

LOOPY is an interactive tool for depicting thinking in complex, technological, sociological, ecological, political, or economic systems.

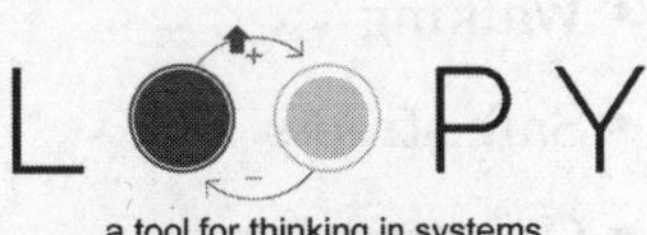

Figure 4.12: *LOOPY*

Playing with simulations helps ask the What if questions and get an intuition of how the system works. There is no coding experience required. Systems can be modelled by simply drawing circles and arrows. It allows us to go from thinking in systems to talking in systems.

The interface helps us add elements and draw arrows depicting relationships and visualize their cause and effect on the final outcomes.

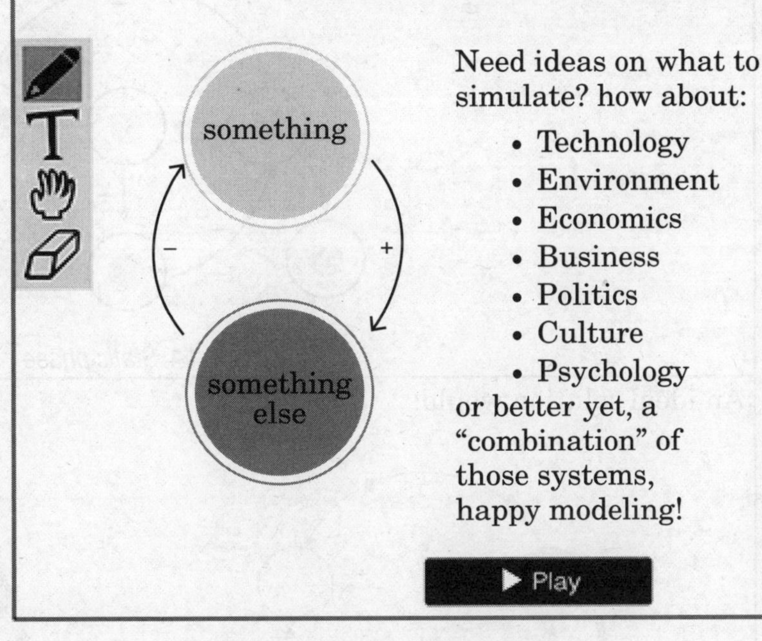

Figure 4.13: *LOOPY interface*

KNOWLEDGE BOT

In LOOPY, you can model systems by simply drawing circles & arrows, like a wee baby.

Activity 4.5

Let us revisit the 4W Problem Canvas for your selected theme and design a system map for the Problem Statement. Mention the system elements whose cause and effect relationship can change the outcomes for the system.

Problem statement: How driving crowds out walking and biking?

Elements of the system:

- Driving
- Biking
- Walking
- Safe streets
- Gas emissions

System Map: Using https://ncase.me/loopy/ interface

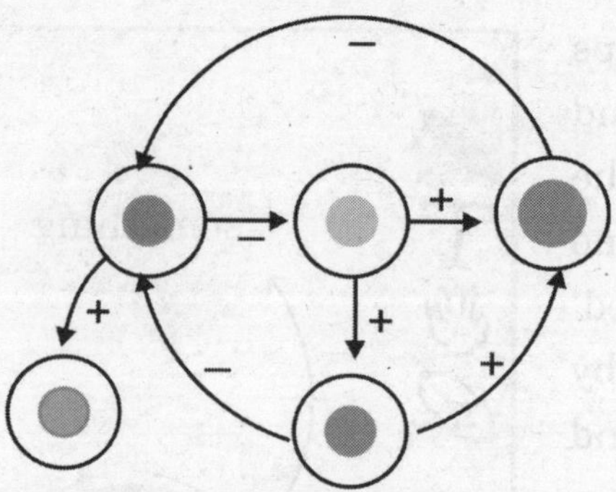

Figure 4.14 *Static phase*

An ideal solution would:

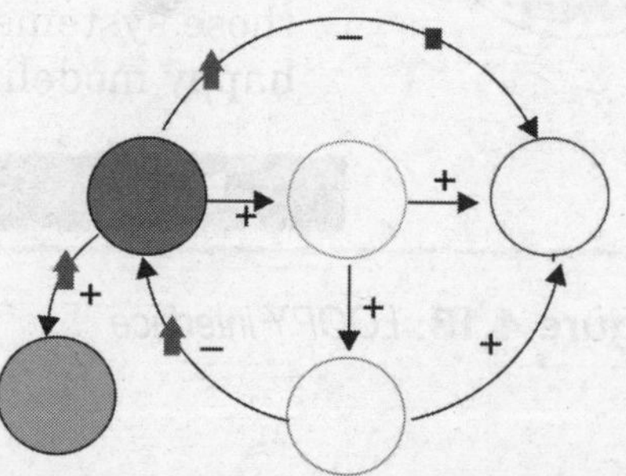

Figure 4.15 *Change of elements*

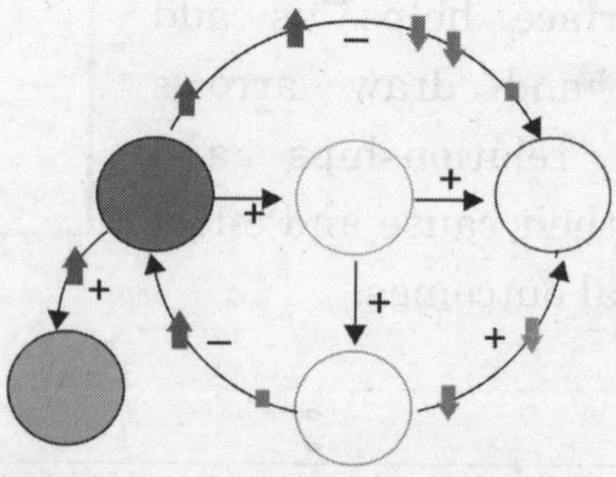

Figure 4.16 *Change of relationships*

Activity 4.6

Let us select a social theme and scope the problem. Design the 4W Problem Canvas for your selected theme for the Problem Statement. Mention the data points and data resources in the given graphic organizer. You can use the theme selected in the previous chapter here.

GOALS	• ______________________ • ______________________	
OUR	[stakeholders] • ______________ • ______________ • ______________	WHO
HAS/HAVE A PROBLEM THAT	[issue, problem, need] • ______________ • ______________ • ______________	WHAT
WHEN/ WHILE	[context, situation] • ______________ • ______________ • ______________	WHERE
AN IDEAL SOLUTION WOULD	[benefit of solution] • ______________ • ______________ • ______________	WHY

Problem Statement:

Elements of the system (Data features):

Data resources

Activity 4.7

Let us revisit the 4W Problem Canvas for your selected theme and design a system map for the Problem Statement. Mention the system elements whose cause and effect relationship can change the outcomes for the system.

Problem Statement:
Elements of the system:
System Map: Using https://ncase.me/loopy/ interface
Static phase
Change of elements/Change of relationships

TECH BOT

- **Data acquisition:** It is defined as the process of collecting and organizing information.
- **Training data:** It is an initial set of data used to help a program understand how to apply technologies like neural networks to learn and produce sophisticated results.
- **Open source website:** It is the government website from where you can get the information.
- **Simulation:** A simulation is an approximate imitation of the operation of a process or system; that represents its operation over time.
- **Loopy:** It is an interactive loop which can be used to play with simulations in real time without using any code.

Recap Bot

- Data is the raw fact which is organized together to form information that needs to be processed further for analysis and data visualization.
- The Artificial Intelligence machine works on the data fed into the machine which is known as the training data and the output/prediction given by the AI machine is the testing data.
- Training data is used to give the machine a set of inputs on which the machine will be assessed later on. The training data needs to be reliable, authentic, and accurate for the AI machine to work efficiently.
- Testing data is used to assess the AI machine for its efficiency and performance.
- Each problem is associated directly or indirectly with some of the factors. These factors are known as data features.
- Data features can be collected from various sources like newspapers, cameras, observations, surveys, questionnaires, and so on.
- Open-sourced websites are the government portals from where the information can be used and referred to. These websites are authentic, accurate, and reliable.
- Some of the open-sourced websites are india.gov.in, nic.in, incometaxindia.gov.in.
- All elements in the system are interconnected and one has to understand the elements and relationships between the elements to understand the system.
- The concept of a loop defines a chain of events in the system and relationships between them. The change in one element affects the consequences in the other.
- As the elements are interdependent, so removing or changing any element in the system will imbalance the whole system.
- Simulation refers to the method of designing a model in a real world where you conduct experiments by changing the values of individual elements and see the effect in the other elements.

A. Multiple choice questions.

1. Which one of the following stands for the second W in the 4Ws Problem Canvas?
   a. Who
   b. What
   c. Why
   d. Where
2. Which one of the following is used to collect data for the AI Project Cycle?
   a. Data Acquisition
   b. Modeling
   c. Evaluation
   d. Project Scoping
3. Data means:
   a. Information
   b. Meaningful information
   c. Visuals
   d. Raw facts
4. Training Data is used in the AI machine for:
   a. Predictions
   b. Testing the model
   c. Giving input to the machine
   d. Processing
5. The training data for AI machine needs to be:
   a. Reliable
   b. Accurate
   c. Correct
   d. All of the above
6. Which of the following is a cybercrime?
   a. Taking someone's notebook
   b. Fighting with someone
   c. Using someone's data from the internet without permission
   d. None of the above

B. Fill in the blanks.

1. Data acquisition is used to ___________ data that has to be authentic and reliable.
2. The second stage in the AI Project Cycle is ________________.
3. A _________ in the system defines a chain of events which signifies the cause and effects among system elements.
4. _____________ is an interactive tool which can be worked without any knowledge of coding.
5. ______________ refers to the method of designing a model of a real system.

6. ________________ is a process used by plants and other organisms to convert light energy into chemical energy.

7. Copying someone's data from the website without permission is a ____________.

C. Match the following.

	Column A		Column B
1.	Data Acquisition	i.	Factors associated with problem
2.	Raw facts	ii.	Interconnected
3.	Data features	iii.	Designing a model of a real system
4.	Testing data	iv.	Collect data
5.	All elements	v.	Data
6.	Energy	vi.	Accurate, reliable, and correct
7.	Simulation	vii.	An interactive tool
8.	LOOPY	viii.	Quantitative property

D. Answer the following questions.

1. Differentiate between training data and testing data.
2. Unscramble the following letters to form a word.
   a. AADT
   b. HEIPHOOSSSYNTT
3. Define the following:
   a. Data Acquisition
   b. Data features
   c. System maps
   d. LOOPY
4. Write the data features for the following:
   a. Fossil fuels
   b. Photosynthesis
5. Name any two open-sourced government portals.
6. Name any four sources to collect information.

Lab Activity

Create the pattern radio: Whale song

It's a new kind of tool that visualizes audio at a vast scale and uses AI to make it easy to explore and make discoveries.

1. Go to the link: https://patternradio.withgoogle.com/

   The following page appears.

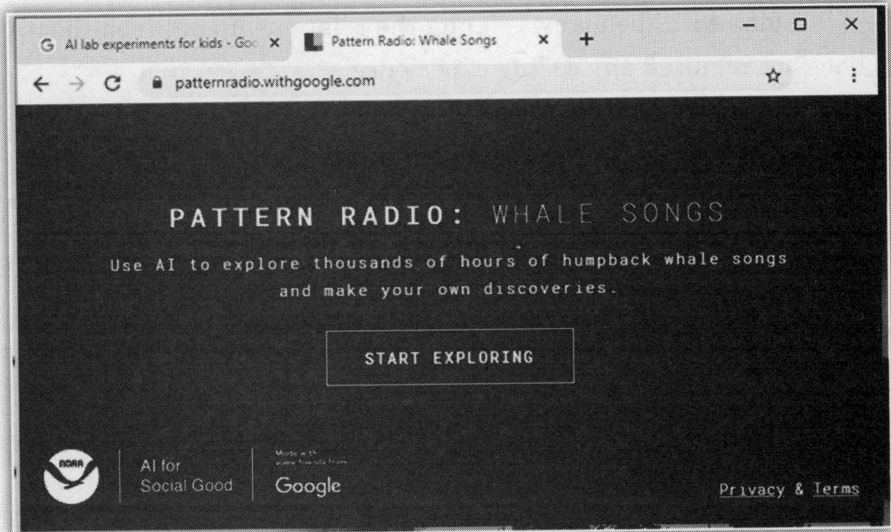

2. Click on the START EXPLORING button. The following screen appears.
3. The desired whale song will be produced.

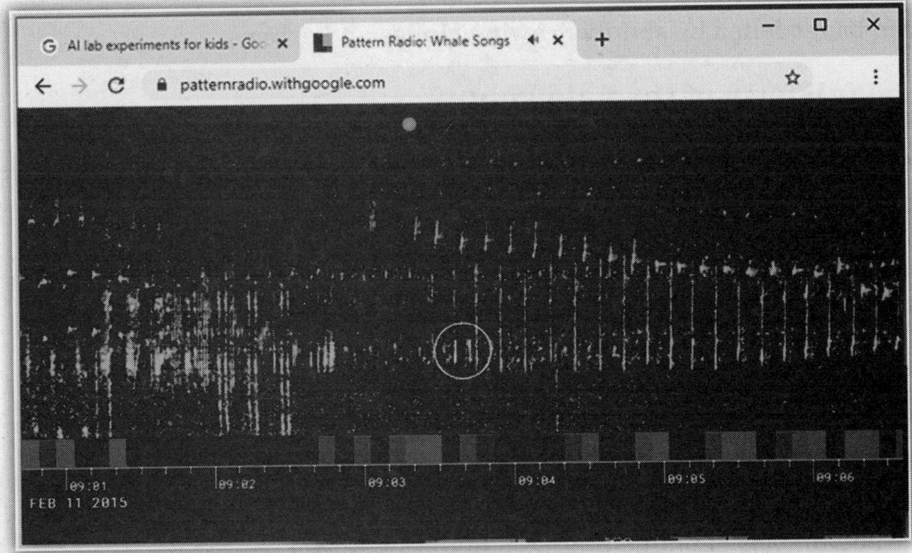

Worksheet

A. Fill in the blanks.

1. ____________________is used to pen down all the elements that are directly or indirectly affecting the problem of the project.
2. ____________________is used to collect data for the problem scoped and this data has to be reliable, authentic and efficient.
3. Removing or ____________________any element relationship will imbalance the system.
4. The + and _______signs with the arrows signify the relationship between them.
5. ____________does not required any coding experience.
6. ___________________is an open-sourced website.
7. All elements in ____________________are interconnected.
8. Energy is a______________property which changes its form but is neither created nor destroyed.

B. State whether the following statements are True or False.

1. In System Map, you can either change the elements or change their relationship.
2. In LOOPY, the longer arrow is referred as time delay.
3. India.gov.in is a platform for supporting open data initiative of Government of India.
4. Data can be collected from survey only.
5. You can copy someone's data without any permission.
6. Accessing using one's finger prints out of the set which is already fed in is known as training data.
7. The official website with information on trains, fares and availability is known as nic. in.
8. Systems can be modelled by simply drawing circles and arrows.

C. Write down the full form of the following.

1. NIC ____
2. API ____
3. gov ____

D. Answer the following questions.

1. Write down the various purposes of data acquisition.
2. How data can be collected from various sources?
3. Explain some of the open-sourced Indian government portals.
4. Explain one example of System Maps.
5. Discuss the advantages of online process simulation portal.

QUIZ CARD

Multiple choice questions.

1. Which data is used to assess the AI machine for its efficiency and performance?
   a. Testing ☐ b. Training ☐
   c. Both a. and b. ☐ d. None of these ☐
2. Which tool is used to play with simulation in real time without using any code?
   a. Simulation ☐ b. Online portal ☐
   c. System Maps ☐ d. LOOPY ☐
3. india.gov.in is a:
   a. Closed-sourced website ☐ b. Double website ☐
   c. Open-sourced website ☐ d. None of these ☐
4. ________________is organised together to form the information.
   a. Data ☐ b. Source ☐
   c. Useful information ☐ d. None of these ☐
5. Which data is used to give machine a set of inputs on which the machine will be assessed later on?
   a. Training ☐ b. Testing ☐
   c. Loopy ☐ d. Both a. and b. ☐
6. The change in one element affect the consequences in the other is known as:
   a. Simulation ☐ b. Online portal ☐
   c. System Maps ☐ d. LOOPY ☐
7. ________________allows us to go from thinking in systems to talking in systems.
   a. Simulation ☐ b. Online portal ☐
   c. System Maps ☐ d. LOOPY ☐
8. ____________________let us assume the mere appearance of a process, without the reality.
   a. Simulation ☐ b. Online portal ☐
   c. System Maps ☐ d. LOOPY ☐
9. All elements in the energy cycle influence the energy______________.
   a. Input ☐ b. Output ☐
   c. Both a. and b. ☐ d. None of these ☐
10. Two or more elements are connected with each other by ____________arrows which signify the relationship between them.
    a. Directional ☐ b. Bi-directional ☐
    c. Both a. and b. ☐ d. None of these ☐

5 Data Exploration

Structure Bot

In this chapter, we will discuss the following topics:

- Introduce different types of data visualisation methods
- Elaborate multiple data visualization techniques
- Design a graph as per a given data set
- Compare and contrast different types of data visualisation methods
- Explore everyday examples of applications using Data Exploration such as Spotify, Google Maps

Objective Bot

After studying this chapter, you should be able to:

- Summarize the need for data visualization
- To interpret and classify data visualization into different categories
- Illustrate multiple graphical tools for representing acquired data such as charts, graphs, mind maps, sketches, and so on
- To construct and evaluate patterns and trends effectively

The term visualization is defined as a creation of a mental image or something. In context of data, data visualization can be perceived as the representation of a set of information as a chart, process, diagram or a picture. Let us revisit a few concepts covered in the previous chapters to further delve into a proper understanding of the chapter title.

Activity 5.1

Match the following statements as per your understanding.

Data Acquisition	⇒		⇐	Valid option for Data Acquisition
Web Scraping	⇒		⇐	Part of Problem Scoping stage
For X → Y, X – Y means	⇒		⇐	If X increases, Y decreases
4Ws Canvas	⇒		⇐	Second stage of AI Project Cycle

In generic terms, information is processed data. Data or raw facts are the important element basis for any process, cycle or relationship. The time spent exploring a set of data helps set a premise for predicting the sense of data. Data visualization helps us comprehend the trends and patterns present in data to decide your strategies and course of action in your AI Project Cycle. Another added advantage is the easy communication of the said facts in a visual representation.

Data visualization is an integral part of competitive intelligence that encompasses data analysis to help gain an edge in its better understanding. Data is a complex entity. It requires a necessary skill to identify the patterns in it to comprehend the trends.

Definition Bot

Data visualization is the graphical representation of information and data.

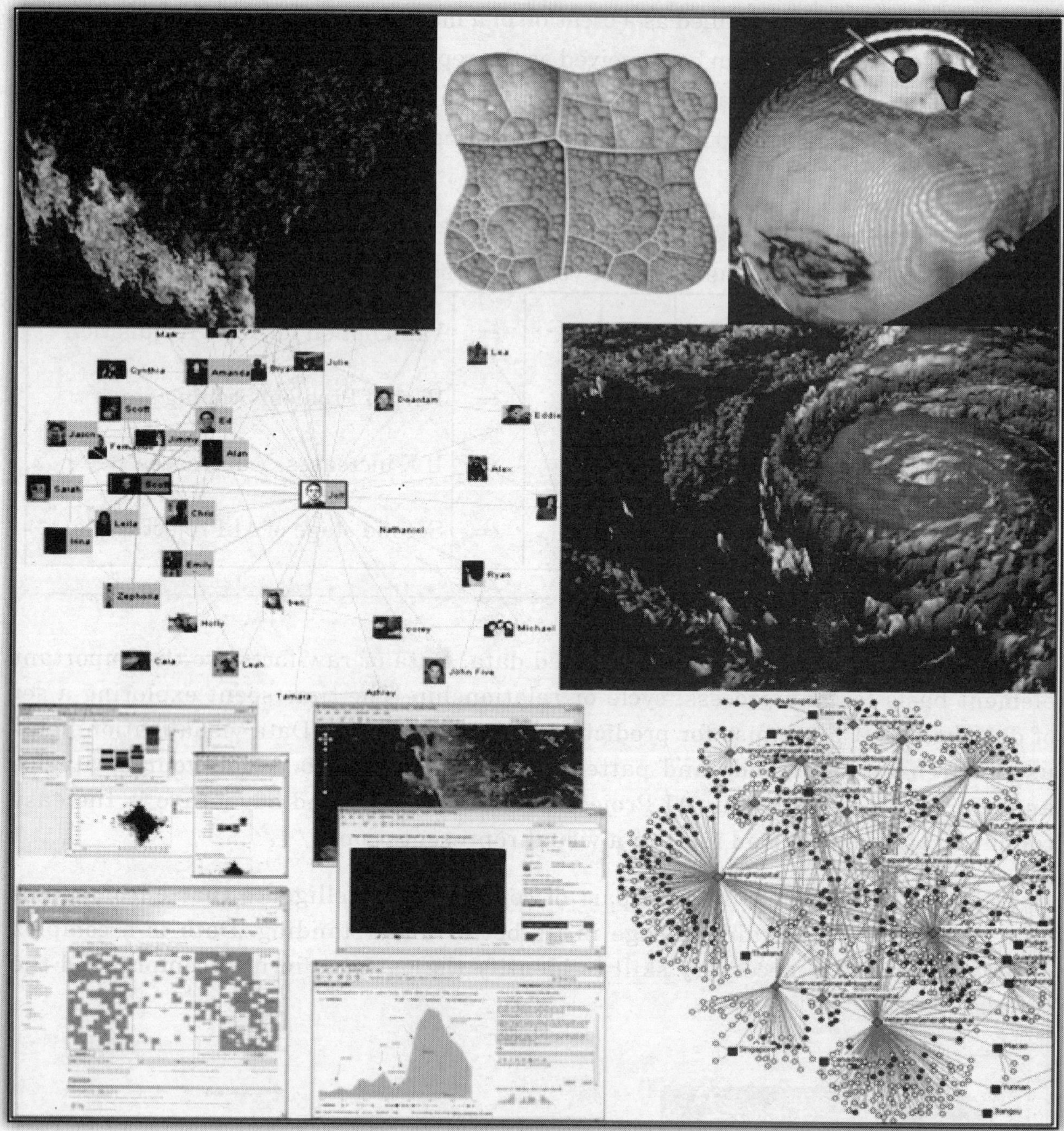

Figure 5.1: *Multiple ways to represent Data*

Activity 5.2

Let us identify and name the types of graphical charts in the given table.

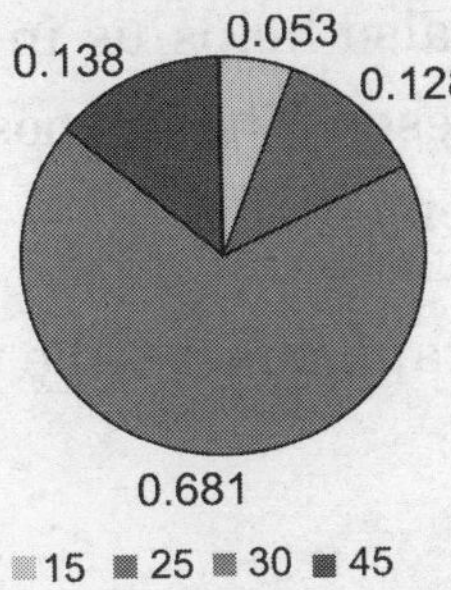 0.138 0.053 0.128 0.681 ■15 ■25 ■30 ■45	
 Frequency 16 14 12 10 8 6 4 2 0	
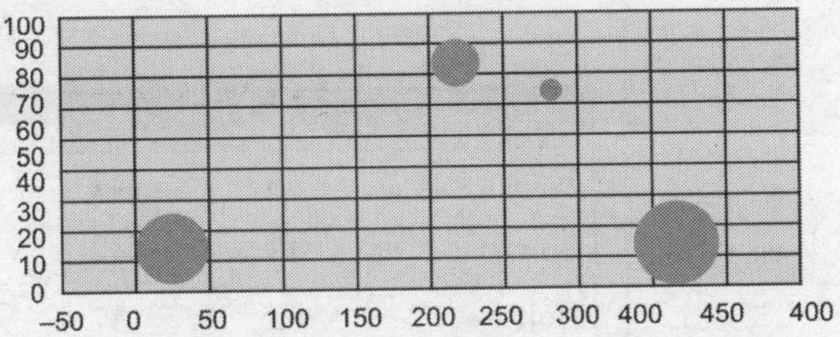 100 90 80 70 60 50 40 30 20 10 0 –50 0 50 100 150 200 250 300 400 450 400	
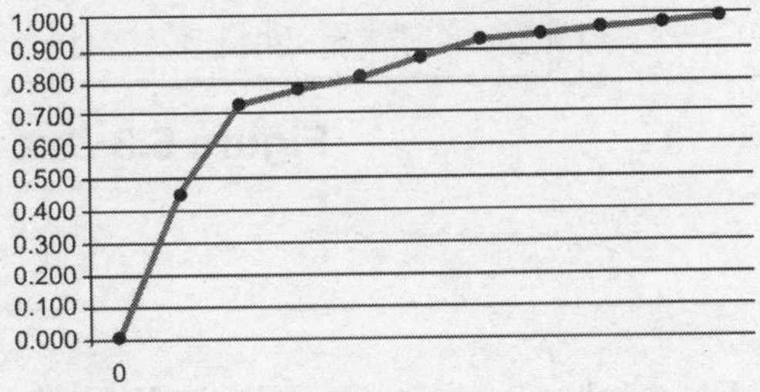 1.000 0.900 0.800 0.700 0.600 0.500 0.400 0.300 0.200 0.100 0.000 0	
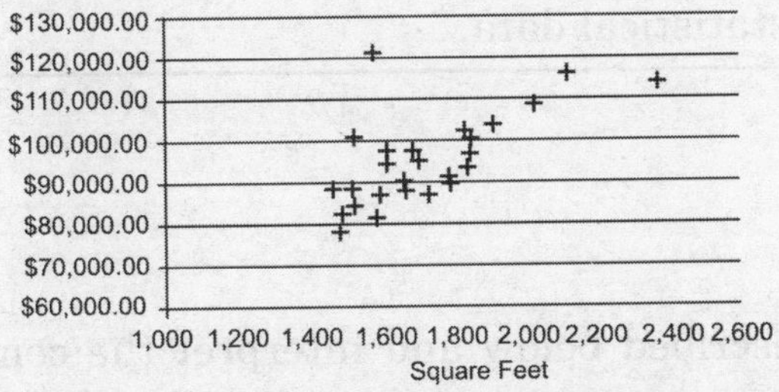 $130,000.00 $120,000.00 $110,000.00 $100,000.00 $90,000.00 $80,000.00 $70,000.00 $60,000.00 1,000 1,200 1,400 1,600 1,800 2,000 2,200 2,400 2,600 Square Feet	

How to decide which graph chart to use for data visualisation?

The deciding factor for finalising which graph chart to use depends on the nature of data. Significantly, the purpose of graphical representation also helps us in getting the sense of trends, relationships and patterns to reach a hypotheses. The purpose helps us set the path to look at multiple solution for your Problem Statement.

Some questions which help us in deciding the type of graph chart to be used are:

- Do you wish to compare values?
- Do you wish to see the composition of something?
- Do you wish to understand the distribution of data?
- Are you interested in analysing trends in the data set?
- Do you wish to understand the relationship between value sets?

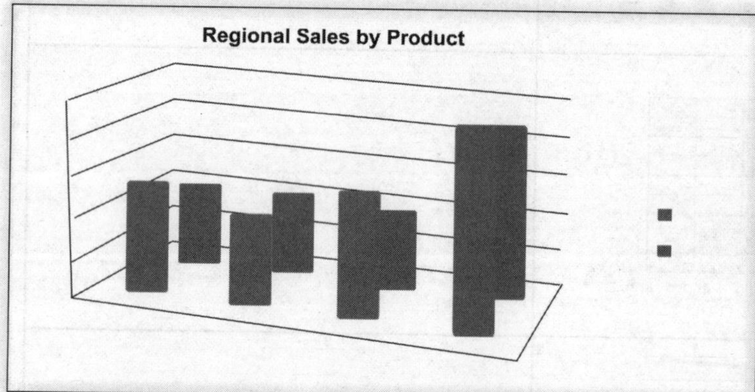

Figure 5.2 *Graph Chart*

Region	Book	DVD	Total
East	58	42	98
North	43	42	95
South	62	37	99
West	100	90	190
Total	261	211	472

Figure 5.3 *Data*

FACT BOT

In 1644, Michael Florent Van Langren, a Flemish astronomer, is believed to have provided the first visual representation of statistical data.

How to read a graph chart?

It is helpful to follow a two-step process described below and interpret the conclusions after having made a graph.

1. **Step One:**

   Describe: This part explains how the figure/table is set up.

   a. Representation on the axes: This step defines the x-axis and y-axis. The x-axis runs horizontally and represents the independent variable; which is the value being manipulated. The dependent variable "depends" upon x-axis and is plotted on the vertical y-axis.

   b. Units on the axes: This step helps us quantify the relationships between variables.

   c. Scale on each axis.

   d. Symbols and legend on a figure: They might be represented by different symbols, dotted lines, colour patterns, and so on.

   e. Observe the patterns in the data.

2. **Step Two:**

   Interpret: This part explains how to interpret the data. It is important to understand how to draw conclusions from the patterns described. You could draw a few inferences based on the graph by asking some of the following questions:

   a. Does the graph support or reject the study's hypothesis? It can be helpful to sketch out what the graph would look like if the hypothesis was supported and what it would look like if it was not.

   b. Are there alternative explanations for the pattern in the data?

   c. Do new or unexpected results generate new hypotheses?

https://datavizcatalogue.com/

The website explores multiple types of data visualisation techniques which can be used to depict the data. The charts are easily categorised by their data visualization functions or by what has to be communicated to an audience. A singular type of chart can be used for both analysis and communication needs.

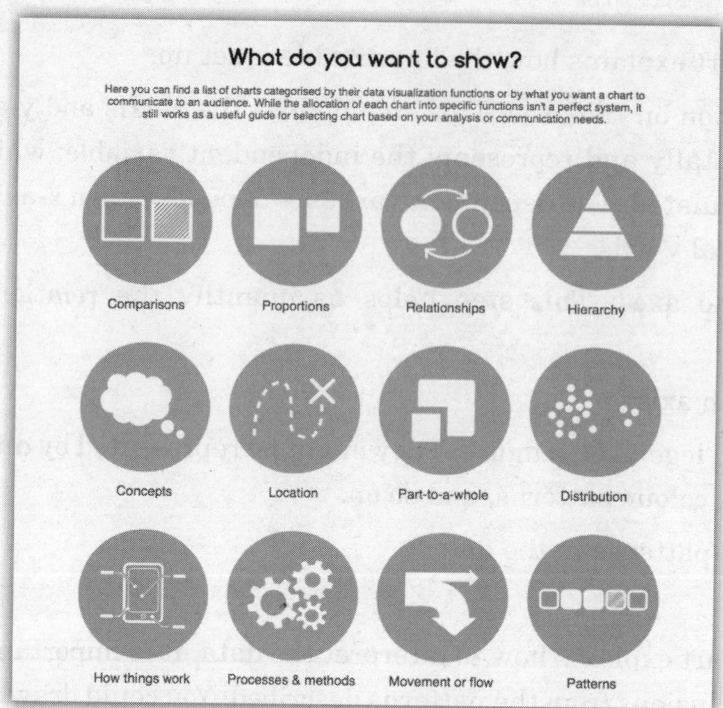

Figure 5.4 *Data visualization catalogue*

Figure 5.5 *Data visualization catalogue - Comparisons*

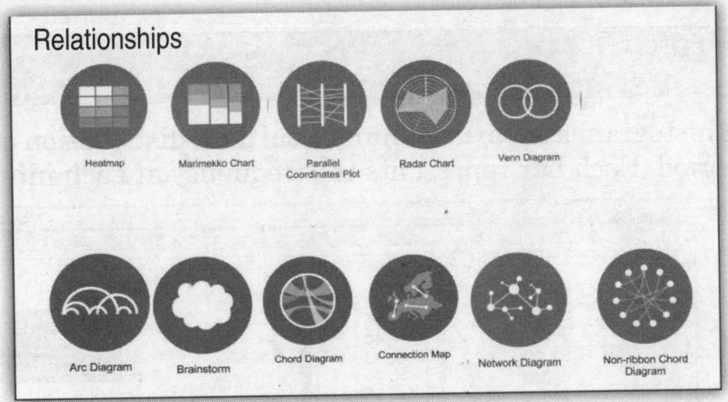

Figure 5.6 *Data visualization catalogue- relationships*

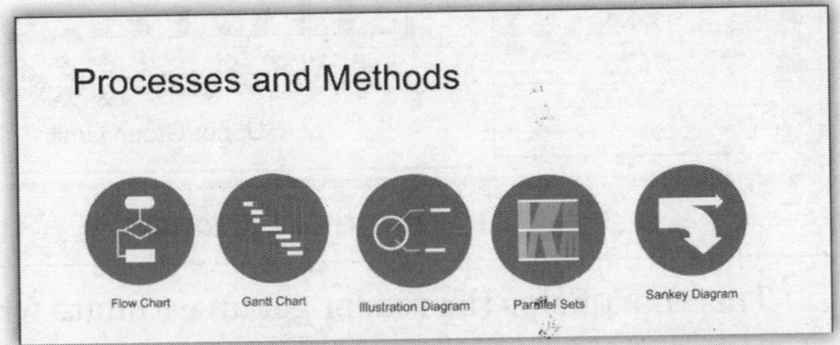

Figure 5.7 *Data visualization catalogue – Processes and Methods*

Exploring a Few of the Data Visualization Techniques

<table>
<tr><th colspan="2">Bar Graph</th></tr>
<tr><td>Description</td><td>A bar graph chart is used to show a comparison among different items horizontally or vertically over an interval.</td></tr>
<tr><td>Example</td><td> 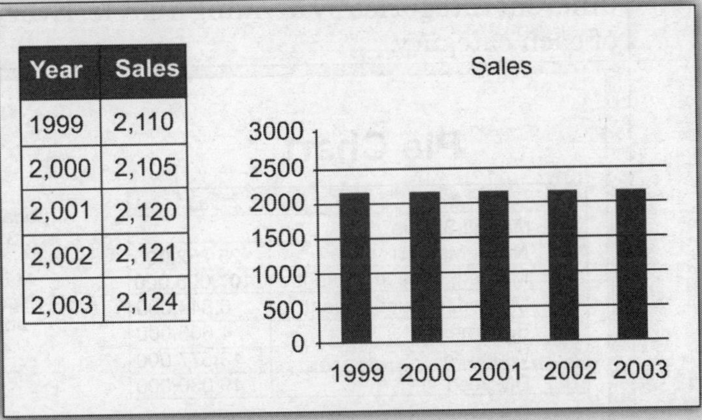
<table>
<tr><th>Year</th><th>Sales</th></tr>
<tr><td>1999</td><td>2,110</td></tr>
<tr><td>2,000</td><td>2,105</td></tr>
<tr><td>2,001</td><td>2,120</td></tr>
<tr><td>2,002</td><td>2,121</td></tr>
<tr><td>2,003</td><td>2,124</td></tr>
</table>

Figure 5.8 Bar Graph Chart</td></tr>
<tr><td>Purpose</td><td>• A bar graph chart works with specific categories on one axis and discrete value scale on the other.
• It helps the reader answer the question of how many.
• It improves readability as it is a diagrammatic comparison of discrete values.</td></tr>
</table>

Histogram

Description

A histogram displays the numerical data distribution over a certain time period. Each bar represents the frequency at each interval.

Example

	A	B
1	Upper Group Limit	Frequency
2	0	0
3	13000	42
4	25000	26
5	35000	5
6	52000	3
7	65000	6
8	78000	5
9	91000	3
10	104000	3
11	117000	1
12	130000	2
13		0

Histogram

10 groups with a $ 13,000 group width

Frequency

Upper Group Limit

Figure 5.9 *Histogram*

Purpose

- This chart helps the reader get an estimate where the values are placed over a continuous interval.
- It helps the user identify the gaps and extremes.
- It is different from a bar chart as it represents frequency distribution of values over a continuous interval.

Pie Chart

Description

A pie chart presents data by depicting percentages/proportion amongst different categories by dividing a circle. Every arc represents a proportion of each category.

Example

Pie Chart

	A	B
18	**Marital Status**	
19	Never Married	25,752.000
20	Married, spouse present	107,008,000
21	Married, spouse absent	6,844,000
22	Separated	4,605,000
23	Widowed	13,577,000
24	Divorced	19,030,000

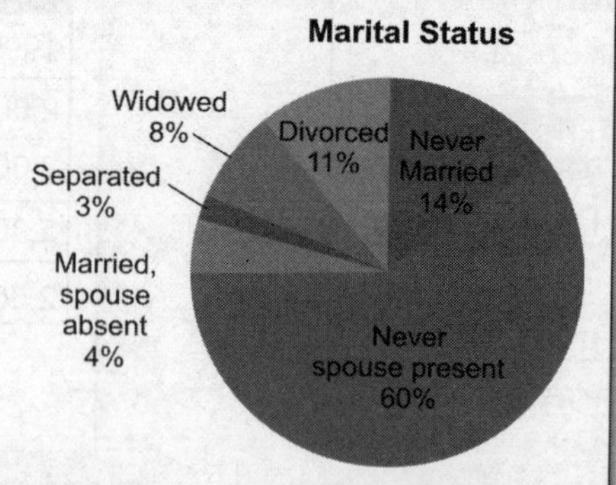

Figure 5.10 *Pie Chart*

MEMORY BOT

Histogram plots the data by chunking it into intervals called 'bins'.

Purpose	• It gives the reader a quick idea of the proportional distribution of data. • The chart is most helpful with smaller amount of data only. • It is visually simpler than other types of graphs.

Line Graph	
Description	A line graph depicts quantitative values over a continuous time interval. The direction of the lines display an indicative trend of the dataset.
Example	**Figure 5.11** *Line graph chart*
Purpose	• The line's journey in the graph can create patterns that reveal trends in the given data. • There can be a presence of more than one data series, which helps the reader compare individual lines to understand different categories of data better.

TIP BOT

Always choose the simplest way to convey your information.

Activity 5.3

Explore the data visualization catalogue at https:// datavizcatalogue.com/ to understand multiple techniques. Collate your understanding about any such two techniques in the given graphic organizer.

Data Visualization Technique 1:	
Description	
Example	
Purpose	• • •

Data Visualization Technique 2:	
Description	
Example	
Purpose	• • •

Tools to Generate Visualisation

- MS Excel
- Apple Numbers
- Google Charts
- Google Docs
- OnlineChartTool.com
- Python Graph gallery

Data Visualization: An example

Once the data regarding the problem is collected, the next step is to put that data in a meaningful form. The step will be required to analyse the data for identifying patterns and trends in the dataset. Hence, you start with understanding the data, scoping the problem and extracting meaningful authentic data. You explore the data and present it using different graphs. The hypotheses which helps us in taking strategic steps in solving your problem statement.

Figure 5.12 *Figuring out data Visualization steps*

Activity 5.4

Let us identify a problem statement: Air Pollution. Design the AI Project Cycle steps learnt so far to depict predicted trends and strategies required.

Step 1: Background information: Air Pollution is one of the major issues which you are dealing with nowadays. You have been observing that the air quality after Diwali deteriorates. You can refer to different sources of information regarding the causes of air pollution like newspaper, internet, news channel, and so on. At the same time, you should also know the effects of air pollution in your physical health and environment as a whole.

Step 2: Let us look at the newspaper article in Figure 5.13.1 and a picture of a graph in Figure 5.13.2 showing the air quality of Delhi.

Air quality is expected to improve on Thursday; people told to avoid outdoor physical activities

The air quality of Delhi worsened to "severe" category on Tuesday, with an Air Quality Index (AQI) of 413 at 8.30 a.m., according to the Central Pollution Control Board (CPCB). The air quality is expected to improve to "very poor" category on Thursday.

'Severe' air quality can cause respiratory problems to healthy people and serious health impact on people with lung or heart diseases, according to authorities.

Figure 5.13.1 *Newspaper article*

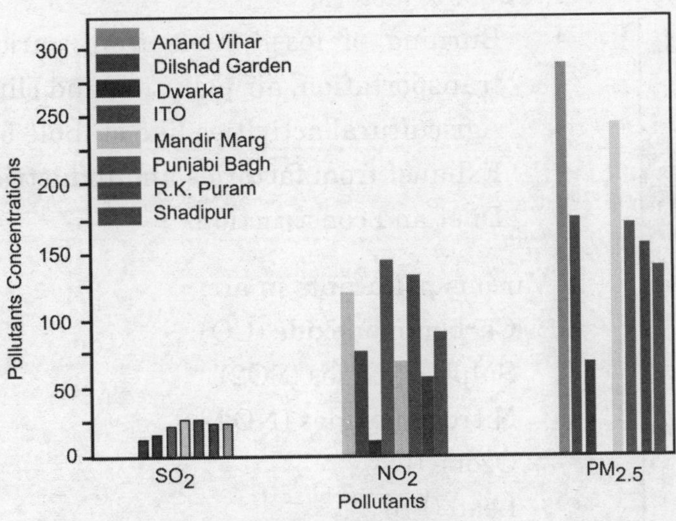

Figure 5.13.2 *Graph*

Which figure gives more information to us, is easy to depict and understand?

The information can easily be depicted and understood using figure 5.13.2. Using this figure, one can easily tell that there are majorly three pollutants which are used to calculate the Air Quality Index with their concentration level in a particular area. It is clearly illustrated in the figure above that how the concentration of one pollutant varies from one area to another.

The graph is a pictorial form of representing whole lot of information which gives clear picture of the air quality. In this graph, it is showing the various components of air pollutants and also the minimum and maximum value of it in the air.

Various websites to check the air quality data are:

- dpccairdata.com by the Delhi Pollution Control Committee, Govt. of NCT of Delhi.
- cpcb.nic.in by Central Pollution Control Board (CPCB) India.

Step 3: Let us recall what you have already done in the previous chapters with regard to collection of data and then use it for tabulating it to create Chart/ Graph. Mention a few data features of air quality.

The air quality can be referred either using the factors causing it or checking the levels of pollutants in the air.

Data features of air quality can be taken care in the following two ways:

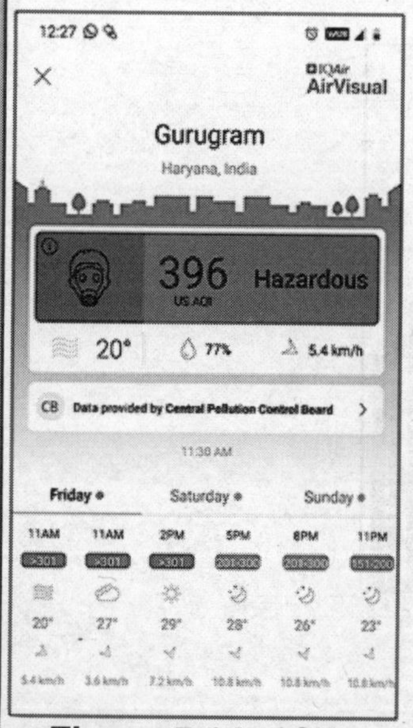

Figure 5.14: *AQI level*

1. Causing factors:
   - Burning of fossil fuels from various sources like transportation, air pollution and climate change.
   - Agricultural activities like stubble burning.
   - Exhaust from factories and industries.
   - Dust and construction.

2. Various pollutants in air:
   - Carbon monoxide (CO)
   - Sulphur oxides (SO2)
   - Nitrogen oxides (NO2)
   - Ozone (O3)
   - Lead (Pb)
   - PM (Particulate Matter)

Step 4: Tabulate the data regarding the main reasons of air pollution and create a pie chart using that data so as to understand it better.

Data for the sources of air pollution are:

Domestic Cooking	7%
Diesel Generators	9%
Transport	14%
Stubble burning	17%
Dust & Construction	45%
Industries	45%

Pie chart for the data collected:

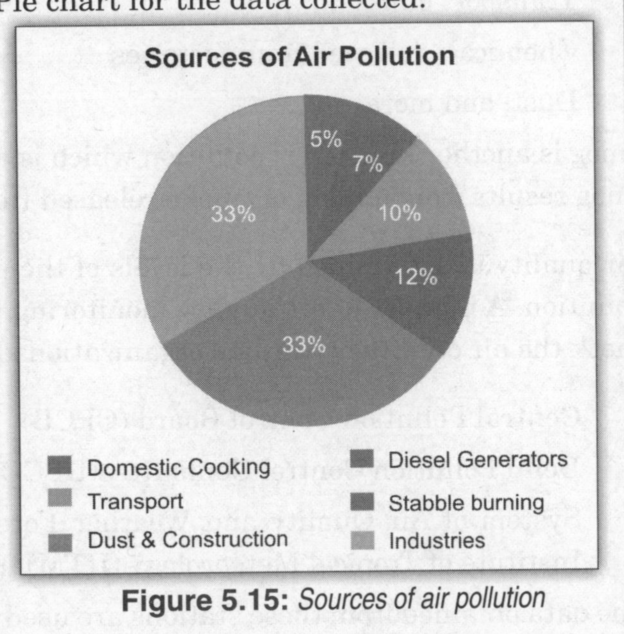

Figure 5.15: *Sources of air pollution*

Brief description

Air contains oxygen which makes life possible on earth.

Air pollution refers to release of gases into the atmosphere which imbalances the components of the air, affect the health of human beings and imbalance the nature of the planet as a whole.

These hazardous gases include:

- Sulphur dioxide
- Nitrogen dioxide
- Carbon monoxide
- Particulate Matter

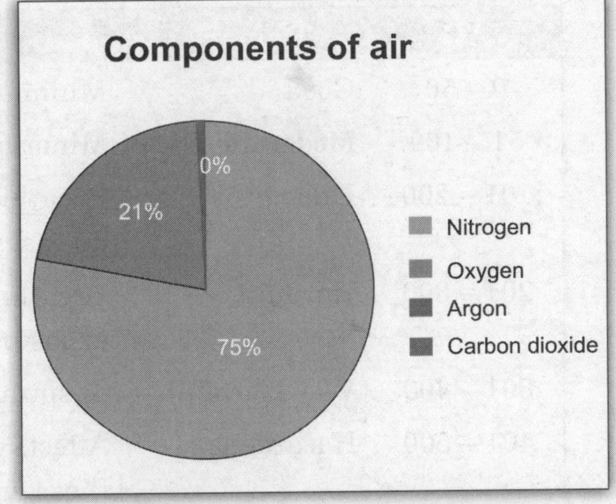

Figure 5.16: *Components of air*

Various sources of these gases are emitted into the air from:

- Stubble burning
- Transport emission
- Chemicals released from factories
- Dust, and more

Smog is another kind of air pollution which is a mixture of smoke and fog. But these days, smog results from mixing of smoke released from coal burning and sulphur dioxide.

Air quality is determined by the levels of the pollutants so as to understand the trend of pollution. A number of air quality monitoring stations are placed across the city so as to check the air quality by various organizations like:

- Central Pollution Control Board (CPCB)
- Delhi Pollution Control Committee(DPCC)
- System of Air Quality and Weather Forecasting and Research (SAFAR) of Indian Institute of Tropical Meteorology (IITM)

The data obtained from these stations are used for the determination of Air Quality Index.

Air Quality Index (AQI) is a tool which is used to monitor the air quality in urban cities on a real-time basis to spread awareness for the general public. The AQI measures the air quality on five air pollutants (Particulate matter, sulphur dioxide, carbon monoxide, nitrogen dioxide and ozone) on the scale of 0 to 500.

The level of PM 2.5 in the air detects the quality of air for your health. Following are the index levels and possible health impacts:

AQ	Remark	Possible Health Impacts
0 – 50	Good	Minimal impact
51 – 100	Moderate	Minor breathing, discomfort
101 – 200	Unhealthy	Breathing issues to those who have asthma or heart diseases
201 – 300	Harmful	Breathing issues to those who have prolonged exposure
301 – 400	Very Harmful	Respiratory illness on prolonged exposure
401 – 500	Hazardous	Affects healthy people and seriously impacts on those with existing diseases

Activity 5.5

Let us tabulate the data for the major pollutants (PM2.5, PM10, O_3, NO_2, SO_2, CO) from 1st November - 10th November 2019 and create bar graph using it. Data for this activity is collected from aqicn.org/city/delhi/r.k.-puram/ in any of the spreadsheet form as shown below.

Dates	PM2.5	PM10	O_3	NO_2	SO_2	CO
1/11/2019	260	430	15	27	4	10
2/11/2019	370	281	11	17	5	10
3/11/2019	288	561	11	16	5	10
4/11/2009	474	206	17	15	5	9
5/11/2019	290	149	18	15	6	10
6/11/2019	250	113	14	14	5	11
7/11/2019	155	171	8	5	5	9
8/11/2019	222	145	17	3	5	12
9/11/2019	199	131	17	9	5	8
10/11/2019	188	145	22	13	6	14

Once the data is tabulated, let us create the following graph using this data:

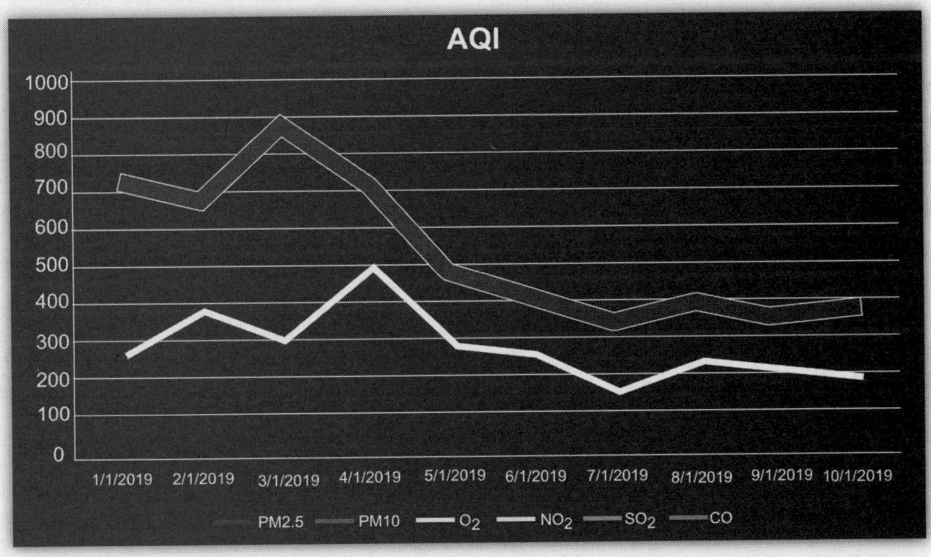

Figure 5.17: *AQI Chart for a given dataset*

The AQI tools are actually collecting real time data and then using the previous data it is predicting the trends. Artificial Intelligence is playing a major role for meteorology department in collecting the data and then analysing of data to predict weather in the form of weather forecasts.

Activity 5.6

Go through the Indian Meteorological department website: http://www.imd.gov.in. Write about the types of services provided by this website.

Service	______________________
	______________________
	______________________

Activity 5.7

Write the various ways with the help of which you can solve the problem of air pollution.

- Use of solar panels at home.
- Use of energy efficient devices like CFL bulb.
- Conserve energy.
- Use of public transportation, car pooling.
- Make use of reduce, reuse and recycle material.
- Avoid burning leaves, trash.
- Plant trees and take care of the trees.

Activity 5.8

Write the various effects of air pollution.

- Heart Disease
- ______________________
- ______________________
- ______________________
- ______________________
- ______________________
- ______________________

Activity 5.9

Identify a Problem Statement in your neighbouring area. Design the AI Project Cycle steps learnt so far to depict predicted trends and strategies required.

Problem statement:
Brief description:
Data sources (newspapers, magazines, articles, journals, internet, and so on)

Tabulated data	Graph Chart
Effects	Solutions

Tip Bot

AQI is important, especially for those suffering from illnesses caused by exposure to air pollution.

Knowledge Bot

The purpose of the AQI is to help people know how the local air quality impacts their health.The higher the AQI value, the greater the level of air pollution and the greater the health concerns.

TECH BOT

- **Data Visualization:** It is the graphical representation of data. It is an effective tool to communicate.
- **Chart:** A chart is a diagram, picture, or graph which is intended to make information easier to understand.
- **AQI:** The AQI is an index for reporting daily air quality.
- **Bar Graph:** It is a chart that uses bars to show comparisons between categories of data.
- **Histogram:** It is a graphical representation that organizes a group of data points into user-specified ranges.
- **Pie chart:** It is a special chart that uses "pie slices" to show relative sizes of data.
- **Line graph:** It is a graph in which points representing values of a variable for suitable values of an independent variable are connected by a broken line.

Recap Bot

- Data visualization is a technique which is used to represent the information in a more meaningful form using chart, process, diagram or a picture.
- Various components of chart are Data series, axes (x-axis and y-axis), plot area, chart area, legend, and so on.
- Use data visualization catalogue to understand different types of graphical tools and their purposes.
- Various tools to generate visualization are MS-Excel, Apple Numbers, Google Charts, Google Docs, OnlineChartTool.com, Python Graph gallery and many more.
- The most abundant gas in the air is Nitrogen.
- Air pollution is a change in the quality of air in your environment that affect the health of living beings and imbalances the nature of the planet.
- Air pollution is the cause for ozone depletion.
- Smoke and other pollutants combined with fog is referred to as Smog.
- Data exploration is the third stage of AI Project Cycle in which the data is put in a meaningful form to analyse data.
- Graph is a pictorial form of representing data. It is a visualization method for analysing data, evaluation patterns and predicting trends effectively.
- Various data visualization tools are used to discover the trends and communicate the results effectively.

A. Multiple choice questions.

1. Which tools are used to formulate the information in more meaningful form for making decisions?
   a. Data
   b. Data Visualization
   c. Information
   d. None of the above
2. Information is:
   a. Computer readable data
   b. Data in meaningful form
   c. Raw facts
   d. Presentation
3. What does the y-axis represent in the following graph?
   a. Distance (in km)
   b. Time (in hours)
   c. (0, 1)
   d. Distance (in meters)

   Time (in hours)

   Distance (in km)
4. Which one of the following is the highest percentage in air?
   a. Carbon dioxide
   b. Nitrogen
   c. Oxygen
   d. Methane
5. Air Pollution causes:
   a. Respiratory problems
   b. Global warming
   c. Soil erosion
   d. Deforestation
6. Which one of the following is not a Greenhouse Gas?
   a. Carbon dioxide
   b. Methane
   c. Ozone
   d. Oxygen
7. The percentage of oxygen in air is:
   a. 78%
   b. 1%
   c. 21%
   d. 0.04%
8. Which one of the following is not a visualisation tool?
   a. Pie chart
   b. Map
   c. Histogram
   d. A Paragraph
9. Which of the following is the use of visualisation technique?
   a. Handle and understand big data
   b. Able to do comparisons easily
   c. Use ordering, layout and hierarchy to prioritize
   d. All of the above
10. Which of the following pollutants are included to measure Air Quality Index?
    a. Sulphur dioxide
    b. Carbon Monoxide
    c. Ozone
    d. All of the above

B. Fill in the blanks.

1. The third stage in AI Project Cycle is ___________ .
2. ________________ helps in better understanding the information and comprehend the trends and patterns.
3. The _________ runs horizontally and represents the independent variable.
4. ____________ on the axes helps us to quantify the relationships between variables.
5. _____________ website explores multiple types of data visualisation techniques.
6. Burning of ________________ is one of the cause for air pollution.
7. ____________ gases creates global warming.
8. The act or result of cutting down or burning the trees is known as ____________ .

C. Match the following.

Column A	Column B
1. Most severe impact on human health	i. AQI
2. Nitrogen	ii. Data visualisation tools
3. O_3	iii. Helps in comprehending trends & patterns
4. PM	iv. Most abundant gas in air
5. Graph	v. AQI 401 – 500
6. Air Quality Index	vi. Ozone
7. Graph and chart	vii. Pictorial representation
8. Data visualisation tools	viii. Particulate Matter

D. Answer the following questions.

1. Write the full form for the following organisations.
   a. CPCB b. DPCC
2. Define the following:
   a. Data Exploration b. Air Pollution
3. Write one purpose each for the following chart types:
   a. Bar Graph b. Histogram
4. Write any two advantages of using visualisation techniques.
5. Name any two visualisation techniques with their purpose.
6. Differentiate between chart and graph.
7. Write the data features for air pollution on the basis of causing factors.
8. Name any two websites to collect the data for air pollution.

9. Write any two effects of air pollution.
10. Write any two solutions where you can contribute to solve the problem of air pollution.
11. How Artificial Intelligence is helping in solving the air pollution?
12. Write any four major pollutants to calculate the air quality.

Lab Activity

Change noise based generative biomes:

Biomes created by Marpi is a WebGL experience that generates pixelated 3D biomes based on noise randomization. With additional colors, this demo looks stunning and definitely requires a good graphics card.

Noise based generative biomes, click Randomize to create new or customize them yourself.

1. Go to the link: https://experiments.withgoogle.com biomes

   The following page appears.

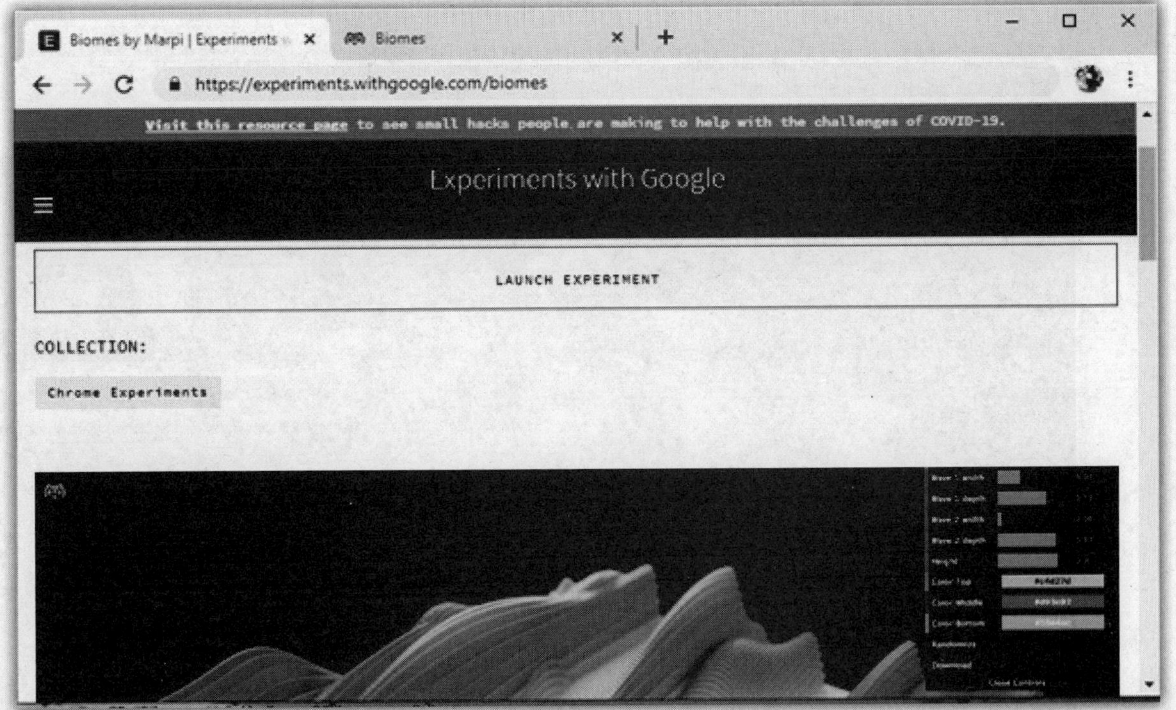

2. Click on the Launch Experiment button. The following screen appears.

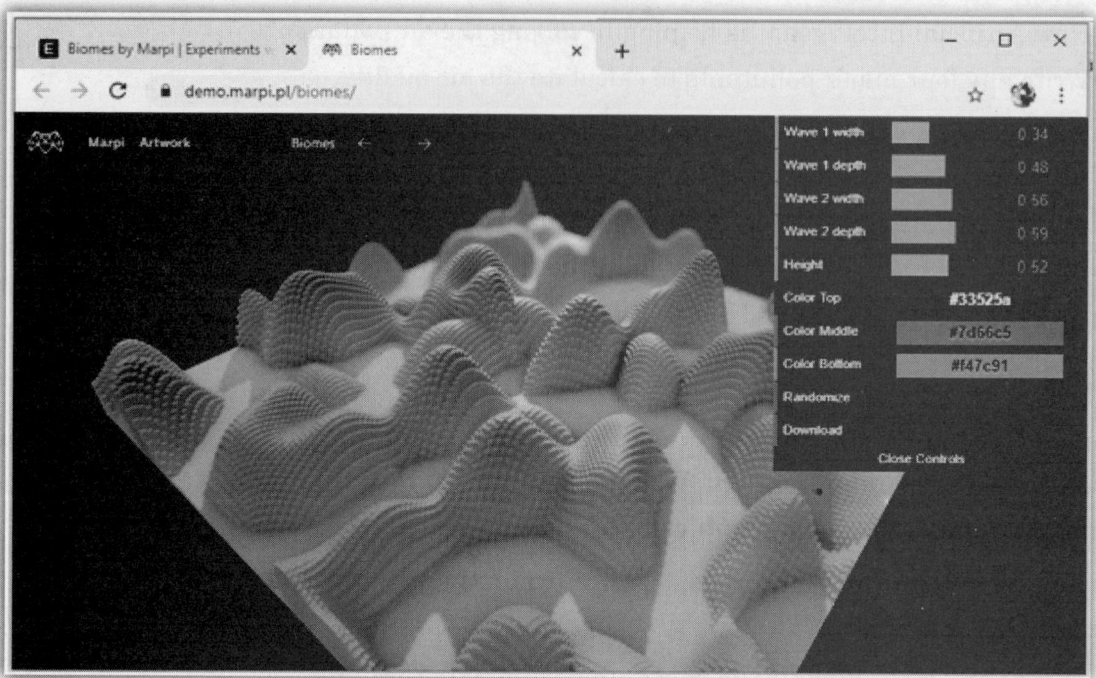

3. Change the Color Top, Color Middle and Color Bottom of your choice. The following screen will change noise based generative biomes.

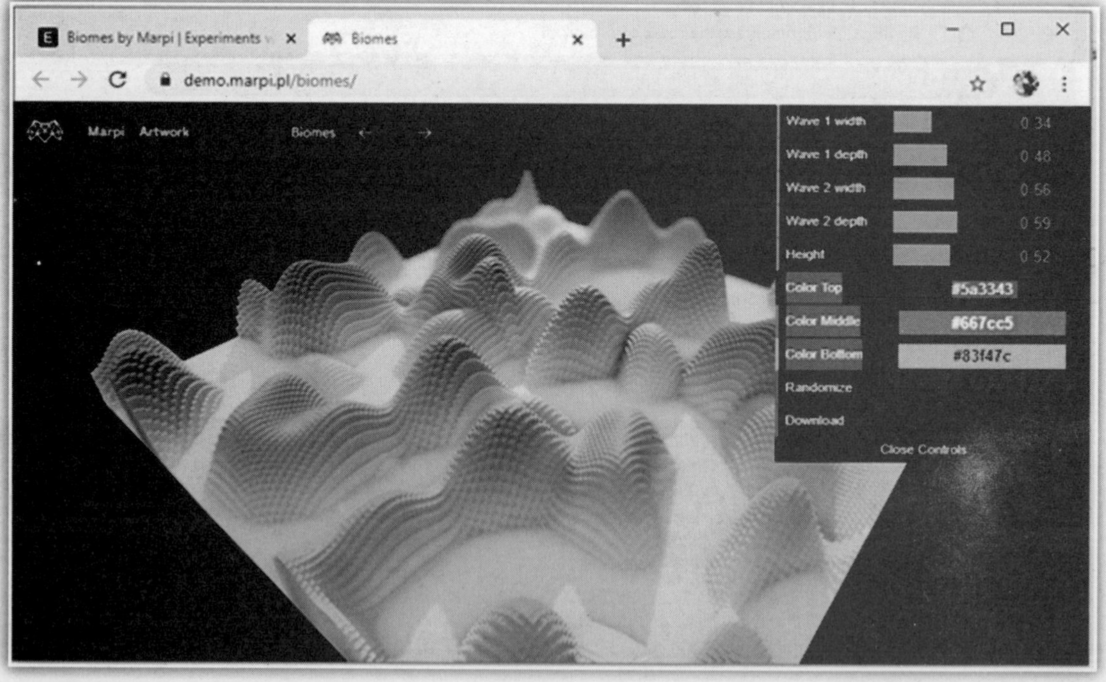

Worksheet

A. Fill in the blanks.

1. ____________________is a creation of a mental image or something.
2. __________________is an advantage of the easy communication.
3. A ____________________displays the numerical data distribution over a certain time period.
4. ______________helps the reader answer the question of how many.
5. ________________is a pictorial form of representing data.
6. Most abundant gas in the air is ______________________.
7. ________________is a mixture of smoke and fog.
8. MS Excel is a ____________to generate visualisation.

B. State whether the following statements are True or False.

1. A Pie chart depicts quantitative value over a continuous time interval.
2. A Histogram is visually simpler than other types of graphs.
3. Data visualisation requires a necessary skill to identify the patterns in it to comprehend the trends.
4. Bar graph helps the user identify the gaps and extremes.
5. Google charts is a tool to generate visualisation.
6. Air Quality Index can be referred either using the factors causing it or checking the levels of pollutants in the air.
7. AQI shows the maximum and minimum value of it in the area.
8. Air quality is determined by the levels of the pollutants so as to understand the trend of pollution.

C. Write down the full form of the following.

1. AQI ____
2. CPCB ____
3. DPCC ____
4. SAFAR ____
5. IITM ____

D. Answer the following questions.

1. Write down the various pollutants in air.
2. What do you mean by data visualisation?
3. Give one example of data visualisation.
4. What is the purpose of histogram?
5. Write down the tools to generate visualisation.

QUIZ CARD

Multiple choice questions.

1. Which chart is most helpful with smaller amount of data only?
   a. Bar ☐ b. line ☐
   c. Pie ☐ d. Histogram ☐
2. A ______________ type of chart can be used for both analysis and communication needs.
   a. Singular ☐ b. Double ☐
   c. Triple ☐ d. None of these ☐
3. Which can be perceived as the representation of a set of information as a chart, process, diagram or a picture?
   a. Line graph ☐ b. AQI ☐
   c. Data visualisation ☐ d. Both b. and c. ☐
4. Who measures the air quality on five air pollutants on the scale of 0 to 500?
   a. Line graph ☐ b. AQI ☐
   c. Data visualisation ☐ d. Both b. and c. ☐
5. Which contains oxygen which makes life possible on earth?
   a. CPCB ☐ b. DPCC ☐
   b. Air ☐ d. Sulphur dioxide ☐
6. Which tool is/ are used to generate visualisation?
   a. Apple Numbers ☐ b. Google Docs ☐
   c. OnlineChartTool.com ☐ d. All of these ☐
7. Which graph improves readability as it is a diagrammatic comparison of discrete values?
   a. Pie ☐ b. Histogram ☐
   c. Bar ☐ d. Line ☐
8. Which axis runs horizontally and represents the independent variable?
   a. x-axis ☐ b. y-axis ☐
   c. Both a. and b. ☐ d. None of these ☐
9. Which is a complex entity?
   a. Data visualisation ☐ b. Data ☐
   c. AQI ☐ d. Line graph ☐
10. Which gives the clear picture of the air quality?
    a. Data ☐ b. AQI ☐
    c. Graph ☐ d. None of these ☐

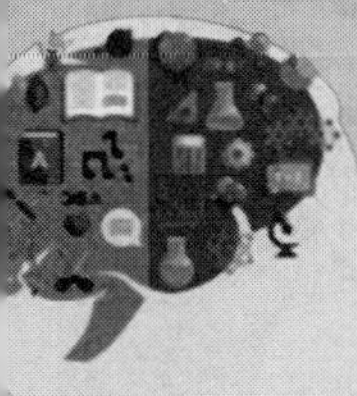

6 Data Modelling

Structure Bot

In this chapter, we will discuss the following topics:

- Differentiate between Artificial Intelligence, Machine Learning and Deep Learning
- Classification of AI Models: Rule based approach and Learning based approach
- Inspect the data set while creating the decision tree and remove redundant data
- Deduce how the computer classifies images as well as reads them using the Pixel-It activity
- State the steps covered while devising an intelligent machine learning model

Objective Bot

After studying this chapter, you should be able to:

- Demonstrate the use of Machine Learning, Deep Learning and Artificial Intelligence
- Demonstrate, develop and formulate the concept of decision trees
- Articulate a computer's ability to identify alphabets and handwritings

Artificial Intelligence (AI) is the software engine that drives the Fourth Industrial Revolution. The ability of machines to perform cognitive tasks like thinking, recognizing, learning, problem solving, and decision making has evolved in many ways. Soon, you will have more of self-driving cars, robots stocking warehouses and caring for the young and elderly. Deployment of a variety of tasks has enhanced productivity manifold due to latest developments in data collection and computation.

Figure 6.1: *A robot*

Artificial Intelligence is gaining the spotlight across applications in your personal and professional lives. Much aligned to this are the Sustainable Development Goals (SDG) that focus on the well being of the planet.

The core idea is building digital machines and algorithms which are capable of performing computational tasks.

In the previous chapter of Data Exploration, you have learned the following:

- Collected the data using data acquisition techniques after exploration for the problem of air pollution.
- After collecting the data, you represented the data using graphical tools to visualize the trends and patterns of the data collected like sources of air pollution/ components of air/various pollutants causing air pollution.

Once various trends/patterns are visualised on the acquired data, you can develop different strategies/techniques in designing an Artificial Intelligent machine to help in solving the problem. The different models will be evaluated by checking their advantages, disadvantages and efficiency. The best model which gives the most efficient and reliable result will be selected. This component of AI Project Cycle is known as Data Modelling.

Figure 6.2: *Predicting the trends*

The model selected will be evaluated for its efficiency on the basis of the results expected from it while comparing with the results you have. This component of AI Project Cycle is known as Evaluation.

Activity 6.1

Fill in the table for the information which you learnt so far.

Sr. No.	Term	Description	Role played in your daily lives
1.	NLP		
2.	AI Ethics		
3.	Problem Scoping		
4.	Data Acquisition		

Definition Bot

Evaluation is the method of understanding the reliability of an AI model, evaluation is based on the outputs which is received by feeding the test dataset into the model and then comparing the output with the actual answers.

Artificial Intelligence works on algorithms after collection of data. The algorithms can be based on a certain type of human reasoning, knowledge and expertise to make the machines work intelligently. These are used for calculations, data processing and reasoning.

Let us understand the differences between Artificial Intelligence, Machine Learning and Deep Learning as these terms are usually used interchangeably.

Artificial Intelligence means creating intelligent machines that can make your work easy, efficient and reliable by using a set of rules/algorithms.

Machine Learning is a domain of Artificial Intelligence which helps the machines to work intelligently and take decisions from their experiences i.e. the machine is learning by themselves using the data and make predictions. In this, the data is given to the machine for training and the machine process the data and perform prediction.

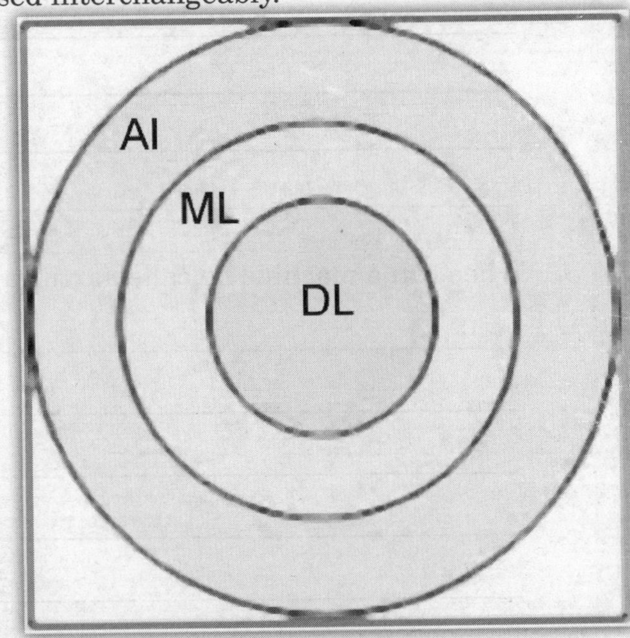

Figure 6.3: *AI Umbrella*

Deep Learning is a subset of Machine Learning which helps the machine to take decisions and learn from large datasets. In this, the information is processed on large amount of data entered just like human brain identifies patterns based on various information in the brain. The new data set is entered then that is compared with the previous data to make sense of it.

FACT BOT

The name Machine Learning was coined in 1959 by Arthur Samuel.

Activity 6.2

Based on your previous knowledge and research work, answer the following questions.

1. Write any two examples of Artificial Intelligence from everyday life.

____

____

____

____

2. What makes a machine work intelligently?

____

____

____

____

____

3. When can a machine be called artifically intelligent?

____

____

____

____

____

KNOWLEDGE BOT

Deep learning was inspired by the structure and function of the brain, namely the interconnecting of many neurons.

Artificial Intelligence is an umbrella term which has Machine Learning (ML) and Deep Learning (DL). As seen in the Figure 6.3, Machine Learning is a subset of AI and DL is a subset of ML.

Modelling refers to develop algorithms/models which is trained in such a manner that generates effective, efficient and reliable results.

There are two approaches while building an AI models:

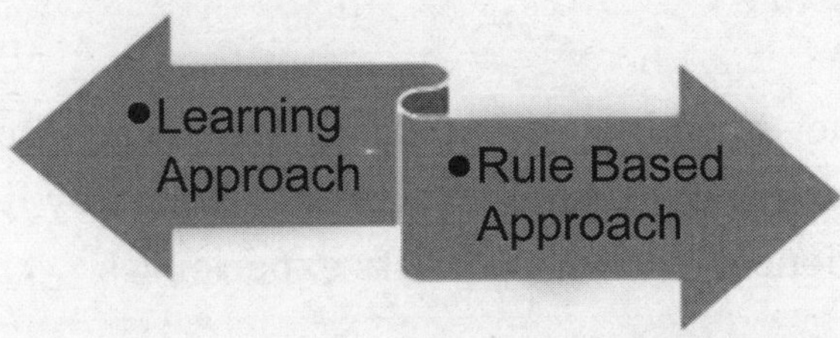

As explained earlier, the various graphical tools used for representing data aid in visualizing it for better understanding of data and helping in discovering trends and patterns out of it. In the same manner, when you talk about a machine accessing and analysing the data, it needs to be in the language which is understandable by the machine. The machine understands binary language (that is, the language of 0 and 1). The mathematical approach is the heart and soul of data analysis. The probability factor of the elements help form a basis for AI models which can further be classified either on rule based or learning based approaches.

AI Models can be classified as shown in the Figure 6.4 given below:

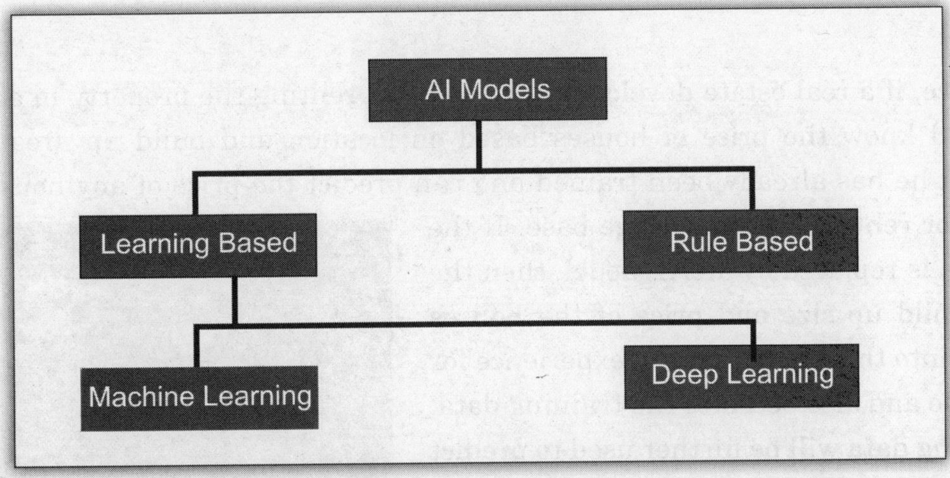

Figure 6.4: *AI Models*

Activity 6.3

Let us differentiate between Learning-based and Rule-based approaches.

Learning-based approach	Rule-based approach
AI machine uses machine learning technique to accomplish task is called learning-based system.	AI machine uses rule-based technique to accomplish task is called rule-based system.
Learning-based approach takes input data and compares it with the data set which is already present in the system and process the output based on it.	Rule-based approach uses rules in the form of if-else statements (as you did in Story speaker activity).
In this approach, the machine keeps learning and make changes by itself over the time with its experiences.	In this approach, rules are predefined and cannot change by itself over the time with its experiences.

Learning-Based Approach

In this approach, the machine learns through experience. It uses the models and algorithms to perform tasks. These tasks are performed on the sample data which is also known as training data. In this approach, the programmer needn't to tell what to do. The machine is fed in with the data and it simply compares it with the previous data sets and learns from that.

For instance, if a real estate developer, who deals in renting the property in a particular area, would know the price of houses based on location and build up area size. This means that he has already been trained and can predict the price of any house which is available for rent on his knowledge base. If the said person is replaced by an AI model, then the location, build up size and price of the houses will be fed into this model, i.e. the experience for the machine and also becomes the training data. This training data will be further used to predict the price of new house available for rent.

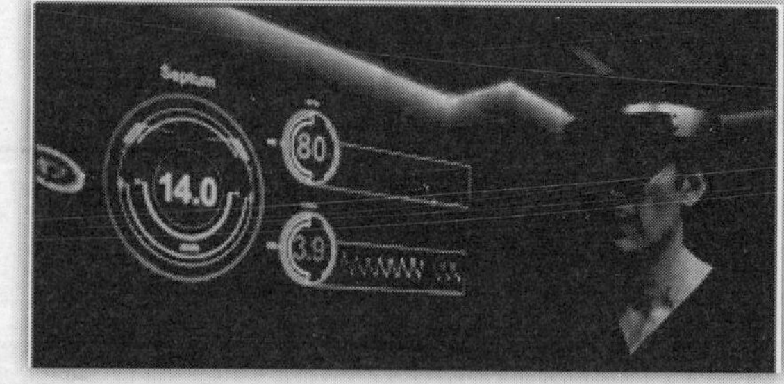

Figure 6.5: *Learning-based model*

Activity 6.4

Research and write a few examples of Machine Learning from your daily lives.

- Google Search and Google Maps use Machine Learning by providing suggested search items in the box automatically as you start typing based on your past searches, popular searches, or any related terms.
- Smart Reply is a new feature in your inbox that suggests three ready replies based on the e-mails you receive. This response will keep improving over time as the system learns.
- ______________________________
- ______________________________
- ______________________________
- ______________________________
- ______________________________
- ______________________________

Activity 6.5

Open the following in the web browser to get the estimated time of arrival on the basis of real-time traffic conditions: https://maps.google.com. Answer the following on the basis of different modes of transport.

Source Location			
Destination Location			
Distance between these two points			
Estimated time taken to reach the destination	Foot	Car	Public Transport
Calculate the speed			

Rule-Based Approach

This approach is based on the data set and rules that are fed into the system to process and gives the result. In this approach, the rules and regulations are already fed in by the developer. The dataset entered is already fed into the AI model along with their attributes that is, each data is labelled. While testing the model with an image, this image is compared with the training data according to the labels of the data.

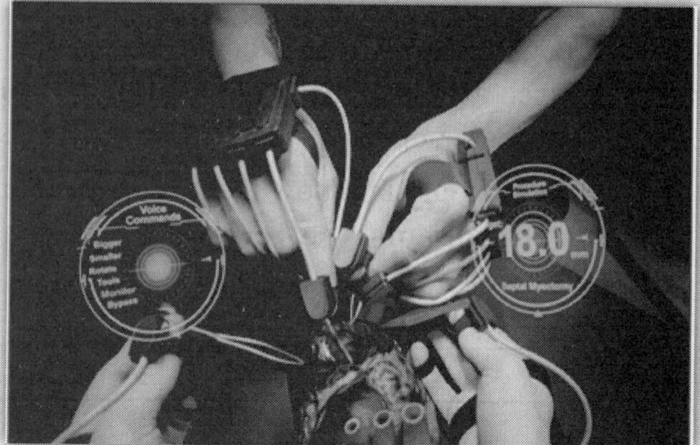

Figure 6.6: *Rule-based model*

A rule-based approach uses rules as the knowledge representation. These rules are coded into the system in the form of if-then-else statements. The main idea is to capture the knowledge of a human expert in a specialized domain and embody it within a computer system. To summarize, knowledge is encoded as rules.

Decision tree

- It is the process which uses the concept of representing the data in the form of a tree.
- This is used in the examples of classifications where the result is in True or False.
- It is also known as a binary tree.

The Decision Tree has the following components:

- Root node represents the top node from where the tree starts.
- Decision nodes which results in splitting of data in multiple data segments and it represents features/attributes.
- Directional arrows route the course of action to be taken.
- Leaf nodes represents an outcome.

The decision trees classify the examples by sorting them down the tree from the root to some leaf node as shown in Figure 6.7, with the leaf node providing the classification to the example. Each node in the tree is the case which branches out to another case or corresponds to one of the possible answers.

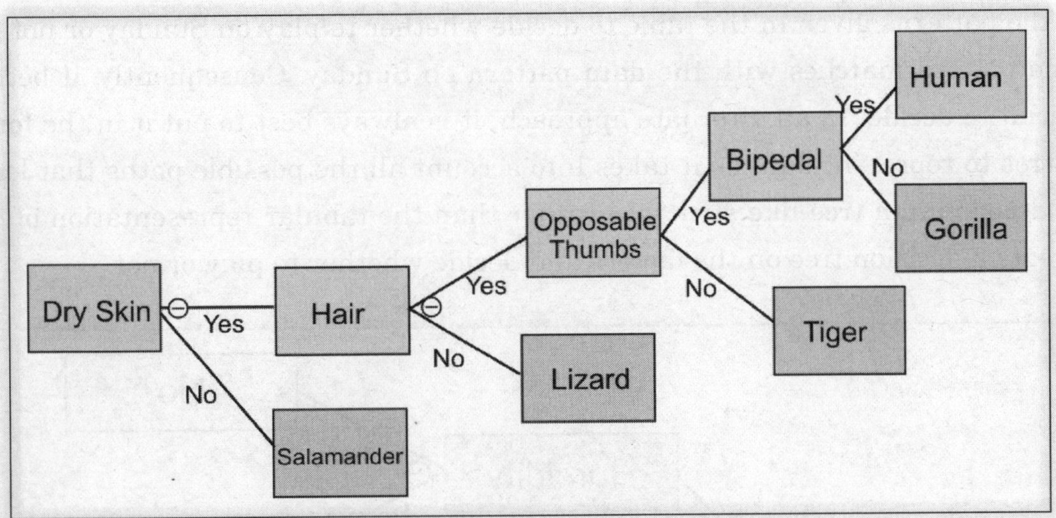

Figure 6.7: *Decision tree example*

TIP BOT

Decision tree can be applied to both regression & classification.

This process is ongoing in nature and is repeated for every subtree. Let's illustrate this with the help of an example. You want to play volleyball on Sunday and a number of factors needs to be checked to decide whether to play or not. These factors can be hot or cold, speed of the wind and humidity, weather is sunny, cloudy or rainy. Hence, let us tabulate all these factors for the past ten days as shown in the following table:

Day	Weather	Temperature	Speed of Wind	Humidity	Play
1	Sunny	Hot	Weak	High	No
2	Cloudy	Hot	Weak	High	Yes
3	Sunny	Mild	Strong	Normal	Yes
4	Cloudy	Mild	Strong	High	Yes
5	Rainy	Mild	Strong	High	No
6	Rainy	Cold	Strong	Normal	No
7	Rainy	Mild	Weak	High	Yes
8	Sunny	Hot	Strong	High	No
9	Cloudy	Hot	Weak	Normal	Yes
10	Rainy	Mild	Strong	High	No

Observe the patterns given in the table to decide whether to play on Sunday or not. But, what if no pattern matches with the data pattern on Sunday. Consequently, it becomes very difficult to decide. In an alternate approach, it is always best to put it in the form of decision tree to represent data as it takes into account all the possible paths that lead to the final decision in a tree-like structure rather than the tabular representation of data. Let us create a decision tree on the factors and decide whether to play or not.

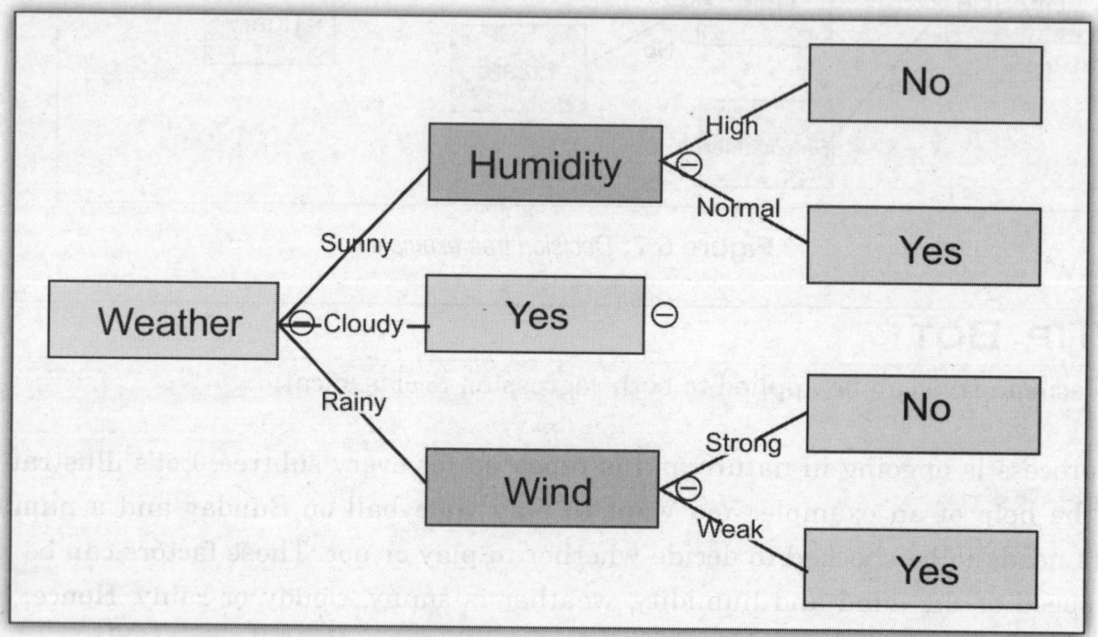

Figure 6.8: *Decision tree*

The Decision tree can also be expressed in rule format using if-else statement:

- If Weather = Sunny and Humidity = High, then play = No
- If Weather = Sunny and Humidity = Normal, then play = Yes
- If Weather = Cloudy, then play = Yes
- If Weather = Rainy and Wind = Strong, then play = No
- If Weather = Rainy and Wind = Weak, then play = Yes

MEMORY BOT

Splitting is a process of dividing a node into two or more sub-nodes.

Activity 6.6

Create the decision tree for the following data table to show what kind of weekend is it.

Weekend	Weather	Parents coming?	Category (in terms of money)	Decision
W1	Sunny	Yes	Rich	Cinema
W2	Windy	Yes	Rich	Cinema
W3	Rainy	Yes	Poor	Cinema
W4	Rainy	No	Rich	Stay in
W5	Windy	No	Rich	Shopping
W6	Sunny	No	Rich	Tennis
W7	Rainy	Yes	Poor	Cinema
W8	Sunny	No	Rich	Tennis
W9	Windy	Yes	Rich	Cinema
W10	Windy	No	Poor	Cinema

Decision tree

Pixel-It

Understand and visualize computer's ability to identify alphabets and handwritings.

- To create an AI Model to classify handwritten letters.
- Develop a model to classify handwritten letters by diving the alphabets into pixels.
- Pixels are then joined together to analyse a pattern amongst same alphabets and to differentiate the different ones.

Photographs are a valuable tool for obtaining information and making decisions based on them. One such example is to ascertain demographics of wildlife populations in nature. There are several computer-aided photomatching algorithms which efficiently match images of unique individual images in databases with thousands of image databases of varying image quality.

Algorithm performance differed greatly with recognition rates ranging from 100% to limiting the review to the 10 highest ranking images. Recognition rate could be improved considerably with a higher number of matching images in the database. Pixel-based matching of images exhibits superior recognition rates compared to any other approaches. By choosing this technique, image databases of huge sizes that are unfeasible to match by eye as a user can be easily translated to accurate individual comparisons for correct estimates.

Hence, it is clearly understandable that in a Rule-based AI Model, the computer algorithm has a data set which is used for matching pixel by pixel to identify the image. Here, knowledge is the rule. It only gets better if the database is large and better-quality images which can be used for comparison. In contrast with a Learning-based AI Model, the algorithm generates further algorithm code to create new sub datasets by clustering based on patterns observed by machine; such as colour, size, and so on.

Activity 6.7

Let us conduct an activity in the classroom to figure out how the computer matches the pixels with patterns to match the correct combinations.

Step 1: Cut out a matrix of a 6x6 matrix table and label as follows. Write any alphabet across the table to cover maximum boxes. Let's say you write "E".

1						2
2						3
3						4
4						5
5						6
6						7

Step 2: Colour the boxes to cover all boxes. Now cut along the rows horizontally.

Step 3: String the cut rows in a continuous sequence.

Step 4: The coloured boxes would represent 1 and empty boxes would represent 0 for the computer. The computer algorithm matches the above pattern with the stored pattern of character "E" of English language to tell the computer that the pattern matches.

Many process oriented departments such as weather forecasting and state assessment departments use the pixel matching algorithms to compare originally created to compare screenshots. The most highlighted features used are accurate antialiased pixel detection and perceptual colour difference matrices.

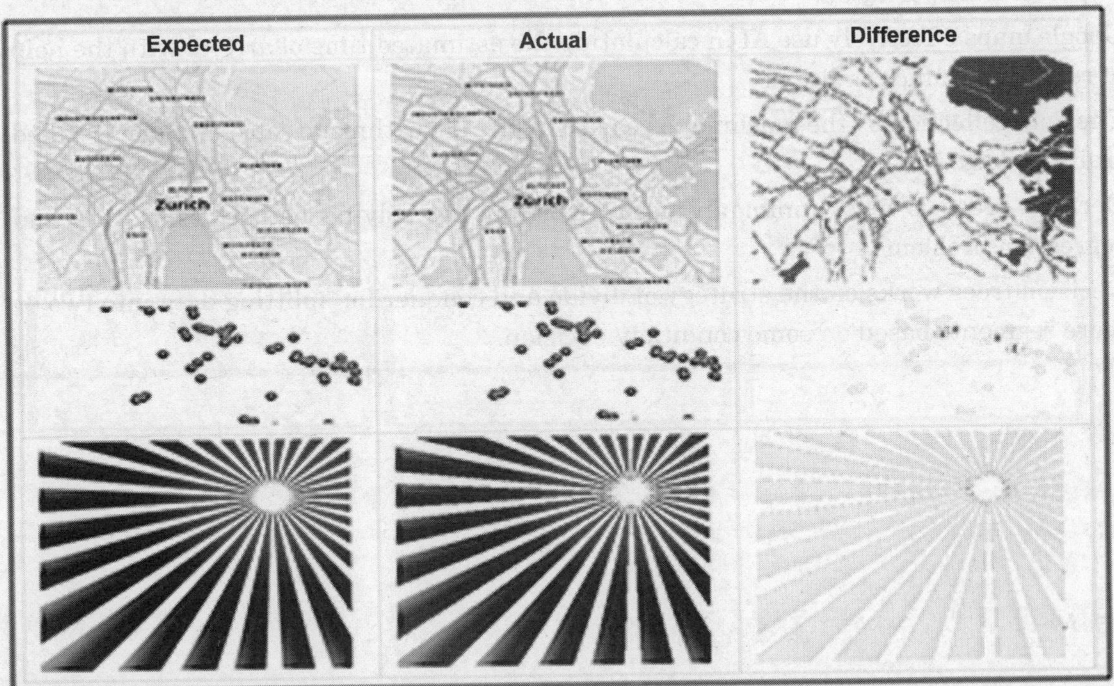

Figure 6.9: *Example Output metrics*

TECH BOT

- **Modelling:** Modelling of Artificial Intelligence means to present the results of the modern researches in the artificial intelligence.
- **Deep Learning:** It is an Artificial Intelligence function that imitates the workings of the human brain in processing data and creating patterns for use in decision making.
- **Machine Learning:** It is the field of study that gives computers the capability to learn without being explicitly programmed.
- **Decision tree:** It is a tree in which each internal (non-leaf) node is labelled with an input feature.

Recap Bot

- Algorithm is a step by step process which helps in taking decisions and Artificial Intelligence uses training data to process and take decisions.
- Artificial Intelligence means making machine work intelligently where the machine is not becoming intelligent by itself, is created by humans and that is why called artificial.
- Google Maps is a web mapping service developed by Google. It offers satellite imagery, aerial photography, street maps, 360° panoramic views of streets (Street View), real-time traffic conditions, and route planning for traveling by foot, car, bicycle and air (in beta), or public transportation.
- Google maps effectively use AI in calculating the estimated time of arrival with the help of real-time traffic conditions.
- The data collection by the machine to be used by the algorithms to solve problem is called training data.
- Decision trees is most commonly used algorithm for solving both classification and regression problems.
- Decision trees works on the strategy of divide and conquer for splitting data into two or more segments based on some condition/ decision.

A. Multiple choice questions.

1. Which component of AI Project Cycle chooses the best model by checking their advantages, disadvantages and efficiency?
   a. Data Modelling
   b. Data Visualization
   c. Data Exploration
   d. None of the above
2. The model selected will be evaluated for its efficiency on the basis of the results while comparing with the results you already have is known as:
   a. Computer Application
   b. Evaluation
   c. Patterns
   d. Problem Scoping
3. Machine Learning is a subset of:
   a. Data Exploration
   b. Data Modelling
   c. Deep Learning
   d. Artificial Intelligence
4. Rule-based approach uses rules in the form of:
   a. Training data
   b. Data set
   c. If-else statement
   d. None of the above
5. A tool which uses a tree-like structure of decisions and their possible outcomes:
   a. Decision tree
   b. Chart
   c. Graph
   d. Network
6. Choose the components of decision tree:
   a. Nodes
   b. Branches
   c. Leaf
   d. All of the above
7. How many test conditions are there in a decision tree to get the output?
   a. One test condition
   b. Two test condition
   c. Doesn't have any condition
   d. Sequence of test conditions
8. A decision tree can be used to solve the following problems:
   a. Regression problems
   b. Classification problems
   c. Both a. and b.
   d. None of the above
9. Which approach is followed in a decision tree?
   a. Bottom-up
   b. Top-down
   c. Both a. and b.
   d. None of the above

10. Higher the Air Quality Index (AQI) of the region means the region is more polluted in the air.

a. True

b. False

c. Can't say

d. None is mentioned

B. Fill in the blanks.

1. Data modelling is the __________ stage in AI Project Cycle.
2. Artificial Intelligence is an __________ term which has ML and DL.
3. Deep Learning is a subset of ______________.
4. ______________ helps machine to take decisions and learn from large data sets.
5. AI models can be classified either on __________ or __________ approaches.
6. __________ approach takes input data and compares it with the data set which is already present in the system.
7. In __________ approach, rules are predefined and cannot change by itself over the time.

C. Match the following.

Column A	Column B
1. Modelling	i. Language of 0's and 1's
2. Graphical tools	ii. Uses if-else statements
3. Deep Learning	iii. Learning-based approach experience
4. Rule-based approach	iv. Develop algorithms/models
5. Training data	v. Learn from large data sets
6. Binary language	vi. Helps in visualization for better understanding
7. Machine learns through	vii. Smart reply, Google search and experience Google maps, and so ons
8. Learning-based approach	viii. Sample data

D. Answer the following questions.

1. Write the full form for the following organisations.

   a. ML

   b. DL

2. Define the following:

   a. Data Modelling

   b. Testing data

   c. Learning-based approach

3. Write one purpose each for the following tools:

   a. Google Maps

   b. Smart Reply

4. Write any two advantages/applications of using learning based approach.
5. Name any two advantages/ applications of using decision trees.
6. Write briefly about the components of decision tree.

Lab Activity

Thing Translator: Take a picture of something to hear how to say it in a different language.

Thing Translator is a web app that lets you point your phone (or laptop) at stuff to hear to say it in a different language. It was developed as part of Google's AI Experiments project.

1. Go to the link:. https://experiments.withgoogle.com/thing-translator

   The following page appears.

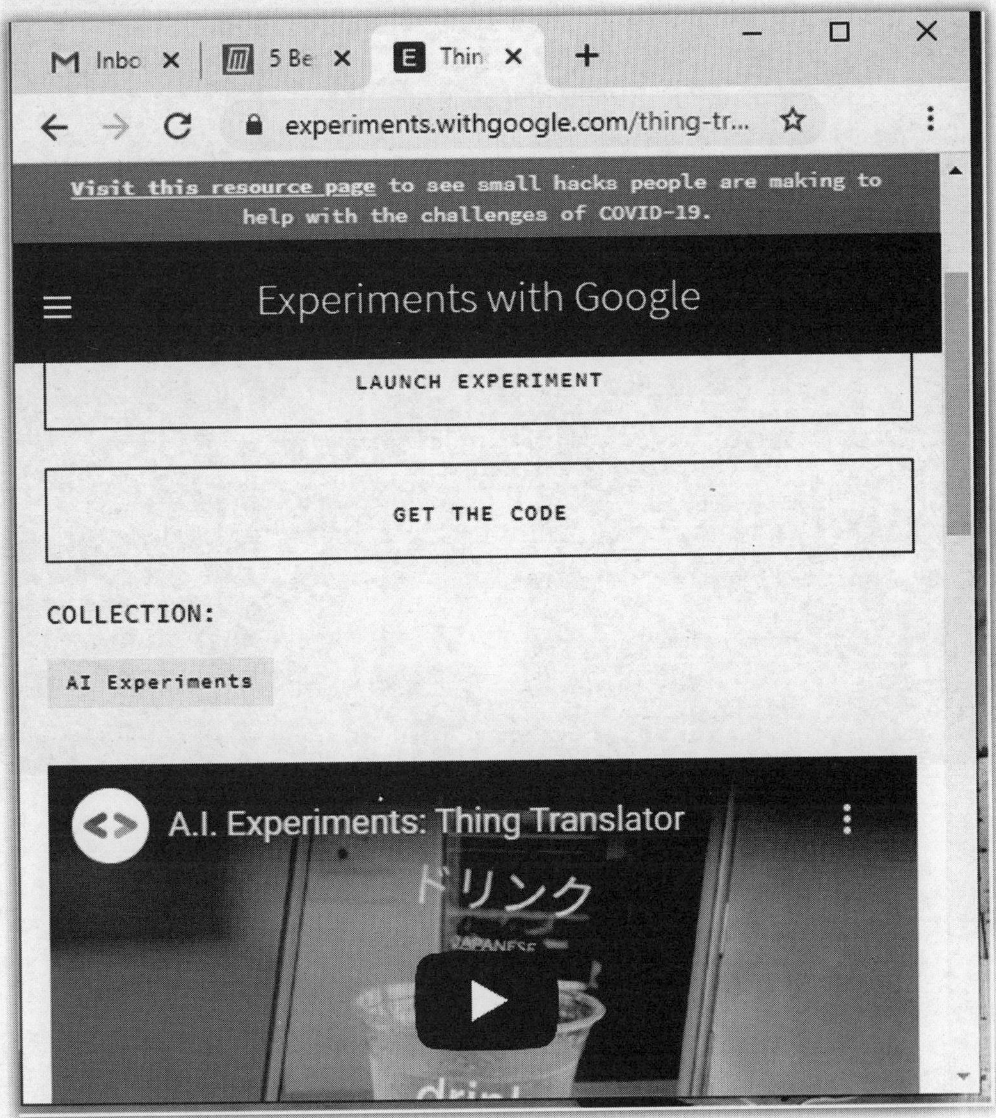

2. Click on the Launch Experiment button.

3. Take a picture of the desired object with Thing Translator and translated the image. So when choosing which language you would like the image translated to, you aren't restricted. Set the language you would like the item translated to (I am choosing Spanish here).

Worksheet

A. Fill in the blanks.

1. ________________________ is the software engine that drives the fourth industrial revolution.
2. AI is an umbrella term which has ML and ______________.
3. There are ___________ approaches while building an AI models.
4. AI machine uses rule-based technique to accomplish task is called as ______________________.
5. Decision tree is also known as______________.
6. _____________is a web mapping service developed by Google.
7. In decision tree, leaf nodes represent an ______________.
8. _____________uses the models and algorithms to perform tasks.

B. State whether the following statements are True or False.

1. Rule-based approach uses rules in the form of if-else statements.
2. Data refers to develop algorithm/models which is trained in such a manner that generates effective, efficient and reliable results.
3. Machine Learning works on algorithms after collection of data.
4. Deep Learning is a subset of AI.
5. The machine understands binary language.
6. AI models can be classified into three types.
7. Rule-based approach, the machine learns through experience.

C. Write down the full form of the following.

1. ML ____
2. DL ____
3. AI ____

D. Answer the following questions.

1. What do you mean by decision tree?
2. Explain Pixel-It.
3. Write down one difference between rule-based and learning-based approaches.
4. Discuss Google maps.

QUIZ CARD

Multiple choice questions.

1. Which AI machine approach uses machine learning technique to accomplish task?
   a. Learning-based ☐ b. Rule-based ☐
   c. Both a. and b. ☐ d. None of these ☐
2. Which feature is a new feature in your inbox that suggests three ready replies based on the e-mails you receive?
   a. Google Search ☐ b. Smart Reply ☐
   c. Google Maps ☐ d. None of these ☐
3. Which uses the concept of representing the data in the form of a tree?
   a. Binary tree ☐ b. Decision tree ☐
   c. Both a. and b. ☐ d. None of these ☐
4. ________________matching of images exhibits superior recognition rates compared to any other approaches.
   a. Learning-based ☐ b. Rule-based ☐
   c. Pattern-based ☐ d. None of these ☐
5. Which is the most commonly used algorithm for solving both classification and regression problems?
   a. Binary tree ☐ b. Decision tree ☐
   c. Both a. and b. ☐ d. None of these ☐
6. The data collection by the machine to be used by an algorithms to solve problem is called as:
   a. Testing data ☐ b. Algorithm ☐
   c. Training test ☐ d. None of these ☐
7. Which node represents the top node from where the tree starts?
   a. Leaf ☐ b. Decision ☐
   c. Root ☐ d. None of these ☐
8. Which AI project cycle gives most efficient and reliable result will be selected?
   a. Evaluation ☐ b. Problem Scoping ☐
   c. Data Acquisition ☐ d. Data Modelling ☐
9. ML is a subset of:
   a. AI ☐ b. DL ☐
   c. Both a. and b. ☐ d. None of these ☐
10. Which nodes which result in splitting of data in multiple data segments and it represents features?
    a. Leaf ☐ b. Decision ☐
    c. Root ☐ d. None of these ☐

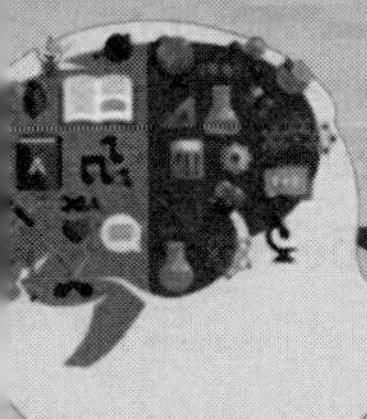

7 Understanding the Neural Network Framework

Structure Bot

In this chapter, we will discuss the following topics

- How Neural Network works and its relationship with the human nervous system?
- Demonstrate the use of Common AI models: Regression, Classification, and Clustering
- Illustrate the features and layers of the Neural Network
- Comparative study between Neural Networks and the Human Nervous System

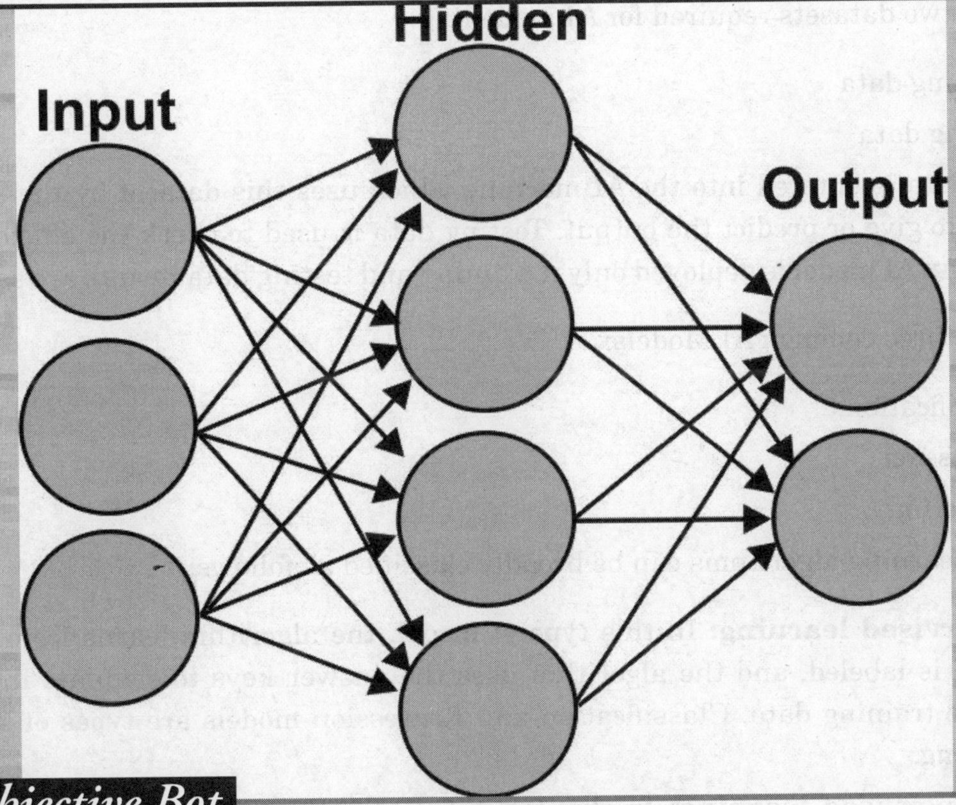

Objective Bot

At the end of this chapter, you should be able to

- Interpret the correlation between the Neural Network and nervous system in the human body
- Understand and appreciate the concept of the Neural Network through gamification

As learned earlier, an algorithm is known to be artificially intelligent if it gets trained properly to make decisions and predictions by its own. This is possible only if the machine is trained with a large and reliable dataset.

Let us say if an AI machine is created to classify images of thumbs up sign. The machine has to be trained with a huge dataset of many different pictures of thumbs up gesture. During the AI machine training process, the machine keeps extracting images from the existing image database based on various sub features, which helps in classification in any of the image of thumbs up. The same process is done with any other type of images. This happens when you upload an image to your Facebook account. It automatically reflects the name tagging by looking at the image dataset already existing in one's photo albums.

The efficiency of the AI machine depends on the results. If it is able to classify correctly, then the machine is efficient otherwise it has to be retrained with a larger dataset.

There are two datasets required for AI modelling:

- Training data
- Testing data

Training data is entered into the AI machine which uses this dataset by the algorithms and rules to give or predict the output. Testing data is used to check the efficiency of the AI model. An AI model is deployed only if training and testing data results are satisfactory.

There are three common AI Models:

- Classification
- Regression
- Clustering

Machine Learning algorithms can be broadly classified as follows:

- **Supervised learning:** In this type of model, the algorithm learns from a dataset which is labeled, and the algorithm uses the answer keys to evaluate its accuracy on the training data. Classification and Regression models are types of supervised learning.
- **Unsupervised learning:** In this type of model, the algorithm learns and makes sense by extracting features/patterns from the unlabeled dataset provided.
- **Reinforcement learning:** In this type of model, the algorithms are working towards accomplishing the goal or try to improve the performance in a particular task. This is used in gaming.

Classification is a type of supervised learning model. Classification models work on datasets which are labeled and then predict the label of the testing dataset.

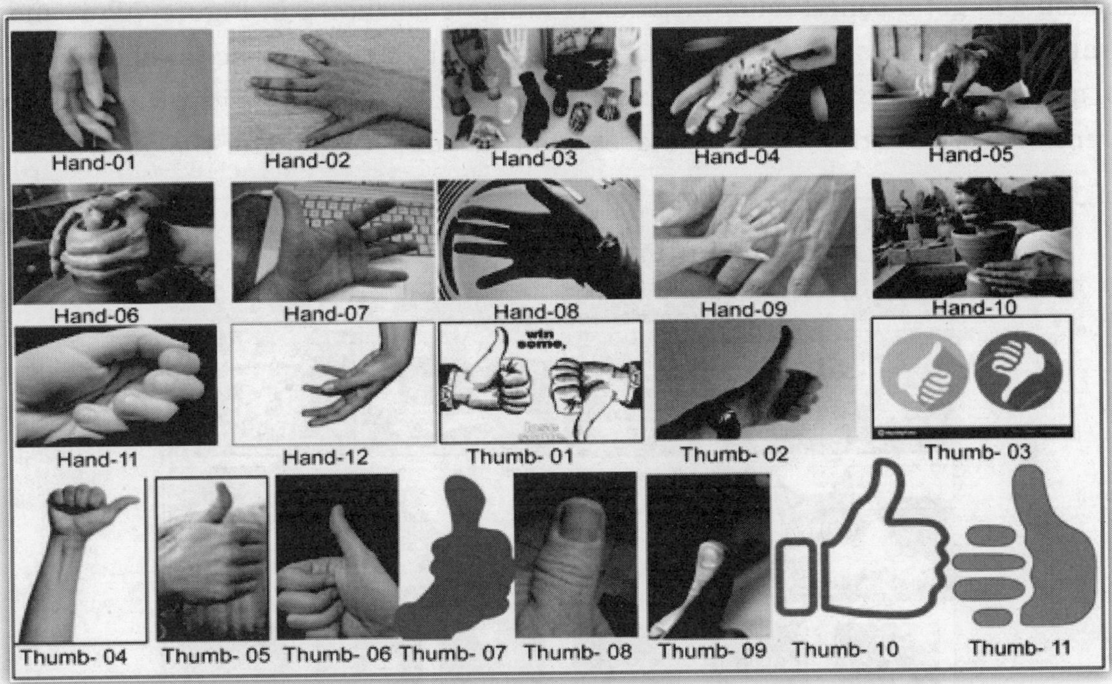

Figure 7.1: *Labeled images of hands and thumbs up*

For example, if you take various images of thumbs up and your hand as a training dataset, then these images have to be labeled as Thumbs up or Hand, respectively as shown in Figure 7.1. This dataset entered in the machine extracts features from the dataset for training and understanding regarding the various features of a full hand or only thumbs up. While testing, the machine compares the input image and extracts features from it which are then compared with the features already marked under the labels. Depending on the degree of similarity, the AI machine will label the testing image. This whole process is known as Classification.

The spam filters in an e-mail is an example of how classification works. Once it is marked spam from a particular e-mail, the next time the e-mail from that source will automatically moved to spam as the system has learned it.

Regression is a type of supervised learning model where the problems are based on continuous data. For example, an algorithm is able to predict the price of an apartment in a particular location with different kinds of facilities. It is able to find out the relationship between the set of data and then predicts the output based on the input variables.

Clustering is a type of unsupervised learning model which uses an algorithm that helps in making sense by extracting features and patterns from an unlabeled dataset. For example, it's possible to get a collection of pictures of animals as shown in Figure 7.2(a) and then separate these pictures into various groups based on their resemblance as shown in Figure 7.2(b) and Figure 7.2(c). In this example, the AI machine generates its own algorithms to differentiate between the training dataset and thus uses it to cluster the data.

Figure 7.2 (a): *Unlabelled dataset of animals*

Figure 7.2 (b): *Pictures of one group of objects that is a cat*

Figure 7.2 (c): *Pictures of another group of objects that is a monkey*

What is a Neural Network?

Neural comes from the word neuron of the nervous system. The neuron is a cell within the nervous system which is the basic unit of the brain used to process and transmit information to all the other nerve cells and muscles. A network of such neurons is called a Neural Network. The same type of behavior is embedded into an artificial machine and thus called Artificial Neural Network. It can adapt to changing inputs and hence the network generates the best possible outcome without making any changes anywhere as the human brain does.

ANeural Network is a series of algorithms that achieves the output after creating relationships on the dataset and processes it in a manner similar to the human brain. Therefore, a neural network means a system of neurons that are working in a form of network. It helps in trading based on algorithms, security classification, forecasting, and so on.

MEMORY BOT

- ANNs are capable of learning, which takes place by altering weight values.
- Supervised learning allows you to collect data or produce a data output from the previous experience.

Activity 7.1

Write the applications of a neural network.

Various applications of a neural network are:

- Trading
- ________________________
- ________________________
- ________________________
- ________________________

Why do you use Neural Networks?

Neural networks are one of the most commonly, powerful, and widely used algorithms which actually use Deep Learning algorithms. They are used to solve real-life complex problems. These networks can learn and create the relationships between all the inputs and gives the result. They can handle non-linear and complex problems very effectively. They can even work and give output if the data is missing. The main advantage of neural networks is that they are able to extract data features automatically without needing any input from the programmer.

Artificial Neural Networks (ANN) are very famous these days and also considered to be very interesting topics due to their applications in chatbots to make your work easy like auto replying the e-mails, suggesting e-mail replies, spam filtering, Facebook image tagging, showing the items of your interest in the e-shopping web portals, and many more.

How does a Neural Network Work?

An Artificial Neural Network consists of neurons that process the information and consists of multiple layers of interconnected nodes. Figure 7.3 shows the representation of neural networks. The three layers in this model are:

- Input layer
- Hidden layer
- Output layer

Each layer is further divided into several blocks called nodes as shown in Figure 7.3. Each node is assigned a particular task to perform and that is further passed to the next layer.

Input Layer

- It is the first layer of a Neural Network.
- It is used to take data as input using this layer and thus gives input to the Neural Network.
- The input layer is responsible to feed in the input and no processing takes place here.

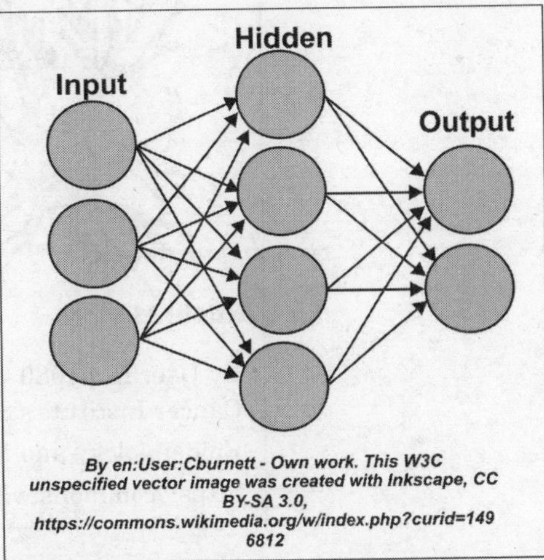

Figure 7.3: *Neural network model*

Hidden Layer

- It is a layer between the input and output layers.
- This layer is responsible for processing the input fed into the system.
- Processing is not visible to anyone and thus is called the hidden layer.
- Each node of the hidden layer has its own functionality, and hence,the defined Machine Learning algorithm gets executed on the data received from the input layer.
- The processed information is then given to the subsequent hidden layer in the network.
- The number of hidden layers in a neural network system totally depends on the complexity of the function for which the network has been designed.

Output Layer

- It is the last layer of the Neural Network.
- It displays the results as given by the system.

Relationship between the neural networks and the human nervous system

Let us see the functionality of a neuron in the human nervous system.

Neurons are the basic units of your nervous system. Every neuron is made up of soma, axon, and dendrites.

Dendrites are tree-like structures which are used to take the input. Soma is the cell body of the neuron and acts like a processing unit. Axon is used to give the output.

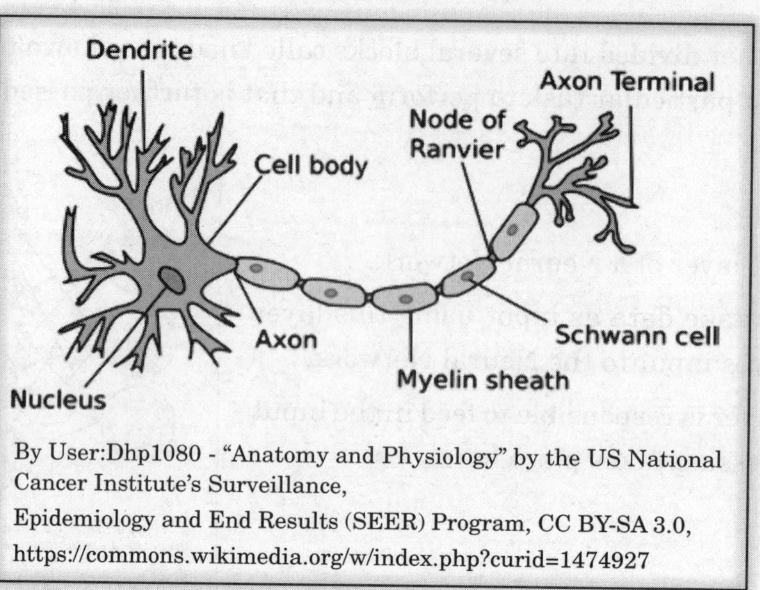

By User:Dhp1080 - "Anatomy and Physiology" by the US National Cancer Institute's Surveillance, Epidemiology and End Results (SEER) Program, CC BY-SA 3.0, https://commons.wikimedia.org/w/index.php?curid=1474927

Figure 7.4: *Picture of neuron*

The similarities between the Artificial Neural Network (ANN) and Biological Neural Network (BNN) are given in the following table.

Artificial Neural Network	Biological Neural Network	Function
Input Layer	Dendrites	Takes input for the system.
Node	Soma/Cell body	Responsible for processing of the information.
Interconnections	Synapse	These are the connections between the input and output.
Output Layer	Axon	This sends out the result.

FACT BOT

The first Artificial Neural Network was invented in 1958 by psychologist Frank Rosenblatt.

Activity 7.2

Write the differences between the Artificial Neural Network (ANN) and Biological Neural Network (BNN) based on the conditions mentioned in the following table.

Criteria	ANN	BNN
Processing capability		
Learning capability		
Storage capacity		

Definition Bot

AI model is a Neural Network model that is based on mathematical calculation with few linear formulas.

Activity 7.3

Let us play a game to understand the working of the Neural Network.

- Divide the whole class into four groups in such a manner that each group represents one layer of the neural network. The first group of X students represents the layer 1, i.e., the input layer, the second group of Y students as the hidden layer 1, the third group of Z students as hidden layer 2, and the fourth group of 1 student as the output layer.
- The input layer takes in the data which is passed on to hidden layers for some processing. The output layer finally gets all information from the hidden layer and gives meaningful information as the final result.

Let us give one problem to the input layer and the final solution/output is delivered by the output layer after all the processing is done by the hidden layers. To understand this hierarchy and concept of layers, let us take an example of Panchayati Raj.

Before playing the game, answer the following questions as per your knowledge:

1. What problems did the villages have?

 ____

2. How was this problem solved?

 ____

3. What is the importance of Gram Sabha?

 ____

4. Is there any relationship between Gram Sabha and Gram Panchayat?

 ____

5. What is the difference between Gram Sabha and Gram Panchayat?

 ____

As you all know that each and every game is associated with certain set of rules and thus, you have to follow a set of rules in this game too that are listed below:

- No one is supposed to talk to one another. Whatever comes to your mind that is your take on it and just keep doing as a part of game.
- In this game, one has to behave like a system to take input silently and write it on a slip and pass on. Also, time efficiency matters in this game, so play it taking as less time as possible.
- There needs to be proper spacing between the layers so that game can be played honestly.
- Only one word per chit is allowed to write.

Let us see how you will play the game now:

- **Input Layer:**
    - All students (for example,seven students) are treated as nodes to the input layer.
    - An image is shown to all the students and each student needs to write six different words on six different chits. The word to be written has to describe the image in the best possible way.
    - One chit is passed to each node of the hidden layer 1.

Analogy with Panchayati Raj: Gram Panchayat being the very first stage of Panchayati Raj acts like an input layer. So, the common people of a village will approach the Gram Panchayat for their problems/issues.

- **Hidden Layer 1:**
    - All students (for example,six students) are treated as the nodes for the hidden layer 1.
    - Each node in this layer will receive one chit from each node in the input layer. Therefore, each node will get seven chits. Now, after reading seven chits, they have to process it and write only four words in four different chits. They can use the same word or any other word as per their understanding.
    - These four chits are to be given randomly to any four nodes of the hidden layer 2 in such a manner that each node of the hidden layer 2 should get the same number of chits.

Analogy with Panchayati Raj: The problem/issues have been received by the Gram Panchayat. Gram Panchayat looks into the matter and tries to solve the issue The Gram Panchayat holds a meeting to take out the solution and takes the matter the Gram Sabha if the problem is critical.

- **Hidden Layer 2:**
    - All students (for example,six students) are treated as the nodes for the hidden layer 2.

- Each node will get some chits from the hidden layer 1. They will have to perform the same task as the hidden layer 1 to list down two different words on two different chits and pass it on to the output layer.

Analogy with Panchayati Raj: Once the information is received by the Gram Sabha,it is the duty of Gram Sabha to check whether the problem is resolved properly by Gram Panchayat. Gram Sabha needs to inform this problem and the kind of solution to the Zila Parishad for its consent.

- **Output Layer:**
  - The output layer will receive 12 chits in all. Using these 12 words from 12 chits, the student has to understand all the words and guess the image shown to the input layer.
  - This layer has to summarize all the words and make the description of the image shown.

Analogy with Panchayati Raj: As the Zila Parishad is the topmost level in Panchayati Raj, the information from the people goes to the Gram Panchayat which is passed to Gram Sabha and thus reaches the Zila Parishad. The Zila Parishad holds responsible for implementation of policies in their district, showcasing the progress of their district as per their effective and efficient implementation.

The output layer presents the summary to the whole class along with the image.

Note: If the summary matches with the image, then the whole network wins the game otherwise they lose.

Watch the following YouTube video to understand how Artificial Intelligence improves the quality of your life.

https://www.youtube.com/watch?v=VwRbvVrUXTc&feature=youtu.be

Activity 7.4

Write any three advantages of Artificial Intelligence from the above mentioned video.

____

____

____

____

Knowledge Bot

- The human brain is composed of 86 billion nerve cells called neurons.
- Neural Networks include various technologies like Deep Learning, and Machine Learning as a part of Artificial Intelligence (AI).

Activity 7.5

Let us understand the Neural Network using this application which is known as **Autodraw**.

To work with Autodraw, let us perform the following steps:

Step 1: Open the application using any one of the following links:

https://experiments.withgoogle.com/autodraw> click on Launch Experiment.

OR

https://autodraw.com>click on Start Drawing.

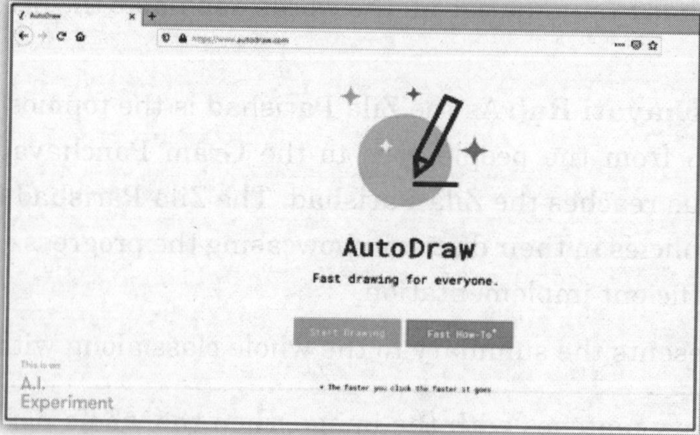

Figure 7.5: *Image shot of Autodraw*

Step 2: Select the first icon from the left-hand side toolbar as shown in Figure 7.6. This icon is used to activate the AI element of the tool.

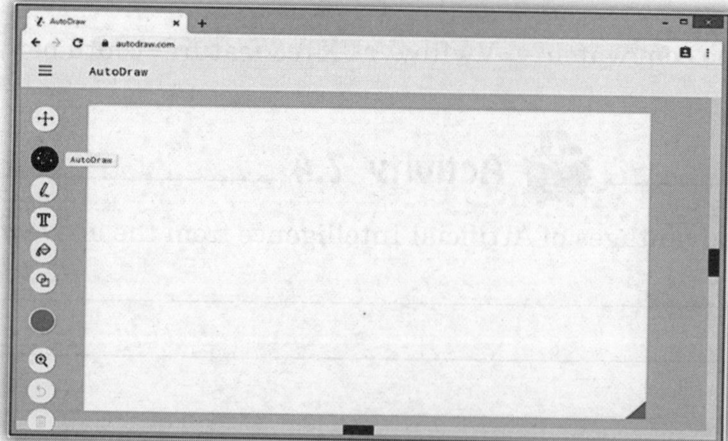

Figure 7.6: *Screenshot of the Autodraw startup canvas*

Step 3: Now, you can draw anything, and you will observe that the AI algorithm predicts all the possible drawings that matches with your artwork. These drawings are shown on the top row. Now, you can choose the image you wanted to draw as it is shown in Figure 7.7.

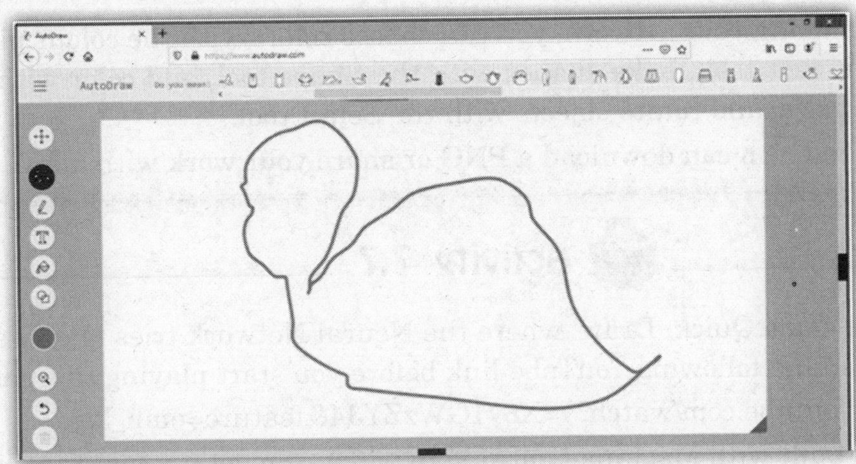

Figure 7.7: *Screenshot of the drawing created with the pencil tool*

Step 4: You will find the image selected on the canvas and now you can choose the colour from the palette and fill it in the image as per your requirement as shown in Figure 7.8.

Figure 7.8: *Screenshot of the drawing once selected from the predicted images by the machine.*

You can play this as a game by just thinking about any image. Start drawing and see what all possible images are displayed after analyzing and predictions made by the AI algorithm.

Activity 7.6

Let us see what more can you do with Autodraw.

To work with Autodraw, let us perform the following steps:

- You can also make your own drawing with the draw tool if you are good at drawing on computers.
- While making your artwork, you can choose colors with the colour picker, add text with the text tool, make shapes with the Shape tool, add color with the Fill tool, move, resize, and rotate objects with the Select tool.
- At the end, you can download a PNG or share your work with a link.

Activity 7.7

Let us play a game Quick, Draw! where the Neural Network tries to guess what you're drawing. Open the following YouTube link before you start playing this game.

https://www.youtube.com/watch?v=X8v1GWzZYJ4&feature=emb_logo

This game is built with Machine Learning in which you get a prompt to draw an image of a written text in 20 seconds in such a manner that the neural network can identify it. The more you play with the machine, the more it will keep learning.

This is an example of how the machine learns over time using Image Recognition and Optical Character Recognition.

It keeps adding the drawings to the world's largest doodling datas et so as to help machine learning research.

When you play this game, it will ask you to draw six objects one by one. One object specified in 20 seconds.

Step 1: Click on the following link to play this game:

https://quickdraw.withgoogle.com/

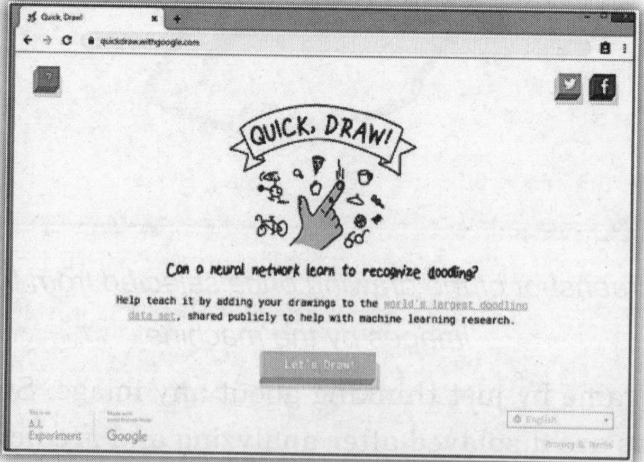

Figure 7.9: *First screen of the app*

Step 2: Click on Let's Draw! and then keep following the instructions given by the system.

Figure 7.10(a) *Autodraw will prompt to draw six pictures one by one*

Figure 7.10(b): *Will keep prompting while you are drawing whichever object is detected from the shape you are making*

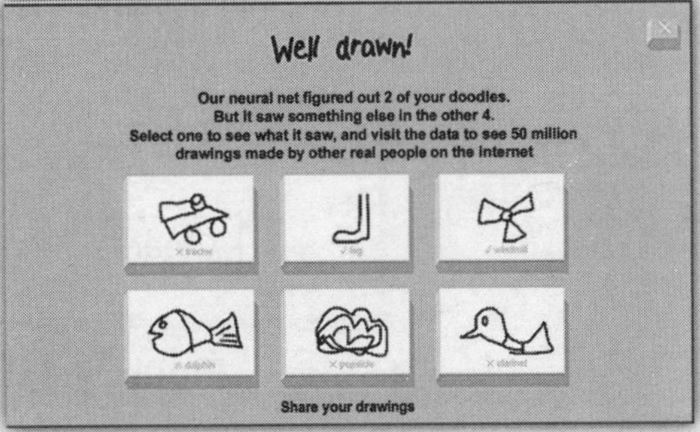

Figure 7.10(c): *Once all six images are drawn, it will display the result as shown*

Activity 7.8

Let us do the activity Sketch2Code by the Microsoft web-based solution which can convert your handmade design into HTML code using Artificial Intelligence.

There are three easy steps to work with the Sketch2Code app:

1. Upload Design.
2. Sketch2code is at work once the design is uploaded.
3. Download your HTML code once HTML is designed by the AI.

Note: You can also view the predicted objects from your sketch which will display three models in a row, that is, Sketch, Predicted objects in the sketch, and the HTML code.

TIP BOT

Sketch2Code is available for developers on GitHub and its code is independent of HTML.

Steps to be followed:

Step 1: Create a handmade drawing of your choice. Click and save it in your system. An example is shown in Figure 7.11.

Admission Form

Enter Your Name :

Date of Birth : Day Month Year

Father's Name :

Mother's Name :

Class :

Clear Submit

Figure 7.11: *Handmade layout*

Step 2: Open the following link:
https://sketch2code.azurewebsites.net/

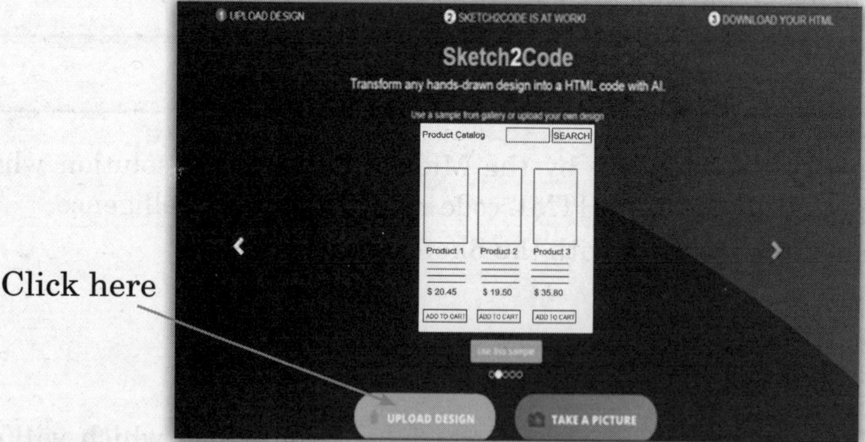

Figure 7.12: *Main screen of Sketch2Code*

Step 3: Click on Upload Design and choose the picture which you want to be converted to the HTML code. An example is shown in Figure 7.13:

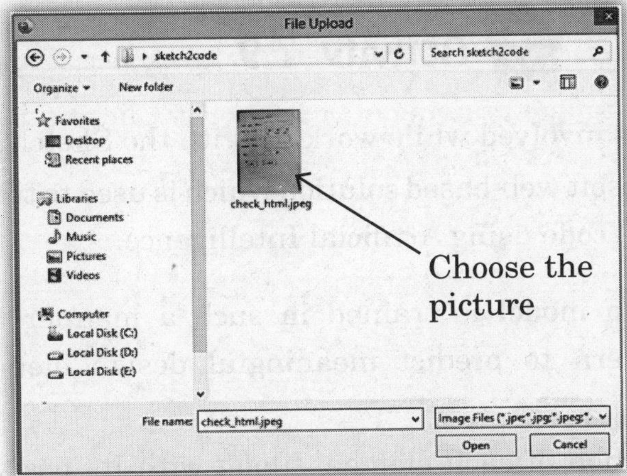

Figure 7.13: *Choose the handmade file*

Step 4: Once the image is uploaded, the Sketch2Code will do its work and show the image file as well as the HTML code with it as shown in Figure 7.14.

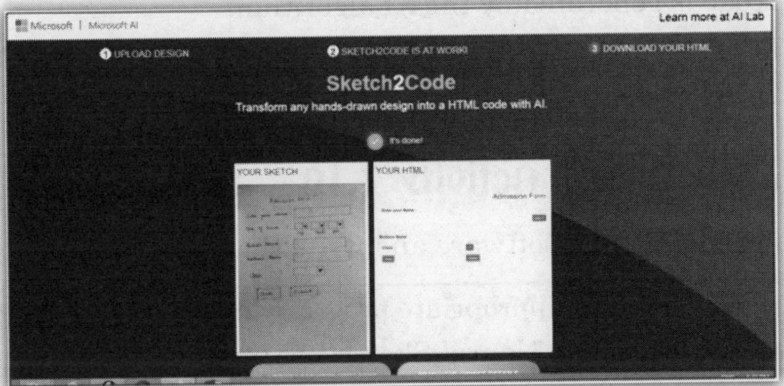

Figure 7.14: *Sketch2Code converted the image to HTML code*

Step 5: You can also check what all elements are predicted by the machine as per your drawing by clicking on the Predicted Object Details button below the HTML code as shown in Figure 7.15.

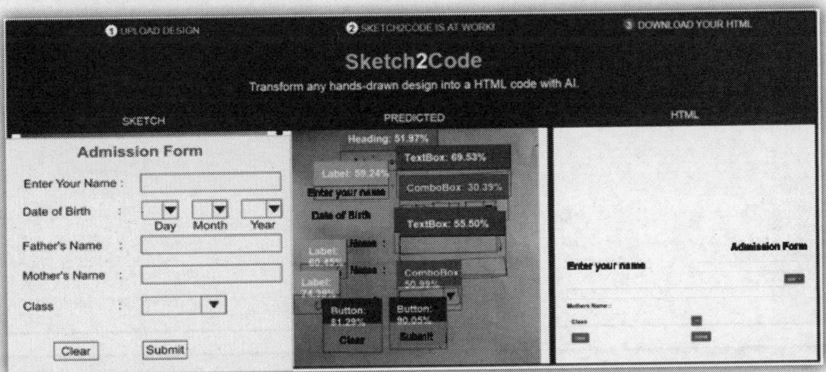

Figure 7.15: *Shows the handmade design, elements predicted by AI algorithm and HTML code*

Activity 7.9

Write the various steps involved while working with the Sketch2Code activity.

Sketch2Code is a Microsoft web-based solution which is used to transform any handmade designs into the HTML code using Artificial Intelligence.

- A computer vision model is trained in such a manner that it recognizes the handwritten pattern to predict meaningful design elements from the image captured.
- Now, text recognition of each element along with its position from the image is used to extract the content.
- The algorithm fetches all the information along with its position from the image and generates the HTML structure.
- The HTML code is generated by the AI algorithm.

Activity 7.10

Research the following AI tools/software and write their purposes.

Bayou	Generate an appropriate program in Java using the query. It uses a method called Neural Sketch Learning.
DeepCode	
Embold	
PyCharm	
Sketch2Code	

Activity 7.11

Open the following link to understand the handwriting with a Neural Network.

https://experiments.withgoogle.com/handwriting-with-a-neural-net

Play with a Neural Network that generates the handwriting based on your style.

Activity 7.12

Write a few advantages of Artificial Intelligence.

- Increases productivity.
- Helps experts to do a better job in less time with AI capabilities.
- Customer service.
- Improves the customer and employees' experiences with AI assistants.
- AI for financial services.
- ______________________________
- ______________________________

TECH BOT

- **Neural Network:** It is a computer program that operates in a manner inspired by the natural Neural Network in the brain.
- **Quick Draw!!:** It is an online game developed by Google that challenges players to draw a picture of an object or idea and then uses a Neural Network Artificial Intelligence to guess what the drawings represent.
- **Sketch2Code:** Microsoft has developed an AI-powered web design tool that can turn sketches of websites into functional HTML code, called Sketch2Code.

Recap Bot

- Machine Learning is a component of Artificial Intelligence that leans from previous dataset.
- Supervised learning models can make predictions based on labeled datasets.
- Classification is a systematic grouping of observations into categories.
- Classification and clustering works on discrete datasets.
- Applications of classification are speech recognition, biometric identification, handwriting recognition, and so on.
- Regression works with continuous data.
- Deep Learning learns by itself, that is, using a neural network that acts like a human brain and then analyzes the data as humans do.
- Examples of Deep Learning are chatbots, automatic translation of text, adding colors to mono colour images, autonomous vehicles, computer vision, text generation (use of punctuation and grammar), and so on.
- The function of an axon in neuron is to transmit information to different neurons, muscles, and glands.
- The function of a dendrite in neuron is to send messages to the neuron cell body for the cell to function.
- The cell body is also called soma which connects to the dendrites so as to bring information to the neuron and the axon which sends information to other neurons.
- Autodraw is a tool by Google Creative Lab.
- Autodraw is a fast drawing tool that acts like a magic wand for everyone to create anything visual and quick.
- Autodraw is collaboration between machine learning and the artist community. It can guess hundreds of drawings and more drawings will be added over time.
- The nervous system is responsible for coordinating and controlling all the activities of the body.
- The Neural Network is defined as a combination of algorithms to understand the relationship between various sets of data to process and then takes out some meaningful information from it.
- Panchayati Raj system of India follows a three-tier system that is Gram Panchayat, Gram Sabha, and Zila Parishad.

A. Multiple choice questions.

1. Which one of the following is used to take the input from the user?
   - a. Hidden Layer
   - b. Input Layer
   - c. Output Layer
   - d. None of the above
2. Which one of the following is not the function of the hidden layer ?
   - a. To display the result
   - b. Receive data from the input layer
   - c. Process the data
   - d. Give the data to the output layer
3. Which one of the following is not a part of a neuron?
   - a. Axon
   - b. Dendrite
   - c. Cell body
   - d. Lobe
4. Which body system is responsible for coordinating and controlling all the activities?
   - a. Stomach
   - b. Muscles
   - c. Nervous system
   - d. Organ system
5. Which is used to send signals away from neurons in the nervous system?
   - a. Nucleus
   - b. Cell body
   - c. Dendrites
   - d. Axons
6. How many tiers are there in the Panchayati Raj system in India?
   - a. 1-tier
   - b. 2-tier
   - c. 3-tier
   - d. None of the above
7. Autodraw is a tool by ____________________.
   - a. Microsoft AI Learning
   - b. Intel AI Models
   - c. Google Creative Lab
   - d. None of the above
8. Sketch2Code is a Microsoft web-based solution to transform any handmade designs into HTML code using Artificial Intelligence.
   - a. True
   - b. False
   - c. Can't say
   - d. None is mentioned

B. Fill in the blanks.

1. Machine Learning is a component of ________________________.
2. ________________ and ________________ works on discrete data.

3. Classification is a ______________ grouping of observations into categories.
4. In ______________ learning, the algorithm learns from a dataset which is labeled.
5. ______________ learning is used in gaming.
6. ____________ data is used to check the efficiency of the model.
7. ______________ is the first stage in Panchayati Raj which acts like an input layer.
8. Bayou uses a method called ______________ Learning.
9. ____________ is a game by Google where neural net tries to guess what you're drawing.
10. ______________ app is used to convert handmade drawing into the HTML code.

C. Match the following.

Column A	Column B
1. Input Layer	i. Fast drawing tool
2. Synapse	ii. Responsible for processing
3. Axon	iii Input layer
4. Hidden Layer	iv. Labeled dataset
5. First layer of Neural Network	v. Soma
6. Supervised learning	vi. Interconnections
7. Cell body	vii. Dendrites
8. Autodraw	viii. Output layer

D. Answer the following questions.

1. Write the full form for the following organizations.
   a. ANN b. BNN
2. Define the following terms.
   a. Deep Learning b. Neural Network
   c. Regression
3. Write any one important feature of the following application.
   a. Autodraw b. Sketch2Code
4. Write the functions of the following:
   a. Dendrites b. Axon
   c. Soma
5. Name any three applications of classifications.
6. Write any two examples of Deep Learning.
7. What is the need of Neural Networks in Artificial Intelligence?
8. Name any two datasets required for Artificial Intelligence modeling.

9. Write the procedure how AI is helping in tagging images in Facebook once an image is uploaded.
10. Differentiate between supervised and unsupervised learning models.
11. Write the three levels of Panchayati Raj along with their functionality.
12. Write the three easy steps to work with Sketch2Code application.

Lab Activity

AI Duet: This experiment lets you play a duet with the computer. Just play some notes, and the computer will respond to your melody. You don't even have to know how to play piano—its fun to just press some keys and listen to what comes back. You can click the keyboard, use your computer keys, or even plug in a MIDI keyboard.

1. Go to the link: https://experiments.withgoogle.com/ai-duet

   The following page appears.

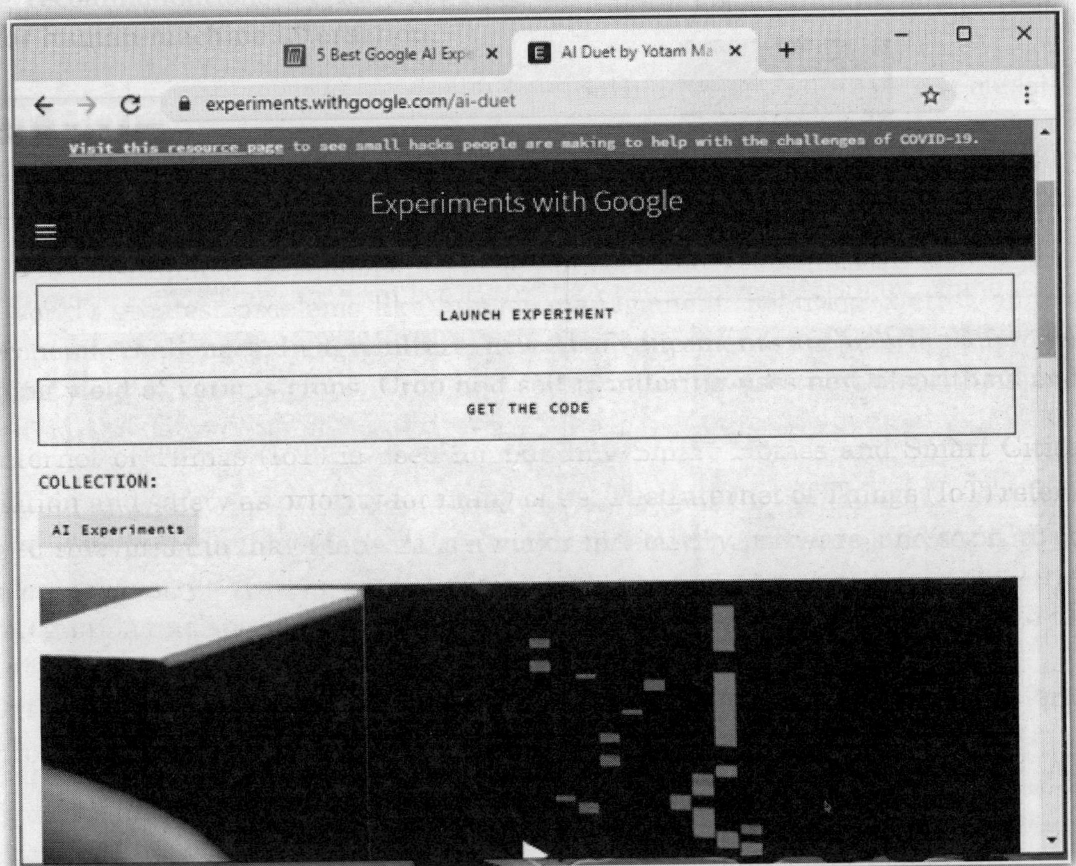

2. Click on the Launch Experiment button. The following screen appears.

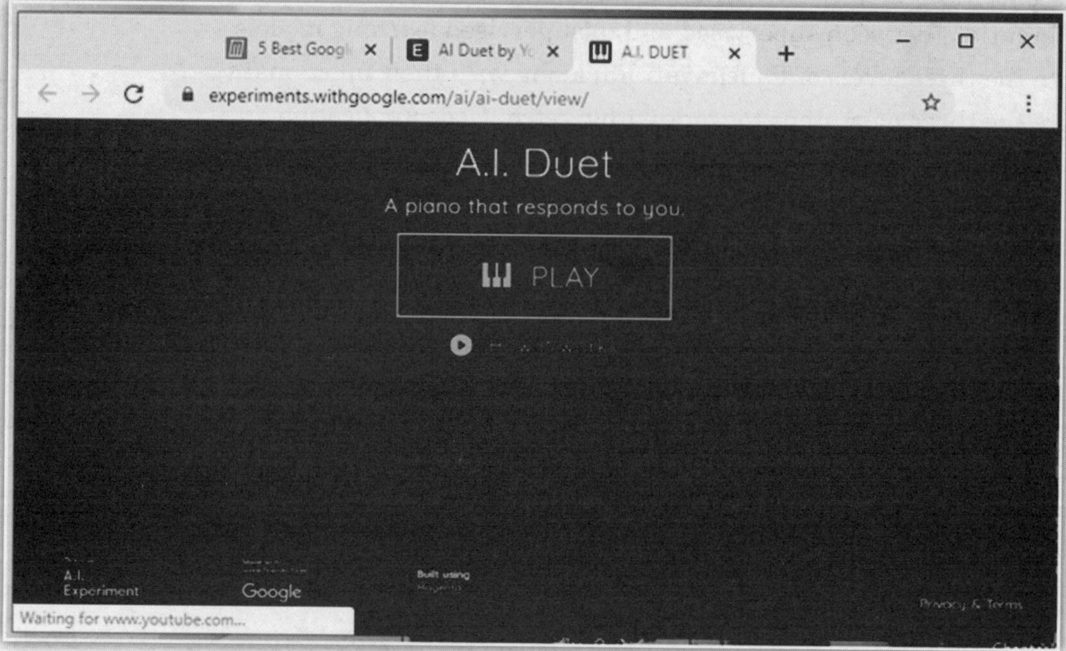

3. Click on the PLAY button.

4. Click on any key of the keyboard. The desired sound will be produced.

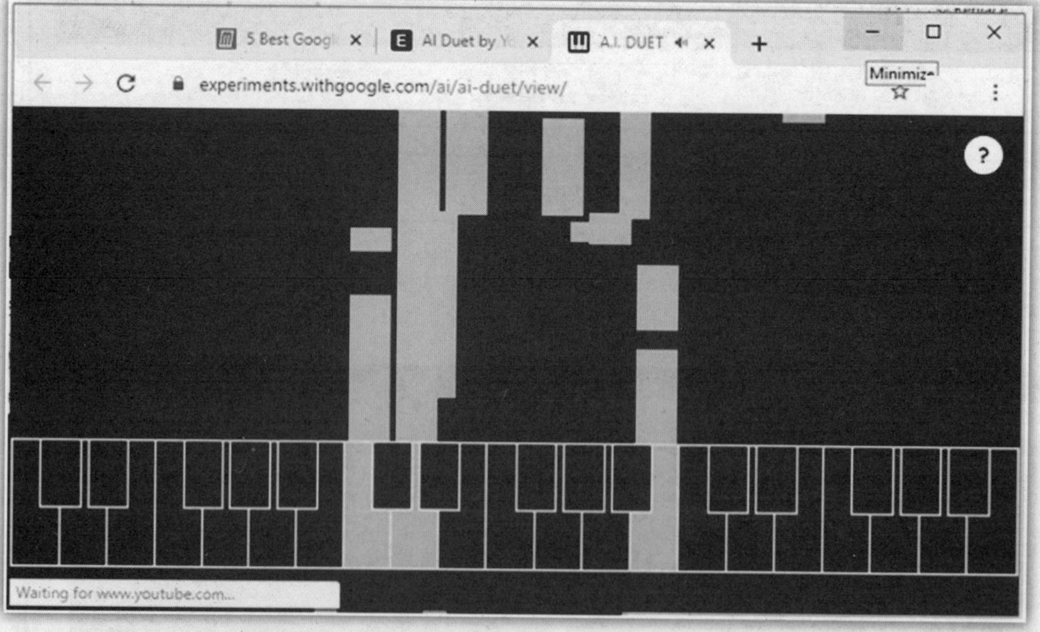

Worksheet

A. Fill in the blanks.

1. ________________is a type of supervised learning model.
2. A network of such neurons is called a ________________.
3. ______________is the first layer of a Neural Network.
4. ________is used to give the output.
5. ______________send out the result.
6. ____________works with continuous data.
7. Classification and clustering works on ____________datasets.
8. ______________is a tool by Google Creative lab.
9. The _________code is generated by the AI algorithm.
10. ____________layer is responsible for processing the input fed into the system.

B. State whether the following statements are True or False.

1. Dendrites are tree-like structures which are
2. Each layer is further divided into several blocks called nodes.
3. Neural Network helps in trading based on algorithms only.
4. Unsupervised learning is used in gaming.
5. The efficiency of the AI machine depends on the results.
6. Regression model work on datasets which are labelled and then predict the label of the testing dataset.
7. Neural comes from the word neuron of the nervous system.
8. Neural Network are used to solve real-life complex problems.

C. Write down the full form of the following.

1. ANN ______________________________
2. BNN ______________________________
3. HTML ______________________________

D. Answer the following questions.

1. Write down the function of soma.
2. What is Autodraw?
3. What is the responsibility of nervous system?
4. Explain regression and clustering.

QUIZ CARD

Multiple choice questions.

1. How many common AI models are there?
   a. 2 ☐ b. 3 ☐
   c. 4 ☐ d. 5 ☐
2. Classification is a type of:
   a. Supervised learning ☐ b. Unsupervised learning ☐
   c. Reinforcement learning ☐ d. None of these ☐
3. Which model algorithm are working towards accomplishing the goal or try to improve the performance in a particular task?
   a. Supervised learning ☐ b. Unsupervised learning ☐
   c. Reinforcement learning ☐ d. None of these ☐
4. ______________data is entered into the AI machine which uses this dataset by the algorithms and rules to give or predict the output.
   a. Training ☐ b. Testing ☐
   c. Information ☐ d. None of these ☐
5. Which filter in an e-mail is an example of hoe classification works?
   a. Spam ☐ b. Trash ☐
   c. Inbox ☐ d. Compose ☐
6. Which learning model tells where the problems are based on continuous data?
   a. Clustering ☐ b. Classification ☐
   c. Regression ☐ d. None of these ☐
7. __________is a type of unsupervised learning.
   a. Clustering ☐ b. Classification ☐
   c. Regression ☐ d. None of these ☐
8. Which is the last layer of the Neural Network?
   a. Input ☐ b. Hidden ☐
   c. Output ☐ d. None of these ☐
9. ____________________is the cell body of the neuron and act like a processing unit.
   a. Dendrites ☐ b. Soma ☐
   c. Axon ☐ d. None of these ☐
10. ______________are the connections between the input and output.
    a. Dendrites ☐ b. Soma ☐
    c. Axon ☐ d. Synapse ☐

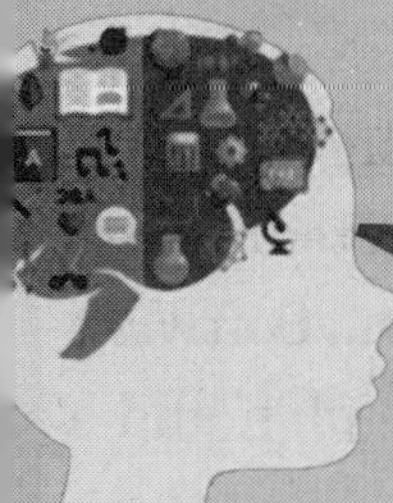

8 Understanding the Programming Basics

Structure Bot

In this chapter, we will discuss the following topics:

- Learn basic programming skills through gamified platforms
- Explore online portals like Code Combat to understand coding basics

Objective Bot

At the end of this chapter, you should be able to:

- Play online games that encourage trial-and-error, critical thinking, and creativity
- Apply the coding skills learned by developing their in project-based solutions

Whenever you want to use a computer for a specific task, a chronological order of instructions have to be given to the computer which can be easily understood and interpreted. These set of logical instructions written in a high-level language forms a program. Software development incorporates various intermediate tasks that follow an organized plan and a series of sub tasks for application development.

Definition Bot

Program is a set of instruction to perform a particular task using any of programming language.

Program Development Stages

- Analyzing a problem requires a clear definition of the problem statement, inputs, processing and desired outputs, and user interfaces.
- Designing the program involves a clear logical plan explaining the algorithm and flowchart of the program activities.
- Coding involves translating the design into an application using a programming language.
- Testing and Debugging requires making the program error free.
- Documentation involves preparing an information manual for the end user.

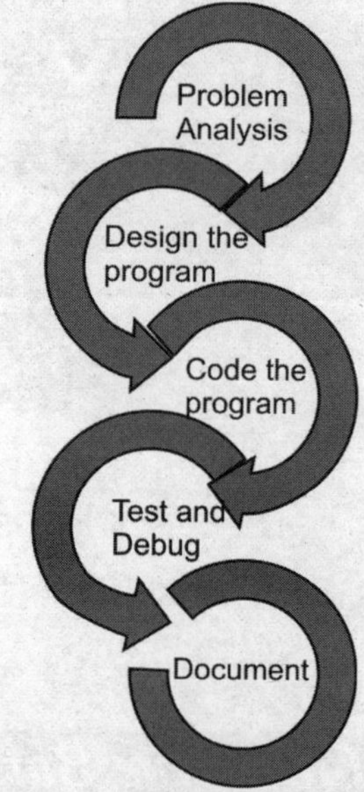

Figure 8.1: *Application Development*

Let us delve a little deeper into the concept to understand it better. Computers are used to perform various tasks to get the results accurately in less time. To perform any task, you always need to follow steps in a particular order. Therefore, step-by-step instructions should be given to solve any problem. Thus, solving a problem depends on how the problem is defined, how the problem is designed and then implemented using a programming language. To represent the steps for problem solving, you need to follow the given steps.

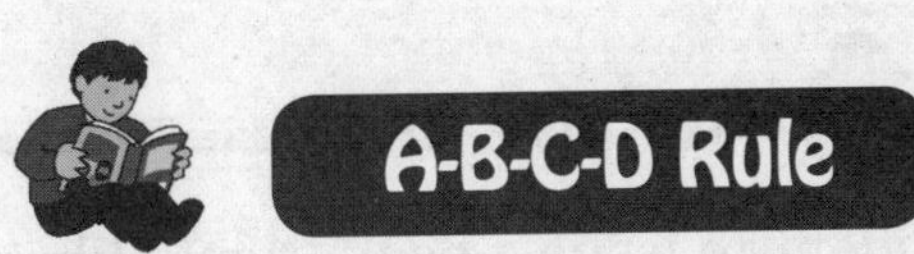

Analyzing the problem
- Try to understand the given problem.
- Read the problem carefully to understand the basic functionalities.
- Figure out what are the inputs required and what all calculations need to be performed on the input to get the desired output.

Broadcast the developed algorithm
- Chalk out a plan of action before writing a program.
- The solution is represented in English language and is called an algorithm.
- An algorithm is like a well-written recipe for preparing a dish with proper steps.

Code it
- After writing the algorithm, convert it into the form which is understandable by the computer to give the desired output. Different languages can be used.

Debug and Test
- The program can then be tested by giving various inputs and checking the outputs for those set of inputs.
- No output will be generated if the code has syntax errors.
- If the code is giving wrong output, then you need to check the logical errors.

An Algorithm can be defined as a set of steps which when followed solve the problem and perform a particular task. It can be described as a set of instructions written in plain English language that take an input and provide an output. In simple terms, it can also be defined as a set of intermediate steps to complete a job.

KNOWLEDGE BOT

- Machine language consists of 0's and 1's which is also known as binary language and is understandable by the computer.
- The assembly language uses symbolic codes known as mnemonics for programming.

Activity 8.1

Write an algorithm for a student to issue a book from a library.

Various applications of a neural network are:

1. ______________________________
2. ______________________________
3. ______________________________
4. ______________________________
5. ______________________________
6. ______________________________
7. ______________________________
8. ______________________________
9. ______________________________
10. ______________________________

Activity 8.2

Write an algorithm to calculate the average of any five natural numbers.

1. Start
2. Accept five natural numbers; a, b, c, d, e
3. Declare Sum: = (a + b + c + d + e)
4. Declare Average: = Sum / 5
5. Print the Sum
6. Stop

Activity 8.3

Write an algorithm to calculate the average of any five natural numbers.

1. Start
2. Accept five natural numbers; a, b, c, d, e
3. Declare Sum: = (a + b + c + d + e)
4. Declare Average: = Sum / 5
5. Print the Sum
6. Stop

Activity 8.4

Mention a few characteristics of a good algorithm.

- **Precision:** The steps are properly mentioned and defined well.
- **Uniqueness:** IPO (Input – Process – Output) cycle.
- **Finiteness:** The algorithm has to stop after a particular number of steps.
- **Input:** To get the data from the user.
- **Output:** To display the process information.

A Flowchart is a diagrammatic representation of an algorithm which explains a step-by-step approach for solving a task. It is made up of boxes, diamonds, and other shapes, connected with an arrow. Each shape represents a step and the arrow represents the order of thinking.

Flowchart symbol	Meaning	Function
	Start/End	An oval represents a start or end point.
	Input/Output	A parallelogram represents the input and output statements.
	Process	A rectangle represents a calculation or intermediate steps.
	Decision	A diamond indicates a decision to divert the flow of the program based on the validity of a condition.
	Arrow	A line is a connector that shows relationships between the representative shapes.

FACT BOT

Flowchart was first developed by Herman Goldstine and John Von Neumann in the 1940s.

DRAW.IO Online Platform

A flowchart can be drawn on a paper as well as using freely available online tools. You can explore the website www.draw.io online portal to draw a flowchart. You can login using your Google e-mail id and authorize the portal. You can further create the flowchart to understand the workflow of the problem statement or a process.

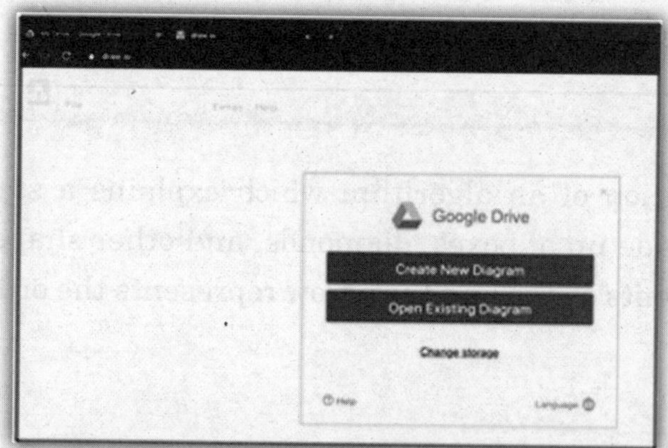

Figure 8.2: *www.draw.io*

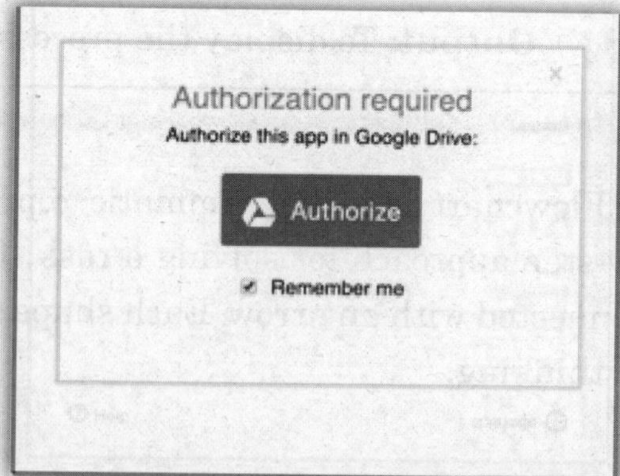

Figure 8.3: *Authorize with e-mail id*

TIP BOT

DRAW.IO supports powerful tools for showing your ideas with diagrams.

Activity 8.5

Draw a flowchart using www.draw.io portal to calculate the average of any five natural numbers. Make use of the algorithm in Activity 8.2.

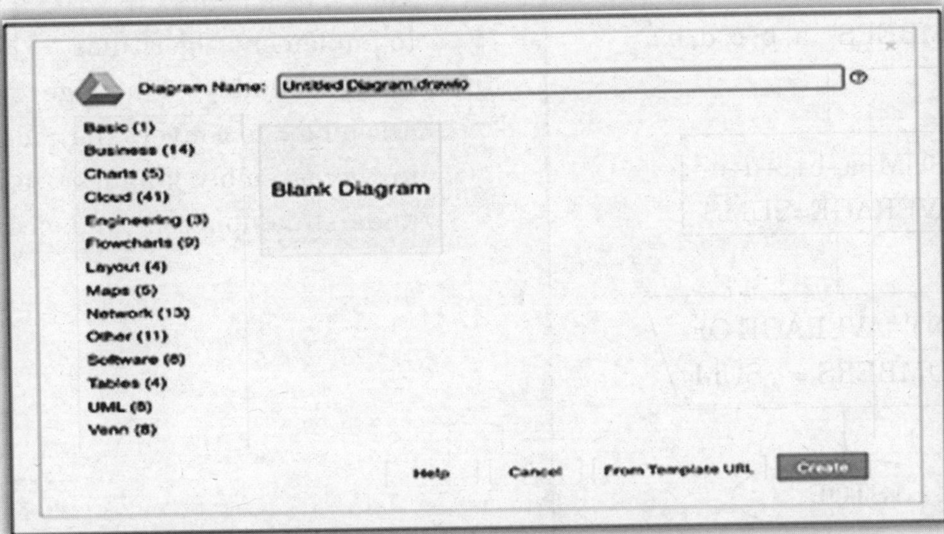

Figure 8.5: *Using a basic template to design the flowchart*

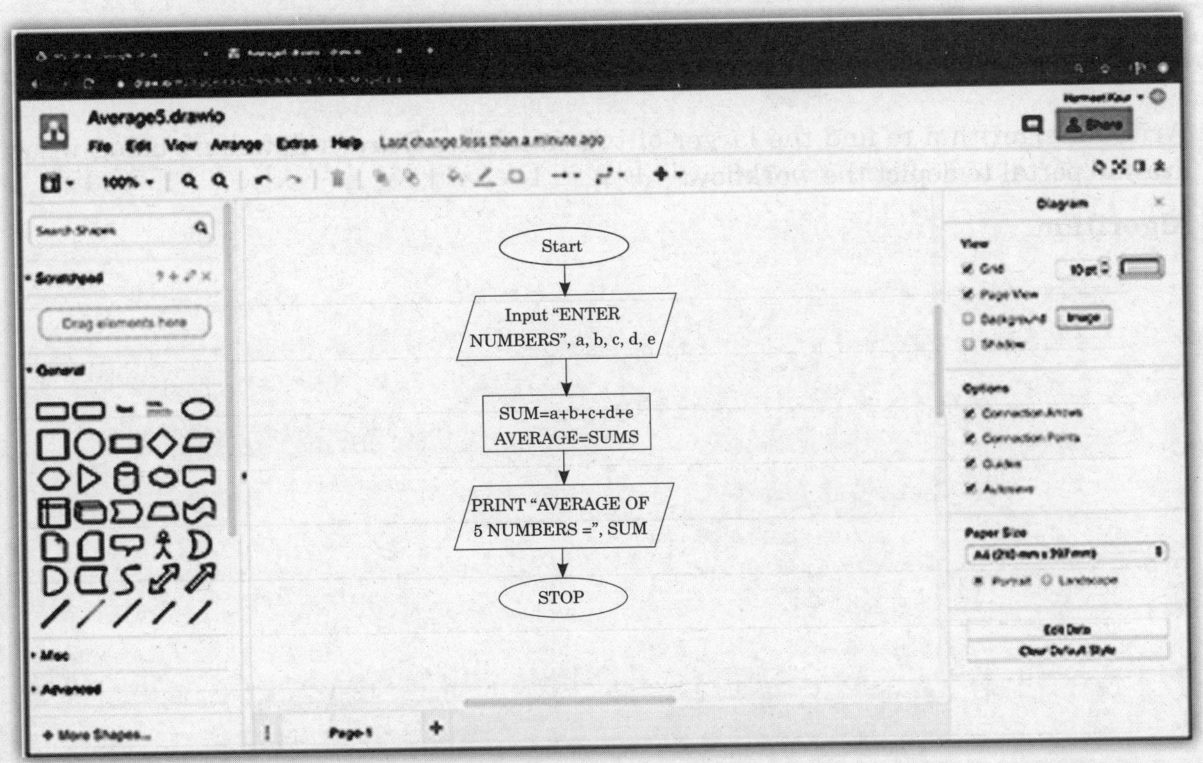

Figure 8.4: *Create a new flowchart*

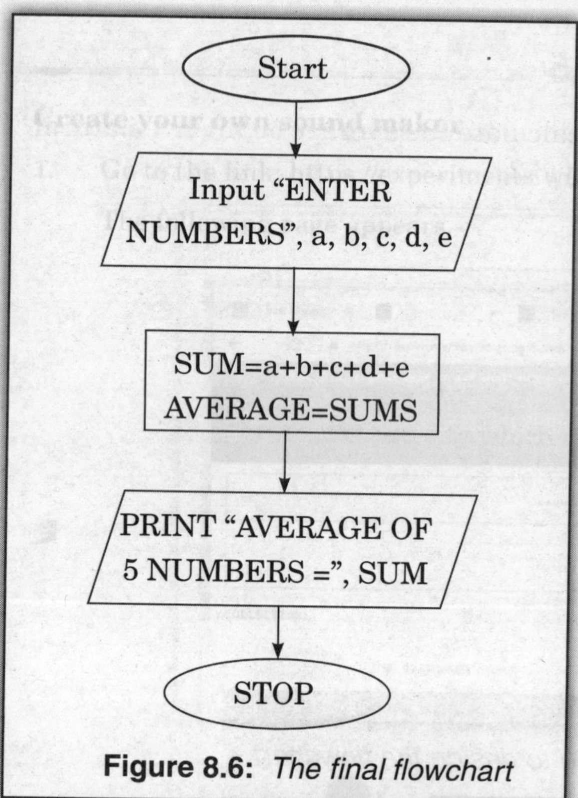

Figure 8.6: *The final flowchart*

EXTRA BYTE

- A programming language is a language which follows a set of rules known as a syntax to write a program to implement algorithms.
- The Assembly language uses an assembler to convert the code written in the assembly language to machine understandable code and vice versa.

Activity 8.6

Write an algorithm to find the larger of two numbers. Draw a flowchart using www.draw.io portal to depict the workflow.

Algorithm

1.
2.
3.
4.
5.
6.
7.
8.
9.
10.

Flowchart:

Gamification

Gamification is the use of game concepts in a non-gaming environment. Learning a programming language has become much easier with the availability of various online gaming portals. It is much easier to understand programming logic since the layout of the game is designed with various methods to encourage the user to solve the challenges and win various levels of the game. It is an immense motivation for the player to practice study and exchange ideas.

There are many such gaming portals available online which have encouraged students and helped them in learning coding or improving their coding skills.

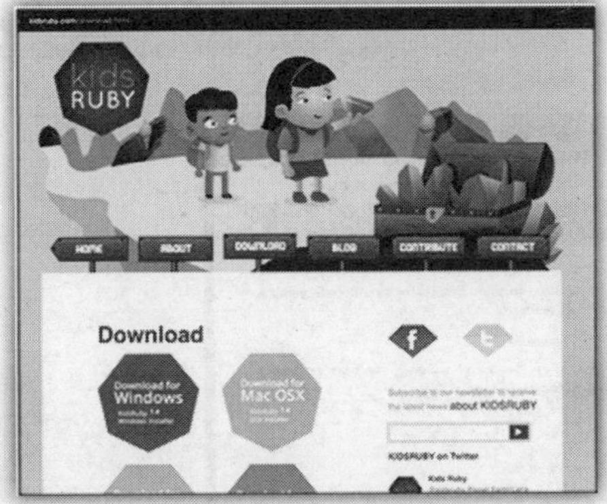

Figure 8.7: *www.kidsruby.com*

Figure 8.8: *www.codemonkey.com*

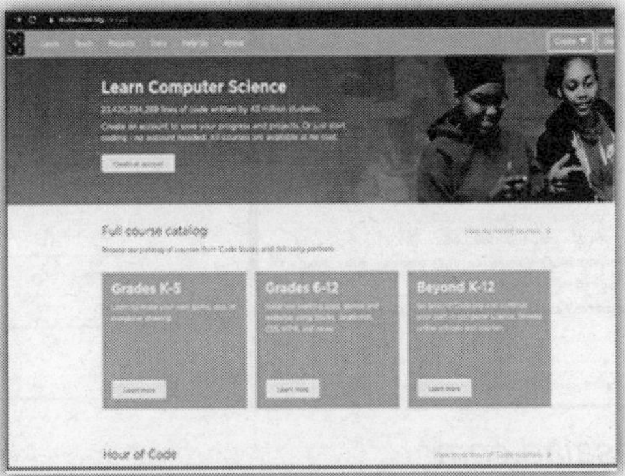

Figure 8.9: *www.code.org*

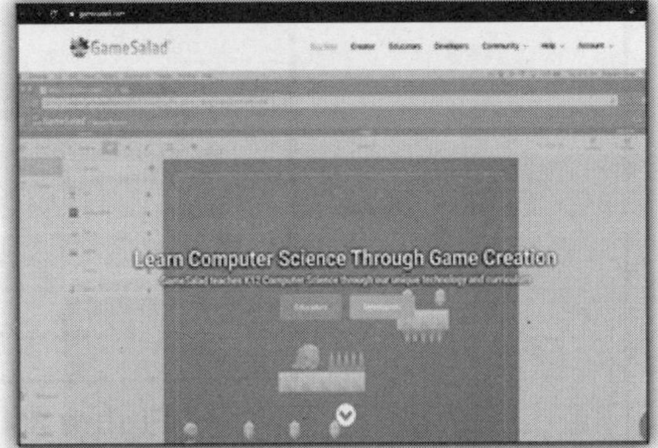

Figure 8.10: *www.gamesalad.com*

The CodeCombat portal

Coding is an incredibly useful skill to have these days. Code Combat uses the trick of turning hard work into a fun game. Code Combat's free Role-Playing Game (RPG) adventures do a great job of turning the basics of coding into fun games for kids. The portal offers worksheet examples which work on the A-B-C-D Rule. The problem statement can be broken down into a series of steps of the algorithm before actually coding the challenge.

MEMORY BOT

- CodeCombat portal uses real typed code and personalized learning to teach computer science with no teacher training needed.
- A Compiler converts the whole program in one go whereas an Interpreter converts the program one line at a time.

Activity 8.7

Explore the URL www.codecombat.com and create a 'Student Account'. You can explore multiple levels and challenges to get a certificate for the course 'Introduction to Computer Science – 1'.

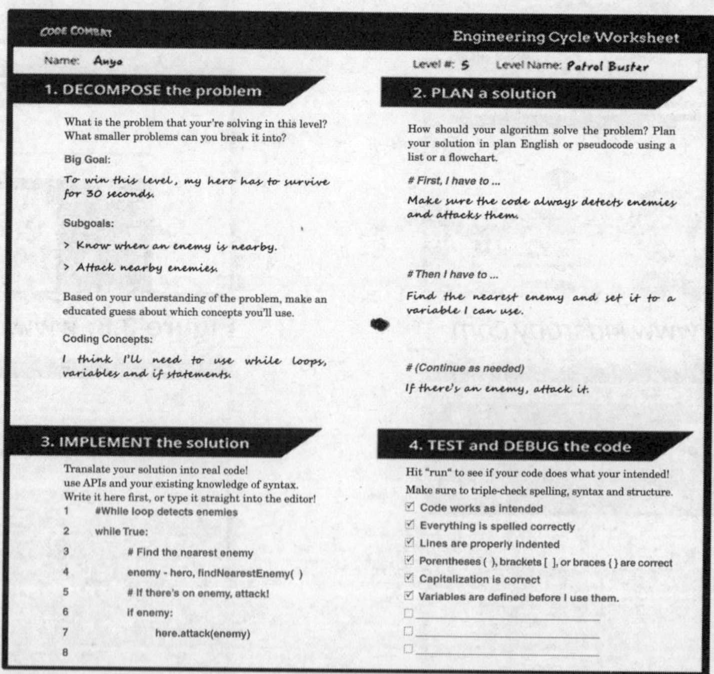

CODE COMBAT

Engineering Cycle Worksheet

Name: *Anya*

Level #: *5* Level Name: *Patrol Buster*

1. DECOMPOSE the problem

What is the problem that your're solving in this level?
What smaller problems can you break it into?

Big Goal:

To win this level, my hero has to survive for 30 seconds.

Subgoals:

> Know when an enemy is nearby.

> Attack nearby enemies.

Based on your understanding of the problem, make an educated guess about which concepts you'll use.

Coding Concepts:

I think I'll need to use while loops, variables and if statements.

2. PLAN a solution

How should your algorithm solve the problem? Plan your solution in plan English or pseudocode using a list or a flowchart.

 # First, I have to ...

Make sure the code always detects enemies and attacks them.

 # Then I have to ...

Find the nearest enemy and set it to a variable I can use.

 # (Continue as needed)

If there's an enemy, attack it.

3. IMPLEMENT the solution

Translate your solution into real code!
use APIs and your existing knowledge of syntax.
Write it here first, or type it straight into the editor!

```
#While loop detects enemies
while True:
        # Find the nearest enemy
        enemy - hero, findNearestEnemy( )
        # If there's on enemy, attack!
        if enemy:
                here.attack(enemy)
```

4. TEST and DEBUG the code

Hit "run" to see if your code does what your intended!
Make sure to triple-check spelling, syntax and structure.

- ☑ Code works as intended
- ☑ Everything is spelled correctly
- ☑ Lines are properly indented
- ☑ Porentheses ( ), brackets [ ], or braces { } are correct
- ☑ Capitalization is correct
- ☑ Variables are defined before I use them.
- ☐ ______
- ☐ ______
- ☐ ______

Figure 8.11: *www.gamesalad.com*

Figure 8.12: *Register as a 'Student' on www.codecombat.com*

(a)

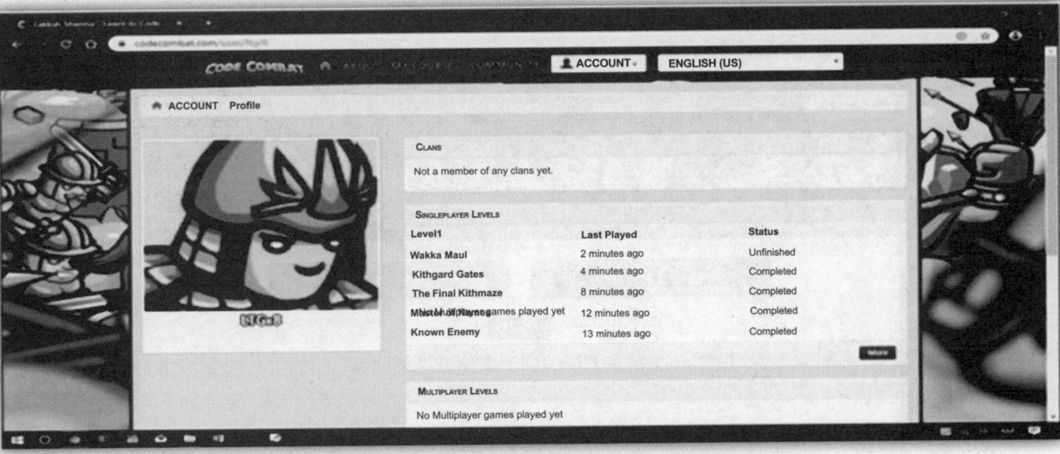

(b)

Figure 8.13: *Student Dashboard*

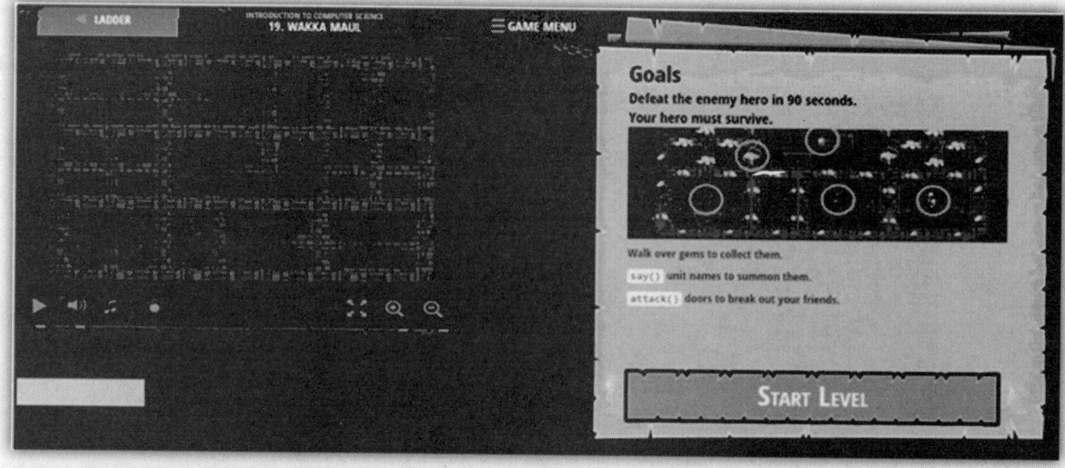

(a)

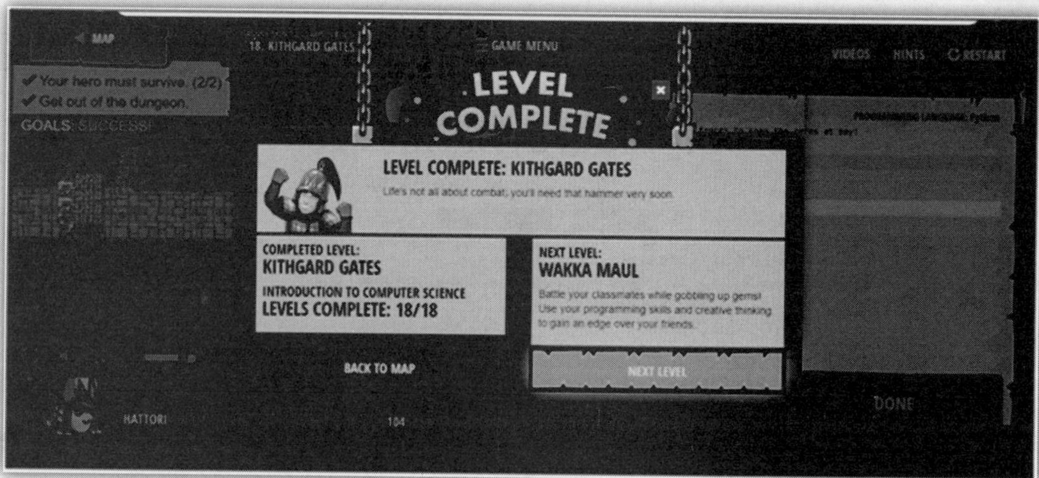

(b)

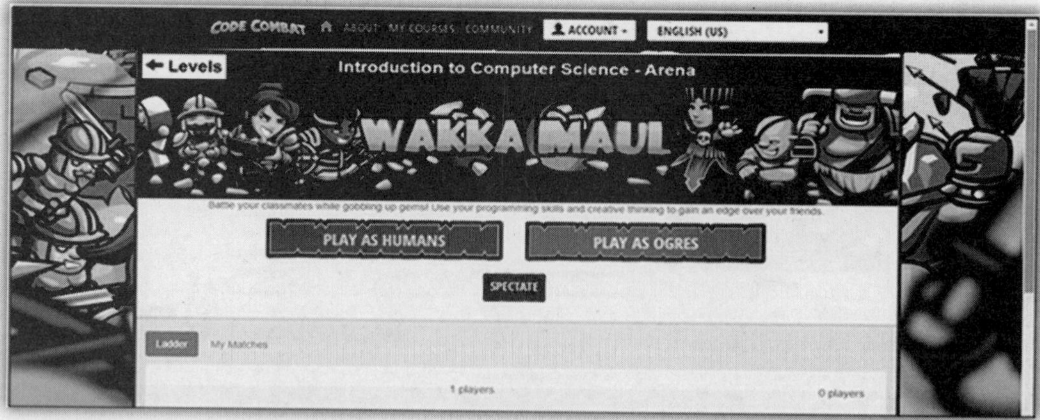

(c)

Figure 8.14: Student Playground

Explore the website Kodu Lab https://www. kodugamelab.com/ to create a game with all possible scenarios and characters. Kodu can be used to teach creativity, problem solving, and storytelling while learning coding skills.

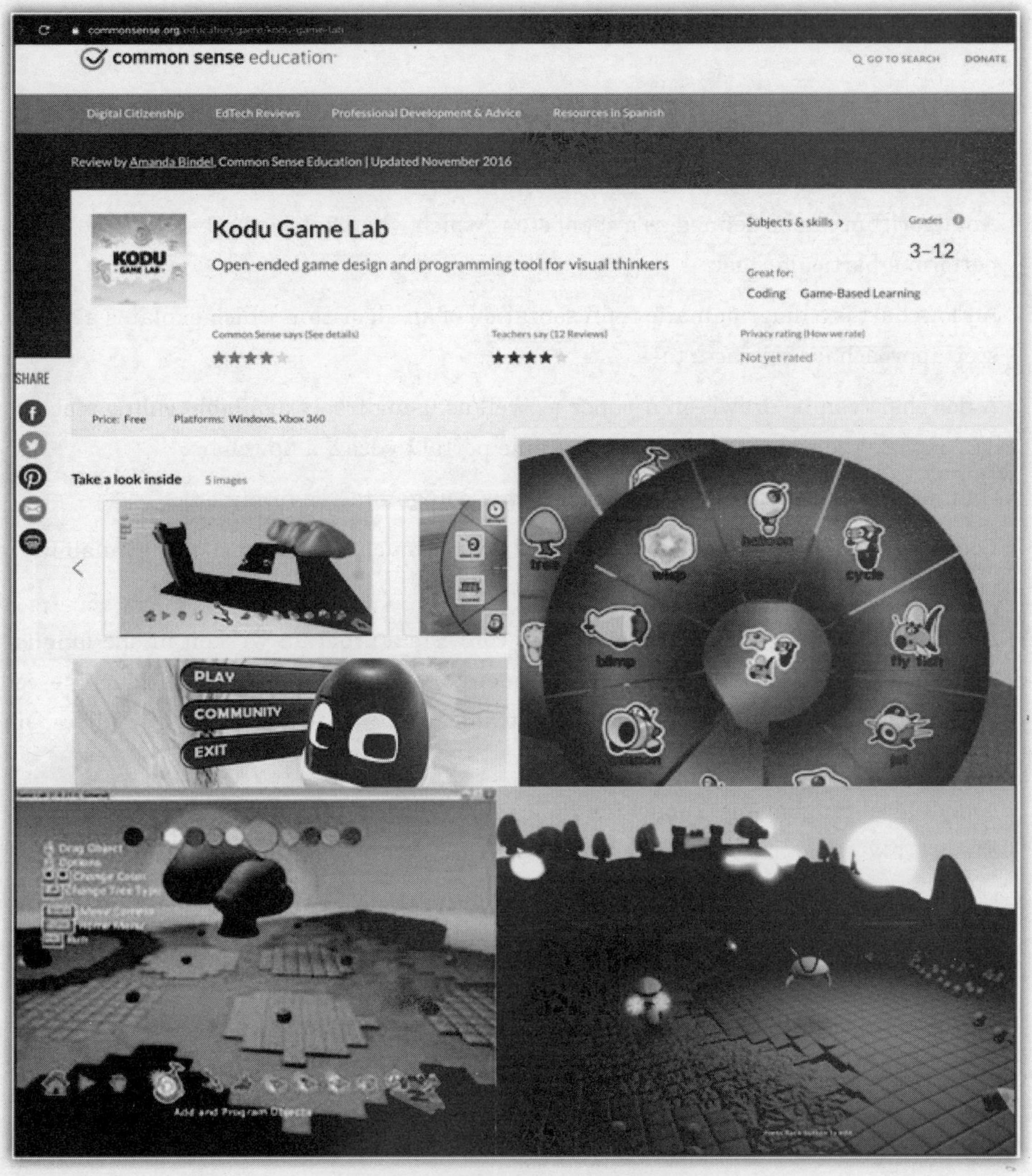

Figure 8.15: *Kodu Game Lab*

TECH BOT

- **Algorithm:** It is a step by step method of solving a problem.
- **DRAW.IO:** It is free online diagram software for making flowcharts, process diagrams, org charts, and network diagrams.
- **CodeCombat:** It is an educational video game for learning software programming concepts and languages.

Recap Bot

- An Algorithm can be defined as a set of steps which when followed solve the problem and perform a particular task.
- A Flowchart is a diagrammatic representation of an algorithm which explains a step-by-step approach for solving a task.
- A flowchart can be drawn on a paper as well as using freely available online tools. You can explore the website www.draw.io online portal to draw a flowchart.
- Gamification is the use of game concepts in a non-gaming environment.
- Learning a programming language has become much easier with the availability of various online gaming portals.
- A computer translator is a processor that converts a program written in one language (known as source code) into machine understandable form (known as machine code or object code). Examples of computer translators are Assemblers, Compilers, and Interpreters.
- A high-level language is a machine independent code which uses languages that uses English like structure to create a program.
- HLL uses an interpreter or a compiler to convert the code into machine language and vice versa. Examples of high-level programming languages are Python, C++, C#, Visual Basic, Perl, PHP, Java, and many more.
- CodeCombat uses the trick of turning hard work into a fun game.

A. Multiple choice questions.

Multiple choice questions.

1. Which translator is used to convert the assembly language code into machine language?
   a. Interpreter b. Assembler
   c. Compiler d. None of the above
2. Symbols used in a diagram to represent the flow of instructions are known as:
   a. Flowcharts b. Algorithms
   c. Communication diagrams d. Diagrams
3. Symbolic codes used in the assembly language is also known as:
   a. Source code b. Object code
   c. Intermediate code d. Mnemonics
4. Data and information is entered into the computer using the:
   a. Output unit b. Memory unit
   c. Input unit d. Processing unit
5. Which of the following is not a programming language?
   a. Python b. Java
   c. Microsoft Windows d. C#
6. Draw.io is a free online diagram software for making:
   a. Flowcharts b. Process charts
   c. Organization charts d. All of the above

B. Fill in the blanks.

1. Analyzing a problem requires clear definition of problem statement, __________, processing and __________.
2. ______________ the program involves a clear logical plan explaining the algorithm and flowchart.
3. Coding involves translating the design into an __________ using a programming language.
4. ______________ involves preparing an information manual for end user.
5. Each shape in a ____________ represents a step.
6. An arrow is a connector that shows ____________ between the shapes.
7. ______________ is an online portal to draw a flowchart.
8. Gamification is the use of game concepts in a non-gaming ___________.
9. _____________ uses the trick of turning hard work into a fun game.

C. Match the following.

	Column A		Column B
1.	Draw.io	i.	Start/End
2.	◆	ii.	Diagrammatic representation
3.	■	iii.	Online tool to draw flowchart
4.	Flowchart	iv.	Step-by-step procedure
5.	Algorithm	v.	Decision
6.	D in A-B-C-D stands for	vi.	Code - It
7.	▬	vii.	Process
8.	C in A-B-C-D stands for	viii.	Debug and Test

D. Answer the following questions.

1. Write the full form for the following organizations.
   a. HLL b. A-B-C-D c. RPG
2. Define the following terms:
   a. Flowchart b. Algorithm c. Program
3. Write any one important feature of the following application
   a. Code Combat b. Draw.io
4. Write the functions of the following.
   a. Translator b. Code Combat
5. Name any three applications of gamification which are used for learning programming skills.
6. Draw a flowchart to read two numbers and display the sum, difference, multiplication, and division of these two numbers.
7. Write an algorithm to print the bill depending on the price and quantity of an item. Also, print the GST, which is calculated as 18% of tax on bill.
8. Write an algorithm and draw a flowchart to print five multiples of a number.
9. Write the stages involved in program development.
10. Define A, B, C and D in A-B-C-D rule for problem solving.
11. Write the steps required in analyzing the problem.

Lab Activity

1. Draw flowchart to find largest of three numbers.
2. Draw a flowchart to add three numbers entered by user.
3. Write an algorithm to find the Fibonacci series till term≤100.
4. Write an algorithm to find sum of first N numbers.

Worksheet

A. Fill in the blanks.

1. Testing and __________ requires making the program error free.
2. ____________ is made up of boxes, diamonds, and other shapes, connected with an arrow.
3. ____________ uses the trick of turning hard work into a fun game.
4. A low level language can be ________________.
5. C++ is a ________________ language.
6. The steps are properly mentioned and well-defined in ____________________.
7. ______________________ website online portal to draw a flowchart.
8. The ___________ has to stop after a particular number of steps.
9. _______________ can be defined as a set of intermediate steps to complete a job.
10. _________________ involves translating the design into an application using a programming language.

B. State whether the following statements are True or False.

1. In A-B-C-D rule, D is Debug and Test.
2. The full form of IPO is Input-Output cycle.
3. Gamification is an immense motivation for the player to practice study and exchange ideas.
4. Algorithm uses shapes to represent a different purpose or action.
5. Assembler is an example of computer translator.
6. Machine language is also known as Binary language.
7. An algorithm can be drawn on a paper only.
8. Documentation involves preparing an information manual for the end user.

C. Write down the full form of the following.

1. HLL ____
2. IPO ____
3. RPG ____

D. Answer the following questions.

1. Explain Assembly language.
2. Write down the examples of computer translators.
3. Write down one difference between compiler and interpreter.
4. Give three examples of high-level language.
5. Write down the function of flowchart symbols.

QUIZ CARD

Multiple choice questions.

1. Which can be defined as a set of steps which when followed solve the problem and perform a particular task?
   a. Algorithm ☐ b. Flowchart ☐
   c. Testing ☐ d. Program ☐
2. Who converts the whole program in one go?
   a. Interpreter ☐ b. Compiler ☐
   c. Assembler ☐ d. None of these ☐
3. Which language consists of 0's and 1's?
   a. Assembly ☐ b. HLL ☐
   c. Machine ☐ d. None of these ☐
4. A ________is a set of instructions to perform a particular task using any of programming language.
   a. Programmes ☐ b. Program ☐
   c. Language ☐ d. Both a. and b. ☐
5. A ___________is a visual representation using step-by-step approach.
   a. Algorithm ☐ b. Flowchart ☐
   c. Testing ☐ d. Program ☐
6. Which language is a machine dependent?
   a. Assembly ☐ b. HLL ☐
   c. Machine ☐ d. None of these ☐
7. A programming language is a language which follows a set of rules known as a ___________________.
   a. Assembly ☐ b. HLL ☐
   c. Machine ☐ d. Syntax ☐
8. Another name of machine code is:
   a. Source ☐ b. Object code ☐
   c. Both a. and b. ☐ d. None of these ☐
9. Python is a:
   a. HLL ☐ b. Low-Level Language ☐
   c. Both a. and b. ☐ d. None of these ☐
10. CodeCombat is a:
    a. Website ☐ b. Portal ☐
    c. Blog ☐ d. None of these ☐

9 Python Programming Language

Structure Bot

In this chapter, we will discuss the following topics:

- Features of Python, Character Set, Token and Identifiers, Keywords
- Introduction to Python programming: process of writing a program, running it, and print statements
- Demonstrate the knowledge of simple data-types: integer, float, string
- Discuss the purpose of Single line and Multi Line Comments
- Understand the purpose of a variable and how to manipulate it
- Illustrate accepting input, assignment statements and writing expressions
- Understand different types of operators: Arithmetic, Relational, and Logical
- Introduce Conditional statements: if, if-else, if-elif-else
- Writing simple programs
- Notion of iterative computation and control flow: for, range ( )

Objective Bot

At the end of this chapter, you should be able to:

- Appreciate the use of Graphical User interface and Integrated Development Environment
- Understand the design for the programming environment for creating Python scripts and programs
- Understand the concept and usage of different data types and operators in Python
- Create Python scripts using basic control flow statements

Python is a modern computer programming language. It supports the development of many applications ranging from text processing to WWW browsers to games. The simplicity of writing an English-like program code helps the programmer focus on the solution rather than the language itself. It is an Open Source Software; the user can freely distribute copies of the software, read and make changes and redistribute again to the community.

The Python program can be run directly from the source code. The interpreter converts the code into bytecodes which is translated into the computer's native language to run it. The programmer need not worry about the compiling and linking of libraries to run the code. Hence, making Python a favorable option since it is portable by nature and work independently on every computer. It can be can be used for both scientific and non-scientific programming and can be embedded with other customizable applications.

Fig. 9.1: *Python Logo*

Python was created by Guido Van Rossum when he was working at National Research Institute for Mathematics and Computer Science in Netherlands. Python can be used to follow both Procedural approach and Object Oriented approach of programming. It is free to use.

Some of the most popular features are as follows:

- Python is case-sensitive language.
- It is a very simple high-level language with vast library of add-on modules.
- It is excellent for beginners as the language is interpreted and hence, gives immediate results.
- The programs are easily readable and understandable.
- It is easy to learn and use.

To write and run Python program, you need to have the Python interpreter installed in your computer. IDLE (GUI integrated) is the standard Python development environment. IDLE is an acronym of Integrated Development Environment and can be downloaded from www.python.org. The programmer can edit, run, browse and debug Python Programs from a single interface with the latest version, 3.7.

Definition Bot

Python is considered a scripting language, like Ruby or Perl and is often used for creating Web applications and dynamic Web content.

There are two ways to use the Python interpreter:

- Interactive mode
- Script mode

The interactive mode allows execution of individual Python statements instantaneously whereas the script mode is used to create and edit Python source files.

You will be using an interactive online Python editor https://colab.research. google.com/ for writing your programs. Google Colab is a free to use Python editor with 12 GB RAM graphics processing unit free support. The program developer is allowed to use and share the program Notebooks with other developers and community like Google Docs. The editor has an added advantage of all major libraries and modules being pre-installed for the developers.

FACT BOT

The first version of Python was released in 1991.

print() in-built function

print() function is used to print information on the screen.

Syntax:

print (message) or print (variable value)

For example:

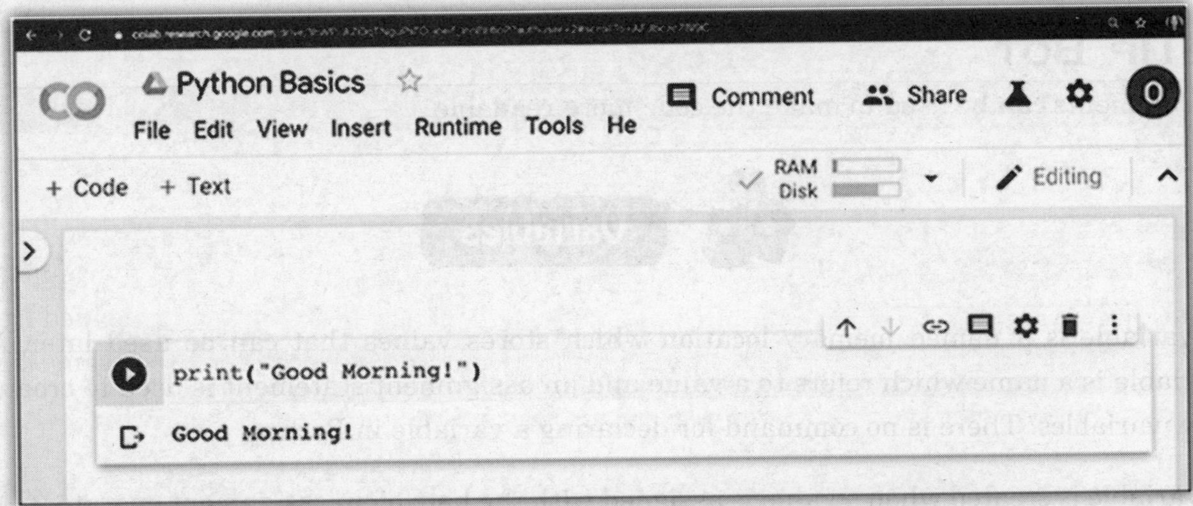

Figure 9.2: *Image Screenshot of Colab Notebook (interactive mode)*

Comments

Comments are the statements added with the code which are not executed by the interpreter. They help the developer understand the code better while referring to it later.

A comment starts with # (hash sign). Statement following after # till the end of the line is treated as a comment and the interpreter ignores it while executing the statement. The sole purpose is to add readability to the code.

There are two types of comments:

- Single line comment using #
- Multiline comments use triple-quoted string (' ' ') in the starting and at the end will also be ignored by the Python interpreter and any statements within them will be treated as comments.

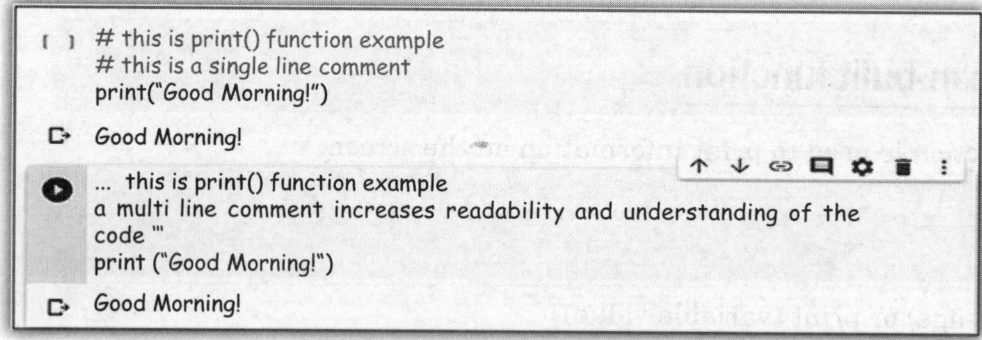

Figure 9.3: *Python comments*

TIP BOT

Comments can be used to make the code more readable.

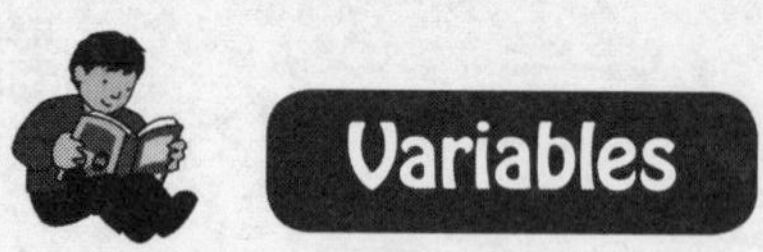

Variables

A variable is a named memory location which stores values that can be used later. A variable is a name which refers to a value and an assignment statement is used to create new variables. There is no command for declaring a variable in Python.

A variable is created when a value is assigned with the help of an assignment operator (=). The print() statement is used to display the values of variables.

The rules for naming a variable in Python are as follows:

- The name should begin with an uppercase or a lowercase alphabet or an underscore sign (_). This may be followed by any combination of characters a–z, A–Z, 0–9 or underscore (_). A variable cannot start with a digit.
- It can be of any length. It is preferred to keep it short and meaningful.
- It should not be a keyword or reserved word.
- Special symbols like !, @, #, $, %, and so on cannot be used in variables.

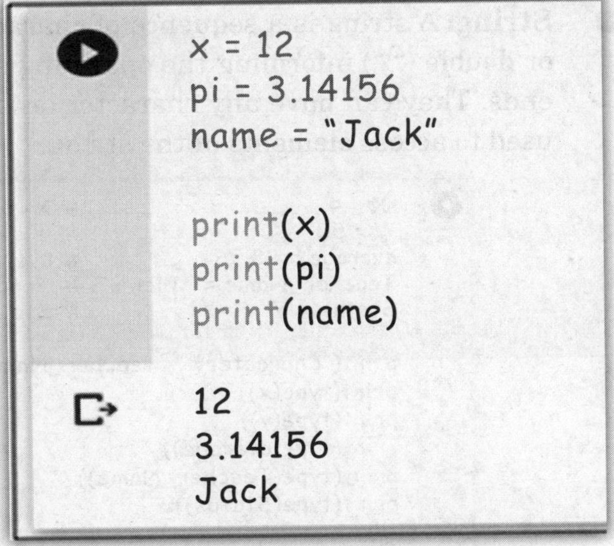

Figure 9.4: *Variables*

A variable in Python can be assigned any of the following types of data.

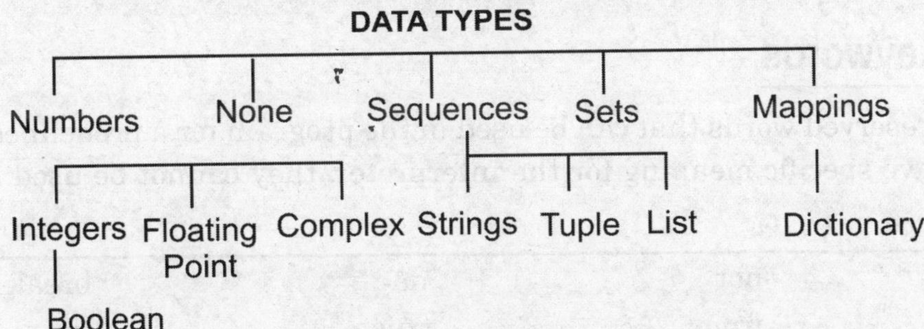

- **Integers:** These are the whole numbers consisting of + or – sign with decimal digits. When working with integers, the developer need not to worry about the size of integer as a very big integer value is automatically handled by Python.
- **type ( ):** This function is used to check data type of variable or value.
- **Floating Point:** Numbers with fractions or decimal point are called floating point numbers. A floating point number will consist of sign (+,-) sequence of decimals digits and a dot such as 0.0, -215.967, 0.3328, 315.3.

- **String:** A string is a sequence of characters which are enclosed in single quotes (' ') or double (" ") informing the operating system where the string constant begins and ends. They can have any character or sign, including space. Square brackets can be used to access elements of the string.

```
X = 4                              # X is an integer
Y = 55                             # y is an integer
average = 98.56                    # average is a floating poitn number
Teacher_Name = "Jack"              # Teacher_Name is a string
Status = 'Y'                       # Status is a single character

print("Character= ", Teacher_Name(3))
print(type(x))
print(type(y))
print(type(average))
print(type(Teacher_Name))
print(type(Status))
```

```
Character= k
<class 'int'>
<class 'int'>
<class 'float'>
<class 'str'>
<class 'str'>
```

Figure 9.5: *Data types*

KNOWLEDGE BOT

Python provides us the type() function which returns the type of the variable passed.

Python Keywords

Keywords are reserved words that can be used in the program for a predefined purpose. As these words have specific meaning for the interpreter, they cannot be used for any other purpose.

and	not	or	break
for	from	raise	try
class	print	return	if
else	while	elif	finally

```
No = 5
Print(No)
```

```
---------------------------------------------------------------------------
NameError                                 Traceback (most recent call last)
<ipython-input-9-983757a66e8b> in <module>()
      1 No = 5
----> 2 Print(No)

NameError: name ;Print; is not defined
```

Figure 9.6: *Error message encountered for invalid keyword usage*

Operators and Operands

Operators are special symbols which represents computation which are applied on operand(s), which can be values or variables. An expression is created when operators are applied on operands. Same operator can behave differently when applied on different data types. Operands are values and variables when used with operators. Operators are categorized as Arithmetic, Relational, Logical and Assignment.

MEMORY BOT

Operators are either represented by keywords or special characters.

Arithmetic Operators: Arithmetic operators are used with numeric values to perform common mathematical operations.

Operator	Name	Example
+	Addition	[10] 55+45 [→ 100 [11] 'Good' + 'Evening' [→ 'GoodEvening' [12] 76-45 [→ 31 [13] 56*34 [→ 1904
–	Subtraction	
*	Multiplication	
/	Division	[16] 78/5 [→ 15.6 [17] 78/5.0 [→ 15.6 [12] 78.0/5 [→ 15.6 [13] 2**3 [→ 8 [20] 26**0.5 [→ 5.0990195135927845
%	Modulus	
**	Exponentiation	

Figure 9.7: *Arithmetic operators*

//	Floor Division	[21] 9.0//2 [→ 4.0 9//2 [→ 4 **Figure 9.8:** *Floor Division*

Relational Operators: It compares the values. It either returns True or False according to the condition.

Operator	Name	Example
>	Greater than	print(90>8) print(100<100) print(88<109) print(99==99) print(100==110) print(100!=102) print(100>=102) print(102<=200) [→ True False True True False True False True **Figure 9.9:** *Relational operators*
<	Less than	
==	Equal to	
!=, <>	Not equal to	
>=	Greater than or equal to	

Logical Operators: These operators are used to combine conditional statements.

Operator	Name	Example
and	Returns True if both the statements are true.	x=12 print(x>50 and x<100) print(x>50 or x<100) print(not(x>50 and x<100)) [→ False **Figure 9.10:** *Logical operators*
or	Returns True if any one of the statement is true.	
not	Reverse the result, returns False if the result is True.	

An expression is a combination of values, variable and operators which generates a single value.

Example:

```
s = 18
t = 25
u = s + t
print("value =", u)
value = 43
```

```
a = 9.0/5 + (16 - 13.0) + 2**3
print("result =", a)
[→    result = 12.8
```

Figure 9.11: *Expression*

Precedence of operator: Higher precedence operator is worked on before lower precedence operator which determines the order of evaluation of operands or values. When the operators are of the same precedence, and are not grouped by parenthesis, the order of execution is based on operator associativity. An operator may be Left-associative or Right –associative. In left associative, the operator falling on left side will be evaluated first, while in right associative operator falling on right will be evaluated first. In Python '=' and "**" are right associative. The precedence is listed below in the order of high precedence to low precedence.

Operator Description

Operator	Description
**	Exponentiation (raise to the power)
+ , -	Unary plus and minus
* , /, %, //	Multiply, divide, modulo and floor division
+ , -	Addition and subtraction
<, <=, >, >=	Comparison operators
==, !=	Equality operators
% =, / =, // = , - =, + =, * =	Assignment operators
not and or	Logical operators

input() function

The input() function is used to accept data from the user of the program.

Syntax of input()

input ([prompt])

If the prompt is present, it is displayed on the screen after which the user can provide the data from keyboard. The function takes the data and converts it to string and assigns it to the variable.

```
[1]  name = input("Enter your name : ")
     english = input("Enter your marks in english : ")
     maths = input("Enter your marks in maths : ")
     science = input("Enter your marks in science : ")
     total = english + maths + science
     print ( name, " has scored ", total, " marks. " )

[→   Enter your name : JACK
     Enter your makrs in english : 78
     Enter your makrs in maths : 89
     Enter your makrs in science : 87
     JACK has scored 788987 marks.
```

Figure 9.12: *input() statement*

You would have observed that the final output is very different from the expected output. This happens due to the default setting of string datatype for any variable accepted with the input() function. In the final answer, the interpreter has merely concatenated all the numbers assuming them to simple characters. Therefore, you have to convert the input variable values into a numeric datatype type for any further manipulation.

The type conversion method from one datatype to another is called as typecasting. You will be making use of int() or float() functions to achieve your desired results in this example.

```
[2]  name = input("Enter your name : ")
     english = int(input("Enter your marks in english : "))
     maths = int(input("Enter your marks in maths : "))
     science = int(input("Enter your marks in science : "))
     total = english + maths + science
     print ( name, " has scored ", total, " marks. " )

[→   Enter your name : JACK
     Enter your makrs in english : 78
     Enter your makrs in maths : 89
     Enter your makrs in science : 87
     JACK has scored 254 marks.
```

Figure 9.13: *using int() function along with input statement*

```
[2]  name = input("Enter your name : ")
     english = float(input("Enter your marks in english : "))
     maths = float(input("Enter your marks in maths : "))
     science = float(input("Enter your marks in science : "))
     total = english + maths + science
     print ( name, " has scored ", total, " marks. " )

[→  Enter your name : JACK
     Enter your makrs in english : 78.5
     Enter your makrs in maths : 99
     Enter your makrs in science : 67
     JACK has scored 244.5 marks.
```

Figure 9.14: *using float() function along with input statement*

Control statements in Python

There are three types of control statements in Python:

- **Selection/Conditional:** Python uses selection statements for decisions and branching of flow of control; that is, choosing between two or more alternative paths.
- **Repetition/Iteration:** Repetition is used for repeating a set of Python code multiple times in a row.
- **Sequential:** The Python statements execute from top to bottom in a sequential order.

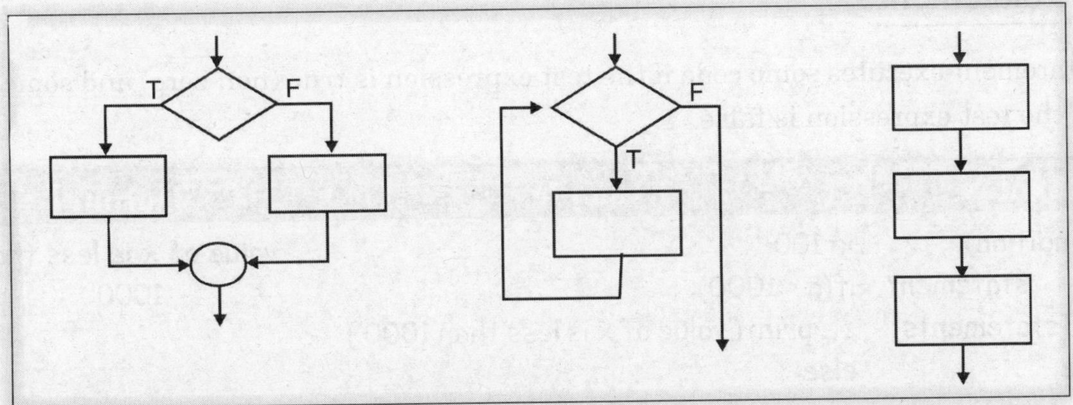

Figure 9.15: *Selection* **Figure 9.16:** *Repetition/Iteration* **Figure 9.17:** *Sequential*

Selection Statement – if statement

The flow of statement execution sometimes requires decision-making. Specific actions have to be taken as per the conditions occurring during the execution of a program. The selection statement evaluates multiple expressions, which produce TRUE or FALSE as the output. The course of action is determined by which statements to execute if the output is TRUE or FALSE otherwise.

if statement

The if statement evaluates a set of statements depending upon the validity of statements.

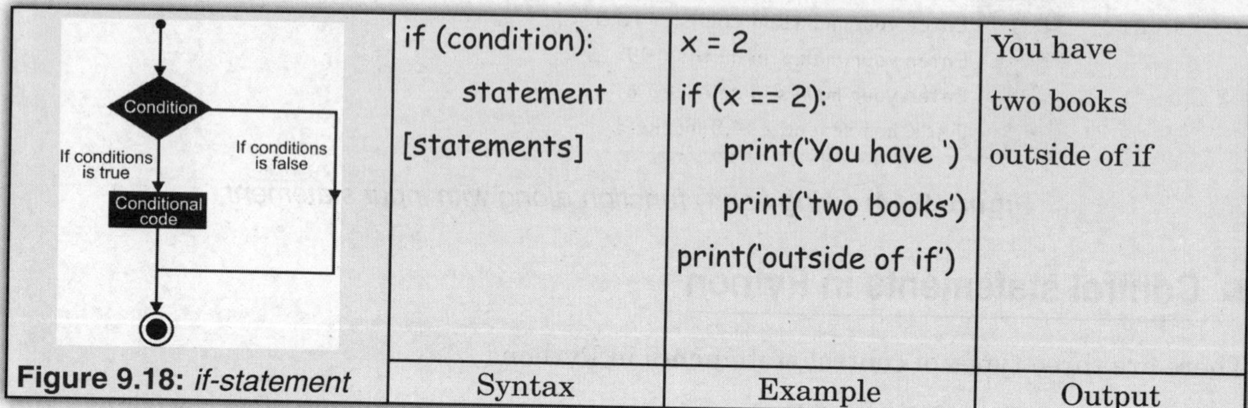

Syntax	Example	Output

if (condition):
    statement
[statements]
	x = 2
	if (x == 2):
	    print('You have ')
	    print('two books')
	print('outside of if')
		You have
		two books
		outside of if

Figure 9.18: *if-statement*

A block of Python code is indicated by indenting each line of the block by the same amount. In above example, both the print statements are part of the if condition because of both are at same level indented but not the third print statement.

if..else statement

This statement executes some code if the test expression is true (non-zero) and some other code if the test expression is false.

Syntax	Example	Output

if (condition):
    statement
    [statements]
else:
statement
    [statements]
	x=100
	if(a < 1000):
	    print('value of x is less than 1000')
	else:
	    print('value of x is more than 1000')
	x=97
	if (x>=90 and x<=100):
	    print('Grade A')
	else:
	    print('Grade is B')
		value of x is less than 1000'
		
		Grade A

Nested if

This statement allows you to check for multiple test conditions and execute different set of statements for more than two conditions.

Example	Output

num = float(input("Enter a number: "))
if num>= 0:
if num == 0:
print("Zero")
else:
print("Positive number")
else:
print("Negative number")
	Enter a number: 34
	Positive number
	
	Enter a number: -34
	Negative number

if..elif..else

This statement allows you to check the validity of multiple conditions for TRUE and execute a block of code as soon as one of the conditions evaluates to TRUE. The elif statement is optional.

Syntax	Example	Output

if expression1:
statement(s)
elif expression2:
statement(s)
elif expression3:
statement(s)
else:
statement(s)
	amount = int(input("Enter amount: "))
	if amount<5000:
	discount = amount*0.03
	print ("Discount given = ",discount)
	elif amount<5000:
	discount = amount*0.05
	print ("Discount given = ",discount)
	else:
	discount = amount*0.10
	print ("Discount given = ",discount)
	Net = amount-discount
	print ("Net payable amount", Net)
		Enter amount:
		5700
		Discount
		given = 171
		Net payable
		amount: 5871

Iteration - for statement

A for loop is used for repeating or iterating over a sequence. There are multiple Python datatypes such as list, tuple, dictionary, string, and so on. With the for loop, a set of statements are executed once for each element in a list and string datatype object.

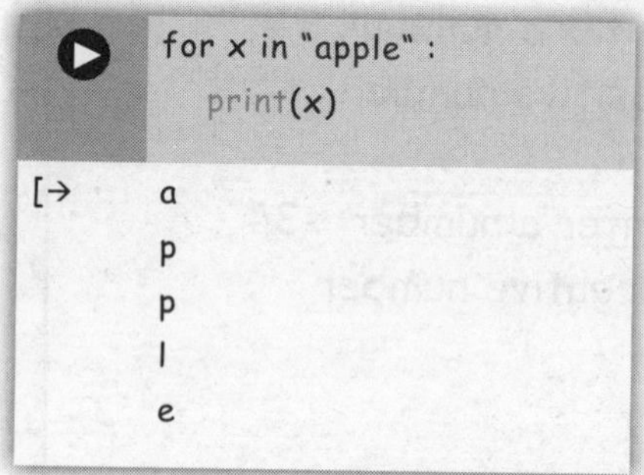

Figure 9.19: *Example of for loop*

```
#Print each stationary item in a stationary list:

stationary = ["pen", "pencil", "eraser"]
for a in stationary
    print(a)
```

```
pen
pencil
eraser
```

Figure 9.20: *Print each stationary item*

The break statement is used to stop the loop when an exit condition is met.

```
# Print each stationary item in a stationary list
# Exit the loop when a is "eraser" :

stationary = ["pen", "pencil", "eraser"]
for a in stationary
    print(a)
    if a == "pencil":
        break
```

```
pen
pencil
```

Figure 9.21: *for statement with break command*

range() function

The range() function is used to repeat a set of statements for a specified number of times. It returns a sequence of numbers, starting from 0 by default and increments by 1 till it ends at the specified number. The upper limit is excluded.

Example 1:

```
[6]  for a in range(10) :
         print(a)

[→   0
     1
     2
     3
     4
     5
     6
     7
     8
     9
```

Example 2:

```
[8]  for a in range(2 , 8) :
         print(a)

[→   2
     3
     4
     5
     6
     7
```

Example 3:

```
     for a in range(10, 25, 2) :
         print(x)

[→   10
     12
     14
     16
     18
     20
     22
     24
```

Figure 9.22: *range() function*

Sequential flow

The Python interpreter follows the sequential order of statements to give the final desired output for the problem statement.

```
[3]   # Python program to find the square root
      # Take the input from the user

      num = float(input("Enter a number: "))

      # '**' exposent operator is used to find the square root
      sq_root = num ** 0.5

      # str() functiion is used to convert a numeric data type into string data type
      # '+' is used in the print statement to add two or more strings for display

      print("The square root of " + str(num) + " is " + str(sq_root))

[→    Enter + number : 16
      The square root of 16.0 is 4.0
```

Figure 9.23: *use of str() function*

```
# Python Program to find the area of triangle
''' If a, b and c are three sides of a triangle.
    Then Semi parimeter is,
        = (a + b + c)/2
    area = V(s(s - a) * (s - b) * (s - c)) '''
#Take inputs from the user
a = float(input("Enter first side of the triangle: "))
b = float(input("Enter second side of the triangle: "))
c = float(input("Enter third side of the triangle: "))
#calculate the semi-parimeter
s = (a + b + c) / 2
#calculate the area of the triangle
area = (s*(s - a) * (s - b) * (s - c)) ** 0.5
print("The area of the triangle is : " + str(area))
```

```
Enter first side of the triangle: 11
Enter second side of the triangle: 10
Enter third side of the triangle: 7
The area of the triangle is : 34 . 292856398964496
```

Figure 9.24: *The area of triangle*

```
[7]  # Python Program to convert kilometers into miles
     # Conversion factor: 1 mile = kilometers * 0.621371
     # Taking kilometers input from the user
     kms = float(input("Enter value in kilometers: "))
     c = 0.621371
     # calculate miles
     miles = kms * c
     print(kms, "Kilometers is equal to " + str(miles) + "miles.")
```

```
Enter value in kilometers : 27.5
27.5 Kilometers is equal to 17.0877025 miles
```

Figure 9.25: *Convert kilo meters into miles*

```
[9]  # Python Program to convert temperature in Celsius to Fahrenheit
     # Conversion Formula, celsius * 1.8 = fahrenheit = 32
     c = float(input("Enter temperature in Celsius: "))
     # calculate fahrenheit
     f = (c * 1.8) + 32
     print(f, " degree Celsius is equal to " + str(f) + "degree Fahrenheit.")
```

```
Enter temperature in Celsius: 41.8
107.24   degree Celsius is equal to 107.24 degree Fahrenheit.
```

Figure 9.26: *Convert temperature in celsium to Fahrenheit*

```
[12]  # Python Program to check if the input number is odd or even.
      '''A number is even if division by 2 gives a remainder of 0.
       If the remainder is 1, it is an odd number.'''
      number = int(input("Enter a number: "))
      if (number # 2) = =  0:
         print(number, "is an even number." )
      else:
         print(number, " is an odd number. " )
```

```
Enter a number: 456
456    is an even number.
```

Figure 9.27: *If the input number is odd or even*

```
[12]  # Python Program to check if year is a leap year or not
      '''A leap year is exactly divisible by 4
       except for century years (years ending with 00).
       The century year is a leap year only,
       if it is perfectly divisible by 400.
       For example,
          2019 is not a leap year
          1900 is a not leap year
          2012 is a leap year
          2000 is a leap year '''
      # Accept year from the user
      year = int(input("Enter a year: "))
      if  (year % 4) = = 0:
          if  (year % 100)  = = 0:
             if  (year % 400)  = = 0:
                    print(year, " is not a leap year")
             else:
                  print(year, " is not a leap year")
          else:
             print(year, " is a leap year. " )
      else:
          print(year, " is not a leap year. " )

[→    Enter a year:  2018
      2018     is not a leap year.
```

Figure 9.28: *If year is a leap year or not*

```
# Python program to print sum of odd numbers between 1 and 15.
sum = 0
for a in range(1, 15, 2):
    print(a)
    sum = sum + a
print("Sum of odd numbers between 1 and 15 is  " ≠ str(sum) )

[→   1
     3
     5
     7
     9
     11
     13
     Sum of Odd numbers between 1 and 15 is 49
```

Figure 9.29: *Sum of odd numbers between 1 and 15*

```
# Python program to print even numbers between 1 and 15.
for a in range(1, 15):
     if a % 2 = = 0 :
        print(a)

[→   2
     4
     6
     8
     10
     12
     14

[15]  # Python program to print even numbers between 0 and 15.
      for a in range(0,  15,  2):
            print(a)

[→    0
      2
      4
      6
      8
      10
      12
      14
```

Figure 9.30: *Even number between 1 and 5*

```
# Python program to print multiplication table of a number
# Take input from the user
number = int(input("Multiplication table of: "))
for a in range(1, 11):
    print(number, 'x', a, '=' , number*a)
```

```
Multiplication table of: 15
15 × 1 = 15
15 × 2 = 30
15 × 3 = 45
15 × 4 = 60
15 × 5 = 75
15 × 6 = 90
15 × 7 = 105
15 × 8 = 120
15 × 9 = 135
15 × 10 = 150
```

Figure 9.31: *Multiplication table of a number*

A Python program may not execute or may generate wrong output when a programmer enters a wrong input or there is an error in the syntax of the source code. The process of identifying and removing errors and bugs from a program is called debugging. Errors occurring in programs can be categorized as:

- Syntax errors
- Logical errors
- Runtime errors

Syntax Errors

Python has its own rules of the programming language that determine its syntax. The Python interpreter interprets and executes the statements only if it is syntactically correct. In case of an error, the interpreter shows error message(s) and stops the execution there.

For example, parentheses must be in pairs, so the expression (90 + 21) is syntactically correct, whereas (7 + 11 is not due to absence of right parenthesis.

Logical Errors

A logical error results in an undesired output without abruptly terminating the execution of the Python program. Since the program interprets successfully, it is sometimes difficult to identify these errors. They are also referred as semantic errors as they occur when the meaning/semantics of the program is not correct.

```
[20]  75 + 65 + 83/300*100
[→    167.66666666666666
      (75+65+83)/300*100
[→    75.33333333333333
```

Figure 9.32: *Logical Error*

Runtime Error

A runtime error causes abnormal termination of program while it is executing. It does not appear until after the program starts running. For example, you have a statement having the division operation in the program. By mistake, if the denominator entered is zero, then it will give a runtime error like "division by zero".

Activity 9.1

Write Python scripts for the following. Test the codes for correct outputs.

1. Write a program to calculate the electricity bill. Accept the last meter reading and current meter reading and the rate per unit from the user. Calculate the number of units and total bill consumption for the user.
2. Write a program to enter the name and height of the user. Convert the height in inches (1 Feet = 12 inches).
3. Write a program to swap two variable values.
4. Write a program to find simple interest.
5. Write a program to check for the correct password.
6. Write a program to display maximum and minimum of two numbers.
7. Write a program to find the largest of three numbers.
8. A company decided to give bonus of 5% to employee if his/her year of service is more than 5 years. Write a program to ask the user for their salary and year of service and print the net bonus amount.

9. A school has the following rules for the grading system. Write a program to ask the user to enter marks and print the corresponding grade as per the following table.
   - Below 25 - F
   - 25 to 45 - E
   - 45 to 50 - D
   - 50 to 60 - C
   - 60 to 80 - B
   - Above 80 – A
10. Write a program to print the discount in Rupees for a salesman. The discount is based on the following conditions.

Sales	Discount%
<Rs. 5000	5%
Rs. 5000 to Rs. 10000	8%
Above Rs. 10000	10%
[Discount= Sales * Discount%) /100]	[Total Amount = Sales - Discount]

TECH BOT

- **Algorithm:** It is a step by step method of solving a problem.
- **Operator:** Python operator is a symbol that performs an operation on one or more operands.
- **Operand:** It is a variable or a value on which we perform the operation.
- **Variable:** A Python variable is a symbolic name that is a reference or pointer to an object.
- **Data type:** Data types represent a kind of value which determines what operations can be performed on that data.
- **Control Statements:** They are used to control the order of execution of the program based on the values and logic.
- **Debugging:** An error in a program is called bug and removing this error is called debugging.
- **Syntax error:** It is an error in the syntax of a coding or programming language, entered by a programmer.
- **Logical error:** It is a mistake in a program's source code that results in incorrect or unexpected behavior.
- **Runtime error:** It is a program error that occurs during the execution of the program.

Recap Bot

- Python is a platform independent programming language which can be used for both scientific and non-scientific purposes.
- Python is case-sensitive language with very vast library. It is free and an open source programming language.
- Python can be used in two ways: Interactive mode and script mode.
- The interactive mode in Python allows the interpreter to execute individual statements and display the output.
- The script mode is used to create and edit Python programs. Program is a sequence of instructions to perform any task.
- Keywords are the reserved words and have special meaning for interpreter. Therefore, these cannot be used for any other purpose.
- An identifier is a name given to a variable, object, class, function, and so on, to differentiate it from one another.
- Comments are the remarks that are added for the programmer to understand the code later and are not executed by the interpreter.
- Single line comment and multiple line comments are the two types of comments that can be used in Python.
- A comment starts with '#' outside a quoted string and ends at the end of a line. Comments are not part of statement. They may occur on the line by themselves or at the end of the statement. They are not executed by interpreter.
- Datatype declares type of an object which identifies the type of value an object can hold and the kind of operations to be performed on that object.
- Numbers in Python can be stored in various forms like integer, Boolean, floating point (decimal numbers) and Complex numbers.
- Numbers, None, Sequence (String, List, and Tuple) are different types of data types in Python.
- Operators are special symbols which performs some action on operands. Operands hold the value and operators perform action on it.
- Arithmetic operators, Relational operators and Logical operators are different categories of operators.
- Expression is a Python statement which is a combination of operators and operands.
- Each and every program requires three stages: Input – Process – Output.
- The input is taken from the user using input() statement or declared within the program.
- Processing statements are the formulas and functions used after the input given.
- The output is the result which is displayed after processing statements using print() statement.
- Indentation is used to represent the Python statement(s) in a compound statement. All statements of a compound statement must be indented by a set number of spaces (usually four).
- White space in the beginning of line is part of indentation, elsewhere it is not significant.
- Wrong indentation can give rise to syntax errors.

BRAIN BOT

A. Multiple choice questions.

1. One of the following is not true for a variable name:
   a. Spaces are allowed
   b. It begins with a lowercase alphabet
   c. Letters, numbers and (_) underscore characters are allowed
   d. Special characters like @, *, % are allowed
2. The file extension for a Python program is ______.
   a. .py
   b. .pyt
   c. .ph
   d. .python
3. The function used to convert a string of digits into an integer.
   a. convert()
   b. int()
   c. string()
   d. str()
4. Strings can be created by enclosing characters inside these:
   a. Single quotes (‘ ’)
   b. Double Quotes (“ ”)
   c. Triple quotes (“ “ “ “ “ “)
   d. Any of them
5. All control flow statements in Python end with:
   a. Semicolon (;)
   b. Hash sign (#)
   c. Colon (:)
   d. Full Stop (.)
6. This statement checks if a is less than equal to b.
   a. if a is less than equal to b:
   b. if a <= b:
   c. if a < == b:
   d. if a >= b:
7. Number of white spaces used for indentation:
   a. 4
   b. 5
   c. 3
   d. 6
8. A process where a set of instructions are repeated in a sequence for a number of times until a condition is met.
   a. Looping
   b. Iteration
   c. Sequential
   d. Selection
9. The function range(4) will return a sequence:
   a. 1, 2, 3, 4
   b. 1, 2, 3
   c. 0, 1, 2, 3
   d. 0, 1, 2, 3, 4
10. The function range(10, 0, -5) will return a sequence:
    a. 10 5
    b. –5 0
    c. 5 10
    d. 0 5 10

B. Fill in the blanks.

1. Python is a ________________ language.
2. ________________ function in Python is used to display the information on the screen.
3. __________ are the statements which are not checked for errors by the interpreter.
4. A variable is a named __________ location which stores values that can be changed later.
5. ____________ function is used to check the data type of a variable or value.
6. ____________ is a sequence of characters which are enclosed in single or double quotes.
7. ____________ are the reserved words that can be used in the program for a predefined purpose.
8. Operators are special ____________ that perform some computation/operation on operands.
9. An expression is a combination of values, variables and ____________ which generates a single value.

C. Match the following.

Column A	Column B
1. Arithmetic operators	i. Function used to display the result
2. input()	ii. Iteration
3. Typecasting	iii. (+, -, *, /, %, **, //)
4. if statement	iv. Process of identifying and removing errors
5. for statement	v. Function used to accept data from user
6. Relational Operators	vi. Type conversion from one data type to another
7. print()	vii. Selection statement
8. Debugging	viii. (>, <, <=, <=, ==, !=, <>)

D. Answer the following questions.

1. What is a variable? Give examples.
2. Mention the important points while creating a variable in a Python program.
3. What is input() function? Give syntax and an example.
4. Which of the following are invalid variables?
   Sum_total, $Name, float, 12rupees
5. What is the difference between = and == operators?
6. How is if..else statement executed?
7. Why is indentation important while using if statements.
8. What will be the output of the following statements?
   a. if (89<100):
      print ("X")
      else:

print ("Y")

b. if (7 < 7):

print ("X")

elif (5 < 7):

print ("Y")

else:

print ("Z")

print ("Program over!")

9. What do you understand by loops and why do we need them?
10. Explain the range() function with an example.
11. What is output for Y?

Y = 0

for a in range (0, 10):

Y = Y + a

print (Y)

a. Is the output for the following code correct?

for row in range(4):

print("##"*row)

Output: ##

####

######

12. What do you understand by debugging?
13. Explain the different types of errors incurred while executing a Python Script.

Lab Activity

1. Write a simple program to enter height of two persons and check whose height is greater than other.
5. Write a program to find the lowest number out of three numbers.
6. Write a program to find the sum of first 10 even numbers.
7. Write a program to enter the marks of 5 subjects and find the percentage.
8. Write a Python program to print the following series using range() function.

a. 3 5 7....19

b. 2 4 6 8 20

c. –2 –3 –4 –5 ......–10

9. Write a program to enter a character and check if it is a vowel or consonant.

10. Find the output of the given code.

```
i = 1
while True:
    ifi % 3 == 0:
      break
print(i)
i + = 1
```

11. What would be the output of the following code?

```
Y = 1
X = 7
X+ = 2
if (x = = 9):
print("Now the value of x is 9")
else:
print("Now the value of x is not 9")
```

12. Find the output of the given code.

```
x = 1
for x in range(1,10):
print(x)
```

13. Consider the given code and find the output.

```
x = 1
y = 5
for x in range(1,y):
print(x,y)
```

Worksheet

A. Fill in the blanks.

1. The acronym of IDLE is____.
2. The first version of Python was released in ________________.
3. Python is a/an _________________source language.
4. The python statement execute from top to bottom in a sequential order.
5. A ____________loop is used for repeating over a sequence.
6. Wrong indentation can give rise to ______________errors.
7. There are _______types of errors.
8. Operators are special symbols which performs some action on ______________.
9. An error in a program is called a _____________.
10. Each and every program requires _______________stages.

B. State whether the following statements are True or False.

1. There are two types of comments in Python.
2. Python is a platform dependent programming language.
3. Python can be used in one way only.
4. Break statement is used to stop the loop when an exit condition is met.
5. Sequential is used for repeating a set of a Python code multiple times in a row.
6. Arithmetic operator is a type of operand.
7. Numbers with fractions or decimal point are called as Integer.
8. The script mode is used to create and edit Python source file.
9. Python is free to use.
10. Python program cannot run directly from the source code.

C. Write down the syntax of the following.

1. print() ____
2. input() ____
3. if statement ____
4. if...else statement ____
5. Nested if ____
6. If...elif...else ____

D. Answer the following questions.

1. Write down the names of control statements in Python.
2. Explain relational operator.
3. What are the rules for naming a variable in Python?
4. What is the use of string data type?

QUIZ CARD

Multiple choice questions.

1. Which statement allows you to check for multiple test conditions?
   a. Nested if ☐ b. if...elif...else ☐
   c. for ☐ d. if ☐
2. Which python statement execute from top to bottom in a sequential order?
   a. Conditional ☐ b. Iteration ☐
   c. Sequential ☐ d. Repetition ☐
3. Conditional statement is also known as:
   a. Iteration ☐ b. Sequential ☐
   c. Repetition ☐ d. Selection ☐
4. Which operator is used to combine conditional statement?
   a. Arithmetic ☐ b. Relational ☐
   c. Assignment ☐ d. Logical ☐
5. The type conversion from one data type to another is called as:
   a. float() ☐ b. int() ☐
   c. Typecasting ☐ d. None of these ☐
6. Which mode allows execution of individual Python statements instantaneously?
   a. Script ☐ b. Interactive ☐
   c. Both a. and b. ☐ d. None of these ☐
7. Who was created by Python?
   a. Guido Van Rossum ☐ b. Tim Berner Lee ☐
   c. Charles Babbage ☐ d. John Berger ☐
8. Multiline comment use__________string.
   a. Double-quoted ☐ c. Triple-quoted ☐
   c. Both a. and b. ☐ d. None of these ☐
9. Which function is used to check data type of variable or value?
   a. Integer ☐ b. Floating Point ☐
   c. String ☐ d. type() ☐
10. A/an __________is created when operators are applied on operands.
    a. Operator ☐ b. Operand ☐
    c. Expression ☐ d. None of these ☐

10 Python List

Structure Bot

In this chapter, we will discuss the following topics:

- Definition and purpose of a list
- **Introduction to Python programming:** process of writing a program, running it, and print statements
- **Simple problem statements:** finding the maximum, minimum, mean, linear search on list of numbers, and counting the frequency of elements in a list

Objective Bot

At the end of this chapter, you should be able to:

- Create simple programs using lists
- Recognize the use of a data structure list to store pieces of information
- Traverse a list and perform various list operations
- Differentiate between various list methods and built-in functions

Before declaring a variable/identifier in your program, you should understand the use of it. In the previous chapter, you saw how the data type plays a very important role in creating the program. Different data types are used in the program as per the requirement of the code. Now, in this chapter, you will understand the concept of one of the collections of the data type known as a list in Python.

Introduction to a List in Python

A List in Python is an ordered collection of one or more elements of different data types.

As you have already studied about the different data types in Python as integer, float, string, tuple, or another list.

The various properties of Lists are as follows:

- Lists are mutable, that is, any element in the list can be changed after creation.
- Lists are useful to store multiple types of elements together.
- Elements in the list are enclosed within square brackets.
- Each element in a list is separated by a comma.
- Each element in the list can be referenced with the help of its index location.
- The location of the very first element in the list starts from 0, second one by 1, and so on.
- The last element in the list can be referenced by –1.
- To get the first element, you can also refer it by – n.

Definition Bot

A list is a collection which is ordered and changeable.

TIP BOT

Lists are a useful tool for preserving a sequence of data and further iterating over it.

```
List is the list of 5 integer elements

[ ]   List1 = [10, 12, 15, 19, 20]
      List 1

[→    [10, 12, 15, 19, 20]

List2 is the list of 4 city names (which is of type string)

[ ]   List2 = ['Delhi', 'Bombay', 'Hyderabad', 'Calcutta']
      List2

[→    ['Delhi', 'Bombay', 'Hyderabad', 'Calcutta']

List3 is the list of 3 floating point numbers

[ ]   List3 = [10, 53, 12.534, 198.4]
      List3

[→    [10.53, 12.534, 198.4]

List4 is the list of 4 elements of mixed datatypes - integer, floating point number, string and a list.

[ ]   List4 = [10, 'India', 239.12, [2, 4.7, 'New Delhi']]
      List4

[→    [10, 'India', 239.12, [2, 4.7, 'New Delhi']]
```

Figure 10.1: *Screenshot of different types if lists created in colab.research.google.com*

To access any elements from the list, use the index location as it is used in strings. Let us look at some of the examples to understand how elements can be referenced with the help of its location.

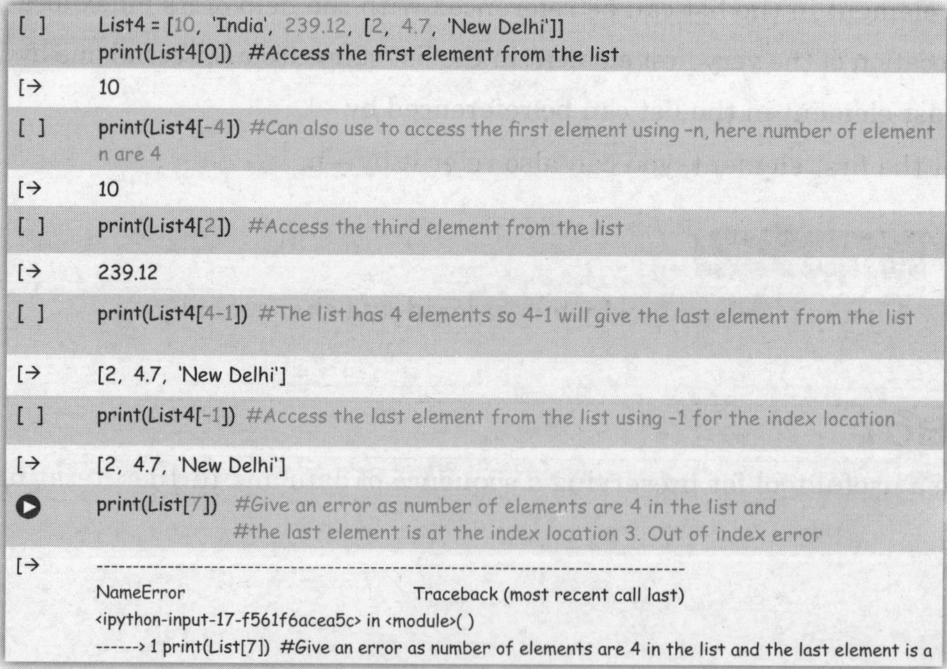

```
[ ]   List4 = [10, 'India', 239.12, [2, 4.7, 'New Delhi']]
      print(List4[0])  #Access the first element from the list

[→    10

[ ]   print(List4[-4]) #Can also use to access the first element using -n, here number of element
      n are 4

[→    10

[ ]   print(List4[2])  #Access the third element from the list

[→    239.12

[ ]   print(List4[4-1]) #The list has 4 elements so 4-1 will give the last element from the list

[→    [2, 4.7, 'New Delhi']

[ ]   print(List4[-1]) #Access the last element from the list using -1 for the index location

[→    [2, 4.7, 'New Delhi']

▶     print(List[7])  #Give an error as number of elements are 4 in the list and
                      #the last element is at the index location 3. Out of index error

[→    ---------------------------------------------------------------------------
      NameError                                 Traceback (most recent call last)
      <ipython-input-17-f561f6acea5c> in <module>( )
      ------> 1 print(List[7])  #Give an error as number of elements are 4 in the list and the last element is a
```

Figure 10.2: *Screenshot of accessing elements from lists created in colab.research.google.com*

The slicing operation can also be used to extract elements from the list. It can be used to access a number of elements together from a particular location to the specified location using the colon (:) symbol between the index locations. The first index location tells from where to start accessing followed by a colon, and then,the next index location means one less than that.

```
List1 = [10, 12, 15, 19, 20, 8, 12, 25]
List 1[1 : 4] #Will display list starting from 2 element to 4th element
              # Or 1 index location to 3rd index location
[12, 15, 19]
List1[0 : 7 : 2] #Start from index lication 0, goes till 6 location and
                 #display alternate elements as the step statement is 2
[10, 15, 20, 12]
List1[0 : 8] #Display all the elements
[10, 12, 15, 19, 20, 8, 12, 25]
List1[-8:-1] #starts from 1st location and goes till second last
             #step statement by default is 1
[10, 12, 15, 19, 20, 8, 12]
List1[-1:-9:-1] #starts from the last location and goes till first
                #step statement is negative as -1-1=-2 and so on
                #use this to display list in reverse order
[25, 12, 8, 20, 19, 15, 12, 10]
```

Fig. 10.3: *Screenshot of accessing elements from lists using the slice operation created in colab.research.google.com*

Traversing a List in Python

Traversing a list means to go through all the elements from the beginning to the last element. To do this, use the index number/location number as seen in the previous example. When you specify the range, the first number specifies the starting index location and the second number specifies that the list will be fetched one less than the second number. If the third number is not specified in the range using a colon, then by default, it is taken as +1. Otherwise, the third number is specified as the step statement,whichmeans it will start fetching the list from the first number, and then, the next element will be the location using the step statement.

MEMORY BOT

In Python, negative sequence indexes represent positions from the end of the array.

You can traverse a list using a for loop or a while loop. The concept of the for loop is already taught in the previous chapter. Let us use the for loop to access elements from the list as shown in Figure 10.4.

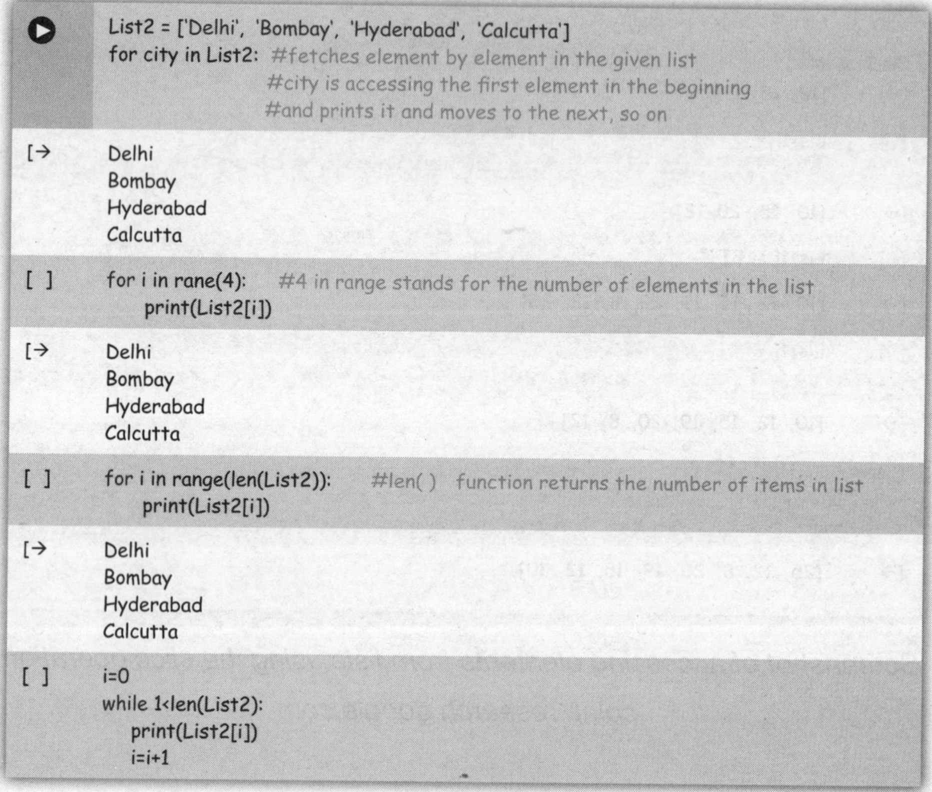

Fig. 10.4: *Screenshot of accessing elements from lists using the for loop using colab. research.google.com*

```
[ ]  i=0
     while i<len(List2):
         print(List2[i])
         i=i+1

[→   Delhi
     Bombay
     Hyderabad
     Calcutta
```

Fig. 10.5: *Use of while loop*

The while loop can also be used to access the elements from the list as shown in Figure 10.5.

Python has built-in functions that can be used to perform various operations on a list. Python built-in functions are those which are already defined with the system for a specific purpose and syntax.

<table>
<tr><th>Built-in Function</th><th>Meaning, Syntax, and Example</th></tr>
<tr><td>len()</td><td>It returns the length of the specified list, that is, the number of elements in the list.

Syntax:

len(list_name)

Example:

<pre>List1 = [10, 20, 30, 25, 8, 9, 10, 22]
print("Number of elements in List: ", len(List1))

Number of lements in List: 8</pre>
Fig. 10.6: len() function</td></tr>
<tr><td>list()</td><td>It creates an empty list if no argument is passed and creates a list if a sequence is passed as an argument.

Syntax:

list()

Example:

<pre>List2=list( ) #creates an empty list
print(List2)
name="artificial"
List3=list(name) #creates a new list using sequence
print(List3)   #passed as argument

[ ]
['a', 'r', 't', 'i', 'f', 'i', 'c', 'i', 'a', 'l']</pre>
Fig. 10.7: list () function</td></tr>
</table>

<table>
<tr>
<td>append()</td>
<td>It adds an element to the end of the list. The element is passed as an argument with the function.

Syntax:

List_name.append(item)

Example `:

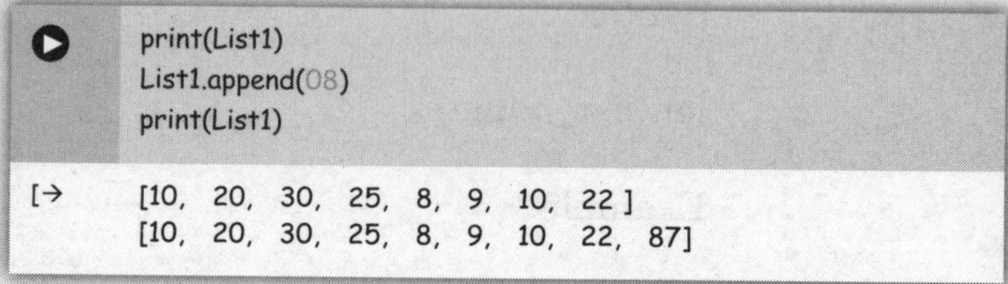

Fig. 10.8: *append() function*</td>
</tr>
<tr>
<td>insert()</td>
<td>It is used to add an element at a particular index in the list. It uses two arguments. The first one is the index location where the element has to be added and the second argument is the number which is to be added.

Syntax:

List_name.insert(index, element)

Example:

print(List1)
List1.insert(2, 129) #add 129 at index 2
print(List1)

[→ [10, 20, 30, 25, 8, 9, 10, 22, 87]
[10, 20, 129, 30, 25, 8, 9, 10, 22, 87]

Fig. 10.9: *insert() function*</td>
</tr>
</table>

<table>
<tr>
<td>index()</td>
<td>

It displays the index location of the first occurrence of the element which is passed as an argument with the function. If the element is not present in the list, it displays the Value Error. It is used to display the location of the element to be searched within the list.

Syntax:

List_name.index(element)

Example:

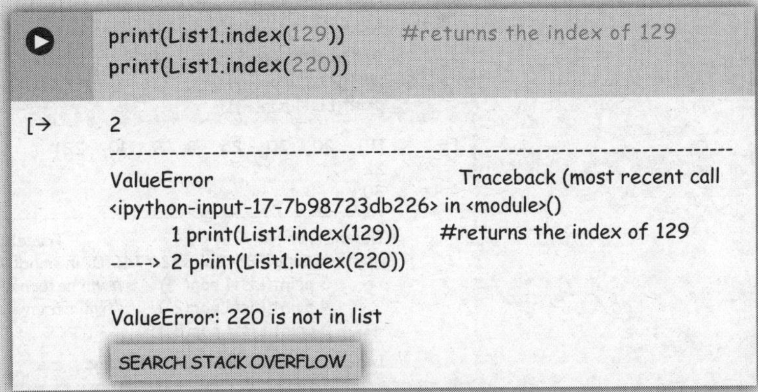

Fig. 10.10: *index() function*

</td>
</tr>
<tr>
<td>count()</td>
<td>

It counts and displays the number of times an element occurs in the specified list.

Syntax:

list_name.count(element)

Example:

```
print(List1)
List1.count(10)
```

```
[10, 20, 129, 30, 25, 8, 9, 10, 22, 87]
2
```

Fig. 10.11: *count() function*

</td>
</tr>
</table>

pop()	It returns and removes the last element from the specified list if no argument is given in the function. If the argument is specified with the function, then the value at that index/location is returned and removed from the list. If the argument specified is not present in the list,then it will display anIndexError. Syntax: list_name.pop(index) / list_name.pop() Example:

```
List1 = [10, 20, 30, 25, 8, 9, 10, 22]
print(List1)
print(List1.pop( )) #will return and remove the last element from the list
print(List1.pop(2)) #will remove element at 2 index location
print(List1.pop(8))
```

```
[10, 20, 30, 25, 8, 9, 10, 22]
22
30
---------------------------------------------------------------------------
IndexError                          Traceback (most recent call last)
<ipython-input-25-85b332#74ff0> in <module>()
      3 print(List1.pop( ))     #will return and remove the last element from the list
      4 print(List1.pop(2))     #will remove element at 2 index location
----> 5 print(List1.pop(8))

IndexError: pop index out of range
```

Fig. 10.12: *pop() function*

remove()	It is used to remove the specified element from the list. It removes the first occurrence of the element from the list if there are many copies of the element to be deleted. If the element is not present in the list, then ValueError is given. Syntax: list_name.remove(element) Example:

```
List1 = [10, 20, 30, 40, 50, 60, 70, 10, 20]
print(List1)
List1 remove(10)   #Remove  the first occurrence of 10
print(List1)
List1.remove(102) #Returns ValueError as 102 is not present in list
```

```
[10, 20, 30, 40, 50,   60, 70, 10, 20]
[20, 30, 40, 50, 60, 70, 10, 20]
30
---------------------------------------------------------------------------------
ValueError                               Traceback (most recent call last)
<ipython-input-30-fa24928b9cce> in <module>()
      3 List1.remove(10)     #Remove the first occrence of 10
      4 print(List1)
----> 5 remove(102)          #Returns ValueError as 102 is not present in list

ValueError: list.remove(x): x is not in list
```

Fig. 10.13: *remove() function*

reverse()	It is used to reverse the order of elements in the specified list.
	Syntax:
	list_name.reverse()
	Example:
	`List1 = [80, 20, 90, 10, 30, 100, 40, 50, 60, 70]`
	`print(List1)`
	`List1 reverse( )`
	`print(List1)`
	`[80, 20, 90, 10, 30, 100, 40, 50, 60, 70]`
	`[70, 60, 50, 40, 100, 30, 10, 90, 20, 80]`
	Fig. 10.14: *reverse() function*

sort()	It is used to arrange the list in ascending order in the original list only. To sort the list in descending order, use reverse=True as an argument of the sort() function.
	Syntax:
	list_name.sort() / list_name.sort(reverse=True)
	Example:
	`print(List1)`
	`List1.sort( )`
	`print(List1)`
	`List1.sort(reverse=True)`
	`print(List1)`
	`[70, 60, 50, 40, 100, 30, 10, 90, 20, 80]`
	`[10, 20, 30, 40, 50, 60, 70, 80, 90, 100]`
	`[100, 90, 80, 70, 60, 50, 40, 30, 20, 10]`
	Fig. 10.15: *sort() function*

sorted()	It creates another list to put the elements in ascending order from the list which is passed as an argument to the function.
	Syntax:
	new_list=sorted(old_list)
	Example:
	`List1=['Delhi', 'Mumbai', 'Calcutta', 'Hyderabad', 'Jodhpur']`
	`List2=sorted(List1) #List2 is created with sorted order from List1`
	`print(List1) #Original List`
	`print(List2) #New list in ascending order`
	`['Delhi', 'Mumbai', 'Calcutta', 'Hyderabad', 'Jodhpur']`
	`['Calcutta', 'Delhi', 'Hyderabad', 'Jodhpur', 'Mumbai']`
	Fig. 10.16: *sorted() function*

min()	It is used to display the smallest element from the specified list.
	Syntax:
	min(list_name)
	Example:
	`List1=[10, 20, 2, 10, 1, 40, 80, 90, 120]`
	`print(List1)`
	`print("The smallest element: ", min(List1))`
	`[10, 20, 2, 10, 1, 40, 80, 90, 120]`
	`The smallest element: 1`
	Fig. 10.17: *min() function*

max()	It is used to display the largest element from the specified list.
	Syntax:
	max(list_name)
	Example:
	`List1=[10, 20, 2, 10, 1, 40, 80, 90, 120]`
	`print(List1)`
	`print("The largest element: ", max(List1))`
	`[10, 20, 2, 10, 1, 40, 80, 90, 120]`
	`The largest element: 120`
	Fig. 10.18: *max() function*

sum()	It is used to display the sum of the elements from the specified list.
	Syntax:
	sum(list_name)
	Example:
	`List1=[10, 20, 2, 10, 1, 40, 80, 90, 120]`
	`print(List1)`
	`print("The sum of elements in the list: ", sum(List1))`
	`[10, 20, 2, 10, 1, 40, 80, 90, 120]`
	`The sum of elements in the list: 373`
	Fig. 10.19: *sum() function*

Knowledge Bot

- append() method only works for addition of elements at the end of the list.
- remove() method in list will only remove the first occurrence of the searched element.

Program 10.1: Write a program to calculate the average marks of a student from the list having marks in five subjects.

```
#Program to calaculate the average marks of a student in 5 subjects
marks = [45,  50,  60,  78,  68]        #store marks in the list
s = sum(marks)                          #store total of a marks in s
num = len(marks)                        #store total number of subjects in num
avg = s / num                 #calculate average as sum divide by number of subjects
print("Total marks scored: ", s)
print("Average score: ",  avg)
```

```
Total marks scored:     301
Average score:          60.2
```

Fig. 10.20: *Source code with output*

Program 10.2: Write a program to calculate the average marks of a student after reading marks in five subjects in the list using the input() statement from the user.

```
#Program to calaculate the average marks of a student in 5 subjects
#marks to be entered by the user using input statement
marks = [ ]      #Create marks as empty list in the begining
                 #Keep adding marks to it one by one
s = 0            #s is to store total marks
for i in range(5)  #Loop to read marks in 5 subjects and
                   #Calculate total simultaneously
  m = int(input("Enter marks in Subject "))
  marks.append(m)      #Add marks m to the end of the list
s = sum(marks)         #Store total of marks in s
num = len(marks)       #Store total number of subjects in num
avg = s / num          #calculate average as sum divide by number of subjects
print("Total marks scored:  ", s)
print("Average score:  ", avg)
```

```
Enter marks in Subject  98
Enter marks in Subject  78
Enter marks in Subject  56
Enter marks in Subject  65
Enter marks in Subject  89
Total marks scored:  386
Average score:     77.2
```

Fig. 10.21: *Output of the given program*

Program 10.3: Write a program to calculate the sum of even and odd numbers from the given list of numbers.

```
#Program to calaculate the sum of even numbers and odd numbers from the given
L1 = [10,  13,  18,  19,  21,  40,  32,  23]  #Given list
sum_even = 0       #sum_even to calculate sum of even numbers
sum_odd = 0        #sum_odd to calculate sum of odd numbers
for i in L1:       #Traverse the elements in the list
    if (i % 2 = = 0):     #To check whether the element is even
        sum_even = sum_even + i        #Calculate sum of even numbers
    else:                              #To check for odd
        sum_odd = sum_odd + i          #Calculate sum of odd numbers
print("Sum of Even numbers: ",  sum_even)
print("Sum of Odd numbers: ", sum_odd)
```

```
Sum of Even numbers:  100
Sum of Odd numbers:  76
```

Fig. 10.22: *The sum of even and odd number*

Program 10.4: Write a program to display the various options to be performed on the list depending on the user's choice.

1. Add a new element.
2. Delete the element.
3. Display the list.
4. Display the list in descending order.
5. Display the list in ascending order.

```
List1 = [10,  30,  40,  2,  6]
print("Choose any option from the following: ")
print("1.  Add an element to the end of the list")
print("2.  Delete an element from the list")
print("3.  Display the list")
print("4.  Display the list in Descending order")
print("5.  Display the list in Ascending order")
choice = int(input("Enter your choice (1-5): "))
if choice == 1:
  print("Elements in the list : ", List1)
  x = int(input("Enter element to be added at the end of list"))
  List1.append(x)
  print("List after adding element: ", List1)
elif  choice = = 2:
  print("Elements in the List:",   List1)
  x = int(input("Enter element to be deleted from list"))
  if x in List1:
    List1.remove(x)
    print("Elements in the List after removing: ", List1)
  else:
    print(x, " not found in the list")
elif choice = = 3:
  print("List: ", List1)
elif choice==4:
  print("List: ", List1)
  List1.sort(reverse = True)
  print("List in descending order: ", List1)
elif choice = = 5:
  print("List: ", List1)
  List1.sort()
  print("List in ascending order: ", List1)
else:
  print("Wroing choice entered")
```

Fig. 10.23: *Output of the program*

The output screenshots based on the program are shown in Figure 10.23:

```
[→  Choose any option from the following:
    1. Add an element to the end of the list
    2. Delete an element from the list
    3. Display the list
    4. Display the list in Descending order
    5. Display the list in Ascending order
    Enter your choice (1-5) : 1
    Elements in the List : [10,  30,  40,  2,  6]
    Enter element to be added at the end of list 45
    List after adding element:   [10,  30,  40,  2,  6,  45]
```

Fig. 10.24: *Output screenshot for option 1 in the program*

```
[→  Choose any option from the following:
    1. Add an element to the end of the list
    2. Delete an element from the list
    3. Display the list
    4. Display the list in Descending order
    5. Display the list in Ascending order
    Enter your choice (1-5) : 2
    Elements in the List : [10,  30,  40,  2,  6]
    Enter element to be deleted from list2
    Elements in the List after removing:   [10,  30,  40,  6]
```

Fig. 10.25: *Output screenshot for option 2 in the program*

```
[→  Choose any option from the following:
    1. Add an element to the end of the list
    2. Delete an element from the list
    3. Display the list
    4. Display the list in Descending order
    5. Display the list in Ascending order
    Enter your choice (1-5) : 2
    Elements in the List : [10,  30,  40,  2,  6]
    Enter element to be deleted from list56
    56 not found in the list
```

Fig. 10.26: *Output screenshot for option 2 in the program*

```
[→  Choose any option from the following:
    1. Add an element to the end of the list
    2. Delete an element from the list
    3. Display the list
    4. Display the list in Descending order
    5. Display the list in Ascending order
    Enter your choice (1-5) : 4
    Elements in the List : [10,  30,  40,  2,  6]
    List in descending order:   [40,  30,  10,  6,  2]
```

Fig. 10.27: *Output screenshot for option 4 in the program*

```
[→  Choose any option from the following:
    1. Add an element to the end of the list
    2. Delete an element from the list
    3. Display the list
    4. Display the list in Descending order
    5. Display the list in Ascending order
    Enter your choice (1-5) : 5
    List : [10,  30,  40,  2,  6]
    List in ascending order:   [2,  6,  10,  30,  40]
```

Fig. 10.28: *Output screenshot for option 5 in the program*

Write Python scripts for the following. Test the code for correct outputs.

1. Write Python statements to perform the following tasks:
   a. Create a list that contains the names of five students of your class.
   b. Print the list.
   c. Add one more name to the end of the list.
   d. Create another list which is the reverse of the previous list.
2. Display both the lists.
3. Write a program to display the minimum number from the given list.
4. Write a program to get the multiples of all the items in a list.
5. Write a program to check whether a number is present in the specified list or not.

TECH BOT

- **List:** A list is used to collect a number of values or variables in an ordered sequence.
- **Traversing:** Traversing means visiting each node of the list once in order to perform some operation on that. This will be done by using the following statements.
- **For loop:** This is a control flow statement for specifying iteration, which allows code to be executed repeatedly.
- **While loop:** This is a control flow statement that allows code to be executed repeatedly based on a given Boolean condition.

Recap Bot

- A List is a sequence in Python which is mutable, i.e., the element in the list can be modified at any point of time.
- Elements in the list are kept in the square [ ] brackets.
- A list within a list can also be created and is known as a nested list.
- List and string indexing is the same and starts with 0 index location.
- There are two ways to traverse elements in the list forward from beginning to end or backward from end to the beginning.
- The In operator is used to check whether an element exists in the specified list or not, and hence,the in operator is called the membership operator. The Not in operator is used in the reverse manner to check whether the element is not present in the list.
- Slicing [:] is used to extract a part out of the specified list.
- Traversing a list can be done using the for loop with len() and range() and while loop.
- The Sort() function arranges the list in ascending order by default and it arranges the list in the original list itself (in place).
- The Sorted() function arranges the list in order by creating another list.

BRAIN BOT

A. Multiple choice questions.

1. __________ command is used to create a list.

   a. Mylist = list()
   b. Mylist = [2, 4, 6, 7]
   c. Mylist = list([2,3,5,6])
   d. All of the above

2. Suppose mylist=[3,5,7,8,9, "artificial"], what is the output of len(mylist)?

   a. 6
   b. 5
   c. 10
   d. None of the above

3. What is the output of max(mylist), if mylist=[3456, 23, 323, 3465, 456]?

   a. 23
   b. 3456
   c. 456
   d. 3465

4. What is the output of sum(mylist), if mylist=[2,4,5,7,1]?

   a. 6
   b. Displays an error
   c. 19
   d. None of the above

5. What is the output of mylist[1:3], if mylist=[2,4,5,7,1]?

   a. [2, 4]
   b. [2, 4, 5]
   c. [4, 5, 7]
   d. [4, 5]

6. What is the output of mylist[-2], if mylist=[2,4,5,7,1]?

   a. 2
   b. 1
   c. 7
   d. 4

7. Which one of the following is used to add a new element to the end of the list?

   a. insert()
   b. add()
   c. push()
   d. append()

8. Which one of the following is used to add an element 23 at index 2 in mylist?

   a. mylist.insert(2, 23)
   b. mylist.insert(23,2)
   c. mylist.add(2,23)
   d. mylist.append(23,2)

B. Fill in the blanks.

1. A List is a __________, that is, the elements can be changed in it.
2. __________ types of elements can be stored in a list.
3. List indexing starts from __________.

4. List indexing is the same as ______________.

5. A List can be traversed ____________ or __________.

6. Elements in a list are kept in ___________ brackets.

7. _______ and _________ are called membership operators.

8. A list within a list is called ___________ list.

9. ____________ function is used to delete an element from the given list.

10. __________ is used to extract a part out of the specified list.

C. Match the following.

Column A	Column B
1. len()	i. To create an empty list
2. append()	ii. To return the number of times an element is found in the list
3. list()	iii. To delete the given element from the list
4. insert()	iv. mylist.append(20)
5. count()	v. To calculate th e number of elements in list
6. index()	vi. Arrange the list in ascending order in the original list
7. remove()	vii. To add an element at the desired index
8. sort()	viii. To return the index location of the element in the list

D. Answer the following questions.

1. Write the various methods which are used to traverse through the list.
2. Define the following terms.
   a. Mutable
   b. List
3. Differentiate between the following functions.
   a. Append and insert
   b. Remove and pop
4. Write the use and syntax of the following functions.
   a. max()
   b. sum()

5. Give the output of the following code:

a.
```
List1 = [ 1, 3, 5, None, (), [] ]
print (len(List1))
```

b.
```
Num = [2, 4, 5, 7, 10]
L= len(Num)
Sum=0
for i in range(1, L, 2):
    Sum + =Num[I]
    print(Sum)
```

6. Using the following expression, write the output of the following statements:

a. max()X = [1, 2, [3, 'amit', 200], 'computer']

b. print(X[0])

c. print(X[2])

d. print(X[-1])

e. print(X[0:1])

7. Write any two features of lists in Python.

Lab Activity

1. Write a Python program to sum all the items in a list.
2. Write a Python program to multiply all the items in a list.
3. Write a Python program to get the largest number from a list.
4. Write a Python program to get the smallest number from a list.

Worksheet

A. Fill in the blanks.

1. A ____________in Python is an ordered collection of one or more elements of different data types.
2. Each element in a list is separated by a _____________.
3. To get the first element, you can also refer it by _________.
4. The ___________________can also be used to extract elements from the list.
5. ____________returns the length of the specified list.
6. ____________adds an element to the end of the list.
7. ______________is used to display the location of the element to be searched within the list.
8. The ___________function arranges the list in order by creating another list.
9. _____________is used to extract a part out of the specified list.
10. Elements in the list are kept in the _______________________.

B. State whether the following True or False.

1. The last element in the list can be referenced by -1.
2. Python has built-in functions that can be used to perform various operations on a list.
3. pop() is used to reverse the order of elements in the specified list.
4. sum() is used to display the largest element from the specified list.
5. List and string indexing is the same and starts with 1 index location.
6. In operator is also known as member operator.

C. Write down the syntax of the following.

1. insert() ____
2. index() ____
3. sum() ____
4. min() ____
5. max() ____

D. Answer the following questions.

1. Explain sort() function in Python.
2. Write down atleast five properties of Lists.
3. Write down one difference between in and not in operators.
4. Write one example of min() in Python.

QUIZ CARD

Multiple choice questions.

1. Which function is used to display the smallest element from the specified list in Python?

   a. max() ☐ b. min() ☐
   c. sum() ☐ d. pop() ☐

2. __________are useful to store multiple types of elements together.

   a. max() ☐ b. min() ☐
   c. sum() ☐ d. List ☐

3. Collection of data type is known as:

   a. max() ☐ b. min() ☐
   c. sum() ☐ d. List ☐

4. The ____________loop can be used to access the elements from the list.

   a. for ☐ b. while ☐
   c. Both a. and b. ☐ d. None of these ☐

5. The syntax of list() is:

   a. list(list_name) ☐ b. list(list_name(item)) ☐
   c. list() ☐ d. None of these ☐

6. __________adds an element to the end of the list.

   a. pop() ☐ b. insert() ☐
   c. index() ☐ d. append() ☐

7. Which function is used to display the location of the element to be searched within the list?

   a. pop() ☐ b. insert() ☐
   c. index() ☐ d. append() ☐

8. ____________a list can be done using the loop with len() and range() and while loop.

   a. Traversing ☐ b. insert() ☐
   c. index() ☐ d. append() ☐

9. In how many ways to traverse elements in the list?

   a. 2 ☐ b. 3 ☐
   c. 4 ☐ d. 5 ☐

10. A list is a sequence in Python which is_________.

    a. Mutual ☐ b. Understand ☐
    c. Probability ☐ d. Mutable ☐

Part – C

VIVA Questions and Answers

1. What type of language is Python?

Ans. Python is a scripting language.

2. How is Python an interpreted language?

Ans. An interpreted language is any programming language which is not in machine level code before runtime. Therefore, Python is an interpreted language.

3. What are Python modules?

Ans. Python modules are files containing Python code. This code can either be functions classes or variables. A Python module is a .py file containing executable code.

4. Name some commonly used built-in modules in Python?

Ans. Some of the commonly used built-in modules are:

a. os

b. sys

c. math

d. random

e. data time

f. JSON

5. Is Python case sensitive?

Ans. Yes, Python is a case sensitive language.

6. Is indentation required in Python?

Ans. Indentation is necessary for Python. It specifies a block of code. All code within loops, classes, functions, etc is specified within an indented block. It is usually done using four space characters. If your code is not indented necessarily, it will not execute accurately and will throw errors as well.

7. How do you write comments in Python?

Ans. Comments in Python start with a # character. However, alternatively at times, commenting is done using docstrings(strings enclosed within triple quotes).

8. How to comment multiple lines in Python?

Ans. Multi-line comments appear in more than one line. All the lines to be commented are to be prefixed by a #.

9. What is the purpose of is, not and in operators?

Ans. Operators are special functions. They take one or more values and produce a corresponding result.

(a) **is:** returns true when 2 operands are true (Example: "a" is 'a').

(b) **not:** returns the inverse of the boolean value.

(c) **in:** checks if some element is present in some sequence.

10. What does len() do?

Ans. It is used to determine the length of a string, a list, an array, etc.

11. Is Python interpreted ?

Ans. Yes, Python is a interpreted language.

12. Is Python Object-Oriented Language ?

Ans. Yes, Python is a Object-Oriented Language.

13. How many modes are available in Python ?

Ans. Interactive mode and script mode.

14. Define Python?

Ans. Python is a high-level, interpreted, interactive and object oriented-scripting language.

15. Who developed Python?

Ans. Python was developed by Guido van Rossum in the late eighties and early nineties at the National Research Institute for Mathematics and Computer Science in the Netherlands.

16. Why Python is easy-to-learn?

Ans. Python has relatively few keywords, simple structure, and a clearly defined syntax. This allows the student to pick up the language in a relatively short period of time.

17. Explain the disadvantages of Python.

Ans. Disadvantages of Python are :

a. Python is not the best for memory intensive tasks.

b. Python is interpreted language and is slow compared to C/C+ + or java.

18. Can Python be easily integrated with C+ + ?

Ans. Yes, Python can be easily integrated with C + +.

19. What is the another name of comparison operators?

Ans. Relational operators.

20. Which operator is used for assigning a value into a variable?

Ans. Assignment operators.

21. Which operator is used for comparison of values?

Ans. Logical operators.

22. What is the use of "+" operator?

Ans. The "+" operator adds values on either side of the operator.

23. What is the use of operator?

Ans. The operator subtracts right hand operand from left hand operand.

24. What is the use of "*" operator?

Ans. The "*" operator multiplies values on either side of the operator.

25. What is the use of operator?

Ans. The 7″ operator divides left hand operand by right hand operand.

26. What is the use of "%" operator?

Ans. The "%" operator divides left hand operand by right hand operand and returns remainder.

27. What is the use of "**" operator?

Ans. The "**" operator performs exponential (power) calculation on operators.

28. What is the use of 7/" operator?

Ans. The 7/" operator results is the quotient in which the digits after the decimal point are removed.

29. What is the use of "= =" operator?

Ans. It checks if the value of two operands are equal or not, if yes then condition becomes true.

30. What is the use of "! =" operator?

Ans. It checks if the value of two operands are equal or not, if values are not equal then condition becomes true.

31. Why do you use "<> "operator?

Ans. It checks if the value of two operands are equal or not, if values are not equal then condition becomes true.

32. Describe the use of ">" operator?

Ans. It checks if the value of left operand is greater than the value of right operand, if yes then condition becomes true.

33. Why you use "<" operator?

Ans. The "<" operator checks if the value of left operand is less than the value of right operand, if yes then condition becomes true.

34. What value has been check by "> = " operator?

Ans. It checks if the value of left operand is greater than or equal to the value of right operand, if yes then condition becomes true.

35. Write syntax for "greater than or equal to" operator.

Ans. a > = b.

36. What value have been check by "< = " operator?

Ans. It checks if the value of left operand is less than or equal to the value of right operand, if yes then condition becomes true.

37. Is "< =" a Assignment operator ?

Ans. No,"< =" is not assignment operator.

38. Optimize these statements as a Python programmer.

1 word = 'word'

2 print word._len_()

Ans. 1 word = 'word'

2 print len(word)

39. How many types of operations are supported by the Python language ?

Ans. Python language supports the following types of operations.

a. Arithmetic operations

b. Comparison (i.e. Rotational) operations

c. Assignment operations

d. Logical operations

e. Bitwise operations

f. Membership operations

g. Identity operations.

40. Why do you use 'break' statement ?

Ans. The 'break' statement can be used to terminate the loop.

41. Write the syntax of an 'if statement1 in Python programming language

Ans. if expression :

statement(s)

42. Write the syntax of an if.....else statement in Python programming language.

Ans. if expression:

statement(s)

else:

statement(s)

43. Define while loops.

Ans. A while loop statement in Python programming language repeatedly executes a target statement as long as a given condition is true.

44. Write the syntax of a while loop.

Ans. The syntax of a while loop in Python programming language is :

while expression :

statement(s)

45. What happened when the condition of while loop becomes false?

Ans. When the condition becomes false, program control passes to the line immediately following the loop.

46. Write the syntax of a for loop.

Ans. The syntax of a for loop look is as follows:

for iterating_var in sequence :

statements(s)

47. What do you mean by "continue statement" ?

Ans. It causes the loop to skip the remainder of its body and immediately retest its condition prior to reiterating.

48. What do you mean by "pass statement" ?

Ans. The pass statement in Python is used when a statement is required syntactically but we do not want any command or code to execute.

49. How can you remove list element ?

Ans. To remove a list element, we can use either the del statement or the remove]) method.

50. Why you use cmp(listl, list2) in Python?

Ans. It compares elements of both lists.

Part – D

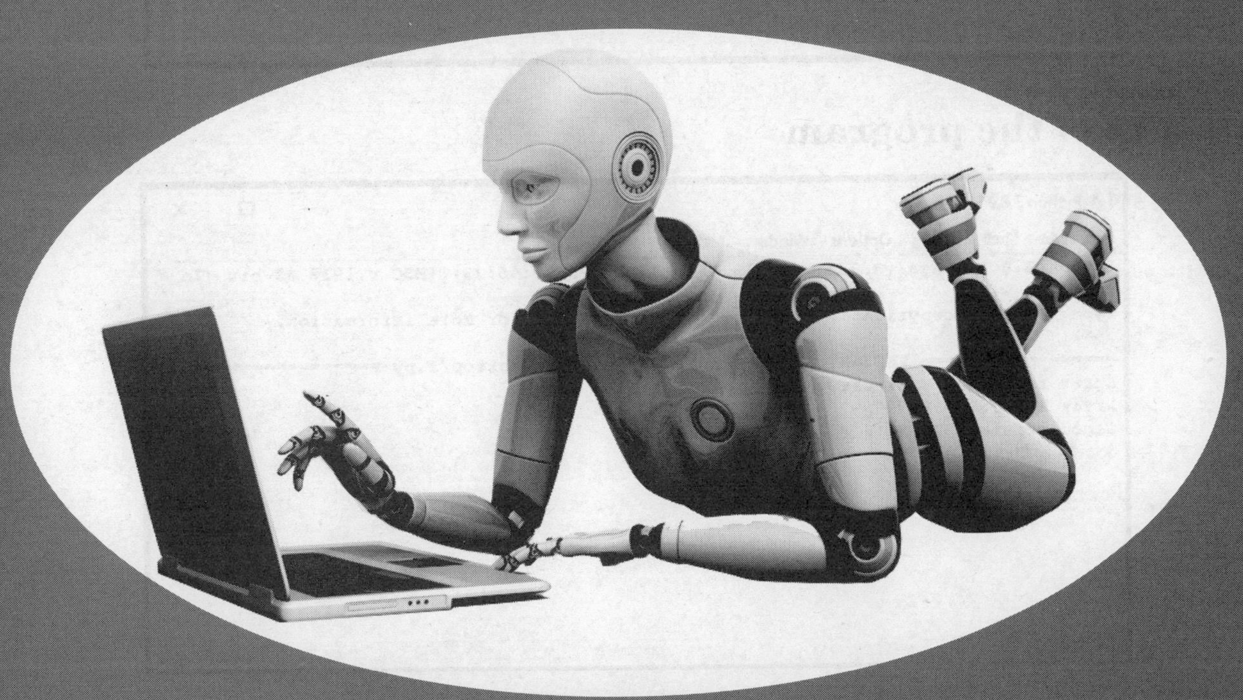

Program 1

Write a program to calculate the area and circumference of a circle.

Code

```
1.py - C:/Users/FamilyMembers/Desktop/1.py (3.8.2)
File  Edit  Format  Run  Options  Window  Help
r=float(input("Enter radius of a circle : "))
area=3.14*r*r
cir=2*3.14*r
print("Area=",area)
print("Circumference=",cir)
                                                  Ln: 1  Col: 0
```

Output of the program

```
Python 3.8.2 Shell
File  Edit  Shell  Debug  Options  Window  Help
Python 3.8.2 (tags/v3.8.2:7b3ab59, Feb 25 2020, 22:45:29) [MSC v.1916 32 bit (In
tel)] on win32
Type "help", "copyright", "credits" or "license()" for more information.
>>>
================= RESTART: C:/Users/FamilyMembers/Desktop/1.py =================
Enter radius of a circle : 12
Area= 452.15999999999997
Circumference= 75.36
>>> |
                                                  Ln: 8  Col: 4
```

Program 2

Write a program to enter number of feet and convert them into inches.

Code

```
*1.py - C:/Users/FamilyMembers/Desktop/1.py (3.8.2)*
File Edit Format Run Options Window Help
feet=int(input("Enter number of feet : "))
inches=feet*12
print("Total number of inches are : ",inches)
Ln: 3 Col: 64
```

Output of the program

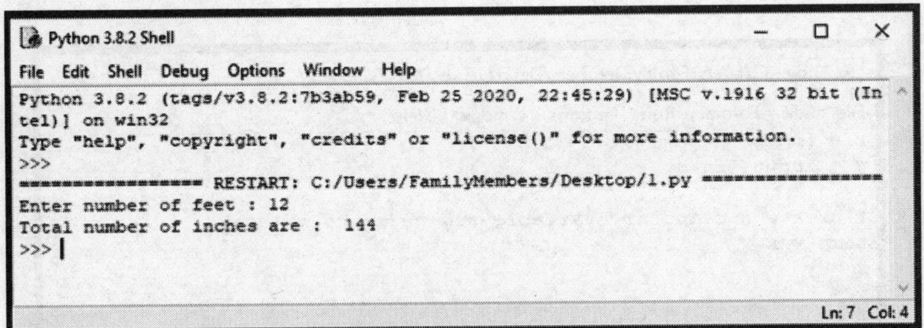

Program 3

Write a program to enter the principal, rate and interest and calculate simple interest.

Code

```
*1.py - C:/Users/FamilyMembers/Desktop/1.py (3.8.2)*
File Edit Format Run Options Window Help
p=float(input("Enter principal amount : "))
r=float(input("Enter rate : "))
t=float(input("Enter time : "))
simple=(p*r*t)/100
print("Simple Interest=", simple)
Ln: 5 Col: 33
```

Output of the program

```
Python 3.8.2 Shell
File  Edit  Shell  Debug  Options  Window  Help
Python 3.8.2 (tags/v3.8.2:7b3ab59, Feb 25 2020, 22:45:29) [MSC v.1916 32 bit (In
tel)] on win32
Type "help", "copyright", "credits" or "license()" for more information.
>>>
================= RESTART: C:/Users/FamilyMembers/Desktop/1.py =================
Enter principal amount : 1666
Enter rate : 12
Enter time : 3
Simple Interest= 599.76
>>> |
                                                                    Ln: 9  Col: 4
```

Program 4

Write a program to enter two numbers and swap them using third variable.

Code

```
*1.py - C:/Users/FamilyMembers/Desktop/1.py (3.8.2)*
File  Edit  Format  Run  Options  Window  Help
x = input("Enter value of x: ")
y = input("Enter value of y: ")

# create a temporary variable and swap the values
temp = x
x = y
y = temp

print("The value of x after swapping: ",x)
print("The value of y after swapping: ",y)
|
                                                                    Ln: 11  Col: 0
```

Output of the program

```
Python 3.8.2 Shell
File  Edit  Shell  Debug  Options  Window  Help
Python 3.8.2 (tags/v3.8.2:7b3ab59, Feb 25 2020, 22:45:29) [MSC v.1916 32 bit (In
tel)] on win32
Type "help", "copyright", "credits" or "license()" for more information.
>>>
================= RESTART: C:/Users/FamilyMembers/Desktop/1.py =================
Enter value of x: 12
Enter value of y: 13
The value of x after swapping:  13
The value of y after swapping:  12
>>>
                                                                    Ln: 9  Col: 4
```

Program 5

Python program to find the factorial of a number provided by the user.

Code

```
*python 5.py - C:/Users/FamilyMembers/Desktop/File/Palvi/python 5.py (3.8.2)*
File Edit Format Run Options Window Help
n = 9

#n = int(input("Enter a number: "))

fact = 1

# check if the number is negative, positive or zero
if n < 0:
   print("Sorry, factorial does not exist for negative numbers")
elif n == 0:
   print("The factorial of 0 is 1")
else:
   for a in range(1,n + 1):
        fact = fact*a
   print("The factorial of",n,"is",fact)
Ln: 5 Col: 4
```

Output of the program

```
Python 3.8.2 Shell
File Edit Shell Debug Options Window Help
Python 3.8.2 (tags/v3.8.2:7b3ab59, Feb 25 2020, 22:45:29) [MSC v.1916 32 bit (In
tel)] on win32
Type "help", "copyright", "credits" or "license()" for more information.
>>>
======== RESTART: C:/Users/FamilyMembers/Desktop/File/Palvi/python 5.py ========
The factorial of 9 is 362880
>>> |
Ln: 6 Col: 4
```

Program 6

Display the multiplication table in Python.

Code

```
*python 5.py - C:/Users/FamilyMembers/Desktop/File/...
File  Edit  Format  Run  Options  Window  Help

n = 9
for i in range(1, 11):
   print(n, 'x', i, '=', n*i)

Ln: 3  Col: 5
```

Output of the program

```
Python 3.8.2 Shell
File  Edit  Shell  Debug  Options  Window  Help
Python 3.8.2 (tags/v3.8.2:7b3ab59, Feb 25 2020, 22:45:29) [MSC v.1916 32 bit (In
tel)] on win32
Type "help", "copyright", "credits" or "license()" for more information.
>>>
======== RESTART: C:/Users/FamilyMembers/Desktop/File/Palvi/python 5.py ========
9 x 1 = 9
9 x 2 = 18
9 x 3 = 27
9 x 4 = 36
9 x 5 = 45
9 x 6 = 54
9 x 7 = 63
9 x 8 = 72
9 x 9 = 81
9 x 10 = 90
>>>
Ln: 15  Col: 4
```

Program 7

Write a program in Python to check whether number is prom or not.

Code

```
python 5.py - C:/Users/FamilyMembers/Desktop/File/P...
File Edit Format Run Options Window Help

n = 203

if n > 1:

   for i in range(2,n):
       if (n % i) == 0:
           print(n,"is not a prime number")
           print(i,"times",n//i,"is",n)
           break
   else:
       print(n,"is a prime number")

Ln: 14 Col: 0
```

Output of the program

```
Python 3.8.2 Shell
File Edit Shell Debug Options Window Help
Python 3.8.2 (tags/v3.8.2:7b3ab59, Feb 25 2020, 22:45:29) [MSC v.1916 32 bit (In
tel)] on win32
Type "help", "copyright", "credits" or "license()" for more information.
>>>
======== RESTART: C:/Users/FamilyMembers/Desktop/File/Palvi/python 5.py ========
203 is not a prime number
7 times 29 is 203
>>> |
Ln: 7 Col: 4
```

Program 8

Write a program in Python to check whether it's a leap year or not.

Code

python 5.py - C:/Users/FamilyMembers/Desktop/File/P...

File Edit Format Run Options Window Help

```
yr = 2000

if (yr % 4) == 0:
    if (yr % 100) == 0:
        if (yr % 400) == 0:
            print("{0} is a leap year".format(yr))
        else:
            print("{0} is not a leap year".format(yr))
```

Ln: 10 Col: 2

Output of the program

Python 3.8.2 Shell

File Edit Shell Debug Options Window Help

```
Python 3.8.2 (tags/v3.8.2:7b3ab59, Feb 25 2020, 22:45:29) [MSC v.1916 32 bit (In
tel)] on win32
Type "help", "copyright", "credits" or "license()" for more information.
>>>
======== RESTART: C:/Users/FamilyMembers/Desktop/File/Palvi/python 5.py ========
2000 is a leap year
>>>
```

Ln: 6 Col: 4

Program 9

Write a program in Python to make a simple calculator.

Code

```
def add(x, y):
return x + y
def subtract(x, y):
return x - y

def multiply(x, y):
return x * y

def divide(x, y):
return x / y

print("Select operation.")
print("1.Add")
print("2.Subtract")
print("3.Multiply")
print("4.Divide")

while True:

choice = input("Enter choice(1/2/3/4): ")

if choice in ('1', '2', '3', '4'):
        num1 = float(input("Enter first number: "))
        num2 = float(input("Enter second number: "))

if choice == '1':
print(num1, "+", num2, "=", add(num1, num2))

elif choice == '2':
print(num1, "-", num2, "=", subtract(num1, num2))

elif choice == '3':
print(num1, "*", num2, "=", multiply(num1, num2))
```

```
elif choice == '4':
print(num1, "/", num2, "=", divide(num1, num2))
break
else:
print("Invalid Input")
```

Output of the program

```
Python 3.8.2 Shell
File Edit Shell Debug Options Window Help
Python 3.8.2 (tags/v3.8.2:7b3ab59, Feb 25 2020, 22:45:29) [MSC v.1916 32 bit (In
tel)] on win32
Type "help", "copyright", "credits" or "license()" for more information.
>>>
======== RESTART: C:/Users/FamilyMembers/Desktop/File/Palvi/python 5.py ========
Select operation.
1.Add
2.Subtract
3.Multiply
4.Divide
Enter choice(1/2/3/4): 3
Enter first number: 12
Enter second number: 13
12.0 * 13.0 = 156.0
>>>
Ln: 14 Col: 4
```

Program 10

Write a program in Python to solve an quadratic equation ax**2 + bx + c = 0.

Code

```
1.py - C:/Users/FamilyMembers/AppData/Local/Programs/Python/Python38-32/1.py (3.8.2)
File Edit Format Run Options Window Help
import cmath

a = 1
b = 5
c = 6

# calculate the discriminant
d = (b**2) - (4*a*c)

# find two solutions
sol1 = (-b-cmath.sqrt(d))/(2*a)
sol2 = (-b+cmath.sqrt(d))/(2*a)

print('The solution are {0} and {1}'.format(sol1,sol2))
Ln: 6 Col: 0
```

Output of the program

```
Python 3.8.2 Shell
File  Edit  Shell  Debug  Options  Window  Help
Python 3.8.2 (tags/v3.8.2:7b3ab59, Feb 25 2020, 22:45:29) [MSC v.1916 32 bit (In
tel)] on win32
Type "help", "copyright", "credits" or "license()" for more information.
>>>
= RESTART: C:/Users/FamilyMembers/AppData/Local/Programs/Python/Python38-32/1.py
The solution are (-3+0j) and (-2+0j)
>>>
Ln: 6  Col: 4
```

Program 11

Write a program in Python to check if a given number is Fibonacci number.

Code

```
*untitled*
File  Edit  Format  Run  Options  Window  Help
num = int(input("Enter a number: "))
sum = 0
temp = num

while temp > 0:
   digit = temp % 10
   sum += digit ** 3
   temp //= 10

if num == sum:
   print(num,"is an Armstrong number")
else:
   print(num,"is not an Armstrong number")
Ln: 13  Col: 42
```

Output of the program

```
Python 3.8.2 Shell
File  Edit  Shell  Debug  Options  Window  Help
Python 3.8.2 (tags/v3.8.2:7b3ab59, Feb 25 2020, 22:45:29) [MSC v.1916 32 bit (In
tel)] on win32
Type "help", "copyright", "credits" or "license()" for more information.
>>>
= RESTART: C:/Users/FamilyMembers/AppData/Local/Programs/Python/Python38-32/1.py
Enter a number: 13
13 is not an Armstrong number
>>>
Ln: 7  Col: 4
```

Program 12

Write a program in Python to print squares of all numbers present in a list.

Code

```
1.py - C:/Users/FamilyMembers/AppData/Local/Programs/Python/Python38-32/1.py (3.8.2)
File  Edit  Format  Run  Options  Window  Help
num = [1, 2, 4, 6, 11, 20]

sq = 0

for val in num:
    sq = val * val

    print(sq)

Ln: 9  Col: 0
```

Output of the program

```
Python 3.8.2 Shell
File  Edit  Shell  Debug  Options  Window  Help
Python 3.8.2 (tags/v3.8.2:7b3ab59, Feb 25 2020, 22:45:29) [MSC v.1916 32 bit (In
tel)] on win32
Type "help", "copyright", "credits" or "license()" for more information.
>>>
= RESTART: C:/Users/FamilyMembers/AppData/Local/Programs/Python/Python38-32/1.py
1
4
16
36
121
400
>>> |
Ln: 11  Col: 4
```

Program 13

Write a program in Python to print the sum of first 10 natural numbers using range() function.

Code

```
*1.py - C:/Users/FamilyMembers/AppData/Local/Programs/Python/Python38-32/1.py (3.8.2)*
File  Edit  Format  Run  Options  Window  Help

sum = 0

for val in range(1, 11):

    sum = sum + val

print(sum)

Ln: 8  Col: 10
```

Output of the program

```
Python 3.8.2 Shell
File  Edit  Shell  Debug  Options  Window  Help
Python 3.8.2 (tags/v3.8.2:7b3ab59, Feb 25 2020, 22:45:29) [MSC v.1916 32 bit (In
tel)] on win32
Type "help", "copyright", "credits" or "license()" for more information.
>>>
= RESTART: C:/Users/FamilyMembers/AppData/Local/Programs/Python/Python38-32/1.py
55
>>> |
Ln: 6  Col: 4
```

Program 14

Write a program in Python to remove duplicates from a list.

Code

```
*untitled*
File  Edit  Format  Run  Options  Window  Help
a = [10,20,30,20,10,50,60,40,80,50,40]

dup_items = set()
uniq_items = []
for x in a:
    if x not in dup_items:
        uniq_items.append(x)
        dup_items.add(x)

print(dup_items)
Ln: 10  Col: 16
```

Output of the program

```
Python 3.8.2 Shell
File  Edit  Shell  Debug  Options  Window  Help
Python 3.8.2 (tags/v3.8.2:7b3ab59, Feb 25 2020, 22:45:29) [MSC v.1916 32 bit (In
tel)] on win32
Type "help", "copyright", "credits" or "license()" for more information.
>>>
= RESTART: C:/Users/FamilyMembers/AppData/Local/Programs/Python/Python38-32/1.py
{40, 10, 80, 50, 20, 60, 30}
>>> |
Ln: 6  Col: 4
```

Program 15

Write a program in Python to get the difference between the two lists.

Code

1.py - C:/Users/FamilyMembers/AppData/Local/Programs/Python/Python38-32/1.py (3.8.2)

File Edit Format Run Options Window Help

```
list1 = [1, 2, 3, 4]
list2 = [1, 2]
print(list(set(list1) - set(list2)))
```

Ln: 3 Col: 36

Output of the program

Python 3.8.2 Shell

File Edit Shell Debug Options Window Help

```
Python 3.8.2 (tags/v3.8.2:7b3ab59, Feb 25 2020, 22:45:29) [MSC v.1916 32 bit (In
tel)] on win32
Type "help", "copyright", "credits" or "license()" for more information.
>>>
= RESTART: C:/Users/FamilyMembers/AppData/Local/Programs/Python/Python38-32/1.py
[3, 4]
>>>
```

Ln: 6 Col: 4

Program 16

Print the following pattern in Python.

```
1
1 2
1 2 3
1 2 3 4
1 2 3 4 5
```

Code

```
1.py - C:/Users/FamilyMembers/AppData/Local/Programs/Python/Python38-32/1.py (3.8.2)
File Edit Format Run Options Window Help
print("Second Number Pattern ")
lastNumber = 6
for row in range(1, lastNumber):
    for column in range(1, row + 1):
        print(column, end=' ')
    print("")
                                                        Ln: 6  Col: 13
```

Program 17

Print the following pattern using for loop

5 4 3 2 1

4 3 2 1

3 2 1

2 1

1

Code

```
*1.py - C:/Users/FamilyMembers/AppData/Local/Programs/Python/Python38-32/1.py (3.8.2)*
File Edit Format Run Options Window Help
n = 5
k = 5
for i in range(0,n+1):
    for j in range(k-i,0,-1):
        print(j,end=' ')
    print()
                                                        Ln: 6  Col: 11
```

Program 18

Write a program in Python to check whether the input character is Alphabet or not.

Code

```
1.py - C:/Users/FamilyMembers/AppData/Local/Programs/Python/Python38-32/1.py (3.8.2)
File  Edit  Format  Run  Options  Window  Help
ch = input("Enter a character: ")
if((ch>='a' and ch<= 'z') or (ch>='A' and ch<='Z')):
    print(ch, "is an Alphabet")
else:
    print(ch, "is not an Alphabet")

Ln: 6  Col: 0
```

Output of the program

```
1.py - C:/Users/FamilyMembers/AppData/Local/Programs/Python/Python38-32/1.py (3.8.2)
File  Edit  Format  Run  Options  Window  Help
ch = input("Enter a character: ")
if((ch>='a' and ch<= 'z') or (ch>='A' and ch<='Z')):
    print(ch, "is an Alphabet")
else:
    print(ch, "is not an Alphabet")

Ln: 6  Col: 0
```

Program 19

Write a program in Python to display calendar.

Code

```
1.py - C:/Users/FamilyMembers/AppData/Local/Programs/Python/Python38-32/1.py (3.8.2)
File  Edit  Format  Run  Options  Window  Help
import calendar
# Enter the month and year
yy = int(input("Enter year: "))
mm = int(input("Enter month: "))

# display the calendar
print(calendar.month(yy,mm))

Ln: 7  Col: 30
```

Output of the program

```
Python 3.8.2 Shell
File Edit Shell Debug Options Window Help
Python 3.8.2 (tags/v3.8.2:7b3ab59, Feb 25 2020, 22:45:29) [MSC v.1916 32 bit (In
tel)] on win32
Type "help", "copyright", "credits" or "license()" for more information.
>>>
= RESTART: C:/Users/FamilyMembers/AppData/Local/Programs/Python/Python38-32/1.py
Enter year: 2020
Enter month: 05
      May 2020
Mo Tu We Th Fr Sa Su
             1  2  3
 4  5  6  7  8  9 10
11 12 13 14 15 16 17
18 19 20 21 22 23 24
25 26 27 28 29 30 31
                                                              Ln: 15  Col: 4
```

Program 20

Write a program in Python to check if the number is a Disarium Number or not.

Code

```
*1.py - C:/Users/FamilyMembers/AppData/Local/Programs/Python/Python38-32/1.py (3.8.2)*
File Edit Format Run Options Window Help
def calculateLength(n):
    length = 0;
    while(n != 0):
        length = length + 1;
        n = n//10;
    return length;

num = 175;
rem = sum = 0;
len = calculateLength(num);

#Makes a copy of the original number num
n = num;

#Calculates the sum of digits powered with their respective position
while(num > 0):
    rem = num%10;
    sum = sum + int(rem**len);
    num = num//10;
    len = len - 1;

#Checks whether the sum is equal to the number itself
if(sum == n):
    print(str(n) + " is a disarium number");
else:
    print(str(n) + " is not a disarium number");
                                                              Ln: 16  Col: 19
```

Output of the program

```
Python 3.8.2 Shell
File  Edit  Shell  Debug  Options  Window  Help
Python 3.8.2 (tags/v3.8.2:7b3ab59, Feb 25 2020, 22:45:29) [MSC v.1916 32 bit (In
tel)] on win32
Type "help", "copyright", "credits" or "license()" for more information.
>>>
= RESTART: C:/Users/FamilyMembers/AppData/Local/Programs/Python/Python38-32/1.py
175 is a disarium number
>>>
Ln: 6  Col: 4
```

Program 21

Write a program in Python to find largest number in a list using max() method.

Code

```
*1.py - C:/Users/FamilyMembers/AppData/Local/Programs/Python/Python38-32/1.py (3.8.2)*
File  Edit  Format  Run  Options  Window  Help
list1 = [10, 20, 4, 45, 99]


# printing the maximum element
print("Largest element is:", max(list1))
Ln: 5  Col: 41
```

Output of the program

```
Python 3.8.2 Shell
File  Edit  Shell  Debug  Options  Window  Help
Python 3.8.2 (tags/v3.8.2:7b3ab59, Feb 25 2020, 22:45:29) [MSC v.1916 32 bit (In
tel)] on win32
Type "help", "copyright", "credits" or "license()" for more information.
>>>
= RESTART: C:/Users/FamilyMembers/AppData/Local/Programs/Python/Python38-32/1.py
Largest element is: 99
>>>
Ln: 6  Col: 4
```

Program 22

Write a program in Python to check the validity of password input by users.

Code

1.py - C:/Users/FamilyMembers/AppData/Local/Programs/Python/Python38-32/1.py (3.8.2)

File Edit Format Run Options Window Help

```
import re
p= input("Input your password")
x = True
while x:
    if (len(p)<6 or len(p)>12):
        break
    elif not re.search("[a-z]",p):
        break
    elif not re.search("[0-9]",p):
        break
    elif not re.search("[A-Z]",p):
        break
    elif not re.search("[$#@]",p):
        break
    elif re.search("\s",p):
        break
    else:
        print("Valid Password")
        x=False
        break

if x:
    print("Not a Valid Password")
```

Ln: 23 Col: 33

Output of the program

Python 3.8.2 Shell

File Edit Shell Debug Options Window Help

```
Python 3.8.2 (tags/v3.8.2:7b3ab59, Feb 25 2020, 22:45:29) [MSC v.1916 32 bit (In
tel)] on win32
Type "help", "copyright", "credits" or "license()" for more information.
>>>
= RESTART: C:/Users/FamilyMembers/AppData/Local/Programs/Python/Python38-32/1.py
Input your passwordPalvi@123
Valid Password
>>>
```

Ln: 7 Col: 4

Program 23

Write a program in Python to print alphabet pattern 'G'.

Code

```
*1.py - C:/Users/FamilyMembers/AppData/Local/Programs/Python/Python38-32/1.py (3.8.2)*
File  Edit  Format  Run  Options  Window  Help
result_str="";
for row in range(0,7):
    for column in range(0,7):
        if ((column == 1 and row != 0 and row != 6) or ((row == 0 or row == 6) a
            result_str=result_str+"*"
        else:
            result_str=result_str+" "
    result_str=result_str+"\n"
print(result_str);
                                                                    Ln: 9  Col: 18
```

Program 24

Write a program in Python to check a triangle is equilateral, isosceles or scalene.

Code

```
*1.py - C:/Users/FamilyMembers/AppData/Local/Programs/Python/Python38-32/1.py (3.8.2)*
File  Edit  Format  Run  Options  Window  Help
print("Input lengths of the triangle sides: ")
x = int(input("x: "))
y = int(input("y: "))
z = int(input("z: "))

if x == y == z:
        print("Equilateral triangle")
elif x==y or y==z or z==x:
        print("isosceles triangle")
else:
        print("Scalene triangle")
                                                                    Ln: 11  Col: 26
```

Output of the program

```
Python 3.8.2 Shell
File  Edit  Shell  Debug  Options  Window  Help
Python 3.8.2 (tags/v3.8.2:7b3ab59, Feb 25 2020, 22:45:29) [MSC v.1916 32 bit (In
tel)] on win32
Type "help", "copyright", "credits" or "license()" for more information.
>>>
= RESTART: C:/Users/FamilyMembers/AppData/Local/Programs/Python/Python38-32/1.py
Input lengths of the triangle sides:
x: 6
y: 12
z: 31
Scalene triangle
>>> |
Ln: 10  Col: 4
```

Program 25

Write a program in Python to accept two integer numbers from a user and return their product and if the product is greater than 1000, then return their sum.

Code

```
1.py - C:/Users/FamilyMembers/AppData/Local/Programs/Python/Python3...
File  Edit  Format  Run  Options  Window  Help
def multiplication_or_sum(num1, num2):
  product = num1 *num2
  if(product <= 1000):
    return product
  else:
    return num1 +num2

number1 = int(input("Enter first number "))
number2 = int(input("Enter second number"))

result = multiplication_or_sum(number1, number2)
print("The result is", result)
Ln: 12  Col: 30
```

Output of the program

```
Python 3.8.2 Shell
File Edit Shell Debug Options Window Help
Python 3.8.2 (tags/v3.8.2:7b3ab59, Feb 25 2020, 22:45:29) [MSC v.1916 32 bit (In
tel)] on win32
Type "help", "copyright", "credits" or "license()" for more information.
>>>
= RESTART: C:/Users/FamilyMembers/AppData/Local/Programs/Python/Python38-32/1.py
Enter first number 10
Enter second number 20
The result is 200
>>>
Ln: 8 Col: 4
```

Program 26

Write a program in Python given a string and an integer number n, remove characters from a string starting from zero up to n and return a new string.

Code

```
1.py - C:/Users/FamilyMembers/AppData/Local/Programs/Python/Python3...
File Edit Format Run Options Window Help
def removeChars(str, n):
  return str[n:]

print("Removing n number of chars")
print(removeChars("pynative", 4))
Ln: 5 Col: 33
```

Output of the program

```
Python 3.8.2 Shell
File Edit Shell Debug Options Window Help
Python 3.8.2 (tags/v3.8.2:7b3ab59, Feb 25 2020, 22:45:29) [MSC v.1916 32 bit (In
tel)] on win32
Type "help", "copyright", "credits" or "license()" for more information.
>>>
= RESTART: C:/Users/FamilyMembers/AppData/Local/Programs/Python/Python38-32/1.py
Removing n number of chars
tive
>>>
Ln: 7 Col: 4
```

Program 27

Write a program in Python to given a list of numbers, return True if first and last number of a list is same.

Code

```
*1.py - C:/Users/FamilyMembers/AppData/Local/Programs/Python/Python...
File  Edit  Format  Run  Options  Window  Help
def isFirst_And_Last_Same(numberList):
    print("Given list is ", numberList)
    firstElement = numberList[0]
    lastElement = numberList[-1]
    if (firstElement == lastElement):
        return True
    else:
        return False

numList = [10, 20, 30, 40, 10]
print("result is", isFirst_And_Last_Same(numList))
                                                    Ln: 11  Col: 50
```

Output of the program

```
Python 3.8.2 Shell
File  Edit  Shell  Debug  Options  Window  Help
Python 3.8.2 (tags/v3.8.2:7b3ab59, Feb 25 2020, 22:45:29) [MSC v.1916 32 bit (In
tel)] on win32
Type "help", "copyright", "credits" or "license()" for more information.
>>>
= RESTART: C:/Users/FamilyMembers/AppData/Local/Programs/Python/Python38-32/1.py
Given list is  [10, 20, 30, 40, 10]
result is True
>>>
                                                    Ln: 7  Col: 4
```

Program 28

Write a program in Python to accept n number from user and calculate the sum of all number between 1 and n including n.

Code

1.py - C:/Users/FamilyMembers/AppData/Local/Programs/Python/Python3...

File Edit Format Run Options Window Help

```
sum = 0
n = int(input("Please enter number n"))
for i in range(1, n+1, 1):
    sum += i
print("Sum is: ", sum)
```

Ln: 5 Col: 22

Output of the program

Python 3.8.2 Shell

File Edit Shell Debug Options Window Help

```
Python 3.8.2 (tags/v3.8.2:7b3ab59, Feb 25 2020, 22:45:29) [MSC v.1916 32 bit (In
tel)] on win32
Type "help", "copyright", "credits" or "license()" for more information.
>>>
= RESTART: C:/Users/FamilyMembers/AppData/Local/Programs/Python/Python38-32/1.py
Please enter number n18
Sum is:  171
>>>
```

Ln: 7 Col: 4

Program 29

Add item 7000 after 6000 in the following Python List.

list1 = [10, 20, [300, 400, [5000, 6000], 500], 30, 40]

Code

```
*1.py - C:/Users/FamilyMembers/AppData/Local/Programs/Python/Python...
File Edit Format Run Options Window Help
list1 = [10, 20, [300, 400, [5000, 6000], 500], 30, 40]
list1[2][2].append(7000)
print(list1)
Ln: 3 Col: 12
```

Output of the program

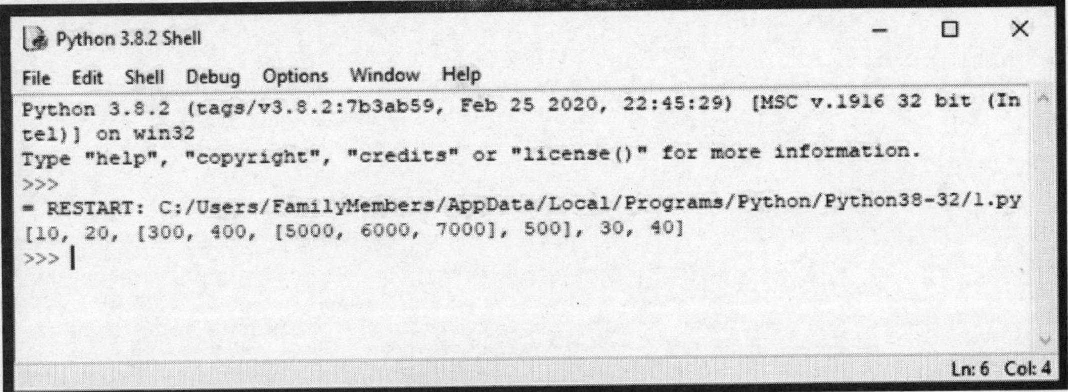

Program 30

Given a Python list, find value 20 in the list, and if it is present, replace it with 200. Only update the first occurrence of a value.

list1 = [5, 10, 15, 20, 25, 50, 20]

Code

```
1.py - C:/Users/FamilyMembers/AppData/Local/Programs/Python/Python3...
File Edit Format Run Options Window Help
list1 = [5, 10, 15, 20, 25, 50, 20]

index = list1.index(20)
list1[index] = 200
print(list1)

Ln: 6 Col: 0
```

Output of the program

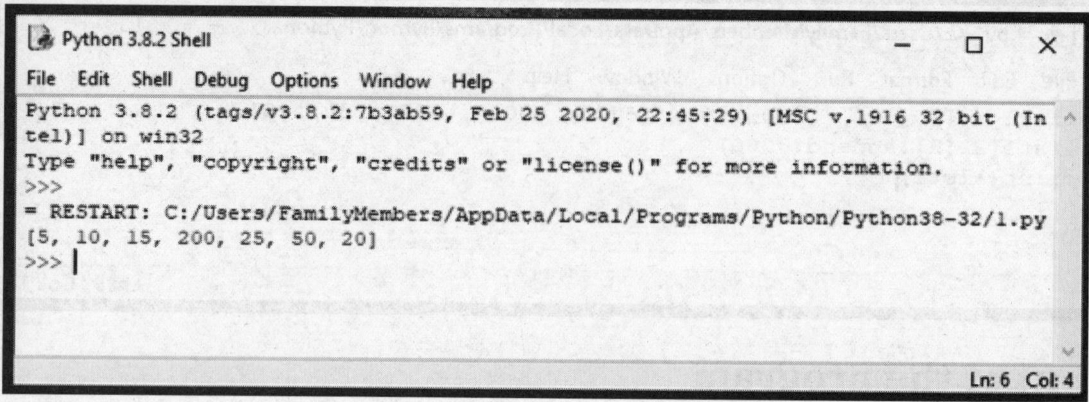

Appendix 1

How to Design a Kahoot?

Kahoot is a game-based learning platform. Kahoots are multiple-choice quiz questions that can be accessed through a web browser or the Kahoot app on a mobile device. The game concept with time-based questions gives the feel of a game show that keeps the players focused. The interface is easy to use so it helps in increasing learning, motivation, concentration, and personalized learning. You can either design a new Kahoot at www.kahoot.com or search for one that is already designed and uploaded in the community.

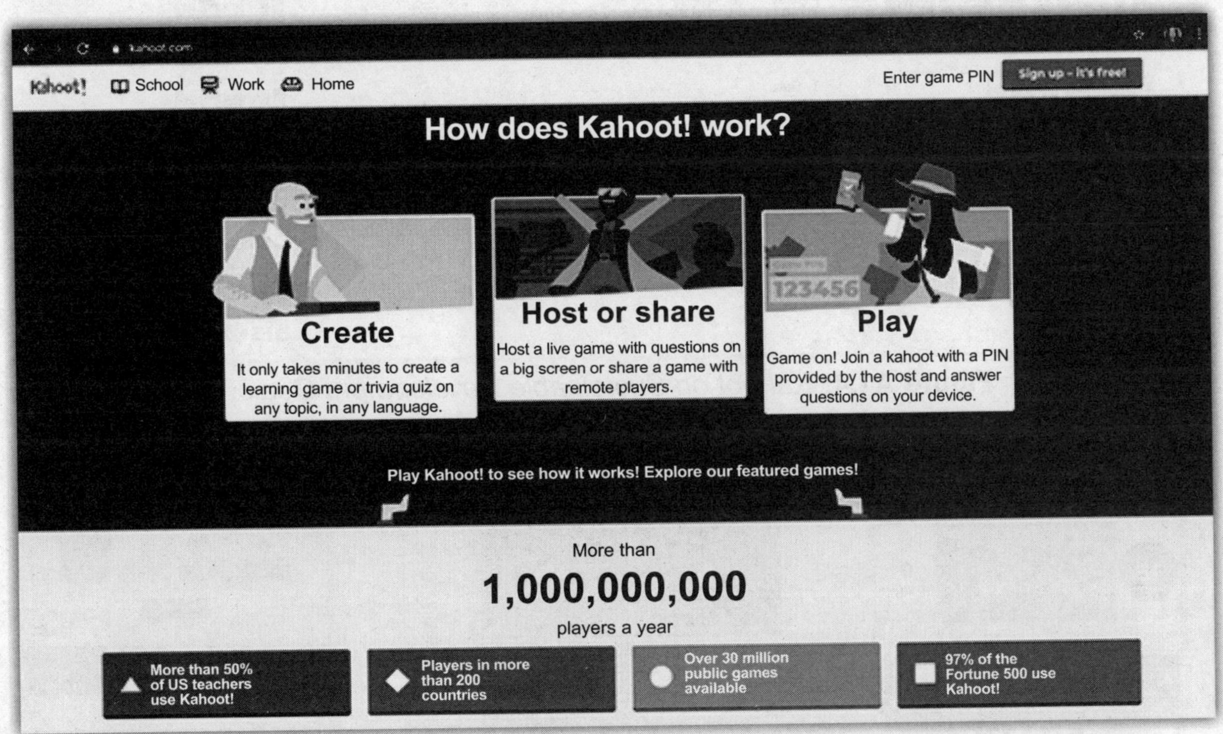

Figure A1.1: *www.kahoot.com*

You can play a game by simply joining in by entering a game pin.

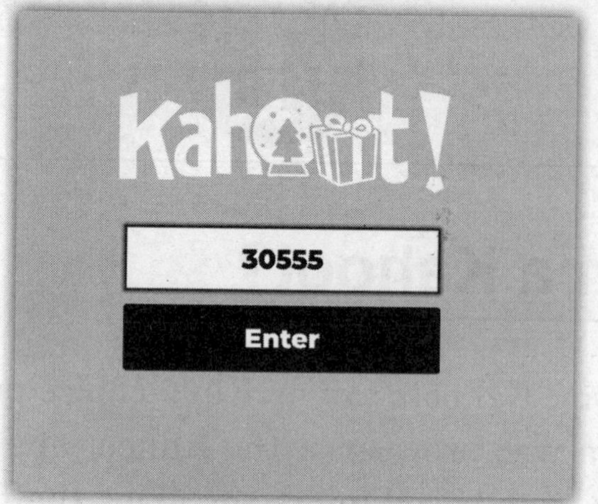

Figure A1.2: *Enter Game Pin*

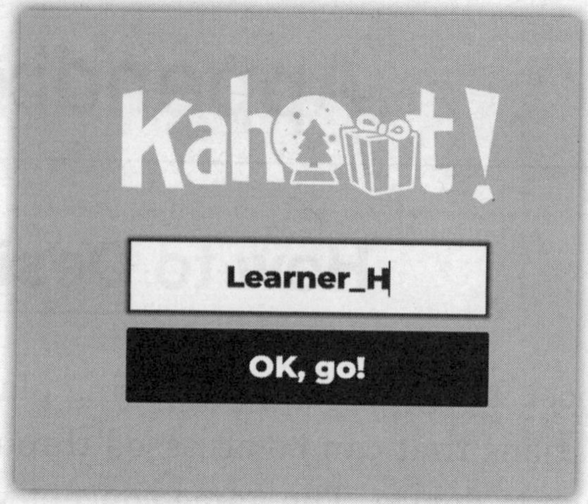

Figure A1.3: *User logged in*

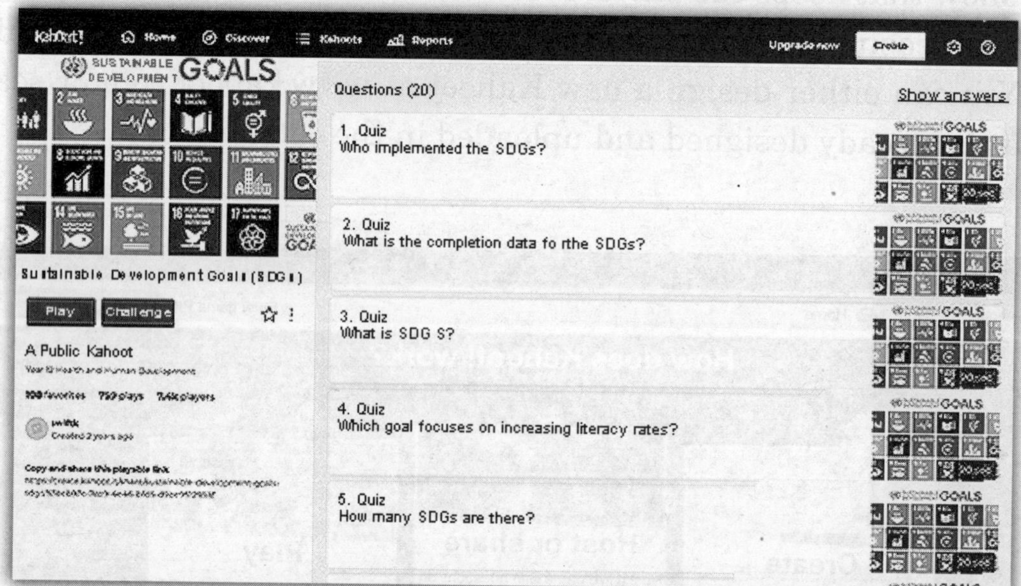

Figure A1.4: *Kahoot on Sustainable Development Goals*

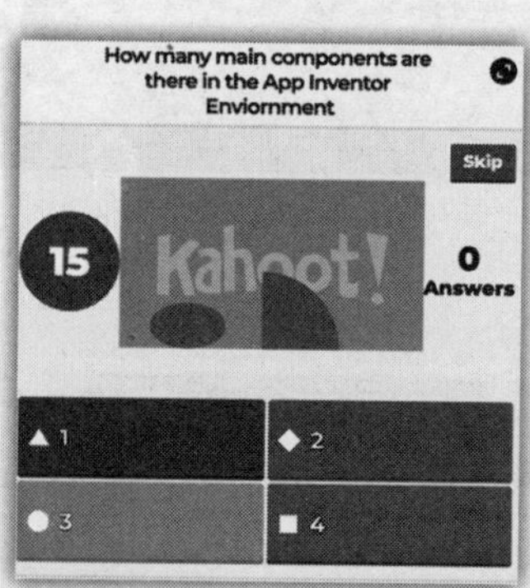

Figure A1.5: *Kahoot Question*

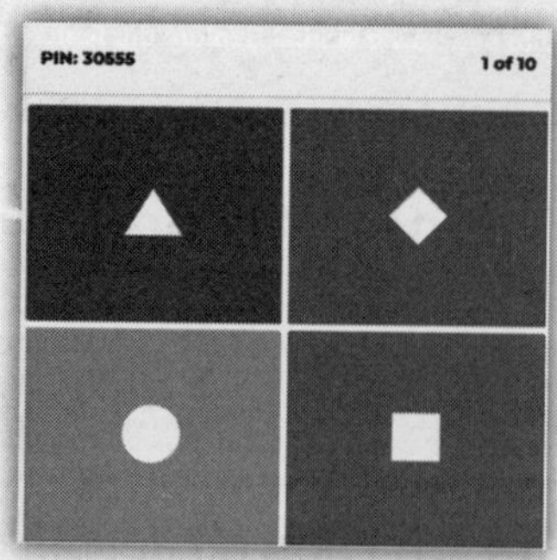

Figure A1.6: *Quiz Choices*

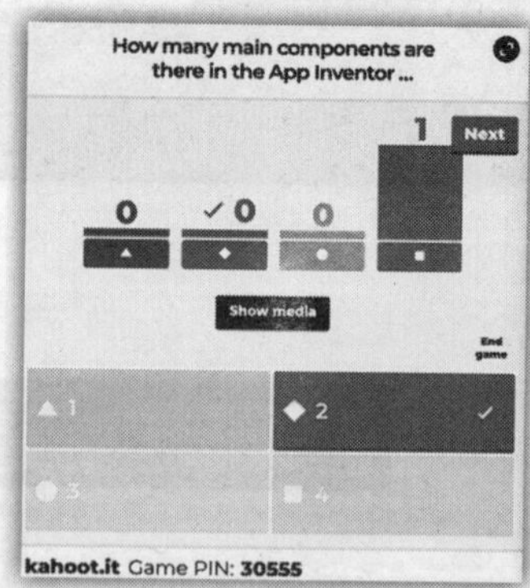

Figure A1.7: *Question Analysis*

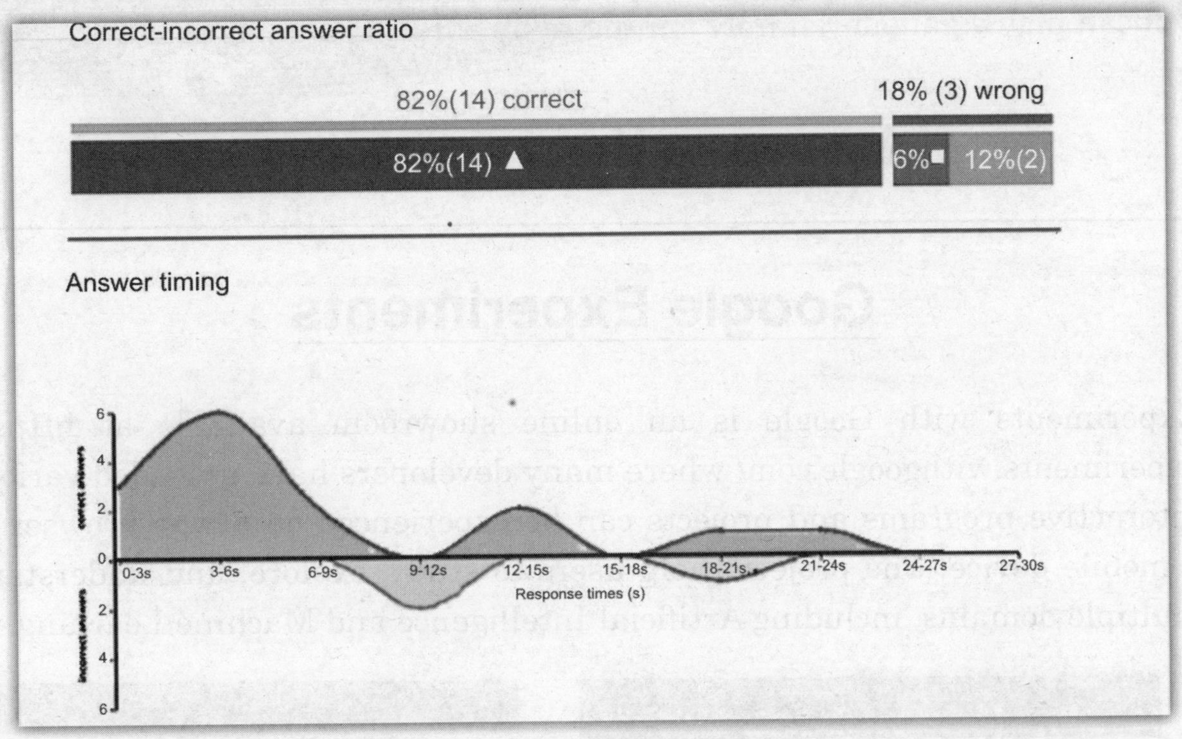

Correct-incorrect answer ratio

82%(14) correct

18% (3) wrong

82%(14)

6%

12%(2)

Answer timing

correct answers

incorrect answers

6 4 2 0 2 4 6

0-3s 3-6s 6-9s 9-12s 12-15s 15-18s 18-21s 21-24s 24-27s 27-30s

Response times (s)

Figure A1.8: *User response analysis*

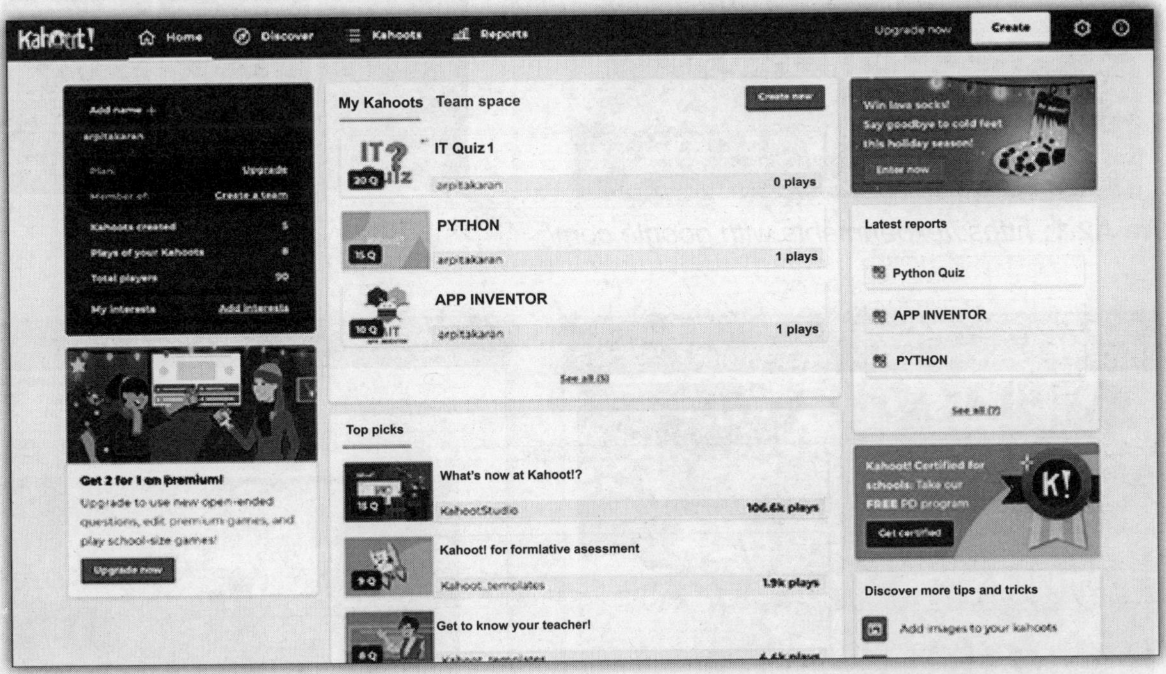

Figure A1.9: *Kahoot User account*

Appendix 2

Google Experiments

Experiments with Google is an online showroom available at https://experiments.withgoogle.com/ where many developers have uploaded various interactive programs and projects can be experienced on a web browser or a mobile device. The projects help users to study, explore, and understand multiple domains, including Artificial Intelligence and Machine Learning.

Figure A2.1: *https://experiments.with google.com/*

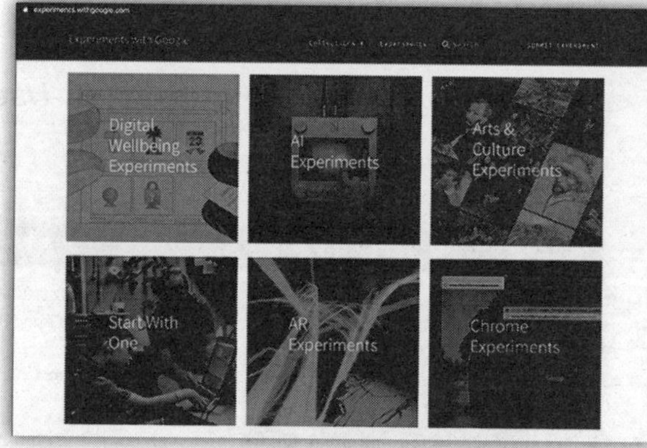

(a)

(b)

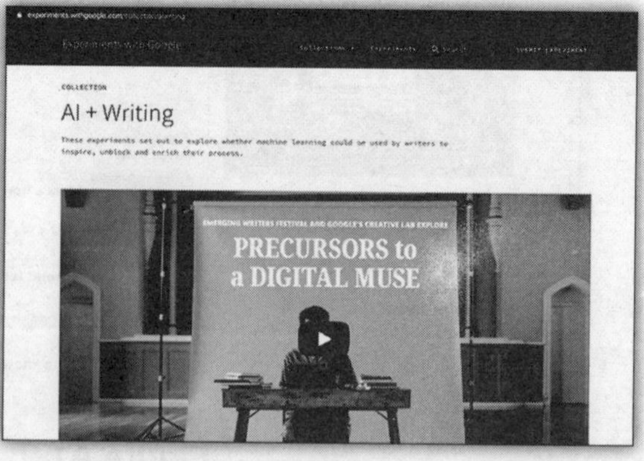

(c)

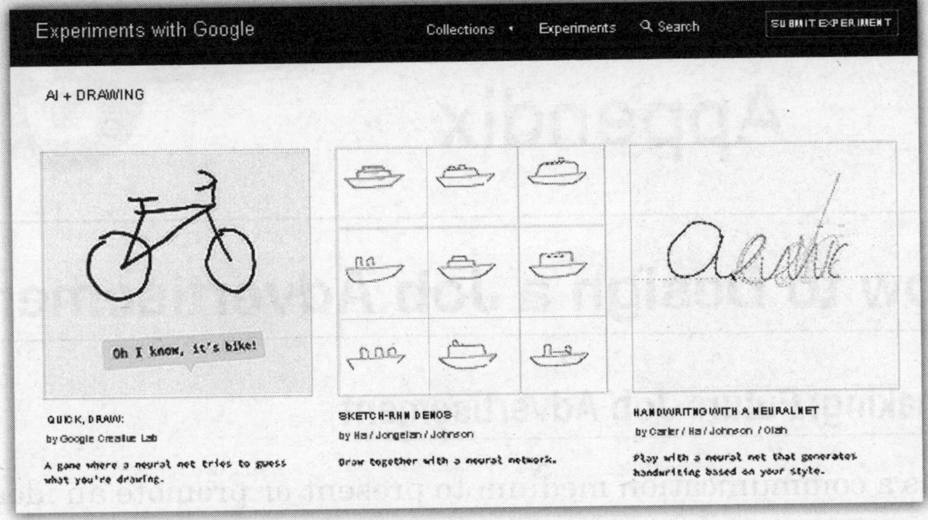

(d)

Figure A2.2: *Multiple learning domains*

(a)

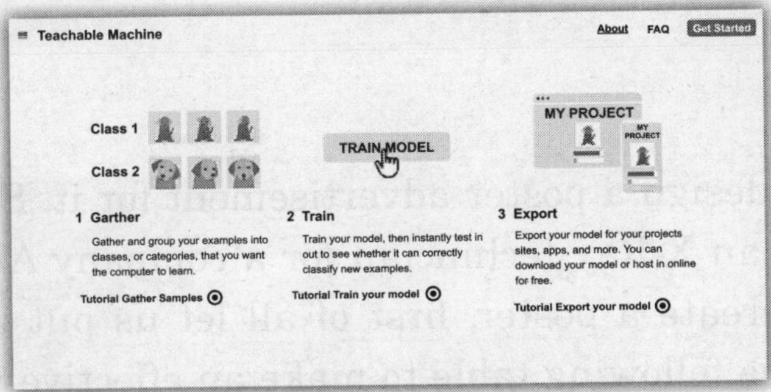

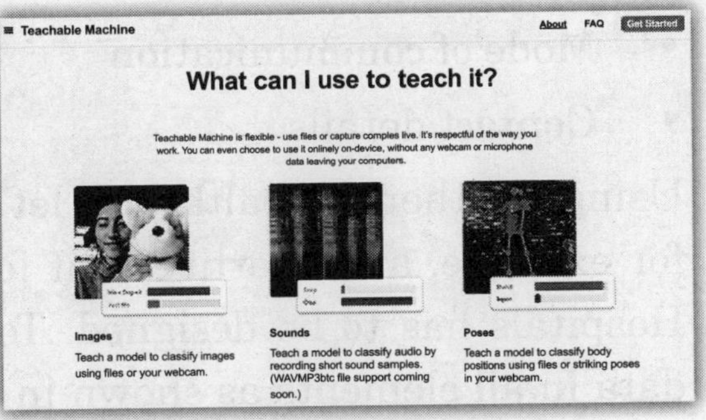

(b) **(c)**

Figure A2.6: *Teachable Machine*

Appendix 3

How to Design a Job Advertisement?

Poster making: Future Job Advertisement

A poster is a communication medium to present or promote an idea/theme to an audience. The focus is on the main idea and has to be presented in such a manner that it talks about the topic clearly by itself. When you need to create a poster for future ready AI jobs' advertisement, then it must have certain key elements in it. The key elements of the poster for such an advertisement are as follows:

- Title of the advertisement (Job designation)
- Short description about the company
- Number of vacancies and the post should be clearly mentioned
- Age and gender for the suitable post
- Location
- Remuneration
- **Qualification:** Educational, technical, and professional experience
- Mode of communication
- Contact details

Using the theme, healthcare, let's design a poster advertisement for it. Say, for example, an advertisement for an X-Ray technician for a company ABC Hospitals has to be designed. To create a poster, first of all let us put the data in all elements as shown in the following table to make an effective job advertisement:

Title of the Advertisement includes the job designation	Radiographer, X-Ray Assistant
Short description about the company	ABC Hospitals has announced a vacancy for X-Ray technician urgently
Number of vacancies and the post should be clearly mentioned for which it is advertised	1
Gender for the suitable post	Male
Location, i.e., state in which it is required	Chennai
Salary	25000 INR
Educational qualification and experience (if any) needed for the post	Graduation with minimum two years of experience
Mode of applying (E-mail, postal, and so on)	Email: hr@abchospitals.co.in
Contact address and phone number for correspondence	ABC Hospitals, Chennai Contact: 1111111111

Once you have the values for the key elements, then you just need to put it in a presentable form in a box. Let us script the data mentioned in the tabular form to see how the above data can be presented in the form of a poster for the job advertisement.

Required X-Ray Technician

ABC Hospitals has announced vacancy for X-Ray technician urgently who is good at communication skills, medical and anatomical skills and mechanical aptitude.

Total Posts: 1

Gender: Male

Location: Chennai

Salary: 25,000 INR

Educational Qualification and Experience: BS in Radiology program

Minimum 2 years of work experience

E-mail your resume at: hr@abchospitals.co.in

Contact: ABC Hospitals, Chennai

#1111111111

Now, as you have studied about the soft skills and technical skills that shall be required for the same job in the next 10 years, let us check out the soft skills and technical skills of the X-Ray technician which you need in your company.

Soft skills:

- Communication skills
- Team work
- Leadership skills
- Adaptability

Technical skills:

- Analytical
- Analysing the equipment problems
- Calibrating and maintaining AI-enabled radiology equipment
- Medical and anatomical skills
- Data analysis
- Machine Learning

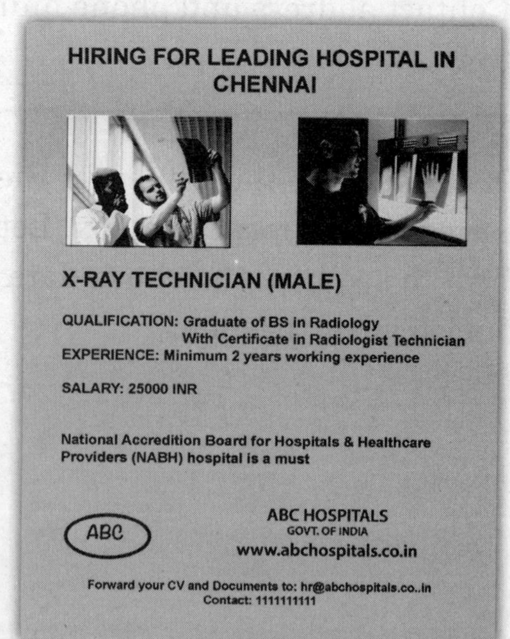

Figure A4.1: *Job Advertisement exemplar (today)*

Poster: Job Advertisement

Figure A4.2: *Job Advertisement exemplar (10 years from today)*

Appendix 4

Python Worksheet

1. Which of the following is a valid name of an identifier?
   a. global
   b. 100abc
   c. average
   d. sol$ution
   e. gameNo1
   f. First_game
   g. Last.name
   h. ?PERCENTage
   i. print
   j. square-area
   k. elIF
   l. FOR
2. What will be the output of the following code:
   a. print(7/2)
   b. print(7//2)
   c. print (8*2 - 2*4)
   d. print (3 + 27/9 - 3**2+3)
   e. print ((4 + 24)/8 - (2**3+3))
3. Which of the following lines is commented?
   a. """First line of a program is a comment"""
   b. # First line of a program is a comment
   c. // First line of a program is a comment
   d. First line of a program is a comment'''
4. Predict the output of the following:
   a. print (2*6)
      print (5+3*7)
      print (2**3)

```
print (8-(6*4))
print( "hello")
print ("sum of 2+5=", 2+5)
```

b.
```
p,q=3,4
p,q,r=10,q,p
p,q,r=r/2,p+4,q*6+2
print(p)
print(q)
print(r)
```

c.
```
maths = 56
english = 23
science = 78
total = maths +english+ science
average = total/3
print( "total" , total)
print ("average: ", average)
```

d.
```
user="John"
if user != "John":
    print ("Invalid user!!")
print ("Entry valid!!")
```

e.
```
x = 100
y = 200
if x%y == 0:
    print ("Divisible")
else:
    print("Not divisible")
```

f.
```
q = 90
r = -9
if x+y> 100:
```

```
    print ("good answer")
elifx+y< 100:
    print ("I wonder")
else:
    print ("wow!!")
```

g.
```
string = "hello world"
for i in range(len(string)-1, 0,-1):
print (string[i])
```

h.
```
num =[10,20,30]
    sum=0
for i in num:
    sum = sum+i
print (sum)
```

i.
```
x=16
y=4
print( x+y)
print (x-y)
print (x*y)
```

j.
```
myList1 = [9, 11]
myList2 = myList1
myList1[0] = 3
print(myList2)
```

k.
```
myList = [1, 2, 3, 4]
myList.append([5, 6, 7, 8])
print(len(myList))
```

l.
```
x = [4, 2, 6, 2, 3, 1]
L1 = a.index(min(x))
L2 = a.index(max(x))
print("The maximum is at position", L1 + 1)
print("The minimum is at position", L2 + 1)
```

5. a. Suppose myList is ['p','r','i','n','t'], what is len(myList)?
   b. Suppose myList is [121, 45, 1090, 34, 52], What is myList[:-1]?
   c. Suppose myList is [8,-1, -3, 12], What is myList * 2?
   d. Suppose myList is [1, 3, 5, 7, 9], what is myList.index(4)?
6. Which of the following types only allows True or False values?
   a. bool
   b. binary
   c. Boolean
   d. None
7. Rewrite the Python code after removing the syntax errors, if any. Underline each correction.
   a.
   ```
   p,q = 90,10
   if p+q< 100
   print ("value less than 100")
   else
   print (value greater than 100)
   end the if
   ```
   b.
   ```
   admn no = eval the input ('enter the admission number')
   if admn_no = 1 or 2:
   print ( "valid admission number")
   ```
   c.
   ```
   a, b = 45 90
   if a>35, b > 85:
   print (" correct range")
   else
   print(" incorrect range")
   ```
8. Which of the following operations will result in 8?
   a. 65//8
   b. 17%9
   c. 2**4
   d. 64**0.5
9. Write a Python program for the following.
   a. Accept marks in five subjects of a student and calculate average. Print the average.

b. Accept the dimensions of a rectangle to calculate its area and perimeter. Print the area and the perimeter.

c. Simulate a phone bill generator. The program should accept the name of the customer and calls made from the user. The bill amount should be calculated @ Rs. 2 per call. The bill generated should also show tax calculation @ 15% of call charges.

Bill generated should look like the following:

Name of Customer : ____________

Call Charges:

calls Made : ____________

Charges : ____________

Bill amount : ____________

Tax : ____________

Net Bill Amount : ____________

Thanks for using our service.

ABC Telecom

d. Simulate a bus ticketing system. Accept the passenger name, number of tickets booked for adults and children, boarding location, and destination. Calculate the bill amount on the following basis:

- ₹ 200 per adult
- ₹ 50 per child
- Add meal charges of ₹ 80 per person

Display the ticket containing all required components.

e. Accept the earnings of an employee and allot commission as per the following table:

Earnings	Commission percentage
>=50000	10
40000 – 49999	8.5
30000 – 39999	7
<30000	5

f. Predict and print the weather conditions based on the degree temperature details accepted from the user as per the following table:

Temperature	Weather
7-15	Winter
16-25	Pleasant spring
26-34	Summer
>35	Hot Summers

g. Generate and print a list containing all odd numbers between 1 and 30.

h. Generate and print a list having squares of all even natural numbers between 1 and 50.

i. Accept five numbers from the user. Traverse the list and print double the value of even numbers and triple the value of odd numbers.

j. Assume a string, mylist = "Programming is fun".
   - Print first five characters
   - Print last five characters
   - Print between 3rd and 10th character
   - Print the string backwards

k. Accept a string from the user and predict the following:
   - Count number of characters
   - Count number of upper and lowercase characters
   - Count number of vowels
   - Count the number of digits
   - Print the string in tOGGLEcASE

Appendix 5

PYTHON IDEs

IDE (Integrated Development Environment) Software

There are two ways to use Python. One way is the interactive mode, where you can simply write the command and get the result of the command. The other is the script mode, where you can type a program which consists of a set of instructions to perform a task and then saves the program code with the .py extension, and executes it as and when required.

An IDLE is used to understand the code and perform the indentation as well. It works better than a text editor. Performing the indentation by itself speeds up your work. Different tools are available as Python IDEs and serves different purposes as well.

Fig. A6.1: *Python logo*

IDLE

It is installed by default when you install Python. It is very easy to work, learn and simple to use. It comes with the Shell Window and the Editor Window. It is possible to use multiple editor Windows to work simultaneously with many programs together.

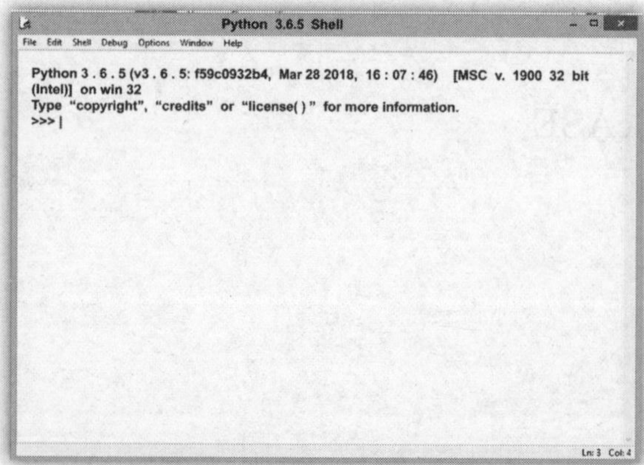

Fig. A6.3: *Python Script mode*

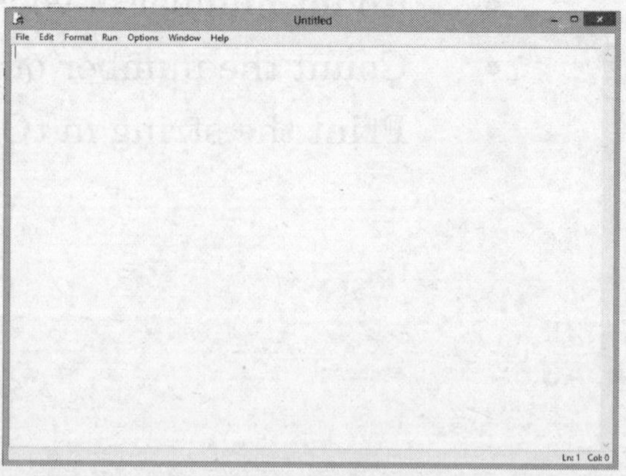

Fig. A6.2: *Python Interactive mode*

PyCharm

PyCharm is an integrated development environment used in programming, specifically for the Python language. It is developed by the Czech company JetBrains.

Fig. A6.4: *PyCharm*

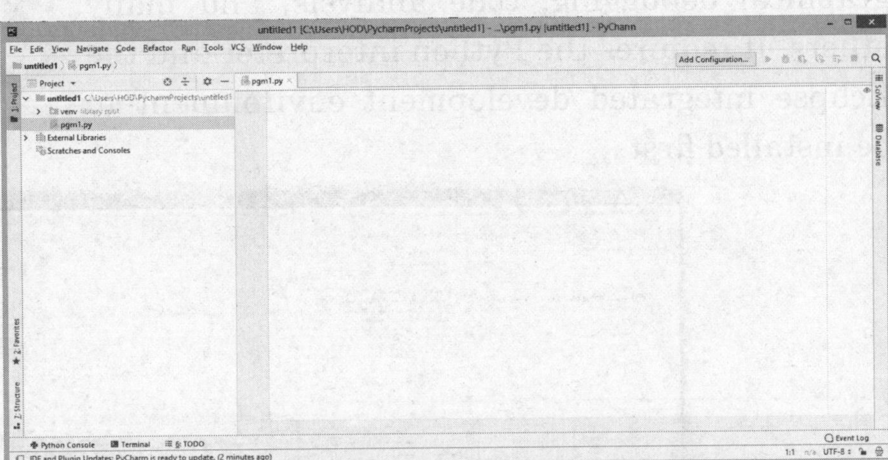

Fig. A6.5: *PyCharm interface*

Spyder

Spyder is an open source cross-platform integrated development environment for scientific programming in the Python language.

Fig. A6.6: *Python Spyder*

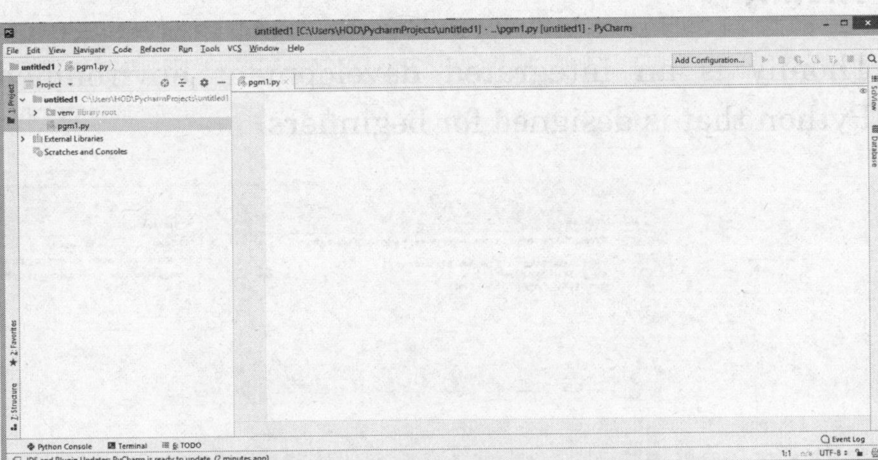

Fig. A6.7: *Python Spyder interface*

PyDev

Fig. A6.8: *PyDev*

PyDev is a Python Development Environment. It is a plugin that supports code refactoring, graphical debugging, code analysis, and many others. It requires the Python interpreter and the Eclipse integrated development environment to be installed first.

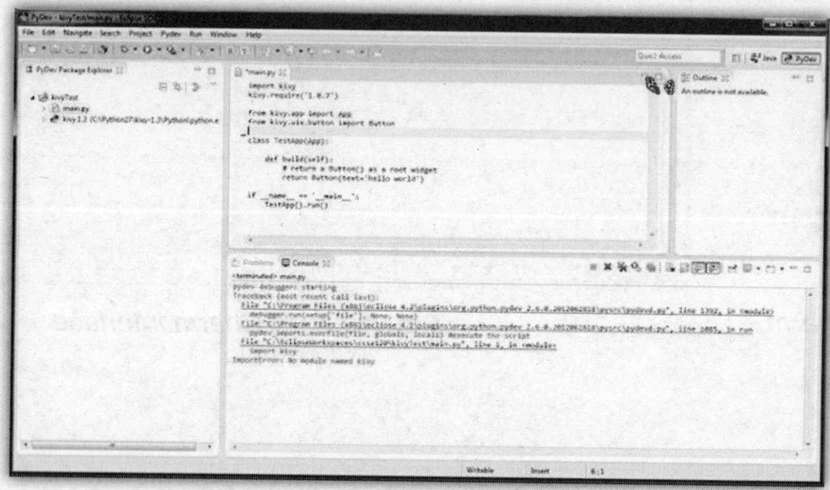

Fig. A6.9: *PyDev interface*

Thonny

Fig. A6.10: *Thonny*

Thonny is an integrated development environment for Python that is designed for beginners.

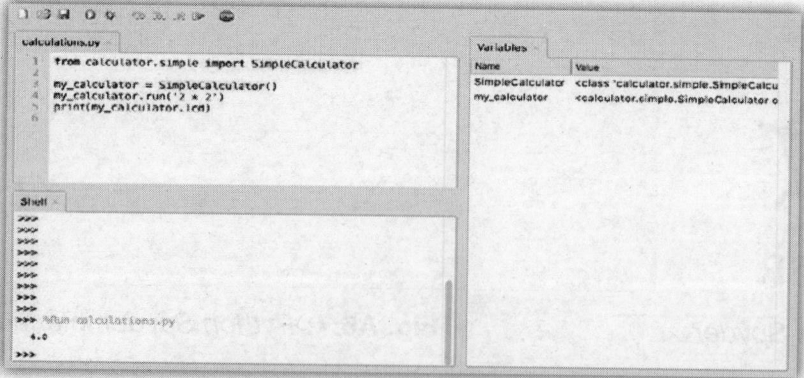

Fig. A6.11: *Python Thonny interface*

Co-curricular Activities

Practical: 50 marks

List of activities that can be assessed under Co-curricular Activities for the practical component.

The following activities from the content can be assessed under Co-curricular activities. A copy of the printed documents of the following can be maintained for the Practical/Assignment File Record.

S No.	Activity	Chapter No. and Name	Activity No.
I.	**Kahoot Quiz:** Conduct an Online Kahoot Quiz on AI concepts learnt in class VIII	**Chapter 1:** Revision of concepts – class viii	Appendix 1
II.	**Kahoot Online Quiz/Pen paper Quiz:** Sustainable Development Goals	**Chapter 1:** Revision of concepts – class viii	Appendix 1
III.	**Article Writing:** Write an article about the problem which you have scoped and write how you wish to solve it using Artificial Intelligence. Use the 4W Problem Statement template for the activity.	**Chapter 3:** Problem Scoping	Activity 3.5
IV.	**Job Advertisement Poster Making:** Create a poster for a job advertisement describing the job created and skills required for the same after 10 years.		Appendix 4
V.	Python Worksheet		Appendix 5
VI.	**Balloon Debate:** Conducting a balloon debate wherein the teams talk in favor of AI and against AI relating it to various domains like agriculture, transport, security, and so on.		
VII.	Write a letter to your future self, mentioning what you have learned about Artificial Intelligence and what are the skills you would like to learn and acquire for availing futuristic job opportunities.		

Sample Paper 1

Time: 2 hours *Marks: 50*

PART A

A. Objective type questions. (Do any four) **(4×1= 4)**

1. The person that receives the message is known as the __________.
   a. Sender b. Message
   c. Receiver d. None of these
2. What do you mean by Management?
3. __________ refers to the characteristics of a particular society, community, or ethnic group reflected in its practices and beliefs.
4. What is the full form of ICT?
5. Business can be broadly classified in five types. (True/ False)
6. The environment are classified into __________ types.
   a. 2 b. 3
   c. 4 d. 5

B. Short answer type questions. (Do any three) **(2×3= 6)**

1. What is the use of ICT in the workplace?
2. What are the causes of environmental degradation?
3. What do you mean by multinational company?
4. What is SWOT? How it is useful?
5. Write down the example of sole proprietorship.

PART B

A. Objective type questions. (Any 20) **(20×1= 20)**

1. __________ is quite relevant in Modern Times.
   a. Artificial Intelligence b. IoT
   c. Both a. and b. d. None of these
2. The __________ template provides the GOTO command.

3. AI plays an important role in ____________ technologies.
   a. Self-driving car b. Metro
   c. Both a. and b. d. None of these
4. Define SDG.
5. Artificial Intelligence was first invented by John McCarthy in 1956. (True/False)
6. SDG fall under the four domain pillars. (True/False)
7. Which app calculate traffic and instruct in order to find the quickest route to user's destination?
8. ____________ is a thinking tool being addressed by AI systems.
   a. E-commerce industry b. Weather prediction
   c. Metro d. None of these
9. Write down the components of AI Project Cycle.
10. Scarcity means:
   a. Shortage b. Lack
   c. Inadequacy d. All of the above
11. ____________ helps us to preserve your environment.
12. In 1963, IBM produced computers which specialized in Data Acquisition. (True/False)
13. What is the purpose of Data Acquisition?
14. Which one of the following stands for the second W in the 4Ws Problem Canvas?
   a. Who b. What
   c. Why d. Where
15. ____________ is the full form of GHG.
16. Burning of ____________ is one of the cause for air pollution.
17. Write down the function of an axon.
18. Give an example of Deep Learning.
19. Which one of the following is used to take the input from the user?
   a. Hidden Layer b. Input Layer
   c. Output Layer d. None of the above

20. Which one of the following is not the function of the hidden layer?
    a. To display the result
    b. Receive data from the input layer
    c. Process the data
    d. Give the data to the output layer
21. Bayou uses a method called _______________ Learning.
22. Classification is a _____________ grouping of observations into categories.
23. Neural Networks include various technologies like Deep Learning, and Machine Learning as a part of Artificial Intelligence. (True/False)
24. BNNs are capable of learning, which takes place by altering weight values.(True/False)

B. Short answer type questions. (Do any four) (2×4= 8 Marks)

1. Write down the application of Neural Network.
2. What are the names of three layers of Neural Network?
3. Which approach uses rules as the knowledge representation?
4. What is the purpose of AQI?
5. Write down the examples of IoT.
6. Explain the use of AI.

C. Long answer type questions. (Do any three) (4×3=12)

1. Explain the role of AI.
2. Discuss process simulation in detail.
3. How to read a graph chart?
4. Write the various steps involved while working with the Sketch2Code activity.
5. Why do you use Neural Networks?

Solutions

PART A

A. Objective type questions. (Do any four) **(4×1= 4)**

1. c. Receiver
2. Management is the art of planning, organising, directing, and controlling the resources and tasks, efficiently and effectively, to achieve a goal.
3. Culture
4. The full form of ICT is Information and Communication Technology.
5. False
6. a. 2

B. Short answer type questions. (Do any three) **(2×3= 6)**

1. It is used in the mining industry for:
   a. Prospecting
   b. Power generation and distribution in power plants
   c. Building and maintaining networks in telecommunication and design
   d. Engineering
   e. Manufacturing
2. Causes of environmental degradation:
   a. Earthquakes
   b. Forest fires
   c. Volcanic eruption
   d. Floods
3. A multinational company is a business that operates in many different countries at the same time.
4. SWOT stands for Strength, Weakness, Opportunity, Threat. It is a technique that helps one to analyse one's own strength and weakness.

5. The examples of sole proprietorship are the grocery store, sweets shop, stationery store, chemist shops, and vegetable shops.

PART B

A. Objective type questions. (Any 20) **(20×1= 20)**

1. a. Artificial Intelligence
2. Advanced
3. a. Self-driving car
4. It is a blueprint to achieve a better and the more sustainable future for all.
5. True
6. False
7. Google Maps
8. b. Weather prediction
9. The components of AI Project Cycle is Problem Scoping, Data Acquisition, Data Exploration, Modelling and Evaluation.
10. d. All of the above
11. Conservation
12. True
13. It enables us to create the content wanted by our audience in contrast to what we thought they wanted.
14. b. What
15. Greenhouse Gases
16. Fossil fuels
17. The function of an axon in neuron is to transmit information to different neurons, muscles, and glands.
18. The example of Deep Learning is chatbots.
19. b. Input Layer
20. a. To display the result

21. Neural Sketch
22. Systematic
23. True
24. False

B. Short answer type questions. (Do any four) **(2×4= 8 Marks)**

1. The application of Neural Network are trading based on algorithms, security classification and forecasting.
2. The three layers of Neural Network are Input layer, Hidden layer and Output layer.
3. A rule-based approach uses rules as the knowledge representation.
4. The purpose of the AQI is to help people know how the local air quality impacts their health.
5. The examples of IoT are security systems, electronic appliances, speakers, cars, and many more.
6. The use of Artificial Intelligence is to create robots that can interact with humans without controls.

C. Long answer type questions. (Do any three) **(4×3=12)**

1. Artificial Intelligence presents and magnifies our understanding to solve complex and interconnected global challenges such as hunger, climate change and life on land and water to name a few. AI processes augment scenarios such as computerizing routine tasks, analyzing big data, and generating intelligent solutions to a wide range of sustainable development issues. A well-designed AI solution can play a transformative role in helping us achieve the SDGs.

   AI is growing exponentially and can give extraordinary results with a correct vision in mind. With the advent of technology, the scales concerning the pros and cons of using Artificial Intelligence to achieve SDGs have dipped in both directions from time to time. The sole purpose of AI usage should be to bring good to humanity as a whole. The development of such technologies should be done in such an inclusive manner that it is equally accessible by all for its benefits.

2. Process Simulation refers to the method of designing a model of a real system. We can conduct experiments with this model by changing the values of individual elements and see how they are related to each other. The purpose of such a change over is to understand the behavior of various operations of the system. In short, simulation lets us assume the mere appearance of a process system, without the reality. The conceptualization of the system shows the system in action and lets us observe the results based on multiple inputs.

3. It is helpful to follow a two-step process described below and interpret the conclusions after having made a graph.

   Step One: Describe: This part explains how the figure/table is set up.

   a. Representation on the axes: This step defines the x-axis and y-axis. The x-axis runs horizontally and represents the independent variable; which is the value being manipulated. The dependent variable "depends" upon x-axis and is plotted on the vertical y-axis.
   b. Units on the axes: This step helps us quantify the relationships between variables.
   c. Scale on each axis.
   d. Symbols and legend on a figure: They might be represented by different symbols, dotted lines, colour patterns, and so on.
   e. Observe the patterns in the data.

   Step Two: Interpret: This part explains how to interpret the data. It is important to understand how to draw conclusions from the patterns described. We could draw a few inferences based on the graph by asking some of the following questions:

   a. Does the graph support or reject the study's hypothesis? It can be helpful to sketch out what the graph would look like if the hypothesis was supported and what it would look like if it was not.

b. Are there alternative explanations for the pattern in the data?

c. Do new or unexpected results generate new hypotheses?

4. Sketch2Code is a Microsoft web-based solution which is used to transform any handmade designs into the HTML code using Artificial Intelligence.

a. A computer vision model is trained in such a manner that it recognizes the handwritten pattern to predict meaningful design elements from the image captured.

b. Now, text recognition of each element along with its position from the image is used to extract the content.

c. The algorithm fetches all the information along with its position from the image and generates the HTML structure.

d. The HTML code is generated by the AI algorithm.

5. Neural networks are one of the most commonly, powerful, and widely used algorithms which actually use Deep Learning algorithms. They are used to solve real-life complex problems. These networks can learn and create the relationships between all the inputs and gives the result. They can handle non-linear and complex problems very effectively. They can even work and give output if the data is missing. The main advantage of neural networks is that they are able to extract data features automatically without needing any input from the programmer.

Artificial Neural Networks (ANN) are very famous these days and also considered to be very interesting topics due to their applications in chatbots to make your work easy like auto replying the e-mails, suggesting e-mail replies, spam filtering, Facebook image tagging, showing the items of your interest in the e-shopping web portals, and many more.

Sample Paper 2

<u>*Time: 2 hours*</u> <u>*Marks: 50*</u>

PART A

A. Objective type questions. (Do any four) **(4×1= 4)**

1. Which of the following helps the user to stay connected with their friends and family?
   a. Talk b. WhatsApp
   c. Art d. All of these
2. All living organisms are included in __________ components of ecosystem.
3. The full form of ITeS is Information Technologies-enabled System. (True/ False)
4. ____________________ is also known as trading or buy and sell business.
5. What does the acronym SMART stands for?

B. Short answer type questions. (Do any three) **(2×3= 6)**

1. How to grow your Initiative skills?
2. What do you mean by printer and its types?
3. Why is it important to converse natural resources?
4. What are the aims of green economy?
5. How do your past experiences affect our perspective?

PART B

A. Objective type questions. (Any 20) **(20×1= 20)**

1. ____________app calculate traffic and instruct in order to find the quickest route to user's destination.
   a. Google map b. Google Music
   c. Both a. and b. d. None of these
2. Who can be controlled through smartphones and smart speakers?
   a. Smart Home Device b. Smart Home

c. IoT

d. Both b. and c.

3. Electronic appliances is an example of ________________.
4. ________________ can write a story in Google Docs.
5. AI makes the machine work intelligently so as to help us in performing the various tasks easily and accurately.
6. Security systems is an example of Internet of Things.
7. Write down the two applications of Artificial Intelligence in your daily lives.
8. Give one use of AI inclusion.
9. Which one of the following is the highest percentage in air?

   a. Carbon dioxide
   b. Nitrogen
   c. Oxygen
   d. Methane
10. Air Pollution causes:

    a. Respiratory problems
    b. Global warming
    c. Soil erosion
    d. Deforestation
11. Artificial Intelligence is an ________ term which has ML and DL.
12. Deep Learning is a subset of ________________.
13. A Pie chart depicts quantitative value over a continuous time interval. (True/False)
14. A Histogram is visually simpler than other types of graphs. (True/False)
15. Write down the various pollutants in air.
16. Give one example of data visualisation.
17. ________________ is a type of supervised learning model.
18. A network of such neurons is called a ________________.
19. Neural Network helps in trading based on algorithms only. (True/False)
20. Each layer is further divided into several blocks called nodes. (True/False)
21. Write down the function of soma.
22. What is Autodraw?

23. How many common AI models are there?

a. 2 b. 3

c. 4 d. 5

24. Classification is a type of:

a. Supervised learning b. Unsupervised learning

c. Reinforcement learning d. None of these

B. Short answer type questions. (Do any four) **(2×4= 8)**

1. What is the responsibility of nervous system?
2. Explain regression and clustering.
3. Write any two advantages/applications of using learning based approach.
4. Name any two advantages/ applications of using decision trees.
5. Explain Smart Home and Smart City.
6. What do you mean by Internet of Things?

C. Long answer type questions. (Do any three) **(4×3=12)**

1. Explain the name and the gaols of SDG.
2. Discuss the components of AI Project Cycle in detail.
3. Define the following:

   a. Data Acquisition b. Data features

   c. System maps d. LOOPY

4. Explain any three applications of classifications in details.
5. Explain the working of Neural Network using Autodraw.

CHAPTERWISE SOLUTIONS

PART A

Chapter 1

Brain Bot

A. Multiple choice questions.

1. c. Both a. and b.
2. a. Understand the message and respond to it
3. c. Both a. and b
4. c. Body language
5. d. Love
6. a. Point of view
7. d. Concise
8. b. An
9. c. Adverbial
10. b. Pronoun

B. Fill in the blanks.

1. Sentence
2. Words
3. Visual communication
4. Information
5. Oral

Chapter 2

Brain Bot

A. Multiple choice questions.

1. c. Management
2. b. Communication skills
3. b. Personal factors
4. d. Positive
5. c. Opportunity
6. b. Others thinking about them
7. c. Realistic

8. c. Initiative
9. d. Self-efficacy
10. a. Threat

B. Fill in the blanks.

1. Cultural factors
2. Physical
3. 3
4. Initiative
5. Self-management

Chapter 3

Brain Bot

A. Multiple choice questions.

1. b. Mobile
2. d. All of these
3. d. RAM
4. c. NIC
5. b. CMOS chip
6. c. Multi-user OS
7. b. Internet Browser
8. b. User name and domain name
9. c. Twitter handle
10. b. Amazon

B. Fill in the blanks.

1. Twitter
2. Friend list
3. Social Tab
4. Carbon copy and Blind carbon copy
5. CPU

C. Match the following.

Column A	Column B
1. Facebook	v. Mark Zuckerberg
2. Non-volatile	ii. RAM
3. Volatile	i. ROM

4.	Monitor	iv.	Output device
5.	Keyboard	iii.	Input device

Chapter 4

Brain Bot

A. Multiple choice questions.

1. d. All of these
2. c. Creativity
3. b. To understand
4. d. All of these
5. a. Service
6. c. Sole Proprietorship
7. c. Takes risks to earn profits
8. c. Sole Proprietorship
9. d. All of these
10. c. Entrepreneurship development

B. Fill in the blanks.

1. Enterprise
2. Pre-training or Initial phase
3. Capital
4. Motivation
5. Entrepreneur

Chapter 5

Brain Bot

A. Multiple choice questions.

1. b. To surround
2. a. Autotrophs
3. d. All of these
4. c. Eutrophication
5. d. High level of microbial pollution
6. d. All of these
7. c. 50 Hz to 15000 Hz
8. a. Glycerol

9. d. Stratosphere
10. a. Ecological disturbance

B. Fill in the blanks.

1. Light, air, soil, water, and minerals
2. Biotic
3. Heterotrophs
4. Ozone layer
5. Reduce, Reuse and Recycle

D. Match the following.

Column A		Column B
1. Environ	iii.	Surrounding
2. Natural environment	i.	Sun
3. Paper bag	iv.	Surrounding
4. 3 R's	ii.	Recycle, Reuse and Reduce

PART B

Chapter 1

Brain Bot

A. Multiple choice questions.

1. c. AI
2. a. Artificial Intelligence
3. a. Smart Home Device
4. b. Transport
5. a. Google Maps
6. a. Self-driving car
7. c. Both a. and b.
8. c. Both a. and b.

B. Fill in the blanks.

1. E-Commerce
2. IoT
3. Story Speaker
4. Advanced
5. 2030

C. Match the following.

1.	SDG	i.	AI Inclusion
2.	TV, AC, fridge	ii.	E-commerce
3.	Healthcare	iii.	17 goals
4.	Benefitted from the application of AI	iv.	Pillars of AI
5.	Economic	v.	Smart Home gadgets

Chapter 2

Brain Bot

A. Multiple choice questions.

1. b. Rainwater harvesting
2. c. Evaluation
3. b. Water Conservation
4. d. All of the above
5. c. Problem Scoping
6. d. All of the above

B. Fill in the blanks.

1. Conservation
2. Data Acquisition
3. Data Acquisition, Data Exploration, Modelling
4. Less, carbon
5. 97%
6. Three-fourth
7. Reliable, accurate
8. Data Exploration

C. Match the following.

	Column A		Column B
1.	Water	vii.	Conservation
2.	Three-fourth	i.	Water
3.	Shortage	vii.	Scarcity
4.	Saving	vi.	Valuable resource
5.	Water conservation	ii.	Global issue
6.	Aim/Goal	viii.	Problem scoping
7.	Data Acquisition	iii.	Collect Data
8.	Data Exploration	iv.	Data arranged in organized manner

D. Answer the following questions.

3. Unscramble the following letters to form a word.
   a. A C E I O O N N S R V T: CONVERSATION
   b. A A C F I II L R T: ARTIFICIAL

Chapter 3

Brain Bot

A. Multiple choice questions.

1. b. Data Analyst
2. d. Project Scoping
3. b. How
4. c. Greenhouse Gas
5. d. All of the above
6. c. Methane

B. Fill in the blanks.

1. Problem Scoping
2. Who
3. What, Where and Why
4. Effect
5. Who
6. Problem statement
7. Carbon dioxide, ozone

C. Match the following.

Column A		Column B
1. Problem Scoping	viii.	Defines the goal of the project
2. 4Ws Problem Canvas	iii.	Who, What, Where, Why
3. GHG	vi.	Greenhouse Gas
4. Increased CO_2 due to	i.	Burning of fossil fuels
5. Greenhouse Gas	vii.	Carbon dioxide
6. Theme	ii.	Broader term
7. Deforestation	v.	Cutting trees
8. Why	iv.	Is the last block of the 4Ws Problem Canvas

D. Answer the following questions.

2. Unscramble the following letters to form a word.
    a. IONCPGS: SCOPING
    b. AACNSV: CANVAS

Chapter 4

Brain Bot

A. Multiple choice questions.

1. b. What
2. a. Data Acquisition
3. d. Raw facts
4. c. Giving input to the machine
5. d. All of the above
6. c. Using someone's data from the internet without permission

B. Fill in the blanks.

1. Collect
2. Data acquisition
3. Loop
4. LOOPY
5. Simulation
6. Photosynthesis
7. Cybercrime

C. Match the following.

	Column A		**Column B**
a.	Data Acquisition	iv.	Collect data
b.	Raw facts	v.	Data
c.	Data features	i.	Factors associated with problem
d.	Testing data	vi.	Accurate, reliable and correct
d.	All elements	ii.	Interconnected
f.	Energy	viii.	Quantitative property
g.	Simulation	iii.	Designing a model of a real system
h.	LOOPY	vii	An interactive tool

D. Answer the following questions.

2. Unscramble the following letters to form a word:

   a. AADT: DATA

   b. HEIPHOOSSSYNTT: PHOTOSYNTHESIS

Chapter 5

Brain Bot

A. Multiple choice questions.

1. b. Data visualization
2. b. Data in meaningful form
3. b. Time (in hours)
4. b. Nitrogen
5. a. Respiratory problems
6. d. Oxygen
7. c. 21%
8. d A paragraph
9. d. All of the above
10. d. All of the above

B. Fill in the blanks.

1. Data Exploration
2. Data Visualization
3. x-axis
4. Units
5. https://datavizcatalogue.com
6. Fossil fuels
7. Greenhouse
8. Deforestation

C. Match the following.

Column A	Column B
1. Most severe impact on human health	iv. AQI 401 – 500
2. Nitrogen	iv. Most abundant gas in air
3. O_3	vi. Ozone

4. PM	viii. Particulate matter
5. Graph	vii Pictorial representation
6. Air Quality Index	i. AQI
7. Graph and Chart	ii. Data visualization tools
8. Data visualization tools	iii. Helps in comprehending trends and patterns

D. Answer the following questions.

1. Write the full form for the following organizations.
   a. CPCB: Central Pollution Control Board
   b. DPCC: Delhi Pollution Control Committee

Chapter 6

Brain Bot

A. Multiple choice questions.

1. b. Data Modelling
2. b. Evaluation
3. d. Artificial Intelligence
4. c. If-else statement
5. a. Decision tree
6. d. All of the above
7. d. Sequence of test conditions
8. c. Both a and b
9. b. Top-down
10. a. True

B. Fill in the blanks.

1. Fourth
2. Umbrella
3. Machine Learning
4. Deep Learning
5. Rule-based, learning-based
6. Learning-based approach
7. Rule-based approach

8. Training
9. Rule

C. Match the following.

Column A	Column B
1. Modelling	iv. Develop algorithms/models
2. Graphical tools	vi. Helps in visualization for better understanding
3. Deep Learning	v. Learn from large data sets
4. Rule-based approach	ii. Uses if-else statements
5. Training data	viii. Sample data
6. Binary language	i. Language of 0's and 1's
7. Machine learns through	iii. Learning-based approach experience
8. Learning-based approach	vii. Smart Reply, Google Search and Google Maps, and so on

D. Answer the following questions.

1. Write the full form for the following organizations.
   a. ML: Machine Learning
   b. DL: Deep Learning

Chapter 7

Brain Bot

A. Multiple choice questions.

1. b. Input Layer
2. a. To display the result
3. d. Lobe
4. c. Nervous System
5. d. Axons
6. c. 3-tier
7. c. Google Creative Lab
8. a. True

B. Fill in the blanks.

1. Artificial Intelligence
2. Classification, clustering

3. Systematic
4. Supervised
5. Reinforcement
6. Testing
7. Gram Panchayat
8. Neural Sketch
9. Quick, Draw
10. Sketch2Code

C. Match the following.

	Column A		Column B
1.	Input Layer	vii.	Dendrites
2.	Synapse	vi.	Interconnections
3.	Axon	viii.	Output layer
4.	Hidden Layer	ii.	Responsible for processing
5.	First layer of neural network	iii.	Input layer
6.	Supervised learning	iv.	Labeled dataset
7.	Cell body	v.	Soma
8.	Autodraw	i.	Fast drawing tool

D. Answer the following questions.

1. Write the full form for the following organizations.
   a. ANN: Artificial Neural Network
   b. BNN: Biological Neural Network

Chapter 8

Brain Bot

A. Multiple choice questions.

1. b. Assembler
2. a. Flowchart
3. d. Mnemonics
4. c. Input unit
5. c. Microsoft Windows
6. d. All of the above

B. Fill in the blanks.

1. Input, output

2. Designing
3. Application
4. Documentation
5. Flowchart
6. Relationships
7. Draw.io
8. Environment
9. CodeCombat

C. Match the following.

	Column A		Column B
1.	Draw.io	iii.	Online tool to draw flowchart
2.		v.	Decision
3.		vii.	Process
4.	Flowchart	ii.	Diagrammatic representation
5.	Algorithm	iv.	Step-by-step procedure
6.	D in A-B-C-D stands for	viii.	Debug and Test
7.		i.	Start/End
8.	C in A-B-C-D stands for	vi.	Code-It

D. Answer the following questions.

1. Write the full form for the following organizations.
   a. HLL: High Level Language
   b. A-B-C-D: Analyzing- Broadcast – Code It – Debug and Test
   c. RPG: Role playing game

Chapter 9

Brain Bot

A. Multiple choice questions.

1. a. Spaces are not allowed
2. a. .py
3. b. int()
4. d. Any of them
5. c. Colon (:)
6. b. if a <= b:

7. a. 4
8. b. Iteration
9. c. 0, 1, 2, 3
10. a. 10 5

B. Fill in the blanks.

1. Case-sensitive
2. print( )
3. Comments
4. Memory
5. type( )
6. String
7. Keywords
8. Symbols
9. Operators

C. Match the following.

Column A		Column B
1. Arithmetic operators	iii.	(+, -, *, /, %, **, //)
2. input()	v.	Function used to accept data from user
3. Typecasting	vi.	Type conversion from one data type to another
4. if statement	vii.	Selection statement
5. for statement	ii.	Iteration
6. Relational Operators	viii.	(>, <, <=, <=, ==, !=, <>)
7. print()	i.	Function used to display the result
8. Debugging	iv.	Process of identifying and removing errors

Chapter 10

Brain Bot

A. Multiple choice questions.

1. d. All of the above
2. a. 6
3. d. 3465
4. c. 19
5. d. [4, 5]

6. c. 7
7. d. append()
8. a. mylist.insert(2, 23)

B. Fill in the blanks.

1. Mutable
2. Different
3. 0
4. String
5. Forward, backward
6. Square
7. In and not in
8. Nested
9. Remove
10. Slicing

C. Match the following.

	Column A		Column B
1.	len()	v.	To calculate the number of elements in list
2.	append()	iv.	mylist.append(20)
3.	list()	i.	To create an empty list
4.	insert()	vii.	To add an element at the desired index
5.	count()	ii.	To return the number of times an element is found in the list
6.	index()	viii.	To return the index location of the element in the list
7.	remove()	iii.	To delete the given element from the list
8.	sort()	vi.	Arrange the list in ascending order in the original list